D0302871

WILLIAM FAULKNER

20│21

Walter Benn Michaels, *Series Editor*

From Guilt to Shame by Ruth Leys

William Faulkner: An Economy of Complex Words by Richard Godden

WILLIAM FAULKNER

An Economy of Complex Words

Richard Godden

PRINCETON UNIVERSITY PRESS

PRINCETON AND OXFORD

Copyright © 2007 by Princeton University Press

Published by Princeton University Press, 41 William Street, Princeton,
New Jersey 08540

In the United Kingdom: Princeton University Press, 3 Market Place,
Woodstock, Oxfordshire OX20 1SY

Library of Congress Cataloging-in-Publication Data

Godden, Richard, 1946–

William Faulkner : an economy of complex words / Richard Godden.
p. cm.

Includes bibliographical references and index.

ISBN-13: 978-0-691-13071-2 (acid-free paper)

LC Control No.: 2006050964

British Library Cataloging-in-Publication Data is available

This book has been composed in Helvetica Neue Typefaces

Printed on acid-free paper. ∞

press.princeton.edu

Printed in the United States of America

10 9 8 7 6 5 4 3 2 1

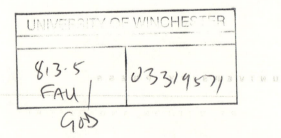

To John T. Matthews and Noel Polk

FOR THEIR WORK AND FRIENDSHIP

CONTENTS

CONTENTS

ACKNOWLEDGMENTS

JOHN T. MATTHEWS, on noting a conference member slump abruptly forward during a paper of mine, once observed that my prose style had finally killed someone. Noel Polk, as a long-time and generous reader of my drafts, worked tirelessly to reduce fatalities. Over the years, both have spotted gaps in my assumptions about Faulkner and suggested means to correction. They, to whom I dedicated the book, are part of a network of Faulknerians whose writing informs the work: I think particularly of Anne Goodwyn Jones, whose delighted skepticism regularly persuades me to reconsider; Peter Nicolaisen, whose clarity I can hope only at some point to emulate; Richard Gray, whose knowledge of southern writing serves as benchmark and rebuke. To write on the South from the perspective of a historical materialist, I have needed southern historians, and have been lucky both at Keele and at Sussex to fall among them: Mary Ellison and Martin Crawford (from Keele) and Trevor Burnard, Richard Follett, and Clive Webb (from Sussex) have been graceful yet direct in countering my ignorance.

Peter Nicholls has little time for the South or for Faulkner, but his eye for the pleasures and strategies of modernist opacity grounds much of what follows. Charles Swann had no time for Faulkner, but remained a friend who regularly and with wit delivered the knee-capping questions necessary to those who would write on that about which much has already been written—since without an enforced shift of perspective, why bother? Colin Richmond, in his insistent curiosity, stands as a distant intellectual example. Rhian Hughes, Tomos Hughes, and Mabli Godden have lived with the work for as long as I have, but with the illuminating conviction that other (sometimes minor) things matter much more; and in mattering so much, must, in the last instance, be brought back to inform the work. I thank them for putting so much into it.

Bits and pieces of what follows were critically read or usefully remarked on by Susan Donaldson, Richard King, Andrew Lawson, Tim Lustig, Sharon Monteith, and Patsy Yaeger. The fifth chapter would not have been possible without an earlier and jointly written essay: for permission to use some of that material in a slightly reinflected form, I again thank Noel Polk. All the above mentioned are in some degree responsible for what follows; I hope that the book does not shame their responsibility.

Research leaves from the Universities of Keele and Sussex and an award from the AHRC have abbreviated what at times felt like an interminable project. Chapters or parts of chapters have appeared in different forms in *ELH*, *The Faulkner Journal*, and the *Mississippi Quarterly*. I am grateful to those journals for permission to reprint that work here.

WILLIAM FAULKNER

INTRODUCTION

M Y TITLE intends no metaphor in its linking of language and economy. Words, as social instruments, exemplifying what Marx calls "practical consciousness,"[1] act upon a reality which they make as much as find. If the real is in a real sense made through words, those words needs must tend to complexity, not least because speakers inherit a language always "already occupied"[2] by prior and unknown users and usage. Since verbal instrumentalists work with a partially known instrument, and in circumstances not of their own design, they, to adapt Marx, are practically unconscious concerning large portions of their practice. Yet that practice, so much incomplete matter made from words, materializes within an economy whose historical conditions form, and take formal complexity from, linguistic work. Five sentences built upon begged questions, compound assumptions, and parabolic bids which it will take an entire study partially to answer, justify, and elucidate. But introductions may perhaps take liberties and should not give the game away.

In a recent anthology of new economic criticism, the editors, Woodmansee and Osteen, note that many who address the intersection of literature and economy argue from analogy: words have their economies—or so the case goes—because language and economy are both arbitrary systems of exchange: "Thus any adequate theoretics of literary economics must begin with the axioms of Saussurian linguistics and post-structuralist theory, that all signs are arbitrary and related syntagmatically—and then address the similarly fictive and constructed nature of money and finance."[3] In contradistinction, *An Economy of Complex Words* reads

Faulkner from within three linked assumptions, none of which derive from Saussure: that economic relations are a guise worn by social relations;[4] that social relations are finally a cause of what stories can and cannot be told (and of the manner of their telling); and that, therefore, economic structures may be read as the generative source of fictional forms. Since I seek to establish a causal rather than arbitrary connection between the work of Faulkner's words and the work of an economy, I had best gloss the economy in question.

Between 1933 and 1938, the New Deal interventions of the Agricultural Adjustment Program in the southern plantation states resulted in an unintended revolution in rural labor relations. Faced with a glutted world market for cotton, the federal government offered to pay southern landowners for ploughing their crops under. Fifty-three percent of the south's cotton acreage went out of production. Since a sharecropper, cropping on a half-the-crop agreement, would by rights receive half the federal payment for the sacrifice of his acres, it paid for the landowner not to sign sharecropping contracts for the following year. Instead, he might hire the same cropper, on an occasional basis and for a wage, to plough the crop under, and reap the entire subsidy himself. Between 1930 and 1940, the tenantry declined by 62 percent in Mississippi. What the labor historian Pete Daniel terms "the Southern enclosure" marks the movement from "capital-scarce, labor-intensive plantation production to capital-intensive, labor-surplus neo-plantation production,"[5] a structural shift most manifest in eviction and black diaspora.

Much of the migration during the thirties was internal, but with the onset of global conflict, the war-driven needs of northern industry ensured that during the 1940s over one million African Americans left the plantation states: Mississippi alone, between 1940 and 1944, experienced a 23 percent decline in its predominantly black farm population. Startling figures for out-migration during the early 1940s should be balanced against equally startling figures for capital inflow during the late 1930s as the enabling condition of that movement of people. Between 1933 and 1939, the federal government's direct expenditure in Mississippi totalled $450 million, while an additional $260 million entered state banks through insured loans.[6]

In effect, the landowning class shifted its pattern of dependency from black labor to northern capital, while the tenantry, increasingly landless and welfare-dependent, waited on the pull of northern employment needs to renew its Great Migration. As the African American historian Jay Mandle puts it, "America's entry into World War II marks the principal point of discontinuity in the black experience of the United States."[7] With blacks less and less in their laboring place and capital more and more in that place, the substance of southern plantation land was transformed—land as "sweat" gave way to land as "capital," though agribusiness and its destruction of "the labor-intensive rural order born of reconstruction" should not be spoken of as fully in place until the 1950s.[8]

Statistics for migration and investment do not adequately convey the impact of what the economist Paul Shuster Taylor in 1937 termed "the greatest revolution since the civil war in the cotton sections of the South,"[9] a breakdown in a regime of accumulation described by Jonathan Wiener *as* "the Second Civil War."[10] The limitations of figures, and arguably of the agricultural, social, and economic histories from which they are drawn, is that they and their sources abstract from the felt experience of the contradiction central to this particular revolution.

Prior to the New Deal (1930s) and the renewed Great Migration (1940s), ethnic relations in the south, resting on a pre- or semimodern regime of constrained labor (debt peonage), had been typified by dependency, growing out of what Mark Tushnett calls "total relations,"[11] that is, relations between owner and cropper that extended to the whole life of the tenant and to the whole life of the landlord. (Under wage labor, employer/employee connections are "partial" in that the wage-payer pays for, and assumes power over, only the working part of the worker's day). In 1935, Johnson, Embree, and Alexander surveyed cotton tenancy and concluded that "[t]he status of the tenancy demands complete dependence."[12]

Dependency cuts two ways, though tacitly: that is to say, within such a regime, the white landowning class, owing their substance to black labor, are blacks in whiteface. Such co-dependence must be denied, though by the mid 1940s, the linked impact of federal funding and enforced black mobility had ensured that historical conditions existed for the extraction of black from white. With the decline of tenantry and the relaxation of structures enforcing dependency, white, in the last instance, had less reason to be black. The proprietors of the forties must loose the bound body of black labor. The trick to the "creative destruction" of themselves,[13] required by a mutation in the form of their capital, is to expel their black substance without self-loss. But where the properties of that selfhood—from face, to skin, to sex, to land—are determined by the laboring other, to loose the other is to lose the self's best parts. In Joel Williamson's terms, commenting on the legacy of southern black/white relations at midcentury, for white to release black is to declare, "I am not going to be me anymore."[14] At which point, federal decisions concerning control of excess cotton production condition the corporeality—the face, sex, skin, and land—of an owning class as it negotiates the expulsion from itself of that which has made it what it is, African American labor.

In *Fictions of Labor* (1997), I argued that Faulkner's major texts of the long 1930s turned on the denial of a social trauma associated with the recognition that the South's singular, coercive, and premodern regime of labor forced black into white, and so made each white black. Since black labor constituted the substance of the labor lord, that lord and his class had to retain the black body, while denying the formative centrality of its presence in their own race, sex, skin, land, and language. The contradiction, white is black, had both to be recognized, or else what is southern about the southern landowner, and to be denied, or else how does the southern landowner "remain me some more"? Few devices operate with greater efficiency in the service of denied recognition (its representation and critique), than Faulkner's famous stylistic difficulty. *Fictions of Labor* suggested, for example, that the prose of *Absalom, Absalom!* (1936) serves its narrators' need to know what they must not know, and not to see what they see. Readers, as they tonally adjust, learn to see its narrators not seeing, and thereby to think what those narrators find unthinkable. Yet during the forties and early fifties, the conceptual habits shared by Quentin Compson and Rosa Coldfield incline to redundancy, as the transformation of their base and motive—a singular regime of labor—required that a class of labor lords become a class of landlords. With African American labor "progressively" forced from the land, onto roads and into cities, landowners no longer found blacks so corporeally in their whiteface. Where *Fictions of Labor* read Faulkner's work of the thirties as thematically and formally generated by a premodern labor trauma, *An Economy of Complex Words* (or, for my purposes here, *Fictions of Labor II*), argues that Faulkner spends the next two decades resolving the impact of that founding trauma's loss. To return to Williamson's formulation: release of the black, however protracted and stylistically occluded, begs the mournful question of "ceas[ing] to be."

In partial response to Williamson's question, my study seeks to trace the demise and reformation of a class by anatomizing the varieties of mourning exhibited by Faulkner's white landowners as they grasped the consequences of modernity in the New Deal's reconstruction of their depressed region. For smaller landowners, grief attended the loss of productive contact with the earth and the descent into wage labor: hence my choice of *The Hamlet* (1940). For larger landowners, grief, in barely acknowledged forms, accompanied the departure of a black work force for the North, as mechanization and agribusiness combined to consolidate land ownership and to demolish the sharecropped plantation, itself a remnant of slavery. I read *Go Down, Moses* (1942) as structured by griefs and longings which dare not state their names. Modernity, so long deferred by a plantocracy whose regime of accumulation (rooted in labor coercion), constituted a counterrevolution running from Emancipation to Depression, was finally confirmed in the South by World War II as it militarized the region's economy. Necessarily, therefore, *An Economy of Complex Words* closes with a reading of *A Fable* (1954), in which the persistent but barely discernible figure of the black jew allows Faulkner a final exercise in swallowed grief on behalf of a class that has ceased to exist.

Malcolm Bull identifies late modernity, of which migration and global conflict are surely features, with an emancipatory impulse through which aspects of the world are "de-alienated" or "drawn closer."[15] So defined, the products of late modernity, among which I would include Faulkner's later fictions, seek to see "unseeable totality,"[16] where sight involves recognition rather than possession. The seen need not be distant (a colony: Tibet in *A Fable*); indeed, sight may involve seeing the already visible in a different way (a black on a southern road: Rider in "Pantaloon in

Black"). The seer who sees in such a manner transforms the different into kin, the far into near, and the near into the intimate, and in so doing suffers all manner of maladies attendant upon emancipation. A brief symptomology may serve to suggest that late modernity, so defined, is inseparable from the contradictory. I would stress that what follows is a worst-case scenario. So to see is to see one's self come apart: to sense oneself as existing on both sides of a divide, whether of race, class, nation, or gender. So to see is to see double and to doubt the coherence, desirability, or relevance of one's own subject position. So to see is to see blind spots: glimpses of the barely known bear witness to the unknown as it comes not into sight, but into hiding,[17] where, an irritant opacity, it "eludes subsumption under ideas."[18] So to see is to suffer "epistemic abjection,"[19] traceable to the recognition that the incompatibility between the seer's reality and that of the newly recognized exists as a contradiction, within which available knowledge serves only to demonstrate that it should no longer serve to sustain the knower. Diagnosis: duplicity, opacity, and contradiction—and the greatest of these is contradiction.

I paraphrase Malcolm Bull's study of late modernity in order to set the experience and formal implications of contradiction at the center of later Faulkner. *An Economy of Complex Words* brings Bull's finally epistemological concerns to an instance of delayed modernization. Until the New Deal, southern planters had effectively refused emancipation, choosing to perpetuate a premodern labor system. The Agricultural Adjustment Program cast them severally toward late modernity in terms of their founding relation to labor; to capital itself, suddenly deprived of human form, as well as to land recast from worked matter to collateral. I read *The Hamlet* (1940), *Go Down, Moses* (1942), and *A Fable* (1954) as studies in deferred modernization and its aftermath, and as such as products of an economic contradiction. To modernize itself the southern landowning class, and Faulkner as its contemporary and historian, had to experience its lived forms—face, skin, sex, land, language—as archaic limits, available either for recuperation (modernity refused) or negation (modernity accepted as "creative destruction"). Since modernization was both abrupt in terms of the initial political intervention (1933–38), and protracted in terms of the lived forms that had to be lived down (1877–1933), refusal and acceptance might occur simultaneously, or, in Faulkner's terms, within the same plot device, character, or turn of word.

Immanuel Wallerstein, historian of capital, catches the intensifying quality of the contradictory in his observation that "contradictions not only provide the dynamic force of historical systems; they also reveal their essential features."[20] So, for example, in 1941, the historical system or regime of accumulation called "the plantation" stood structurally exposed in the south insofar as its largely black and largely bound labor force had been released from dependency by fiscal intervention on a federal scale. Since the "dynamic force" behind the postbellum plantation amounted to the coerced extraction of labor from barely free workers, or, in

Jay Mandle's formulation, from those who were "not slave, not free,"[21] the abrupt discarding of the profit source exposed both coercer and coerced to their own "essential features," even as those features and the system that sustained them changed.

But, to step back for a moment: what does it mean to say that a contradiction *within* bound labor, or *within* the labor lord who binds, provides the dynamism of the plantation system? After Althusser, I would suggest that "dependency," as a cultural logic or ideology, provides "a representation of the imaginary relationship of individuals to their real conditions of existence."[22] Stated crudely, "real conditions" on the postbellum plantation were coercive: yet "dependency," an imaginary proposal of mutual benefit between labor and labor lord, suggested that the "not free" were "not slave," insofar as they had a degree of autonomy over their crop; whilst adding that the lord was himself bound, at least for the length of the growing season, to take responsibility, at a prearranged level, for the subsistence of his labor force. The "representation" is "dynamic" in that it involves both parties in recognized misrecognitions: that is to say, both parties play double and consequently view themselves as surrounded by divided things (split referents), each of which posits alternative and contradictory realities. So, the "not slave" is free (autonomous), but must display deference (dependency): his crop, as that which he has made, he assigns to himself as a signal of his autonomy; yet his signature (if he can write) is nominal, in that he signs as cosignatory, thereby assigning his crop (and the laboring body that made it), to division by the labor lord (and his literacy). The crop and its labor are marked as scenes of contestation. Equally, and within the same "representation," the labor lord experiences lordship *and* contractual obligation; he reads the product of his land as simultaneously his own *and* as the extension of a body of labor, which is, in effect, "being his body for him."[23]

It would, I think, be a mistake to understand Althusser's "representation" as a displacement of a real social contradiction, or in Jameson's terms, as a "purely formal resolution" through which the "insurmountable" force of the contradiction is ameliorated.[24] Rather, because the "representation" retains, even as it misrecognizes, the contradiction which generates it, the forms and practices of the "representation" (to adapt Adorno) wear the lines of their construction in their features.[25] "Representation" may be said to exemplify contradiction's "dynamic force" insofar as it secretes (in both senses of that term) the system's "essential features." A regime of accumulation, even one whose premodern labor form is linked only by its products to global markets, and so to capital's inherent tendency to progress through competition,[26] must transform itself from within. Contradiction, as an impulse to "creative [self-] destruction," drives the system and its transformation. Marx defines "creative destruction" as that tendency whereby an economy dispenses with its own unproductive elements: "the violent destruction of capital, not by relations external to it, but rather as a condition of its self preservation . . . advice to begone and to [make way] for a higher state of social production."[27] As a labor lord, to preserve his land, declares himself unproductive, he divides: as a cropper "cries begone" to Memphis or Chicago, and to a "higher stage of social production," he splits. Both figures, in their duplicities, must master a stylistics for doubt and self-loss; a melancholy aporetics, featuring parataxis, alterity, and ellipsis, not merely as tropes but as practices of mind and hand. To live in contradiction is to be doubled, divided and grieving; to set oneself beside one's self, as she who handles worked things that palpably become other things through her very work. Among those worked items, words and their forms loom large.

At which point, several who address the intersection of literature and economy, reaching for "Saussurian linguistics and poststructuralist theory," will discern heresy. Where I posit language as "practical consciousness," delivering split referents, doubled and divided by specifiable contradiction, they might posit a semantics of deferral and undecidability, within which an epistemic aporia, rather than an historical contradiction, serves best to explain the tendency of language to refer in a complex and incomplete manner. For Derrida, and with him a major strand of contemporary theory, a deep suspicion of referentiality ensures that language cannot deliver the signified as any kind of social index, since it replaces things and ideas with linguistic forms. What replaces "defers" and "differs" from the replaced, establishing (in Derridean terms) the supplementarity of language. For example, the Greek noun "pharmakon" means, "the drug; medicine and/or poison":[28] Derrida argues that the semantic split prompts "indefinite pivoting,"[29] since each option, whatever its context, must allude to, defer, and supplement its opposite, rendering the meaning of "pharmakon" ever undecidable. For Derrida, the semantics of "pharmakon" typify linguistic reference more generally. So perceived, undecidability inheres structurally in linguistic reference—symptom of an epistemological uncertainty which pivots each usage on an absence to which, in the last instance, it must defer. To reiterate: Derrida's version of referential undecidability is an epistemic given.

To follow Vygotsky, Vološinov, and Bakhtin away from Derrida is to recognize that language refers, in the manifest absence of a *corresponding* referent, to that which is anything but absent. Instead, language intends toward the world via the social assumptions and purposes of its user. Linguistic usage, whether as thought, script, or speech, drives a material trace through that toward which, with varying degrees of ontological vehemence, it directs its words. Within a materialist paradigm, the referent is inextricable from the material process of its construction, among which processes language, as "practical consciousness," is pervasive.

Of course, the speaker, living a life "on the borders of someone else's consciousness,"[30] encounters, within her medium, material traces from the linguistic work of others, perhaps long since sedimented into extant social artifacts, activities, and institutions, themselves predicating future utterances and actions. Necessarily, therefore, a user's inflection expresses a divided or, in some circumstances, a contradictory intent. Bakhtin provides a useful summary of the divided nature of the socially indexical sign:

> The word is not a tangible object, but an always shifting, always changing means of social communication. It never rests with one consciousness, one voice. Its dynamism consists in movement from speaker to speaker, from one context to another, from one generation to another. Through it all, the word . . . cannot completely free itself from the concrete contexts into which it has entered. By no means does each member of the community apprehend the word as a neutral medium of the language system, free from intentions and untenanted by the voices of its previous users. Instead, he receives the word from another voice, a word full of that other voice. The word enters his context from another context, permeated with the intentions of other speakers. His own intention finds the word already occupied.[31]

Divided signs yield split referents, but the dynamic of any motion between semantic variables pivots not on epistemic absence, but on a determinable historical trajectory or tension between archaic and emergent social positions. For example, the imperative "go down," in *Go Down, Moses*, by the first decade of the twentieth century might refer either to "fellatio" or to "cunnilingus":[32] Faulkner scholarship, reaching quite properly for an intertextual reference to the spiritual, "Let My People Go: A Song of the Contrabands,"[33] does not hear an alternative inflection. Hearing sexual slang in the title depends on recognizing the allusive and pervasive presence of an erotic African American male body in the subsemantics of *Go Down, Moses*. That body, once glimpsed, justifies and elicits a titular oscillation between "Go Down, Moses" as a political injunction, prompting the renewed out-migration (or exodus) of recently bound black labor (or Jew) from the South (or Egypt); and "Go Down, [on] Moses" as a deeply covert and even unsounded sexual plea.

I fear, at this point, that too much of my game is in evidence. Even so, briefly to continue: contra Derrida's "pharmakon," Faulkner's "go down" is not undecidable. Although it elicits extreme motion between semantic options, the movement can be traced to the contradictory positioning of the divided body of black labor in 1941, a body federally rendered surplus to labor need, but nonetheless much needed in deniable forms.

By way, more typically of less dramatically split instruments, Faulkner, like any verbal instrumentalist, seeks to project singular effects, marking and making the real as a coherent project. Yet in the plantation South, between 1940 and 1954, the real, in economic terms, inclined to incoherence. Consequently, the project of Faulkner's later fiction, a project made partially from words, whose very partiality marks that project with underheard objections and contraries, must wear in the lines on its face the features of contradictions borne . . . must, semantically speaking, whisper with antipathies.

At which point, with the game I trust not quite given away, I give up on my introduction—in order closely to read, through the semantics of Faulkner's complex words, those particular economic complexities from which words in the last instance (an instance that must not endlessly be delayed) take their forms.

Earthing *The Hamlet*

A PRELUDE: regarding leisured New Yorkers of the 1870s from the perspective of 1920, Edith Wharton is much preoccupied with social transition as registered in mannered artifacts, hence her attention to "Worth dresses," in *The Age of Innocence*. Whether it is "vulgar" to wear Parisian fashions bought at Worth in the year of their purchase, or whether custom requires that such garments be "put away" for two years prior to display, concerns those gathered at Mrs Archer's Thanksgiving dinner. One guest, Miss Jackson, blames the banker Beaufort for starting "the new fashion by making his wife clap her new clothes on her back as soon as they arrived: I must say at times it takes all Regina's distinction not to look like . . . like . . ."[1] Beaufort is a banker of uncertain origin and questionable probity, who stabilized his liquidities by marrying Regina Dallas, "a penniless beauty . . . [from] one of America's most honoured families," given "'*droit de cité*' . . . in New York society" by her relation to the Mansons and the Rushworths.[2] Miss Jackson's ellipses contain two options: "like . . . " an advertisement, or "like . . . " a prostitute (ameliorated through such euphemisms as "actress" or "mistress").[3] The missing word transforms the words that surround it, so that if Regina displays her sensuality too overtly for purposes of profit, her name shifts from the regal toward the vaginal (it should be remembered that Wharton names Beaufort's mistress and second wife, Fanny Ring). "Worth" too is destabilized: even as a reduction in the turn-over time of a particular "look" realizes enhanced profits for the fashion house, so retail outlets, like "Worth," will change their emphasis. Plate glass, an invention of the 1870s, allows fashion to be "flaunt[ed]," and mitigates against the laying away of any garment so that it may "mellow under lock and key."[4] Where "Worth" is synonymous with throughput, its value shifts from the register of ethics to that of price.

Miss Jackson's tongue is stopped by a number of awkward conjunctions, spatial, temporal, and social. She pauses, perhaps, as the "marble palaces" (or department stores), which proliferated during the decade, come under pressure from the furnishings, "the heavy carpets, the watchful servants, the perpetually reminding tick of disciplined clocks,"[5] so characteristic of the interiors of the haute bourgeoisie. Her hiatus may owe something to the retrospection of those New York clocks, which ensure that each social season repeats the timetable of the last, as they confront, in the "perpetually renewed stack of cards and invitations on the hall table" beneath them,[6] a temporal "lock and key"—evidence of the need to monitor the meetings of bourgeois sons and daughters in department store and park, the new social spaces oriented to the futurity of display. That Sillerton Jackson should resolve the lapse occasioned by his sister's lost analogy, with "the air of producing an epigram,"[7] marks his attempt tonally to trump the social antagonisms tying his sister's tongue. His solution, "Like her rivals," tacitly reminds Mrs Archer's guests that Regina *has* a rival: the clashing of the spoken and unspoken names is replete with social disparity. That the conversation should pass immediately from the unmentionable mistress to Beaufort's "speculations" indicates how absolutely debates about the proper disposition of a dress displace, and yet reflect, economic tensions between kinds of capital and classes of women. An incomplete analogy has filled the room with different ways of life. The manner in which it is completed, in keeping with the furniture, aestheticizes the unreconcilable, eliciting a murmured "Oh, —" from the ladies present, and allowing the assembled company the comforting thought that form—in this case a form of words—can transform unpalatable social mutation into a repeatable bon mot.

My quasi-archaeological itinerary for an elliptical moment of social awkwardness is both speculative and far from exhaustive, but should serve to show that a garment may be replete with divergent social scenes and interested parties, whose interference with one another materializes its meaning. Such readings seem more suited to Victorian drawing rooms than to southern storefronts, perhaps because —care of Thorstein Veblen's good sense—we assume that manners take time, and that only a leisured class has time to spend on them. As Veblen put it in 1899, "the pervading principle and abiding test of good breeding is the requirement of a substantial and patent waste of time."[8] Wharton's leisure class enjoys a secure property base with which to buy time for training in "invidious differences."[9] To the leisured goes the hard and "useless" work of producing,[10] refining, reading, and rereading distinctions so as to maintain a grip on an information network invested in taste, and adding up to cultural power. However, "conspicuous leisure" is not the only route to the recognition that material objects may be complex indices of the social practices and discriminations sedimented within them.[11] Presumably, any social structure that achieves a degree of continuity, albeit brutalizing and co-ercive, will elicit from coercers and coerced, an ability (often defensive) to read the material minutiae on display at locations associated with enforcing those rules of exchange which validate that structure. Veblen's point would be that leisure time, plus un- or barely earned income, lends legibility to the accumulated taste on show in Mrs Archer's dining room. My point will be that time plus poverty can teach the impoverished to mind their manners, or at least to mind what manners can do at those everyday sites where the continuities of power are exhibited and tacitly de-bated. On which grounds, I turn from Jane Merry's dress, at the first night of the New York Opera (circa 1870), to Flem Snopes's choice of shirt for his first day's clerking in Varner's store (circa the late 1880s). I take both items to be "mannered" and socially encyclopaedic because those who consider them have for different reasons had time to reflect on the proper and improper use of their culturally abun-dant and yet materially slight properties.

I

Flem's "brand new white shirt" is cut from unlaundered cloth and retains the creases and "zebra-like" sun streaks of "each successive fold" in the bolt from its time on the store shelf.[12] Stitched by a "stiff and unaccustomed hand," it is the first in a series of shirts. Flem wears it for a week before replacing it with " a second one exactly like it": "It was as though its wearer, entering though he had into a new life and milieu already channelled to compulsions and customs fixed long before his advent, had nevertheless established in it even on that first day his own particular soiling groove" (777). The shirt opens the opening paragraph of chapter 3 of book 1 of *The Hamlet* (1940). The book is called *Flem*. Since the second paragraph starts, "He rode up on a gaunt mule," it is fair to say that his shirt comes before him and is made to say much about his arrival, achieving max-imum effect with minimum force. So, for example, it is white. Ratliff's shirt, made by his own "accustomed" hand (777), is blue. Ratliff is a merchant who offers credit and whose dog-kennel cart is a mobile version of Varner's commissary, yet Ratliff wears blue—a sartorial decision involving downward aspiration, undertaken in order that his shirts shall complement the clothing of the rural workers of small means who are his market. Flem rises from minimal means: white announces his ascent.

The material itself multiplies the effect of the color, bringing together different spaces in a single image. The cloth proclaims that it is new and from the store; in-deed, the narrator is emphatic, treating the cloth as a synecdoche of Varner's com-mercial "milieu." The wearer, who marks the cloth and its milieu with "his own particular soiling groove," is placed and displaced by Faulkner's choice of double-voiced terms, each of which points simultaneously in discrete social directions. "Soil": Flem is nominally from the soil, and therefore at work in the store is "matter out of place" or social dirt;[13] but his "soilure" marks the cloth with a "groove" which is no longer manual (that of a "hand" "accustomed" to the plough), but legible (or suited to a ledger). The point of Faulkner's semantic valencies would seem to be, not that Flem has become a clerk, or as many Faulkner scholars would have it "homo economicus," but that he is both clerk and cropper, and as such is an anomaly in a white shirt.

The inhabitants of Frenchman's Bend are puzzled, reading black for white. We are told that on the evening of the first day

> they were gathered even before the sun was completely gone, looking now and then to-wards the dark front of Varner's store as people will gather to look quietly at the cold embers of a lynching or at the propped ladder and open window of an elopement, since the presence of a hired white clerk in the store of a man still able to walk and with intellect still sound enough to make money mistakes at least in his own favor, was as unheard of as the presence of a hired white woman in one of their own kitchens. "Well," one said, "I don't know nothing about that one Varner hired. But blood's thick. And a man that's got kinfolks that stay mad enough all the time to set fire to a man's barn—"
>
> "Sho now," Ratliff said. "Old man Ab aint naturally mean. He's just soured." (755)

Flem is blackened on two other occasions in the novel. The narrator likens him, sitting at Varner's knee with "the open ledgers" at the yearly settlement of tenant accounts, to a "native parrot-taught headman in an African outpost" beside a "white trader" (786). In addition, Ratliff obscurely dresses Flem in "long black stockings" so that (at least in Ratliff's imagination) he can penetrate Eula (880).

To make sense of the Bend's latent sense that Flem is black we need to consider his other accessory—the tie, "a tiny machine-made black bow which snapped together at the back with a metal fastener" (783). The tie, like the shirt, receives detailed explication and contains varied social trajectories. Likened to "an enigmatic punctuation symbol . . . cryptically balanced . . . against the expanse of the white shirt" (783–84), it gives pause ("." ":" ";" "," . . . but for how long?) and raises issues of tone (exclamatory [!], interrogative [?]). To suggest that Flem buys the tie out of deference to Will Varner's taste in Sunday best is to miss the point made by those in the store on the day of Ab Snopes's arrival, for whom the son's tie recalls the father's "stiff foot," in that both exhibit a "quality of outrageous overstatement of physical displacement" (784). To men of small means the tie signals Flem's continuity with barn burners. To storeowners, presumably, it indicates Flem's aspiration to own. To Flem it may be the sign of service to two masters.

But before considering Flem's sartorial intent, I had best address why croppers and tenants would link a snap tie to a club foot. The force of their analogy is that both its elements "overstate" and "displace," begging questions as to what they cover up and omit. Since the men on the porch know Ab as an unconvicted barn burner, and since barn burning in the 1880s was a largely anonymous crime, perpetrated by the propertyless against the propertied,[14] it would seem that they suspect his son of harbouring purposes both criminal and political. In "Barn Burning" (1938), Faulkner notes that "the element of fire spoke to some deep mainspring of his [Ab's] . . . being . . . as the one weapon for the preservation of integrity, else the breath were not worth the breathing."[15] Ab is an arsonist, but the burning of a barn by an impoverished cropper directs a quasi-political resentment against an institutional structure associated with a seemingly unchangeable form of labor exploitation. Barns, gins, stables, and storehouses were the preferred targets of the arsonist, in that each was a real and symbolic accumulation of that which owners had stolen from tenants—their labor, which labor was all that the tenant had to sell. The men who sit on Varner's porch are men of small means. Most of them are his tenants: in drawing a resemblance, however strained, between Flem and Ab some among them may be expressing a utopian hope, while others, perhaps of slightly greater means, tacitly hypothesize a disguised crime. Their analogy, resonant with class options, is specific, drawing into resemblance the look of a tie and the sound of a boot. Given that Ab's foot, tracking dirt onto De Spain's "pale" rug,[16] is part of the anecdotal heritage of the Bend, the analogy rests on what Paul Ricoeur might call an "iconic moment,"[17] in which the tie on the shirt and the shit on the rug are drawn into visual alignment. If so, central to the figure of speech is the idea that Flem's putative mark of respectability (the tie *is* for church) obscures and yet contains his dirty purposes.

It is a small step from dirt to ethnicity, at least for those on the porch. We should perhaps recall the narrator's sense that, on the evening of Flem's first day, those who watch the store from Mrs. Littlejohn's boarding house, do so as though "looking quietly at the cold embers of a lynching" (755). Although those who are on conversational terms with men who can afford to pay board may have more means than others who "furnish" out of the commissary, both groups share a sense of Flem's blackness: the lynched in Mississippi have been predominantly black, even as "clerks" and hypothetical "cooks," though white, *should* be black—at least in the mind's eye of those who consider Flem's new position. An ethnic stain might also explain their sense of the new clerk as a potential sexual predator, a sense later elaborated in Ratliff's fantasy of Flem's lower half, theatrically blackened for purposes of Eula penetration. The "embers" in question are complex, combining dirt, arson, and ethnicity in an unstable semantic mix, and focusing on an analogical framework which reaches via the "tie" back through Ab's soiling boot to his "flame."[18] Arson was for the most part anonymous, but was believed to be the preferred weapon of a disaffected black tenantry.[19] For some at least, most probably on Varner's porch, the link between the son's tie and the father's boot, though as ethnically confused as populism's failure to recognize class affinities across the racial line, contains a residual longing that the Snopes in Varner's store, like the Snopes on Varner's land, will remember that his "integrity" resides in the lesson of his class apprenticeship—namely, that the property of the owners derives from the sweat of the owned, and can be burned down.[20]

I have been attending to subsemantic whisperings latent in a ramifying resemblance. Implicit in my reading is an account of the memory of men on different porches as they read Flem's shirt and tie. Michel de Certeau notes that knowledge derived from memory "draws on a multitude of events among which it moves without possessing them (they are all *past*, each a loss of place but a fragment of time), it also computes and predicts 'the multiple paths of the future' by combining antecedent or possible particularities."[21] As I understand him, de Certeau suggests that memory makes temporal metaphors, combinations in which discrete times (and particulars) coexist in a relation of tension, since the similarity and dissimilarity of the two or more moments articulated together implies alternative temporal options. De Certeau adds that the mobilization of memory "is inseparable from alteration." Indeed, he speaks of a "double alteration," of the memory and of the object that prompted its work ("which is remembered only when it has disappeared").[22] Such an account gives to memory an anticipatory edge: we remember a present particular (which vanishes in the degree to which it is drawn into memory) in order to revise an element of the past, in the light of an alternative future. Hence he adds:

> Memory is in decay when it is no longer capable of this alteration. It constructs itself from events that are independent of it, and it is linked to the expectation that something alien to the present will or must occur. Far from being the reliquary or trash can of the past, it sustains itself by *believing* in the existence of possibilities and by vigilantly awaiting them.[23]

To compound de Certeau with Ricoeur at this abstracted point might seem willful, but I am concerned to emphasize and explore the workings and class implications embedded in a single act of memory—that of those men on the porch as they "postulated" (784) a connection between Flem's tie and Ab's foot. Their sense of analogy owes more to metaphor than to simile. To "postulate" is to make a strong claim or demand, in this case for a resemblance—which is to say, they all but make a metaphor. Ricoeur takes a tensional view of metaphor as productive of an "impertinent predication," resulting from the interaction of the terms combined, whose clashing of elements modifies the literal meaning of the metaphoric referent. What results is not the obliteration of the thing referred to (in this case, a tie) to but its conversation into a "split reference" (tie and boot), which confronts receivers of the metaphor with the requirement that they make and remake reality:

> [M]etaphoric meaning does not merely consist of semantic clash but of the new predicative meaning which emerges from the collapse of the literal meaning, that is, from the col-

lapse of the meaning which obtains if we rely on the common or usual . . . value of our words. The metaphor is not the enigma but the solution of the enigma.[24]

The men who recall the sound of Ab's boot on seeing Flem's tie make an "enigma" (or "double alteration") in which the mark of the son's respectability and the evidence of the father's radicalism both resist and yield to each other, their compatibility resting on incompatibilities of class and race and time that will not simply lapse into a generic "Snopes" (enroute for "Snopesism"). Rather, the tie, as metaphor and temporal conjunction, is a disturbing hybrid or "split reference" that creates, for its "readers," a conceptual need to challenge extant versions of what a Snopes is and will be, does and will do.

Or, as de Certeau might put it, the croppers and tenants who make the tie "mean," engage in, the "instant art" of memory to produce an "ensemble" (or "concrete encyclopedia") made from "an unending summation of particular fragments," each "distort[ing]" the others to yield *passages into something else* through 'twisted' relations . . . and reversals":

> The oddest thing is no doubt the *mobility* of this memory in which details are never *what* they are: they are not objects, for they are elusive as such; not fragments, for they yield the ensemble they forget; not totalities, since they are not self-sufficient; not stable since each recall alters them. This "space" of a moving nowhere has the subtlety of a cybernetic world. . . . But all these variants could very well be no more than the shadows—enlarged into symbolic and narrative projections—thrown by the practice . . . that consists in seizing the opportunity and making memory the means of transforming places.[25]

The narrator wants to keep the tie simple, parenthetically noting that after Flem had achieved the presidency of a Jefferson bank "he had them made for him by the gross" (783). In the context of Flem's irresistible rise, his tie might lose its "cybernetic world" were it not that the narrator of *The Hamlet* is one among several voices, and may sit too close to Ratliff for us to take him on trust (more on this later). Sewing machine agents, storekeepers, bankers, and perhaps this narrator have a tendency—inherent in their properties—to look to the future, and to rest easy in market projections about "progress." To men of small means, a tie on a Snopes means more than one thing, even as that Snopes may have more than one purpose and some of them might be crossed.

II

While not simplifying Flem, critics have tended to narrow the focus of his complexity. As Richard Gray puts it, he is prevalently read as "an agent of Capitalism."[26] For James Snead he is "the commercial spirit in its purity," capitalism's "restless centre,"[27] while for Louise Barnett, he acts "according to the impersonal rule of modern capitalism . . . a personified abstraction of Acquisition."[28] The variants are several: from Mauri Skinfill's "New South's capitalist,"[29] through Joseph Urgo's "structural speculator,"[30] to Richard Moreland's "structural Jew," scapegoated by rumour into "the mysteriously unlocalizeable unknown in the workings of the Bend's economy."[31] One variation run on the variants involves arguing over whether or not Flem represents the values of the hamlet, that is, "Does Snopes reflect, extend or parody Varner?"[32] My point is not to deflect from the economic emphasis, but to stress that the economy in question is historically particular, and that Flem may be misread if he is too readily allegorized as the agent of something as generic as "capital."

Indeed, Flem's first significantly independent act on entering Varner's store in 1887 is as contradictory as his shirt and tie.[33] He refuses credit (783): read from the perspective of 1940, his decision is at one with the regional shift from "debt" to "wage," and so is the act of a financial innovator. Varner, we are told, races to the store to reassert the credit option; for him to do anything less would be to connive at the subversion of "cropping" as a system for the coercion of a low-paid work force.[34] Varner needs his tenants and croppers in debt, the extent of their debt being the extent of his control, and so of his profit. Read from the perspective of the late 1880s, Flem's decision is inept, or, perhaps, radical—in a manner that his father might appreciate—since credit-withdrawal is more systemically threatening than barn burning. Nor should we turn too swiftly from the radical option. Jody Varner may take Flem as fire insurance (752), believing that once in the store he will be the store's man, acting on behalf of property in the matter of Ab's inflammatory resentment of proprietors. But Jody forgets the measured nature of Flem's response to his father's radical tradition: Flem gets the job not only because he properly refuses Jody's blandishments, insisting "[a]int no benefit in farming" (750), but also because he stands in the right place—as Varner recognizes too late, "Hell fire . . . [h]e was standing just exactly where couldn't nobody see him from the house" (751). Jody's expletive takes its edge from Ab's "flame," but only because Jody recognizes in Flem's positional sense the son's respect for his father's quasi-populist handiwork. Jody may cheer himself up by forgetting his own delayed insight into class continuity, but the drawers of analogy on the store front have better memories.

Of course the marks of Flem's social ascent are clear and available: his displacement of Jody from the key sites of economic transaction—the counter, the ledger, the gin, the cash box, the ear of the owner, and attendance on the owner's daughter. But the trajectory does not necessarily lead directly from "peasant" to financier, despite the narrator's parenthetical allusion to a Jefferson bank (783). The narrator, like a good speculator, fixes his economic eye on far futurity and encourages us to ignore residual elements in Flem's behavior, and to go for the emergent. Yet Raymond Williams points out that no economic moment is "one thing," its modes of exchange being characterized by archaic as well as innovative patterns of transaction.[35]

The tail end of the 1880s in Mississippi is complex: populism has failed on two counts—failed to distract the ruling landed elite (Varner) from its engagement with the commercial values of the "New South." Note that the store vies with the field as the Bend's focal institution. In addition it has failed to fabricate a union between men of small and yet smaller means, between, that is, petty producers working their own land (the farmer from whose barn Ike steals corn; Houston in decline) and croppers and tenants (Ab and Mink) working the property of speculators in land.[36] Note that Mink's insistence on common grazing rights implies freedom from dependency and cooperative working patterns.[37] Note also that Houston, despite owning a shrinking farm, fails to see grounds for shared interest with Mink. Houston has mortgaged a section of land to Varner, to which land Varner has bound Mink as tenant or virtual peon.[38] Despite a lengthy class apprenticeship to both agricultural and urban labor, as wheat-hand, shepherd, construction worker, long-shoreman, and locomotive fireman (928), Houston cannot recognize that he and Mink are linked as debtors to the same speculator. Varner holds collateral in land against Houston's debt (931) and collateral in labor against what Mink owes; the distinction divides the debtors. But one might have expected antagonism toward Varner to unite them, given that Varner—as "usurer," "owner of most of the good land in the country," and mortgagee "on most of the rest" (733)—is surely a candidate for the twin populist epithets, "money king" and "speculative parasite."

The class plot thickens once the late 1880s in Mississippi are perceived from 1940. Faulkner completes the various elements of *The Hamlet* during a decade of radical class transformation. The influx of federal funding achieved under the Agricultural Adjustment Program (1933–38) effected a revolution, in which the land-owner ceased to be a labor lord (or coercer of "bound" tenants) and became an employer (who might or might not contract for labor); even as the sharecropper was transformed from debt peon to under- or unemployed wage earner.[39] Give that Faulkner writes 1887–1890 from the late 1930s, he necessarily writes about populism's failed labor revolt from the perspective of an unfinished but inescapable revolution in southern labor. Revolt and revolution revise "dependency" and recast how money is made and labor used in the South. Faulkner situates Flem at the nub of a number of awkward and dramatic class transitions, both in the manner of ownership and the ways of work. If, in 1890 as in 1940, owners are unsure of how to own and of what best to own, even as those who work the land are unsure of their ties, both to the land and to those among whom they work, the positioning of Flem between Ab and Varner is calculatedly complex.

Since Faulkner sets *The Hamlet* in a divided time (or times), and locates Flem at an exact juncture between antagonistic classes (further divided against themselves), it would be a mistake to follow the general drift of much Faulknerian scholarship in reading Flem too purely as capital's agent.[40] Consequently, I shall read Flem for his labor latencies and possibly populist remainders. To listen to his silence is, as Michael Millgate points out, to hear only two hundred and forty-four words; but taciturnity allied to a good ear need not necessarily and all at once make of him "a silent tactician and master strategist" on capital's behalf.[41] On the contrary, his career in the Bend offers examples of ineptitude and luck. Whether or not one reads his initial refusal of credit as radical residue or financial innovation, it *is* conspicuously silly in terms of its outcome. Moreover, the requirement that your boss pay publically and to the cent for a small item from his own stock may presage a scrupulous adherence to the viewpoint of exchange, but it might equally indicate a residual and ingrained resentment of the carelessness of the wealthy, while also suggesting that Flem, as yet only an apprentice clerk, lacks the ability to read the fuller economy of Varner's tobacco purchase (780).

Certainly, in the matter of goats, Flem fails to hear Ratliff's calculation, although Bookwright senses that Ratliff's words on the desirability and availability of goats are just too loud to be taken at face value (804). That Flem loses little on the goat deal, despite error, has nothing to do with putative skill and everything to do with a combination of coincidences; first, the fortuitous surfacing of a note to the sum of ten dollars in Isaac Snope's name (800), but payable by Flem (Ike's guardian): second, Ratliff's unwillingness to make claim, because he knows that if Flem redeems the note, he will simply use it again as a form of currency. Flem *may* have assessed that persons unknown (among them Ratliff) might be unwilling to draw, however indirectly, on the limited resources of an idiot, but he did not calculate the lucky break of *that* note appearing in *that* hand, during a deal which he was on the brink of losing. He was just lucky, and my point is that he needed to be, given the conspicuous failure of his purchasing strategy. Luck also attends the achievement of his greatest asset, Eula and her landed dowry. Flem is quite simply in the right place at the right time. Impregnated by the departed Haoke McCarron, Eula is deemed to need a husband, at least according to her father. Flem, boarder in the Varner house, clerk in the Varner store, and apparent trainee manager of Varner's properties, gets the break. I do not mean to suggest that he has not *made* his luck, merely that it *is* luck. Later in *The Town* (1957), he will exchange Eula's sexual favors for a bank. However, in *The Hamlet* his hypothetical inability to service those favors, *could* be read not as price maintenance, but as a withdrawal of pleasures. The claim is unlikely in the light of what we later learn about Flem's sexuality. However, between *The Hamlet* and *The Town*, class-motivated celibacy remained an option ignored by critics. Perhaps the idea of Flem's denying fulfillment has not been considered because, as a notion, it partakes of his apprenticeship to barn burning as an abuse of the master's goods, rather than of his putative commitment to speculative capital.

Flem's tie to the tenantry, if restored, also allows his eventual use of Eula's landed part to be inflected two ways. Joseph Urgo quite properly points out that for Flem the Frenchman's place (like any place) has no "intrinsic value," rather its "monetary value" derives from Flem's skill in restoring a story to the land. Flem, he says, converts a "forgotten property" into "a site of desire" by silently performing the one about the buried gold of the plantocracy, allied in his person to the other one about Flem Snopes the speculator. Ergo for Urgo, Flem having the ground salted by night is a "structural speculator" who creates "speculative property."[42] I would not disagree, but would add the riders that he does it badly, and that he *may* just be blundering in the dark. Some of the coins Flem buries in lieu of the Frenchman's antebellum gold are dated post-1891. The carelessness with which he forges might have alerted those whom he fools to their foolishness, thereby deflating his land's price. My objection to claims for Flem's capitalist acumen approaches hair-splitting, but allied to previous evidence of error, inappropriate action, and luck, his entire scheme for the ruined plantation house joins his refusal of credit as being just possibly little more than a guess on a wing and a prayer, allied to a gift for getting it right should something come of it. Given his complete silence on motive and purpose, one might add that fooling persons with more money than sense by placing fools' gold on ex-planter property, property which his father knew to be "Nigger sweat" with a little "white sweat" added,[43] might well appeal to a residual populist, still alive and functioning in a body soon misguidedly to be allegorized as the fount of Snopesism.

III

I have been reading Flem against the grain, seeking two class trajectories (residual and emergent) where others have found one. The singularity of the prevalent "take" on Flem owes much to Ratliff's critical preferences, both as character and as interpreter of all things Snopesian. Due skepticism over some of Ratliff's judgments is difficult because the narrator tends to drift from indirectly reporting the sewing machine agent's thoughts to unattributed elaborations on those opinions, which, sans cited source, stand in for a narrative position. Nonetheless, Ratliff's perception of Flem needs to be recognized as partial, interested, and class-based. Despite posing as Flem's archrival, and seeming to exist as his antithesis—garrulous where Flem is taciturn; neighbourly where Flem is isolated; a member of the community where Flem is its pariah; manifestly human where Flem is clinically detached—Ratliff shares much with Flem, not least that both quit rented fields for versions of the store. Indeed, it could be argued that similarity of class origin might partially validate Ratliff's judgments regarding Flem were it not that Ratliff's stepping from the agricultural ladder leads him to depoliticize his own antecedents—witness how he gets Flem's father wrong, and thereby prepares the ground for his mistaking of the son.

Since errors with regard to Ab stem from Ratliff's class needs, I had best explore the implications of his mercantile status. Structurally speaking, Ratliff is an outreach worker for Varner's credit mechanisms. Though an independent trader, selling sewing machines most typically on credit—a twenty-dollar note down in exchange for a machine—he depends upon and validates those structures of debt emanating from Varner's store and from Varner's rented fields. Just as Varner calls in his liens on land use and store goods at the end of the growing season, so Ratliff redeems his notes against the yield of his client's crop, as translated into cash at Varner's gin. In that he also takes pleasure in "retailing" a "stock" of "mouthwords" (780) during his tours of the backroads of the Bend, he should be understood as acting as Varner's indirect agent, verifying the credit-worthiness of those among whom he moves. What else is his store-porch version of Ab Snopes, if not a barbed credit rating for a tenant whom the owner may have to watch?

The economic historians Ransom and Sutch note that in 1880 the average "customer" in a southern store generated no more than eighty dollars credit a year,[44] of which Ratliff's twenty is a sizeable portion. Furthermore, Ratliff is the part-owner of a Jefferson restaurant, frequented by drummers, the very salesman whose goods lodged in Varner's store will retail at "credit prices" way above their cash cost to the storekeeper.[45] My point is that for all his benevolence, Ratliff's concern for the planting and cashing of crops complements Varner's. Both are merchants who depend for the "retail" of their "stock" on a system which leaves southern labor with less than little on which to live. Ab Snopes knows as much, commenting on Jody's offer that he "[f]urnish out of the store. . . . No cash." "I see. Furnish in six-bit dollars" (736). A "six-bit" dollar is a dollar worth seventy-five cents,[46] the missing quarter covering the difference in price between a good bought on credit and the same good paid for in cash. Figures detailing the increasing cost of southern credit between 1875 and 1896 read like larceny. Trapped in a credit mechanism, controlled by merchants and land lords, (and I would reiterate that Varner is both), the southern tenant

> was neither owner of his land nor manager of his business. Caught between requirements imposed by the landlord and those imposed by the merchant, his independent decision making was limited to the mundane and menial aspects of farming. The larger decisions concerning land use, investments in the farm's productivity, the choice of technology and the scale of operation—were all made for him. Undoubtedly, as a consequence, his pride, his ambition, and his efficiency as a tiller of the soil were reduced.[47]

Ransom and Sutch place the debilitation of the southern tenantry squarely at the door of the merchant. Ratliff is culpable: not to Varner's degree, but on the same scale of measurement.

Once the sewing machine agent's structural position is recognized as aiding and abetting what Faulkner calls in Varner "usury" (733), several of his judgments on things Snopesian come into class focus. In the matter of Ab, Ratliff's "retailing" casts a barn burner as a "soured" but negotiable tenant (756–73). Ratliff is a revisionist, his "fool about a horse" recomposes Faulkner's earlier "man with a flame." In 1938 Faulkner published "Barn Burning," wherein Ab, equipped with a "niggard fire" (three times reiterated within the space of two pages) and a frock coat cut from the "tin" of Conrad's *The Nigger of the Narcissus*,[48] burns barns in a manner eminently readable as a version either of the Southern Farmers' Tenant Union's cross-racial resistance to picking prices, or (cast back in time from 1910 to the 1880s) of populist intransigence. I lack the space to detail my grounds for such a claim,[49] but the very fact that Ratliff digests "Barn Burning" into four pages for Jody, and spends the equivalent of some twenty-five pages on Ab's defeat in a horse trade, for the men on Jody's porch suggests that he seeks to deradicalize his subject. Politicized tenants, who leave farms burned prior to ginning, are no more in Ratliff's interest than in Varner's. Just as Ratliff "whitens" Ab, so he shifts his exploiter from an in-county landowner (be he Harris, de Spain, or Varner) to an out-of-state trader, the Texan Pat Stamper (761). Moreover, the issue at stake in the trade is not even equine, but "them eight cash dollars . . . actual Yoknapatawpha County cash dollars" (761) that Stamper got from Beasley Kemp. Kemp is local, and Ratliff's Ab trades to regain county honor abused by a "stranger" (761). Cash is to blame, not credit. Furthermore, Ab's loss of his only stock animal—that which grants him minimal independence in the matter of farming—is blamed, not on a regime of accumulation which "left farmers with enough to survive . . . [but] removed most of the gains from whatever growth took place,"[50] but on a "stranger" and his "magician" camped by a roadside (761). Ratliff knows his audiences: to Jody he gives a depoliticized warning about a member of the workforce; to the workforce he gives distractions.

Having told his stories, Ratliff visits their subject with a gift of whiskey:

> He halted the buckboard at the fence. The plow had reached the far end of the field. The man turned the team, their heads tossing and yawning, their stride breaking as he sawed them about with absolutely needless violence. Ratliff watched soberly. Just like always he thought. He still handles a horse or a mule like it had done already threatened him with its fist before he even spoke to it. (774–75)

The passage is dense with ignored political residues. But who is ignoring what exactly? Ratliff "watche[s]," but the judgment as to "needless[ness]" properly belongs to the narrator, since although it epitomizes Ratliff's subsequent "thought[s]," it is not of them. Moreover, the Faulkner of "Barn Burning" and of the account in "The Long Summer" of Mink's destitution knows that a tenant's relation to a mule (which may imminently or actually be the property of his landlord) better approximates to a fixed fight than to productive labor. Faulkner does not believe his narrator's Ratliff-led suggestion that a tenant has no need of violence.

Since the narrator at times parrots Ratliff, it is perhaps unsurprising that the voice of the merchant carries the critical day. Yet Faulkner provides structural materials for a contextualizing of Ratliff's voice, which once it is heard as class-inflected yields sufficient internal evidence for a critique both of the merchant and of his sometime amanuensis. Ratliff's childhood bound him to Ab, to rented fields, and to a coercive, credit-led labor regime. In the light of such an apprenticeship, his mercantile judgments are marked by residual contradictions, which if pursued expose his limitations as a reader of Snopes. I have space for only two examples, both of them related to Flem's simultaneous achievement of the body of Eula and of her landed part (the Old Frenchman's place), given in dowry by her father. Ratliff cannot accept these losses. Glossed, his response might run: outwit Flem to regain Varner's ear. Do so by purchase of the place, which place as surrogate for Eula grants admission, through her landed body, to the Varner clan.

At the start of book 3 ("The Long Summer"), and after Eula's departure with Flem on extended honeymoon to Texas, Ratliff approaches the Bend, where the Houston/Mink dispute over the pasturing of Mink's scrub bull is to be adjudicated. He does so, slowly, via a conversation with Varner, outside Varner's house, on the loss of the Place. I am framing his thoughtful saunter toward the store carefully, since his comments there need to be mediated through his fragmented meditation on the bodies of Eula and of the land, both lost to him. Ratliff's elegiac recollection brings soil and soilure out into what, care of Ricoeur out of de Certeau, I would call an "impertinent" clash of "variants" (or quasi-"cybernetic . . . ensemble") whose "split referents" whisper along their schisms of "symbolic and narrative projections." The various trajectories of Ratliff's reverie remain implicit, but readers must draw them out if they are to understand the sewing machine agent's gnomic summation of Flem as a store-bound sexual predator in "long black stockings" (880). For example:

> And yet those buggies were still there. He could see them, sense them. Something was; it was too much to have vanished that quickly and completely—the air polluted and rich and fine which had flowed over and shaped that abundance and munificence, which had done the hydraulic office to that almost unbroken progression of chewed food, which had held intact the constant impact of those sixteen years of sitting down: so why should not that body at the last have been the unscalable sierra, the rosy virginal mother of barricades for no man to conquer scot-free or even to conquer at all, but on the contrary to be hurled back and down, leaving no scar, no mark of himself (That ere child aint going to look no more like nobody this country ever saw than she did, he thought.)—the buggy merely a part of the whole, a minor and trivial adjunct, like the buttons on her clothing, the clothes themselves, the cheap beads which one of the three of them had given her. (877)

Beside Varner's "gapped and weathered picket fence" (876), Ratliff recalls the buggies once tethered there, driven by Eula's displaced suitors. The narrator insists that "[h]e could see them," before rendering the transport transparent via slippage from sight through "sense" to "[s]omething" in residual excess of their having "vanished." The "[s]omething" approximates to that "perceptual cramp,"[51] inherent in the "iconic moment" of metaphor when the visual nature of the "*figure* of speech" requires an impossible image (Ricoeur speaks of it as the visualization of a "split reference").[52] Like a plaster crucifix whose stigmata are deemed to bleed, or like Ike McCaslin's old snake sprouting rudimentary and prelapsarian limbs in order to walk "on two feet and free of all laws of mass and balance,"[53] the buggies have been the impact point for too much narrative for them simply to depart with their actual physical departure, at least in Ratliff's mind's eye. The dash ("—") points to a hiatus in visibility healed by a smell ("polluted . . . air"), and dramatizes the remembered and quasi-iconic nature of the buggies. Under the sign of erasure those vehicles can be reconfigured, as though out of air, as a sliding hybridity into which all that has ridden on them and proceeded by way of them can be summoned, thereby yielding "*passages into something else* through twisted relations" (de Certeau).

The buggies are the focus of an extended metaphor. Standing on Varner's property and carrying Varner's daughter, they mediate the passage of one into the other via courtship and matrimony. But in Ratliff's memory they pass into "something" more copious in its "variants." Sniffing the air, he discovers a "rich" pollutant which in the first instance has equine sources: horses are numerous—those of the suitors, Ratliff's "own two" (877), but most olfactory of all Varner's recently departed "old fat white horse" whose "sonorous . . . entrails" (875) and "internal chord[s]" (876) doubtless perfume the air. But the anal odor derives also from other beasts and is accompanied by additional orifices. Dogs join the horses, in Ratliff's memory, to "snuffle" at the fence posts. Ratliff adds that the "two-legged feice" (877) can, in the absence of Eula, desist from sniffing and raising their legs against the fence. "Feice" is odd, being either a singular or a strange plural of "fice," a small mongrel dog: in the context of "chewed food," its exceptional spelling yields "faeces,"[54] whereupon those drawn to Varner's unnamed daughter are scatologically stained. The "richness" of the smell, equine, canine, human, faecal, and urinary, has only just begun. Nor should one "deodorize" the passage by thematizing Ratliff's vision as "excremental," and moving discreetly on. Ratliff cannot quit the smell which "shape[s]" the buggies, and by extension forms their passenger—realized as mouth, anus, and vagina. "She" (Eula's name is not used and for almost the entire and extended sentence, female pronouns are avoided); she chews. Her body, as an "hydraulic" entity, is one which conveys liquids through pipes: contextually speaking, those liquids are easily identified. Since she chews, her peristaltic "office[s]" "progress" inevitably to that whereon she sits, the "rosy" cheeks of which shield anus and hymen, though the latter is secondary being a matter of some hope on Ratliff's part.

He further notes that despite matrimony "at the last" Eula may yet be "the rosy

virginal mother of all barricades." His leap from Eula's backside to the French Revolution, and more particularly to intimations of the iconic revolutionary female,
Marianne, may at first, second, and third glance seem willful. Yet by casting Eula's
hymen as a mountainous and radical barricade, Ratliff effectively relegates the as-
sailant Flem to a reactionary failure; while elevating Eula, in a gynaecological revision of her French apogee, into a virginal matriarch.[55] The narrator parenthetically
interpolates Ratliff's idiomatic summation of the metamorphosis: Eula and Eula's
child are both immaculate conceptions, being products of autogenesis unmarked
by any male "this country ever saw." In which case, Ratliff, the provider of the barricades, joins Flem among those "hurled back"; by the deep logic of his own
metaphor, he numbers himself among the spent reactionary forces. All of which,
from excremental odor to virgin birth, occurs as an ellipsis, set within a single sentence and framed by marks of excision ("— . . .—"). The implied omission, little
more than a dense ensemble annotating a smell, is further framed by the word
"buggy" ("those buggies . . . the buggy").[56] Since we are told that the "buggy [is]
merely a part of the whole," which w/hole in the text has drawn diverse holes to it,
the vehicle is subsumed within an orifice simultaneously rectal and vaginal. At
which stage in my reading of the residues, I find myself dearly wishing to quit: my
unease complements that of the narrator who represses his own fundamental and
absorptive pun on "whole," for the "buttons," "beads," and "trivial" coverings of the
body in question.

Yet I must persist, fearing that I have given the wrong impression. In passages
of dense metaphoricity, to follow the logic of one associative strand, from its
"focus" to the further reaches of an implied "framework," can be to ignore the semantic consequences of interference from other strands. Perhaps Ratliff leaves
Eula unnamed and rarely grants her a female pronoun during his meditation, because "she" is not for him exclusively a woman; in which case, my pathologizing
of her body may at best be partial. When he first pauses by the triggering picket
fence, Ratliff observes to Varner, "You must have been desperate," but the narrator adds, "He was not even thinking of Varner's daughter's shame or of his daughter at all. He meant the land, the Old Frenchman place" (875). If Eula is a synecdoche for "land" (and land accompanies the marital transfer of her body), her
landed part, already established as an assemblage of holes, takes on an alternative and autochthonous series of associations, extending from the "buggy" seat on
which Eula sat, through Ike Snope's sodomizing of Houston's cow, to Flem's "salting" of a hole he has had dug in the Frenchman place.

But I run far ahead of myself, and if only to escape Ratliff's promiscuous sense
of smell, I offer an interim comment on autochthony. An "autochthon" is one who
springs from the soil which he/she inhabits: Adam formed from dirt, and limping
Oedipus, tagged by this name (meaning "swollen foot") to that from which he
came, are noted carriers of autochthony. *The Hamlet* is replete with autochthonic

limpers: the cretin, Ike, falls down a lot, and although he does not like the "taste of . . . certain kinds of soil," he is a "herbivore" partial to "what his upright kind . . . call filth" (900). Labove, despite his own agility, "cleats" his peasant family to the ground with a series of borrowed "football shoes" (825); among them, his granny, "lik[ing] the sounds the cleats made on the floor" (826) is mightily club-footed. Armstid breaks his leg twice, limps, and is last seen "[digging] himself back into the earth which had produced him" (1069). Eula too can be said to limp, her inertia rendering her slow to walk. Lack of ambulatory ambition involves her in various forms of carriage: from infancy to five or six, "a negro manservant . . . stagger[s] slightly beneath his long, dangling, already indisputably female burden like a bizarre and chaperoned Sabine rape" (818); from eight to fourteen, her daily trips to school (riding double with her brother Jody, since she "calmly and flatly refused to walk" [820]), yield an anthology of "breast," "buttock" and "outrageously curved dangling leg" (823)—all of it drawn earthwards by Eula's preference for "sitting supine and female and soft and immovable" (820). Aptly, given her tendency to inertial overflow, McCarron enters her from above and on the ground, arguably exemplifying the narrator's opening bid, in the first paragraph of book 2 ("Eula"), which casts her as "bursting grapes . . . writhen bleeding . . . beneath the hard rapacious . . . goathoof" (817). *The Town* (1957) specifies the "hoof," indicating that impregnation occurred beneath both McCarron and his horse. On which evidence, Eula might more properly be spoken of less as snagged to the earth by a nascent limp than as the earth's orifice. Given her place in a subterranean but sustained autochthonic ensemble, to enter Eula is to enter the ground and more particularly the Frenchman place, site of the Bend's origin. But of course, Flem has taken the bodily form of that place away, and will at the novel's close corrupt the deep-plot of autochthony, salting the place with coin in order (and eventually in *The Town*) to take a bank out of Eula's "place."

IV

Some of the above, I would argue, lies behind Ratliff's disturbed refusal to name Eula, at the start of "The Long Summer," as he rides from Varner's picket fence to Varner's store. Were he to articulate her name, he would prioritize her gender over her autochthony, her sexual soilure over her iconicity as soil given human form. To say or think "Eula" would be to characterize what the Bend has lost as exclusively female, rather than as a particular relation to the land, partially embodied in Eula's focal form. For sake of clarity, I shall step briefly back from particularities, in order to summarize the purpose of the ensembles of inference whose coagulations I have been tracing. Faulkner creates Eula as a landed place, not to sexualize the earth but to earth sexuality. He gives body to the ground so that place can be read as materializing what bodies do to the earth in that place. Even so, it is clear that by the time Ratliff reaches the store his initial desperation over land predation has drifted toward a more specific, though not necessarily more accurate, anxiety about sexual predation. The form of his anxiety is incomprehensible to those who hear it. Arriving at the store's gallery he tells a story which follows and extends his silent and olfactory meditation on "buggies," but which articulates primarily that strand of it concerned with anality.

Ratliff's preface to his tale of "sex in the store" is a wordplay turning on his conversion of a proper noun ("Snopes") into an improper verb ("to snopes"). Each Snopes seen over the four pages dividing buggy-meditation and dirty-story is anally resonant: Lump, Varner's new clerk, has a "bright-pink mouth like a kitten's button" (878) (I am reminded of the narrator's earlier surrendering of the pun "w/hole" for a "button" [p.159]); Mink's preferred and deleted expletive is "shit" ("---t!" [879]); and I. O.'s "rodent's face" (879) reaches back through Ratliff's earlier reference to a "heifer to catch a rat" (877) to "dung-heap" and "pismire" (878). Ratliff's neologism draws on what he sees, his verb for Snopes is perhaps unsurprisingly a synonym for the verb "to bugger." But where "buggy" displaced inferences of anal penetration into autochthony, here entry into the soiling hole lacks earthly intimation: "Snopes can come and Snopes can go, but Will Varner looks like he is fixing to snopes forever. Or Varner will Snopes forever—take your pick. . . . maybe a new fellow doing the jobbing but it's the same old stern getting reamed out" (879–80). Ratliff's pun is economic, being made on the day and in the place of Varner's "yearly settlement with his tenants and debtors" (786). The pun's logic is inexorable: if "to snopes" (whoever is doing "it") is to penetrate "earth-reeking men" (786) from behind, then what the peasantry are paid is synonymous with semen. Flem Snopes's most marked emission is tobacco spit. Cash, semen, and phlegm are a whispering trinity latent in Ratliff's pun. The narrative impacted in the neologism carries Ratliff directly to his account of Flem and Eula's marriage night. Flem is given "long black stockings," and a screen painted "to look like . . . a wall full of store shelves of canned goods" is set by the bed (880). But Ratliff is saved from having to name Eula in order to set her in the scene, by the arrival of a "little boy" of uncertain age and "innocent" eye, who we will subsequently learn is pimping for Lump in the matter of Ike's sodomizing of the cow. Faulkner's choice of person from Porlock allows the second- or third-time reader dimly to associate Eula's unnamed but imminent orifice with the cow's autochthonous aperture, only to have that association transformed by Ratliff's violent switching of bodies. Under the guise of the boy's interruption, Ratliff shifts his scene from hotel room to store, substituting a black field-hand for Eula. The woman is marked as a "brute" by her "mule"-like sense of smell (882), and by her request for lard from a "bucket with . . . a hog on it" (880). Payment is by sex—and Snopes is rendered bestial by Ratliff, even as Ratliff walks toward the barn in which Ike prepares (all unknown to Ratliff) to seduce a cow. Given that Ratliff's punch-line has the black worker say to Snopes as he approaches orgasm above her, "whut you ax fer dem sardines?" (882), we may speculate that where the price of lard is sex in the missionary position, the price of a luxury like sardines may be a less customary mode of entry—buggery fits on every count.[57]

The field-hand's question closes section 1 of the first chapter of "The Long Summer," it also closes Ratliff's exercise in elegy, which has taken the form of three linked genres (meditation, pun, and dirty story). Each element of the exercise is re-inflected when read through the others. So, put schematically, a primarily autochthonic meditation on a place turns anal under pressure from the pun, whose semantic seed it contains. Yet "reaming" remains residually informed by the "rich" (and "polluted") ensemble attending the "bugg[er]y." Furthermore, despite following the inescapable recognition that "to snopes" is to sodomize in the extraction of usurious profit, the dirty story is cleansed by autochthonous remnants, present care of the outer reaches of the framework attending the body/buggy metaphor, and therefore accompanying Eula's black surrogate. The worker comes afterall, "from the field with the field sweat still drying on her" (882), attended by inferences of mule and pig; furthermore, her punch-line is immediately succeeded by Faulkner's celebratory account of Ike's passage through a cow and into the earth (section 2, chapter 2). My point is that although the focus of Ratliff's grieving anxiety shifts from lost earth to sexual loss (as he moves between fence and store), a reader balancing the various elements involved in that loss need not conclude with Ratliff that Flem Snopes is a synonym for "dirty money."

Three reservations could be raised against Ratliff's pathologizing of his rival, reservations stemming largely from residual elements in Ratliff's case for the prosecution. Firstly: to sexualize Flem, modifying Ratliff's terms, is to neglect the "whole" hole for one part of it. By leaving the "soil" out of "soilure," Ratliff ignores what I have been calling the "autochthonic" ensemble, whose elements matter not just because they are thematically sustained by the novel, but because their persistence implies a social form. Ratliff to the contrary, Eula must remain partly a landed part, rather than a price on its way to being a bank, her earthiness being supportable for as long as the social practices which sustain that meaning in her persist. As the annales historian Fernand Braudel observes, the market has a brief and "modern" history which remains less than ubiquitous: he proposes that beneath any market/money economy lies "the lowest stratum of the non-economy, the soil into which capitalism thrusts its roots, but which it can never really penetrate. The lowest layer remains an enormous one."[58] Arguably, the presence of a nonmarket remainder, with its residual nonmoney modes of exchange, is more likely in a southern soil which, until recently, has been worked toward meaning through a premodern regime of accumulation. Recently, here, may be the 1880s shadowed by chattel slavery, or even 1940 shadowed by debt peonage. Either date allows that the Bend retains practices of exchange which should not simply be assimilated to market terms. Braudel's lowest layer persists among Faulkner's "peasants" as subsistence production for use rather than sale, and as barter where desires are unmediated by price.[59] Of course, in a cash-crop economy, even where that crop yields minimal and occasional cash to the immediate producers, money mediates. But its mediation remains subject to alternative strands of exchange, at least at the residual levels of memory and hope, levels that may impede the explanatory currency of coin.

Eula, prior to marriage, and for a large part of the book that carries her name, embodies, for the Bend just such autochthonic memory and hope. Labove notes "that quality in her which absolutely abrogated the exchange value of any single life's promise or capacity for devotion, the puny asking-price of any one man's reserve of so-called love" (839). However, by the close of a three-fold elegy, Ratliff discards his recessive and class-based intimation of intimacy between body and soil; instead, he translates Eula into purchasable "gal meat" (869), in order to render her, almost but not quite, a black hole in a dirty story. As usual the narrator follows Ratliff's lead. During the rest of "The Long Summer" and for the entirety of "The Peasants" we are permitted only one extended glimpse of Eula (1016), in which, though decorated with the bric-a-brac of fertility—"moon blanched" on a "sap[py]" April night and in the vicinity of a "silver pear tree" about to "make"—she is "spurious" and "marblelike"; a funerary monument to an autochthon. Positioned at a second-floor window, she is distanced from the earth and from the felt structures at work in it. The separation renders her an anthology of mythic labels rather than an iconic focus for a way of life.

Ratliff takes the land out of Eula's sexuality, and so turns away from his own antecedents lodged in a "peasant" or producing class for whom the earth remains human. Consequently, by the close of his tripartite elegy, he sees primarily as a merchant sees, in terms of price—the price of sardines, of Houston's cow, or of a piece of land. Yet, having spent much of his childhood in the company of Ab Snopes, barn burner, even as he prices he considers price a perverse stain, and displaces responsibility for it onto Flem. The meditation contains a double (albeit metaphoric) accusation: that Flem sodomizes a labor force and abuses a field hand, in both instances his semen being associated with rectal dirt and money. Ratliff could not be plainer: he concludes his meditation with Flem firmly lodged inside a worker. But Faulkner's sequencing offers a corrective, whose case might run: for semen, shit, and coin read seed, milk, and earth. Chapter 1, section 1 of "The Long Summer," containing the meditation, is directly followed by a section detailing how Ike Snopes's courtship of Houston's cow yields libations of seed and milk, poured into the earth. Only at the end of the chapter, and after thirty pages of exacting immersion in the bovine, do we return to Ratliff, his face against that "orifice" in the back wall of Mrs. Littlejohn's stable, toward which, thirty pages earlier, he was walking as he talked: "He did look, . . . it was as though it were himself inside the stall with the cow, himself looking out of the blasted tongueless face at the row of faces watching him who had been given the wordless passions but not the specious words" (913). The identification involves more than sympathy. Ratliff finds himself in Ike's position because he has just thought himself into similar holes. An earlier triangulation of Ratliff, Flem, and Eula, in which Eula was the landed love object, Flem the agent of price, and Ratliff a self-denying autochthonous rival, is reconfigured—with the cow playing Eula's part, Ratliff standing in for Flem, and Ike for Ratliff. Ratliff can be in two positions at once because although he does Flem's work, pricing and beefing the bovine mistress, he remains residually the autochthon, from behind whose face he can watch his mercantile self debasing a passion for the earth. Ratliff mutes his affinity for Ike: by emphasizing "tongueless[ness]" he censors his own earlier and unvoiced analogue to the idiot's "passions."

V

All of which may seem at some distance from my earlier claim to be making a case for the fallibility of Ratliff's account of Flem. My first reservation was that by rendering Flem sexually rapacious, Ratliff misrepresents him. The case is neither retrospective nor physiological. I am not saying that given what we learn in *The Town* (1957), Ratliff's attribution of potency to an impotent man is erroneous. I am saying that the increasing exclusivity of Ratliff's eroticization both of Eula and of Flem allows him to simplify what he himself has seen in the soil through the optic of Eula's iconicized body. Ratliff's account of Flem as the rapist of a workforce is finally self-serving. Ratliff, child of a tenant, who recreates himself as an agent of systemic credit, constraining low-paid agricultural labor, needs a story that will ease his own sense of having betrayed his class of origin. Eula as autochthon allowed Ratliff to retain links with the tenantry. By using Flem to abuse her landed part, Ratliff severs his own awkward and increasingly archaic social ties. As a narrative trope, Flem, rampant and emitting dirty money, offers further compensation, allowing Ratliff to situate himself as the better face of the coercive economy which he believes they both serve. Despite the deep logic of his own class necessity, Ratliff cannot quite bring himself to have Flem rape Eula, hence the substitute. I would stress that Ratliff's social needs and not Flem's desires give rise to the orthodoxy concerning Snopes.

Of course, I simplify, creating a class allegory from what amounts to subsemantic whisperings of a Chinese kind, my excuse being that by overarticulating Ratliff's residues I hope to establish that Flem-as-sex-and-cash is a misrepresentation. The narrator may be fooled, but the men on Varner's porch, with an eye for a shirt and tie, sense a different Flem. Which is the substance of my second reservation concerning Ratliffs judgment: that Flem, as Ab's son, retains class continuity with the political violence of a resistant tenantry, a continuity which Ratliff must erase. And so, in quickened succession, to reservation three: that Ratliff knows what Ratliff does—that Ratliff's "Flem" is a calculated fiction in pursuit of which Ratliff can distract himself from his own "modernization," and from its attendant treacheries. The three-fold meditation through which the agent of credit dispensed with autochthony and its tacit social form mirrors an earlier meditation. Both are prompted by the marriage. Both take Eula as their initial subject. Both depart from a buggy. And both have a tripartite structure. Where the second features a reverie on a buggy, a pun, and a dirty story, the first consists of a buggy-born-reverie, a riddle, and a tall tale. Their affinities of form and content are critically missed, perhaps because the meditations fall on either side of the space between books 2 and 3.[60] The gap is a fact of narrative organization, but given that he who meditates is Ratliff, assisted by the narrator in Ratliffian mode, the gap itself may serve the sewing machine agent's purposes, allowing him to interrupt himself at an awkward moment. Yet, and in addition, the break between books effectively bridges the gap which it introduces, nullifying the chronological space between Eula's married departure for Texas (late spring) and Ratliff's return to the Bend from a trading trip (September). Since Ratliff leaves book 2 lamenting, and enters book 3 lamenting we are structurally invited to compare his lamentations, correcting that interruption by way of which he avoided his own worst insights—or so I shall contend.

To compare meditations is to see Ratliff having two goes at the same elegy. I shall refer to the first (in "Eula") as the "ur-elegy," and before detailing Ratliff's displacement of its class implications, I shall gloss its formal affinities with the second, or "revisionist," elegy (in "The Long Summer"). Where the second deploys reverie and wordplay as separate exercises, the first collapses the two into a reverie turning on a riddle. Despite their differences each is triggered by a similar pattern or rhythm of recollection which can be presented as a shared structural element. Aware that I may be straining my reader's patience, I offer a trigger diagram (glossed by the suggestion that those readers for whom such exercises are inherently annoying should skip):

Ur-Elegy [book 2]

Eula as buggies	>	buggies gone	>	"—a word . . . —"	(wordplay as riddle)	>	buggy back sans Eula

Revisionist Elegy [book 3]

Eula as buggies	>	buggies gone	>	"—the air polluted . . . —"	(smell prompts wordplay as pun)		buggy back sans Eula

In the ur-elegy, what comes after the dash and before the restored vehicle is an unspoken word (the riddle). In the revision, the dashes bracket "air," or more particularly a smell. In each instance, air, breathed or sniffed, is the elusive substance of the reverie:

> [Ur-Elegy] one bright brief summer, concentric, during which three fairly well-horsed buggies stood in steady rotation along a picket fence or spun along adjacent roads between the homes and the crossroads stores and the schoolhouses and churches where people gathered for pleasure or at least for escape, and then overnight and simultaneously were seen no more; then eccentric: buggies gone, vanished—a lean, loose-jointed, cotton-socked, shrewd, ruthless old man, the splendid girl with her beautiful masklike face, the froglike creature which barely reached her shoulder, cashing a check, buying a license, taking a train—a word [there follows a seventeen-line speculation concerning the unuttered word]. . . . Even one of the actual buggies remained. (867–68)
>
> [Revisionist Elegy] And yet those buggies were still there. He [Ratliff] could see them, sense them. Something was; it was too much to have vanished that quickly and completely— the air [there follows a ten-line speculation on the "air"]. . . .—the buggy merely a part of the whole. (877)

Since I have already reviewed the content of the air in the second reverie, I had best specify what the air holds in the ur-version:

> - a word, a single will to believe born of envy and old deathless regret, murmured from cabin to cabin above the washing pots and the sewing, from wagon to horseman in roads and lanes or from rider to halted plow in field furrows; the word, the dream and wish of all male under sun capable of harm—the young who only dreamed yet of the ruins they were still incapable of; the sick and the maimed sweating in sleepless beds, impotent for the harm they willed to do; the old, now-glandless earth-creeping, the very buds and blossoms, the garlands of whose yellowed triumphs had long fallen into the profitless dust, embalmed now and no more dead to the living world if they were sealed in buried vaults, behind the impregnable matronly calico of others' grandchildren's grandmothers—the word, with its implications of lost triumphs and defeats of unimaginable splendour—.(868)

I quote at length in order to comment more tersely. The "word," prompted by the courtship buggies, might logically be "Eula" or "love," since "she" is the lost "love" of the Bend's "cabins," "roads," and "field[s]," were it not that neither "Eula" nor "love" quite encompasses the unlovely locations through which the murmur is made to pass—sick beds, death beds, burial chambers, and the vaginal "vault" of a collective grandmother. Noel Polk has intriguingly used the last site to suggest that the word in question is "cuckold."[61] Extrapolated, the argument behind his suggestion might run: the word is transferred primarily between men; some among its synonyms imply penetrative sex ("will," "dream . . . of ruin," "wish . . . of harm"), but the ultimate destination of the would-be-seminal murmur is the womb of an extrafamilial grandmother. Which posits the question, what is the word doing in such a place, if not "cuckolding" or conceiving a bastard? The genealogy available in the phrase "others' grandchildren's grandmothers," is devious, but explicable once it is recognized that the dying and generic old man, care of the word, long since cuckolded someone else (word into "vault" > seed into vagina), to produce an illegitimate line. The bastard progeny, cast as "buds," "blossoms," and "gar-lands," though probably dead ("fallen into the . . . dust"), have doubtless them-selves had families, whose founding illegitimacy is disguised by the "impregnabil-ity" of the offending "matron's" reputation among her "grandchildren." "Cuckold" is the word, at least for Polk. But "cuckold," though intricately persuasive, does not explain the "earth-creeping" emphasis of the riddling term—that passing of the "word" through horticulture ("bud," "blossom") via "dust" into the ground itself ("buried vault" is both a female body and a place of entombment). Once the ur-rid-dle ("the word") is read, for sameness and for difference, through the stencil of its structural analogue in the revised elegy, "the word" is made plain.

"Eula," "love," and "cuckold" do indeed have a place within the "murmur," but "soil" is their generic or containing term. "Eula," married, may well be an enduring figure in the sexual fantasies of the Bend's male population, who would briefly "love" to be in Flem's position, that is, to "cuckold" the unlikely husband. But the word "soil" contains and yet is more than these words. In the revised reverie, the buggies "vanished" (159) prompting Ratliff, care of his Ratliffian narrator, mourn-fully to associate Eula with two opposed holes—a hole in the ground (autochthony) and an anus (stain). In this, the ur-version, the same buggies "vanished" (147) in order for the same duo to take her to similar places, a "vault" that is both an earthly aperture and a soiled sexual hole. In each elegy, reverie plus wordplay writes Eula as "soil" and "soilure," doing so in a way that recalls the very autochthony that is being abused. If she, as a landed place, is "soiled," that stain necessarily retains the "soil" which Ratliff's "Flem" would convert into dirty emissions of coin. Note how, in the ur-version, the dying old men who are the final transmitters of "the word" are first dryadic ("bud," "blossom," "garland") and then embalmed. As arborial corpses they cannot stay down, their resiliency, and that of their silent "word," being caught in Faulkner's problematic phrasing. "[E]mbalmed now and no more dead to the living world if they were sealed in buried vaults," can be inflected in two ways: "embalmed now and no more[,] dead to the living world [as] if they were sealed in buried vaults. Or, "embalmed now and no more dead to the living world [than] if they were sealed in buried vaults." The nub of the difficulty is whether or not to neutralize the troubling phrase "no more dead," whose underpunctuated duplicity reflects Ratliff's class problem: if the dirt-poor farmers of the Bend are not dead, if they are alive in the earth made human by their labor, should Ratliff, fear-ing the redundancy of that form of life, declare them dead? At this point in his ur-reverie, Ratliff has no answer—hence the deep duplicity of the phrase, "no more dead." However, "soil" as a silent solution to the riddle, tacitly answers his unasked question. "Soil" implies that Eula's body, "loved" and "cuckolding," remains the focus of an autochthonic impulse. Though silent, "the word" intimates the presence of recessive social forms, and of the desires inherent in those forms. The riddle is unanswered, but the very asking of it proposes the persistence of troubling remnants and social fragments in the voice of Ratliff and of his narrator.

The structurally equivalent wordplay in the revised version lacks the ambivalence of "soil." "To snopes," meaning "to bugger," is replete with "soilure," meaning "to do dirt": any echo of "soil" in that "soiling" is so recessive as to be virtually a dead sound. By the time Ratliff returns from Jefferson to the Bend he all but believes that the earth resonates only with its price. Crucial to his transformation, and to the class erasure inherent in it, is the final element in the ur-elegy—the Faustian tale of Flem in hell. How Ratliff gets from "the word" to the tall tale is difficult in a way the transitions in the revised version are not. To rehearse the links in the second reverie is to see how smoothly any initially autochthonic potential is drained from the meditation. Memory of the buggies draws an anal ordure from the air, which leads to the pun on "Snopes" as sodomy, apt preface to a sexual story whose punch-line intimates anal penetration. In the ur-elegy the recollected buggies elicit a "murmur" of air, whose exhalation contains what I have been calling "embodied" or "human" earth. How then does Ratliff shift from an autochthonic site to hell?

He changes the subject. His riddle-driven reverie departs from the "vanished . . . buggies" (868) and returns to the remaining buggy (868), but chronologically his trip to Jefferson and four-month absence from the Bend fall between reverie and tall tale, during which, "remembering, still seeing them" (869), Ratliff switches priorities from Eula's "calm beautiful mask" (869) to Flem's tie and jaw (879). The substitution occurs within just over a page, so that the leap from reverie to story, from standard to italic print, from Ratliffian narrator to anonymous tale-teller, and from Bend to Hell, though striking in all these aspects, is more apparent than real:

> It [Eula's face] went fast; it was as if the moving glass [on the train out of Jefferson] were in retrograde, it too merely a part, a figment, of the concentric flotsam and jetsam of the translation, and there remained only the straw bag, the minute tie, the constant jaw:
>   *Until at last, baffled, they come to the Prince his-self. "Sire," they says. "He just wont. We cant do nothing with him."* (869–70)

Continuity resides in the chewing jaw, in so far as Flem's spit, the essence of his name, provides the tale-teller with the substance of Flem's soul, and so with a key plot element—a "soul" deposited in hell and apparently lost by the itinerant devils into whose keeping it has been given. They "*sealed it up in a asbestos matchbox and put the box in a separate compartment to itself*" (870), but on breaking the seal and opening the box they discover only "*a little kind of dried-up smear*" (870).

The "*smear*" has a complex provenance: it reaches back to the initial stage of the meditation and exactly complements the unexpressed "soil," in that it too is "sealed" (868/870) in two boxes, the second of which is tacitly a "vault" (868/870). Since "the word" (868) was seminal by way of its residency in a generic grandmother, the "*smear*" may carry connotations of a sexual deposit. In addition, as Flem's phlegmishness, it necessarily derives from his chewing. Flem chews tobacco, but famously announces to Jody that he likes to "chew up a nickel now and then until the suption is out of it" (751). His essential stain partakes of "suption" and as such is emblematic of money's essence: note the contraction from chewing tobacco to coin, and from coin as a measure of value (a nickel) to coin as liquidity ("suption"), existing to ease the flow of commodities. From such a provenance "*smear*" derives a double trajectory: first, by way of "soil" and its autochthonic ensemble, toward those subsistence producers bound by debt to the ground. Second, from "suption," toward the credit mechanisms that bankroll the owning class. The story is designed to resolve the contradiction inherent in its narrative trigger, the "*smear*." Necessarily, therefore, it is about labor and credit.

Flem offers the Prince his soul, presumably in return for the "*gratifications*" and "*vanities*" (chews and ties). Returning to the location of the agreement (a compression of store and Frenchman's place, both sites of tacit contract), he seeks to redeem his soul and to be judged, only to learn that his soul (or collateral) has vanished, presumed stolen. This much is simply a summary of the implied and given plot. I shall now read the story through the labor/credit relations to which the collateral, or "*smear*" heard as "soil," alludes. Tenants and croppers offer landowners a year of their labor as collateral, in return for which they receive land and a promise of a portion of the cash crop they raise. The logic of the tall tale implies that their collateral is not worth a "spit" within the system that it enables; yet that labor is all they have to offer, and so remains of their essence (or soul). Pursuing the logic—Flem comes to redeem the collateral of his class, only to find that he is to receive nothing because of an obscure vanishing trick or theft, which has vitiated that labor. The trick is called "debt peonage," whereby the land lord/storeowner steals the rural workers' work via the pricing of credit at outrageous levels such that, come cropping time, the workers' efforts will prove worthless, in that their fruits do not pay their debts.

Which exegesis takes us to the point in the tale where Flem states that he knew all along that his soul, like his name, lacked the value of "spit" because, from the first, it belonged to and was created by the Devil. Or, by way of the economic stencil through which I have been reading, he admits always to have known that the labor of his class was the creature and creation of a murderous system of indebtedness. How can such an acknowledgment, seemingly involving the tenantry's agreement to be the tool of systemic exploitation, bring the Devil to his knees?

I can answer my own question only with further questions. Who tells the tale and to whom? Nominally unnamed, the speaker has to be Ratliff. I have encountered few readers who do not assume as much. But, equally, I have yet to find a critic who explains the italics, with their inference of silenced speech and of a displaced speaker. Despite its idiomatic and anecdotal form, the story is told to no one by a narrator who would prefer to remain anonymous. Not the Ratliffian narrator, since "his" vocal register is interrupted by the italicized speech; nor, overtly at least, Ratliff. Faulkner's decision to use italics, the only extended example of such usage in the novel, separates the story from both text and context, implying that the teller tells it quietly to himself, but that he would rather no one knew as much. What then must Ratliff articulate in such a way as almost to hide it from himself?

Again, the answer is in the "*smear*," or rather in the contradictory class options latent in that "*smear*." Ratliff's Flem brings the Devil to his knees simply by acknowledging that his soul—the essence of the tenantry—is not land made human by labor (the "*smear*" as seminal soil), but the land's price (the "*smear*" read for the "suption" in it). Ratliff, the creator of the denouement, is debilitated—not just because Flem's confession dedicates the laboring class, the class of Ratliff's childhood, to the mechanism of indebtedness, but because it expels from the "*smear*" any reassuring and residual inference of the value of human practices, iconicized within the land by Eula and labor. Less gnomically: if the "*smear*" is just liquid assets, then Eula's autochthonous sexuality is worth no more than a dirty story about the value of a fuck—which is virtually how Ratliff will tell it in the second and revised elegy, where "*smear*" becomes "soilure" as rectal dirt.

I would emphasize that the Devil's debilitation is comprehensible only if transferred from the character to the tale's quiet teller. Indeed, unless the story is "about" the teller, its resolution makes no sense, the Devil having no reason to be dethroned by what amounts to confirmation of his authority. Once the story's debate over who creates whom is read as concerning the story's missing teller or "creator," the Devil's fall falls into place. Ratliff, maker of the anecdote, is the tale's absent "creator," and as such is of the Devil's party. Moreover, the casting indicates that he knows as much. Hell is administered by a triumvirate: the Devil (or "*Prince*"), son of a more eminent "*pa*" (Satan), is advised by a wise councillor ("*the old one*"). The arrangement complements that facing Flem on his entry to the Bend. At the start of the novel, Jody (the "*Prince*"), advised by Ratliff ("*the old one*"), agreed on a contract with Flem. Since Will Varner is the owner of the store in which Flem will clerk, and of the fields where Ab will labor, that contract is in the father's (Satan's) name. Much else in the tale echoes the early days of Flem and Ab Snopes: setting, contractual debate, asbestos match box, concluding conflagration, and the *Prince*'s exit—all derive from the details attending Snopesian entry. A tenant farm or commissary, from the perspective of the bound tenant, is close to Hell. Neither Ab nor Flem sign a contract, though during negotiations Jody has frequent recourse to the expletive "hell fire" (739, 744, 745, 748, 751), and there is much talk of matches, struck and unstruck (742, 751). Indeed, an "*asbestos matchbox*" (870) may well be the ideal correlative of Jody's notional "fire insurance" (752). Eventually, in the tale at least, the barn/commissary burns, or, more properly, "Hell" is put to the "fire"; at which point, the Prince is to be seen *"scrabbling across the floor, clawing and scrabbling at the locked door, screaming. . . . . . .* (873). Given how much the tale takes from the first days of the Snopes, it is hard not to hear in its last line an echo of Jody's initial glimpse of Ab: "a pair of eyes of cold opaque gray between shaggy graying irascible brows and short *scrabble* of iron-gray beard as tight and knotted as a sheep's coat" (735–36). Ab was ever a wolf in sheep's clothing, and had Ratliff said as much from the first, crediting the cropper with his proper and populist "integrity," as one for whom "fire" was of the essence, perhaps Ab would not have been granted access to Varner's lands, and consequently his son would have had no route to Varner's store. Jody, and those of his party, are indeed left *"scrabbling at [the] locked door"* of Ab and Flem's unvoiced intent, victims of a councillor's bad council . . . or so the tall tale tacitly runs.

In effect, Ratliff offers a gloss on the early days of Snopes, and finds himself guilty. His advice enabled their entry. He connived at Flem's pricing of the embodied earth. He was complicit in the abuse of the earth's icon, Eula. He, therefore, is the "creator" brought down by the tale that he cannot quite bring himself to tell. I would stress that Flem's confession is Ratliff's creation, and that as such it reveals more about Ratliff's affiliations than Flem's. Note that the inflammatory bric-a-brac which accompanies the story could be read as a realization of the continuing urgency of populist resentment—a Snopes does, after all and in effect, tear down rather than burn down the house made from the stolen sweat of his class. But Ratliff is too busy accusing himself, and hiding from his self-accusation, to pursue this residual option. At the core of the story is the *"smear"*; and Ratliff, by the end of his ur-reverie, is sure that the *"smear"* means dirty money, not human soil. He has not resolved the contradiction out of which his tale grew, he has simply cancelled it. By cancelling the political provenance of the autochthonic ensemble, Ratliff severs his tie to the subsistence class. Freed, and of Varner's party, he can busy himself in the continued creation of a "Flem" onto whom he may displace both his guilt and the worst aspect of his own structural function. Consequently, the contradictions of the ur-elegy as a whole, haunted by populist residues and autochthonous remainders, give way to the clearer accusations of the revised version.

What is lost, particularly in the transition from tall tale to dirty story, is the sense that Flem remains the political child of Ab, rather than Varner's displaced inheritor. Of course, the burden of my argument has been that the lost populist tradition is lost to Ratliff, but not to those readers who see in Flem's inconsistencies, and in the authorial ploy of the double elegy, a route to adequate mourning for the resistant class victims of agricultural modernization.

VI

As a coda to my claims, I offer a brief and doggedly duplicitious account of Flem's "achievements" on his married return to the Bend in book 4. He has a surrogate sell the "painted ponies." He arranges for the salting of the earth of the Frenchman's place. He leaves for Jefferson with the accumulations gained from both ventures. On the surface, he translates his assets into cash, about which hovers more than a suggestion of forgery: the ponies are "painted" and the buried coins are fools' gold. Ratliff's version of Flem as dirty money would seem to be the authorized version. But the residues persist. I have space only to outline how book 4 of *The Hamlet* ("The Peasants") might be read for its considerable remainders.

Look first at what the ponies *do*. They are brought to the Bend bound in fencing wire. The wire recalls Mink and Houston's dispute over Mink's scrub bull, a dispute turning on Mink's failure properly to fence his stock. Mink, a tenant, believes in open range and common-use rights. Houston, an owner, holds to the "fence stock, not crop" principle,[62] the better to protect and increase individual accumulation. As Steven Hahn, an historian of southern populism has argued, stock-law disputes became the focus of the struggle of petty producers against dependency.[63] Fences and wire were politically contentious in Mississippi between 1880 and 1890, since only unfenced or open range ensured the persistence of common grazing rights, and the attendant ability of a destitute tenancy to maintain any stock at all. Once the ponies are cut from the wire, they, like an animate version of Ab's "fire," enter a number of the Bend's institutions—the barn, the boarding house, the court—each of which they thunderously take apart. Eck's barn is the first to go, "exploded into mad tossing shapes like a downrush of flames" to a cry of "Hell fire" (994). As I have pointed out, barns were a preferred target for populist arson, being stores for the real and symbolic accumulation of that which the owner had stolen from the tenant, the tenant's labor. The ponies tie Flem to his radical family tradition, by way of wire and flame.

Mrs. Littlejohn's boarding house receives an equine visitation, during which Ratliff is forced to jump to his bedroom window. Presumably, other merchants and drummers, enablers of indebtedness and of the "credit price" system, are similarly discomforted. More serious damage is done to the institution of horse trading itself. Several of Varner's tenants buy the vicious and uncatchable stock. Some are seriously hurt in efforts to apprehend their purchases. Bystanders are hurt also. The horse trade could be read as one site where men of small means gain an element of independence. Ownership of stock, whether horse or mule, means that a cropper's share of the crop will be larger.[64] The fact that he can plough using his own beast frees him from dependency on the landlord's stock, and so from an element of the landlord's managerial control. But the chief "benefit" of the trade in horses is the "honor" achieved by the successful trader: witness Ab's desire to recoup the "honor . . . of Yoknapatawpha County" (761) from Pat Stamper. Flem's vicious ponies bring home the point that such "honor" is delusional: crippling and damaging their systemically crippled and damaged "owners," they emphasize that any perk or palliative on offer within the system is simply a "painted" screen obscuring a savage regime.

Nor is the law an agency of social justice. When Tull takes his broken body to court, appealing for damages against Eck as "owner" of a painted pony, the justice of the peace, despite his several and venerable patriarchal badges (thick Bible, impeccable linen, resemblance to a "tender caricature of all grandfathers" [1033]), can do nothing. We should be surprised. The ponies do not love a wall, door, fence, gate, or wire, but justice, as in the case of Mink's unfenced scrub bull, will generally find for the fences. In *that* case, Justice of the Peace Varner, early described as being "thin as a fence rail" (733), handed down a predictably class-interested decision against common-use rights in land, and for enclosure, with its attendant shrinking of the meager means of an impoverished tenantry. That Flem's ponies should thwart the reach of the owners' judicial system reiterates their iconoclastic force. Technically, the ponies are not "owned," and so cannot be bound by a jurisprudence designed to protect and litigate in matters of property. They are, like Ab's "fire," an end to property, and consequently they slip the wire, shatter the fence, render bridges impassable and evacuate the Bend's more substantial structures. Ratliff and Varner, the powers that be, attempt to appropriate them as "carnival" for the labor force: called out to set Armstid's leg, Varner notes that the purchasers, "are going to come out even on them things, after all. . . . They'll get the money back in exercise and relaxation." He adds that "[i]f we had just knowed about this in time, we could have trained up a pack of horse-dogs . . . [and held] field trials" (1018–19). Carnival was ever a defense whereby owners controlled the free time of a coerced labor force.[65] But in this case the entertaining ponies are even-hooved in their progress, ruining property-sustaining institutions along with the body of labor (witness Armstid and Tull). Flem, the residual populist and ur-iconoclast, is by this stage the enemy of all relations.

Of course, in that the ponies create a supposed profit for Flem, their mayhem could be attributed to the owner's name, under the heading "creative destruction"—that tendency whereby capital dispenses with its own unproductive elements, glossed by Marx as "the violent destruction of capital, not by relations external to it, but rather as a condition of its self preservation . . . advice to be gone and to [make way] for a higher state of social production."[66] But not in 1940, or indeed 1890. At the time of the long composition of *The Hamlet* (1926–40), Faulkner was concerned with the reformation of labor and its ruination as it was forced out of the forms into which "dependency" and an archaic regime of accumulation, resting on coercion, had cast it. The painted ponies, far from being the destructive essence of competitive capital, are a figuration of the vortex that arises

from Ab's "integrity" as it fails of political purpose and shifts toward social conflagration. That the ponies put money in Flem's pocket is true; that they wreak havoc
in the Bend is true; that this makes Flem capital's epitome is false. Between 1887
and 1890, Flem is Ab's son, at a loss for political agency but loathing a system
which gives rise both to Mink and to Varner. He has nowhere to go but up, though
he is more interested in ruin than ascent. "Come up," his terminal utterance (1075),
need not be inflected as purposive—though that would be Ratliff's way; it might
better be heard as resigned in the face of the insufferability of the available social
options.

Iconoclasm is all that remains to Flem, underpinning his marriage to Eula and
subsequent sale of the Frenchman's place. Whether Eula is read as a utopian embodiment of the social relations of subsistence, or as an iconic piece of class nos-
talgia with which Ratliff cheers himself up, or merely as the daughter of a rich father—Flem brings her down. Eula leaves the Bend with him, on his wagon, among
his household goods, "beautiful" but "corpse-like" (1072). The "froglike" Flem (868)
is an iconoclast adequate to the considerable reach of his wife's iconicity. He even
diminishes her landed part. Recognizing the power of the old stories about the
buried gold of the plantocracy, Flem lets his hireling be seen digging at night in the
ruined garden of the plantation house. That he should catch Ratliff with his employment of a silly story, made sillier by its rewritten resolution, surely gratifies Flem,
once it is seen that he remains his father's son and class descendant. Of course,
Flem clerks for Varner, operates Varner's credit system and graduates to one of his
own. Had he stayed on the bottom rung of the one-runged agricultural ladder, he
would probably have burned with Ab and Mink's murderous but finally ineffective
class resentments. Instead he rises and takes that resentment with him.

To recover Flem's inconsistencies and his lasting radical residues would be to
revise *The Hamlet*, not least because it involves exposing the voices of Ratliff and
"his" narrator as narrowly class-inflected. Revision is overdue in that readers have
generally found Ratliff persuasive, and as a result have tended to cast Flem as
some species of capitalist, and to give him a bad press. Yet he leaves the Bend
with his worldly goods on a wagon, for a tent behind a restaurant in Jefferson—
hardly an achieved bourgeois, and in marked contrast to Will Varner, who fanta-
sizes quitting "the whole shebang" to visit the St. Louis World's Fair, showcase of
late nineteenth-century bougeois capital (820). I would suggest that Flem is the
sometime keeper of revised versions of his father's "fire," and that in 1940, at least,
The Hamlet continues to articulate the radical tug of labor's resentments, even as
the southern laboring class is being modernized beyond such options. Ratliff, hesitantly nostalgic for a utopian version of Flem's class of origin, is the acceptable
face of that modernization—nonetheless, his voice is riddled with contradictions
which the "real" Flem exposes. We tend to miss Ratliff's falsifications, and Flem's
point, because we, like Will Varner, are just too keen to get to the World's Fair.

Comparative Cows:

Reading *The Hamlet* for Its Residues

I

A S RATLIFF returns to the Bend, mourning Eula's departure from it, Mink Snopes awaits his day in court. The point at issue between Mink Snopes and Jack Houston is a fence.[1] Unfenced or open range represented for Mink, and the southern tenantry, access to common use rights. Whereas, the principle, "fence stock, not crop," served the interests of owners such as Houston. Varner, the magistrate, "fence rail . . ., thin,"[2] decides for Houston. His decision can only be read as class-interested. In the late 1880s fencing was the linchpin of the owners' determination to control labor: a cropper or small renter who lacked common grazing rights had to hire a mule from the landowner, buy butter and bacon from the owner's commissary, and, above all, plant the cash crop in order to cover his costs, thereby upping the owner's "share" while ensuring the owner's control. Stock law disputes understandably became crucial for petty producers struggling against dependency.[3]

In the 1880s and early 1890s fences were a live issue in Mississippi, where between 1880 and 1890 thirty-three counties had laws requiring that stock be fenced, while forty-one districts remained entirely open range. Populist strength in the state centered on open counties.[4] The decision over whether or not to enclose lay with the county authorities, who were subject to petition by "freeholders" in the matter. Varner, landholder, beat supervisor, justice of the peace, election commissioner, and putative stuffer of ballot boxes (733) *is* that authority in those counties straddled by Frenchman's Bend (731). In his magisterial capacity, he fines Mink three dollars, to be paid to Houston to cover Houston's pasturing costs over one winter. In *The Mansion* (1957), Mink is required to work off the fine in fence posts. Varner's political irony is inescapable: a man of minimal means must construct for a possessor of pedigree stock (the stallion and the hound) the very means whereby his own lack of substance, and that of his class, shall further shrink. The antagonists in *The Hamlet* are well aware of the symbolic potential of fence posts: going to collect his bull from his neighbor's land, Mink encounters Houston, who stops him by drawing a pistol. Mink protests poverty ("you know I aint got one"). Houston suggests a duel whose ground should be measured in the items that so offend, "they would lay the pistol on a fence-post and back off one post apiece on each side and count three and run for it" (876).

The posts, and the stock laws legitimating them, were part of a long class war fought for the means of production (for use rights in, and control over, land). In 1882, John Stogner of Carroll County, Georgia, wrote, "We were told in 1859 [*sic*] that secession was the greatest thing that the South could do. . . . It was a rich man's war and a poor man's fight, so will the stock law be a benefit to a few landlords . . . while nine-tenths of the people will be in a deplorable condition."[5] Mink's position is deplorable: Houston, plus Varner, plus Flem Snopes, worsen it. Flem, like Mink, deals in "scrub cattle," but manages via a "foreclosed lien" to translate them into a "a herd of good Herefords" (787). Stock improvement is impossible without fences. Arguably, in killing his class enemy, Houston, Mink kills the wrong exemplar (at least in the first instance). Either way the murder should be understood as a politically radical act. Mink uses a class implement: enclosures threatened common hunting rights across once open ground; Mink may be too poor to buy the shells that would enable him to hunt (939), but his choice of the rifle is as politically charged as Houston's suggestion for the duelling ground. And Houston knows it—his dying words accuse Mink not of being a murderer or even of being particularly inept, but of being poor, "God damn it, couldn't you even borrow two shells, you fumbling ragged—" (934).

Once Mink's yearling is read as one locus of class violence, other items in the scant itinerary of the struggle take on political resonance. The wife, the ground, and the hound, like the posts and the gun, can be articulated through class. But strangely, to read attentively is to learn that the residual meaning of the events triggered by the bull derive from archaic structures of feeling associated not with white landlords and white tenants, but with masters and slaves. In effect, Mink's disputed bull prompts a "pre-political act" of populist resentment whose deep structure is that of a slave revolt.[6]

Much of Mink's story fits ill with the populist cast of his crime, and much that is ill fitting fits once it is set within a master/slave dynamic. Mink's is a tale of two bodies, his wife's and Houston's, and of his inability to shed either of them despite considerable effort. I have described elsewhere what I take to be Faulkner's sense of the founding scene of slave production (be it bondage as chattel, or by debt).[7] Here, I shall simply outline the structural core of that scene, stressing the inseparability of the binding bodies from those whom they bind. Given what Mark Tushnett calls the "total relations" of slavery,[8] whereby the master is responsible for all aspects of the slave's life (rather than merely for his labor time), master and slave are continuously proximate. Proximity, according to Hegel, is internalized, leading the master to the fateful and previously repressed recognition that his mastery depends not upon himself but upon the labor of the constrained man.[9] Meanwhile, the slave finds in the work of his hands the substance of his lord, recognizing (via labor), that he makes his master's mastery. The recognition is as uncomfortable as it is radical, not least because the bound man has (up until this theoretical point) lived as an extension of his owner's will. Consequently, if he who is the substance of the lord is logically to displace the master (who contains and masks him), he must die in his old and subservient form, to reinvent himself (through revolt), in a form as yet unknown.

With luck, my gloss on the ur-structure informing, among others, Sutpen and his Haitians, Hegel's "Lordship and Bondage," and Eugene Genovese's *Roll Jordan, Roll* (1976), will serve as an adequate preface through which to address Mink's relation to those who own. Mink is indisputably owned. Witness the rented cabin for which he pays "almost as much in rent in one year as the house had cost to build" (935) and which is his past and his future. Witness, also, his "meagre," "sorry," "stunted" crop (935, 936), whose yield will not yield him enough to release him from small-tenant status at the base of a so-called agricultural ladder: "the paintless two-room cabin . . . not old, yet the roof of which already leaked and the weatherstripping had already begun to rot away from the wall planks and which was just like the one he had been born in which had not belonged to his father either, and just like the one he would die in if he died indoors" (935). Faulkner's account of the cabin's typicality types Mink as the representative of a class having no trajectory beyond more of the kind of labor that will result only in the barest reproduction of its capacity to labor again. Mink has mobility, but it is lateral, limited, and circular. He has "no money," little "stock," no "tools" (936), the merest shelter, and is bound for a year at a time to a means of production (poor land) that he can never own, and from which he can produce only profit for his landlord. The cabins will change, but his condition will not.

Once, when he was twenty-three-years old, he "repudiat[ed] the land" and ran, "seeking the sea" (951). His migration carried him some two hundred miles before being halted by a wife who would prove a surrogate master. Faulkner situates another lord at the land's literal edge ("almost there" [952]), so that Mink's courtship may become a slave revolt in all but name. On the run from one land lord (who is also, though tacitly, the lord of his labor), Mink binds himself to another and overt labor lord, one who uses "convict labor" (952) to clear timber. Mink chooses to work among prisoners in order to take his sexual turn with the owner's daughter. The future Mrs. Snopes is not just marked male ("short hair," "masculine . . . overalls" [953]), she is marked masterful ("the confident lord of the harem" [953]). She exerts absolute authority over an extended and largely black body of bound labor.[10] Faulkner measures her mastery with a single detail: she requires her sexual slaves to act as body servants in a second sense—instructing them to razor-cut her hair "man-short" (954). The razor, a potential and ethnically marked weapon, so used, renders the woman a man even as it feminizes and darkens the men who serve her with it. Mink, by choice and association blackened and bound, penetrates a lord (he is "summon[ed]" from the place of labor [953]). What he does when he is in there is, to say the least, contrary. "He entered," we are told, "not a cave" but "a tumescence" (238). The phallic clash of a female master and an elective slave is further complicated by the presence of other antagonists:

> he not only saw that he must compete for mere notice . . . but that when he did approach her at last he would have to tear aside not garments alone but the ghostly embraces of thirty or forty men; and this not only once but each time and hence (he foresaw even then his fate) forever: no room, no darkness, no desert even ever large enough to contain the two of them, and the constant stallion-ramp of those inexpugnable shades. (953)

"Inexpugnable" is interesting in that one might have expected "inexpungible"; at the very least the latter (meaning "not deleteable," "incapable of erasure"), hovers as an alternative above the former (meaning "incapable of being taken by force," "impregnable"). What is in question is the nature of the "shades": since they are prevalently black, and inside a version of their master, our understanding of the nature and degree of their resistance is significant. If they simply cannot be effaced from the body of their lord, they must be counted part of his substance. If, however, they remain as an invincible presence within the master's body, they should be reconsidered as residually Jacobinical. Either way the lord's white body darkens. Further, the position of Mink, one from among the bound who competes with them, depends upon whether we hear "shades" as lexically linked to "stain" or to "revolt": the latter is on the page, but the former (if only as a whispered antonym) reduces its political force. Mink, I would suggest, is all these things to this masterfull woman. He is one of a company of bound "shades" who constitute her substance; as such, he is "forever" a stain waiting to be expunged and a presence on the brink of revolt. He is also, however, at odds with the company he keeps: being white and a nominal volunteer, he is the master's champion in the matter of blacks.

I have been reading sexual exchange through the template of a particular and coercive labor structure, prompted to do so by Faulkner's presentation of the erotic as a mask worn by the economic. Mink's wife excites him exactly because she "contains" blacks and is of the master's party. In breaking into her, among "high-waym[e]n, murderer[s] and thie[ves]" (953), he penetrates an extension of the lord's body even as it takes delight from an erotic form of labor control. Penetration, at the level of Mink's fantasy, is a revolt of the bound, "Afterward it seemed to him that the afternoon's bedding had been the signal for . . . the collapse of her father's enterprise" (954). Mink's semen is rightly held by her to be inflammatory and poisonous ("too hot. It burns" [954]), because, structurally speaking, what comes from Mink—whether semen or sweat—is the "stuff" (954) that the lord must extract and contain if he is to be a lord, and the "stuff" that will bring his house down.

Mink and his wife, as co-dependent as Hegel's slave and master, are mutually entangled in a persistently erotic economics. Meeting at dusk in the Bend, after Mink has murdered the wrong man, his wife longs to be his executioner:

> "God damn you! If they would just let me do the hanging!" She shook him, her face bent to his, her hard, hot, panting breath on his face. "Not for killing him, but for doing it when you had no money to get away on if you ran, and nothing to eat if you stayed. If they'd just let me do it: hang you just enough to take you down and bring you to and hang you again just enough to cut you down and bring you to—" He slashed out again, viciously. But she had already released him, standing on one foot now, the other foot angled upward from the knee to meet her reaching hand. She took something from her shoe and put it into his hand. He knew at once what it was—a banknote, folded and refolded small and square and still warm with body-heat. And it was just one note. (955–56)

Sexual fluids and cash cojoin as Mrs. Snopes, in reaching for her shoe, enacts a classic erotic pose: that the folded note she retrieves is "warm" with "body-heat" at least implies a vaginal purse, particularly as spending and the male genitalia are tacitly linked in her desire repeatedly to hang her husband. The conjunction of a dash ("—") and "slashed" allows the recognition that what cutting down will bring the hanged man "to—" is sexual release. On only the previous page "the jerk and twitch" of Mink's "spent" body after penetrative sex is detailed, as is the power of his "seed" (955). Since his stuff "burns," it is logical that for Mink anger and emission are homologous, so that "lash" and "slash" (in his case) contain ejaculate: "'God damn you!' [she said] He began to struggle, with a cold condensed fury which did not seem quite able or perhaps ready to emerge yet from his body. Then he lashed suddenly out . . ." (955). Mink believes that the folded ten-dollar note is Varner's—a payment for sexual favors. Her possession of it marks her (at least for him) as one who has returned to servicing the body of the land lord. In which case, the allied trajectories of cash and sex may be said to describe a class narrative. She, of the lord's party, must ingest the bound man's "stuff," since his "spending" is the substance of the lord (hang him); but she cannot let the bound man die, because he *is* the lord's substance (cut him down and sustain him). Her punitive desires accord with the deep structure of an archaic and coercive form of labor. Mink is having none of such sustenance; he rejects the bank note, but the manner of his rejection is telling: "she saw only the slight jerk of his hand and wrist—no coin to ring against his thumbnail or to make any sound among the dust-stiffened road-side weeds where gouts of dusty cotton hung" (956). Contextualized by so much covert "spending," "jerk," "stiffen," and "gout" prove seminal. Mink may reject his land lord's cash, but even as he discards it his lord's land embodies the master's mastery in the form of cash-crop emissions. Of course, the crop is as much the matter of Mink's sweat as it is the property of the master's landed body. Wife, lord, and land embody him even as he substantiates them, and he can no more leave that land and its lord than he can quit his wife. So read Mink's desire for his wife, and hers for him, turns on their functioning as aspects of the master's body and of its impacted labor narrative.

Not for one moment—even the moment when he pulls the trigger on the owner's representative—can Mink escape the subterranean reconfigurations of that ar-chaic social plot. The narrator assures us that in shooting Houston, Mink is "for-ever . . . wedded and twinned" (934) to his victim. What is in effect one act of a class war, whereby a tenantry declares a degree of independence from owners, is redefined by its own semantic residues so that "dependency" rather than "auton-omy" rises like a deep memory from the details of the crime. If Mink, residually, is more "slave" than "populist," and Houston more "master" than "landowner"—Mink must die, for killing that on which he depends. True to Hegelian form Mink quits the scene of the crime and takes to his bed in the posture of a corpse: "lying flat on his back in the darkness with his eyes open and his arms straight beside him, thinking of nothing. . . . he might have been the corpse his attitude resembled" (940). Mink initiates a revised version of Henry Sutpen's extended death: Henry (the master) kills Bon, the black "goods" that are his substance; he consequently van-ishes from *Absalom, Absalom!* (1936). Lacking that which sustains him, he returns only "*To die. Yes. / To die*?".[11] As soon as Quentin takes the labored point, he too—his Harvard place grounded on revenues from the sale of property deriving from slave production—assumes the horizontal. "Rigid" and sick-unto-death on his Harvard bed,[12] Quentin embodies Henry, who embodies the old story of mas-ters who recognize and kill (or speak) the slave within, and in so doing die.

Mink's revised reversal of that story is, however, interrupted: having removed the master from himself, and laid himself out, he finds that the master's body and its representative (the hound) will not release him. Mink is haunted by the residues of his own dependency, in the guise of Houston's hound and its cry. Until the hounds' voicing of the master is silenced, the silence which grows from the shot cannot fill him with its confirmation that his negation of the lord has indeed been a structural suicide. For three nights he hunts the hound, during which period, consuming only sweetened water and the scrapings of a grain tub, he becomes spectral, "as if his body had not substance" (959). His substance is the howl that extends the life of the lord. Believing, after three nights, that he has killed the beast, Mink allows the "tremendous silence . . . broken when the first cry of the hound reached him" finally to affirm his status (sans master) as a piece of funerary art in the making:

> [The] silence . . . roared down about him and, still roaring, began to stiffen and set like cement, not only in his hearing but in his lungs, his breathing, inside and without him too, solidifying from tree-trunk to tree-trunk, among which the shattered echoes of the shot died away in strangling murmurs, caught in that cooling solidity before they had had time to cease. (946)

Of course, the lord/dog is not entirely dead, and so neither is Mink.

I am exaggerating, but only slightly, in order to excavate a deep narrative. Objections to the plot so plotted might fasten upon Faulkner's emphasis on Mink's emergent and seemingly independent "will." The case for Mink as agrarian rebel rather than thwarted slave might run by way of fence post and enclosure dispute to an incipient class consciousness, exemplified by Mink's sense that his "work," after the crime, is "harder than any work he had ever done," but that it involves "excitement" and "novelty" (943). Mink has changed the nature of his labor by killing the owner who denied him access not only to a scrub bull, but to what that stock represented—to use rights in common land; to limited ownership of the means of production; to a degree of independence from the cash crop, and so to subsistence agriculture as self-management. Thus inflected, Mink's disputed bull partakes of the social incandescence of a barn-burning flame in the hands of Ab Snopes, for whom "the element of fire" amounts to "the one [available] weapon for the preservation of [class] integrity."[13] This much I have already argued. Read from within a populist trajectory, Mink's bull and Ab's fire are weapons in the same war, and as such their deployment is a measure of shared class consciousness. How else to explain the absoluteness of Mink's antipathy to Flem? For Mink, dispossessed of an owner, and possessed of a new "will," Flem is a class traitor. Except that, even as Faulkner elaborates on Mink as a hero of the will, so he casts that will into patterns which may be read as a spectral manifestation of an earlier form of labor. In the immediate aftermath of the crime, Mink eats only "raw meal . . . which he did not want and apparently did not even need, as if his body were living on the incorrigible singleness of his will like so much fatty tissue" (943). Read projectively, from the late 1880s forward through the 1940s, toward, that is, the achieved and enforced independence of southern labor,[14] Mink's will has dispensed with a redundant body, constrained by dependency to function primarily in the owner's interest. Withdrawn from labor, and made over into the means for the completion of a social crime (new "work"), his revised body ensures the autonomy (or "singleness") of his will to be rid of the owner's voice. However, read retrospectively, from the 1880s back across debt peonage and toward chattel slavery, the same account can be made to serve the old master narrative. Mink's will, ever bound to the will of the master, wills itself dead, since he [Mink], in killing the master, virtually kills himself. Mink has to force himself to eat and live. Just about sustained, Mink's body denies his structural death, keeping him alive only by vampirically "living on" a will which is the master's in all but name. Which may sound strained, but on the very next page Faulkner appears to dedicate Mink's "will" to Houston, cast as equestrian and so as a planter: "his [Mink's] will, stood like an unresting invincible ungrazing horse while the puny body which rode it renewed its strength" (944). The "puny" body of labor may have unhorsed the lord, but its "will" keeps the "invincible" form of that which it has cast down.

If less allusive evidence were needed, consider how Mink releases himself (albeit briefly) from Lump—another manifestation of southern labor's class options. Lump, the second Snopes to keep Varner's store and to apprentice himself to merchant capital, sees a dead owner not as an inescapable aspect of the laborer's person, but as fifty dollars (950). Lump cannot understand how Mink has failed to recognize the chance to transform his murderous "work" into a wage by robbing the corpse. Mink, read as a creation of an earlier regime of accumulation, refuses to price the body, since to do so would be to alienate a key aspect of himself from himself. Necessarily, in escaping Lump's insistent translation of Houston into wasted profit, Mink acts on behalf of an archaic master. Detouring Lump into his rented barn,

> [he] reached down from its nail in the wall a short, smooth white-oak stick eyed at the end with a loop of hemp rope—a twister which Houston had used with his stallion, which Snopes had found when he rented the foreclosed portion of Houston's farm from the Varners—and turned and struck all in one motion and dropped the cudgel and caught the heavy body as it fell. (964)

The impromptu weapon has a complex provenance. Houston's stick, marked masterful on two counts, both by its application to a stallion and by "one-eyed" innuendo,[15] reaches Mink via two landowners. Left during a foreclosure, it at least implies that owners are diverse and own differently. Such difference is muted by Mink's adoption of the stick to curb a labor modernizer from within his own class. Effectively, Mink allies with Houston and Varner against an alternative version of himself. He puts Lump down, gently, tying him with "a hame string" and "the check rein from his plow gear," as though to reiterate the binding nature of the instruments of labor. That the narrator has Mink improvise a gag from a strip of the clerk's shirt indicates how exactingly Faulkner attends to accessories as class indices. Lump, Flem's follower and imitator, doubtless affects the shirts of his predecessor—those hand-stitched, white (rather than blue) work shirts, into which, weekly, Flem had cut "his own particular soiling groove" (777). The shirts, no less strikingly mannered than those of Jay Gatsby, along with the "machine made black bow tie" (783), might be taken as a cumulative measure of Flem's class ascent. Mink uses a version of Flem's shirts to impede Lump's imitative rise. Given that Mink's choice of murder weapon carried a political charge, his selection of curbs for Lump is positively counterrevolutionary.

Freed from Lump's version of Houston as the wages of crime, Mink reverts to the master/slave dynamic in the matter of weaponry: he seeks an axe with which to release Houston's corpse from the hollow tree where he has hidden it, and to which the lord's voice in canine form, still binds him. The tree is significantly one to which, two years earlier, Mink "had lined a wild bee" (941), which is to say, tacitly, that the master's temporary resting place contains the sweetness of the slave, and that in killing his lord, Mink diminishes his own substance. Nonetheless, his aim is finally to dispose of the body and of its extension (the dog), thereby liberating himself from Houston's mastery. The axe is a "black" axe, stolen from a neighboring African American tenant, and its ethnicity marks Mink's purpose as "revolt." Paradigmatically, once again in possession of the corpse, Mink finds himself possessed by that which he would bury. Houston's body quite simply won't leave him alone, bits of it remaining attached to him to the last, so that when he "hurl[s]" it into the river, "through a long bank of mist like cotton batting, beneath which the water ran," he is compelled to "spring . . . after it, catching himself back just before he follow[s]" (969). Mink's last glimpse of the corpse registers "three limbs where there should have been four" (970). One limb remains in situ, and since we are not told what happens to the hound, it would be fair to say that the lord's extensions continue to haunt the lord's land, and that, therefore, Mink's revolt does not entirely displace the master. Nonetheless, enough of Houston is dead and buried for Mink, subject to the subterranean workings of a residual labor model, to all but die at the climax of his assault on the lord's body. At the very moment when Mink regains the hollow tree, to recover Houston's missing limb (and, in my terms, to expel the remnant of the archaic regime), he is arrested, effectively to be constrained for the rest of his life. He will, of course, "escape" in *The Mansion* (1959), to kill Flem, but it should be remembered that his final act is one of response to the "gentle tug" of the ground. At the close of *The Mansion*, when he lies down to die, the "tug" of the earth may be linked to Houston's missing limb and hound, in that Mink refers to the earth's "old patient biding . . . holt on you" as the work of "Old Moster Himself."[16] Arguably, Mink, at the last, submits his body to a master, embodied in southern soil, from whose mastery he has never entirely freed himself.

A similar structural point can be made by way of the subsemantics of Faulkner's strained account of the decision not to try Mink at the time of his arrest (October) but to leave his case to the following May: "So the case was pretermitted from sheer desuetude of physical material for formal suttee, like a half-cast play" (975). "To pretermit" is "to leave out," "omit," or "disregard." Mink is "left out" apparently because of the "discontinuance" or "disuse" ("desuetude") of materials for the practice of "suttee." A "suttee" is a Hindu widow who immolates herself on her husband's funeral pyre along with the body; by extension, "suttee" may also refer to that act of self-immolation. The legal "play" is "half-cast," presumably because of the absence of the victim's body, but "cast," in the context of Mink's being cast as Hindu window and other "half," is feminized and racialized, becoming "caste." At which point, Faulkner's legalese is reinflected; superficially, "desuetude" was the wrong term, since "cessation" makes sense when applied directly to "suttee," but not in relation to the lost "materials" of the missing corpse. With reference to those "materials," Faulkner needed a legal world for lost evidence. "Suttee" appears to have overdetermined his choice of "desuetude," but the whispered presence of Mink as "half-caste" and as dying with his/her lord, prompts the recognition that what has been "left out of the narrative," or perhaps "overlooked intentionally" ("pretermitted"), is "a discontinuance in the practice" ("desuetude") not of "suttee" but of slavery. Read for the subterranean implications of its curious vocabulary, the decision to defer Mink's trial date sounds like a tacit acknowledgment that there may be no point in hanging a slave for the murder of his master, since the defendant in such a case is all but dead.

II

But why? Why is Mink's dispute with Houston, politically speaking, double voiced? A populist killing sits ill with a slave revolt. Yet, once noticed, the latter residually impairs the emergence of the former. Donald Kartiganer, sensitive to the sudden and seemingly discontinuous appearance of Mink's story in "The Long Summer" (book 3, chapter 2, *The Hamlet*), describes it as a sort of plot explosion, variously "abrupt," "scandalous," "excessive" and "anarchic"; he adds that it is the second detonation in the third book, following the equally disruptive story of Ike's love for a cow (book 3, chapter 1).[17] Both are fairly brief and self-contained narratives which, at least superficially, distract from Faulkner's book-long preoccupation with the Ratliff-Flem-Eula-Varner triangle. Yet they share significant connections, each being bovine in focus, and implicitly appealing to an archaic social form. That Mink's bull has the political properties of Ab's fire should not distract from its species affinity with Ike's cow. Bull and cow are linked not simply as disputed stock, but as beasts through which a Snopes seeks access to use rights in the land.

I had best explain what may, in Ike's case, seem a gnomic assertion. Faulkner details two of Ike's nights with the cow; both share a scenario in which the idiot penetrates his paramour as a prelude to a second penetration of the earth: ergo, his *true* love is the soil. Witness Faulkner's second and extended account of a night between Ike and the cow. Ike passes through the cow and into the earth, the presence of the earth here being represented by a spring, which spring displaces the cow as the earth's orifice. Darkness falls. Milk falls. The figures both drink at "the well of days, the still and insatiable aperture of earth" (903), otherwise described as "tender mouth." The earth's "mouth" is doubly "insatiable": first, because it draws into itself "the all of light" from the sun's passage during the day; and second, because when Ike drinks, his image is kissed by a liquid "aperture" into which it passes and drowns, "he breaks with drinking the reversed drinking of his drowned and fading image" (903). The earth's orifice is capacious. Faulkner moves directly from describing its absorption of Ike's image to detailing its absorption of all the light of day; indeed, the two (Ike and light) fuse in a piece of luminous innuendo:

> until at last the morning, noon and afternoon flow back, drain the sky and creep leaf by voiceless leaf and twig and branch and trunk, descending, gathering frond by frond among the grass, still creeping downward in drowsy insect murmurs, until at last the complete all of light gathers about that still and tender mouth in one last expiring inhalation. He rises. The swale is constant with random and erratic fireflies. (903)

The "mouth" which inhales the "expiring day" inescapably sucks. Since that mouth is "insatiable," fringed and damp, its metamorphosis into aroused vagina is imminent, and affirmed by Ike's reaction. "He rises," physically from the pool and phallically into its "aperture." "Swale," prompted by "rise," doubles as "moist and marshy depression" and "pudendum." The erratic "fireflies," caught in the logic of the innuendo, tend toward the seminal and the erotic. Ike turns from the spring to the cow, who acts as the spring's structural analogue. Both draw light into themselves, the cow being "Blond too in that gathered last of light." Faulkner closes the paragraph and the chapter with a biblical echo, "They lie down together," a phrase which recalls "to lie with" and so summons any number of Old Testament couplings. The immediately subsequent section break is an omission which implies an emission. I would add that Ike's inseminations are milky (he invariably milks the cow, as a prelude to lying with her on the spot that the milk has soaked), and that they are variously productive of "Troy's Helen," bishops, kings, victims, nymphs, and "graceless seraphim" (898, 903). If the ground is haunted, and Ike's semen may be traced to the scene, issues of paternity are at least mooted. I would reiterate that what Ike puts into the earth is emphatically white, consisting of semen and milk, and generative of ghosts.[18]

Since Ike penetrates a cow to sow white spirits in the earth, he may be thought of as autochthonic, or as one who springs from the soil which he or she inhabits. Ike has other earthy credentials: he falls down a lot, and the suggestion that he does not like "the taste . . . of certain kinds of soil" at least implies that he is partial to other kinds of dirt. He is a herbivore who eats "what his upright kind . . . call filth" (900). My point is that Ike's cow grants him access to his true love—the soil, which both nourishes him and is the object of his passion.

Nor is Ike the only tacit autochthon in *The Hamlet*. A brief listing may serve to locate the social form inherent in his obsession. Armstid, a cropper, is doubly autochthonous: he drags a twice broken and "stiffened leg" (1073), most typically into a trench, where "waist-deep" in the ground, he digs "himself back into the earth which had produced him" (1068, 1069). When resting he is "immobile as the lumps of earth he had thrown out of it [his pit]" (1066). The analogy between Armstid and earth is emphatic.

Labove partakes of Armstid *and* Ike. With his "legs haired-over like those of a fawn" (839), and his black hair "coarse as a horse's tail" (827), he "cleats" his peasant family to the ground via a series of borrowed "football shoes" (824). Moreover, La*bove*, whose name contains intimations of the *bovine*, loves Eula not least because she "abrogate[s] . . . exchange value," resembling an unownable field—a field, that is, which should be held in common, rather than be enclosed for private ownership by marriage:

> He could almost see the husband which she would someday have . . . . the crippled Vulcan to that Venus, who would not possess her but merely own her by the single strength which power gave, the dead power of money, wealth, gewgaws, baubles, as he might own, not a picture, statue: a field, say. He saw it: the fine land rich and fecund and foul and eternal and impervious to him who claimed title to it, oblivious, drawing to itself ten fold the quantity of living seed its owner's whole life could have secreted and compounded, producing a thousand fold the harvest he could ever hope to gather and save. (839–40)

"He saw it," is the key to Labove's extended analogy. Faulkner's insistence on the moment of sight, within a metaphoric act uniting body and land, foregrounds the figurative element within that figure of speech. What is seen is horticultural and vaginal (witness "seed" in both senses). Eula, set within the mind's eye of Labove's metaphor, is both land and "parts," and as such she is, at the moment "he saw it," autochthony iconicized. Charles Saunders Peirce stressed that "icons stand for something because they resemble it."[19] Plainly Eula does not resemble a field, but the iconic impulse (the "picturing function" or "figurability" of an instant of sight lodged within a metaphor)[20] defeats the literal by inducing in Labove what Umberto Eco might gloss as "perceptual cramp": "At a certain point the iconic representation, however stylized it may be, appears to be more true than the real experience, and people begin to look at things through the glasses of iconic convention . . . [in a] sort of perceptual cramp caused by overwhelming cultural habits."[21] The problem with Eco's cramping is that although it releases iconicity from the limited notion of dependency upon visual relationships, it is unhelpful about how culture causes cramps. Labove has autochthonous tendencies. But hair, legs, name, and boots would be frivolous without his grounding in a "dirt-farmer tradition and heritage" (837). Labove's childhood involved an apprenticeship to worked "dirt," and his perceptions cramp around Eula's parts because those formative practices, associated with subsistence agriculture, tie bodies closely to the land, without apparent mediation by money. Arguably, he perceives Eula as iconic to the land because of the persistence within him of habits formed by an archaic mode of production which he seeks to quit.

Ike, Armstid, and Labove constitute an autochthonous series, in which Armstid and Labove intimate the social practices inherent in the structures of their feeling. We are not shown the early work of the schoolteacher, though doubtless he would have been put into the field by his father, just as Ab Snopes in counting children counts "field hands" (736). We are, however, party to the labor of Armstid. At the novel's close, he digs in the Frenchman's place, apparently for coin, but in digging he releases uncoinable company. As a crazed autochthon he cannot escape re-semanticization by way of Ike's seminal soil. Read from within his series, Armstid puts back more than he extracts, returning to the earth the secret of his insepara-bility from it. That inseparability is cemented through the enforced practice of sub-sistence as an economy of "use values," that is, of things made to satisfy immedi-ate wants or to fulfill immediate purposes. Money, on entering such an economy, ceases to be money; losing its abstract value and its metamorphic capacity to rep-resent a certain quantity of any and all things, it takes on the specificity of the labor that went into it. So, Mrs. Armstid says of her five dollars, given by her husband to Pat Stamper in payment for a painted pony:

> "I would know them five dollars. I earned them myself, weaving at night after Henry and the chaps was asleep. Some of the ladies in Jefferson would save up string and such and give it to me and I would weave things and sell them. I earned that money a little at a time and I would know it when I saw it because I would take the can outen the chimney and count it now and then. . . . I would know it if I was to see it again." (1036)

Armstid's digging, like his wife's coins, is a summation, expressive of his life's work on and in the land; a labor dedicated to the assumption that it had to be worth something. Part of Armstid may dig for the Frenchman's coin as reminted by Flem and buried in the Frenchman's place, but another part of him digs for his own sweat; that is, to recover from the ground the lifetime's practice that he has put into it. Faulkner's account of the hill farmer, from whose barn Ike Snopes steals grain, might stand as the type of life-work informing Armstid's excavation:

> the constant and unflagging round of repetitive nerve-and-flesh wearing labor by which alone that piece of earth which was his mortal enemy could fight him with, which he had performed yesterday and must perform again today and again tomorrow and tomor-row . . .—this until the day came when (he knew this too) he would stumble and plunge, his eyes still open and his empty hands stiffening into the shape of the plow-handles, into the furrow behind the plow, or topple into the weedy ditch, still clutching the brush-hook or the axe. (908–9)

Having worked so hard, Armstid foolishly believes that there must be something in what he has done and what he has done it to: a belief ratified by his typicality in the Bend, where premodern forms of labor ensure the persistence of non monetary modes of exchange, and therefore of land materialized through practices that impede the explanatory currency of coin.

III

The links between Ike and Mink's stock may now be apparent. Both beasts offer their "owners" access to the land, while implying that the earth is best "appreciated" within a residual social structure, associated with subsistence production and common-use rights. At one point, Faulkner establishes a semioccult link between the animals in their function as apertures to the earth. At night, Ike milks and penetrates his cow in wooded hill country: milk literally soaks the ground into which sperm metaphorically passes. Rising, prior to the dawn, the idiot leaves the cow to steal grain with which to feed her. As he returns from a nearby barn, the dawn "is not decanted onto earth from the sky, but instead is from the earth itself suspired" (898). Faulkner eroticizes the suspiration in an extended description which translates the mingled liquids of the lovers into the source of "upseeding," as "frond by frond . . . it rises and disseminates and stains the sleep-fast earth" (898–99). Lactate, sperm, and soil fuse in an unlikely emission of "light." Elsewhere, the mix is less benevolent. When Mink kills Houston over the bull, or more properly over shared use rights in unfenced ground, the ground itself proves politically correct, insofar as Houston's death issues from the earth in collaboration with Mink's rifle. Thrown from his horse by the shot, Houston saw

> the pain blast like lightning across the gap . . . [between vision and where his feet should have been]. But it came from the other direction: not from himself outward, but inward toward himself out of all the identifiable lost earth. Wait, wait, he said. Just go slow at first, and I can take it. But it would not wait. It roared down and raised him, tossed and spun. (934)

"It" is identifiably "pain," rising from the "earth" as "lightning," which because of its source and form fuses with earlier emissions to make common cause with populist resistance to stock law and enclosure. So cow and bull unite, via the logic of an extended analogy ("lightning" out of the "lost earth"), as that analogy transmutes the earth into an agent dedicated to self-preservation, in the tacit form of a "commonwealth."[22] Faulkner's reasoning, though subterranean, fits with his wider and gradual politicization of autochthony. All of which is very consistent, if one ignores the problematic deep-structure of the bull plot as slave revolt.[23] Furthermore, nothing in my tricky linkage of bull and cow explains their "explosive" co-presence in the larger narrative of *The Hamlet*. Which takes me, trailing problems, to the third and final cow in my comparative exercise, a figure who may yet prove to be the explanatory key.

Eula is both bovine and autochthonous. To the male population of the Bend she is little more than a uterus (835), decorated with mammaries and a ruminant "damp mouth" (848). Ratliff merely focuses the collective lexicon when he declares her a "heifer" (877) with a pedigree descending from Juno (that most cowlike god) by way of Ike's mistress—a Juno among cows (899). The match between Eula and the cow is compounded by a consideration of Eula's all-purpose proximity to soil. Possessed of a landed marriage part, her points of contact with or near the ground, be they buggy seat, school bench, or earth, attract considerable attention. Ratliff metaphorically "snuff[s]" at the buggy in which she was courted (159); Labove "wallow[s]" his face against a "plank still warm from the impact of her sitting" (840); Hoake McCarron penetrates Eula on the ground, his "injured side" lifted by her from below (860). Several persons excavate her marriage portion.

To recognize that Eula is cowlike *and* landed is to modify her sexuality. Indeed, if one takes seriously Faulkner's sustained parallel between the object of Ike's love and Varner's daughter, one needs must argue that just as Ike has sex not primarily with a cow, but with a hole in the ground, so, by association, one strand of the hamlet's obsession with Eula involves a desire for intimacy with the soil, focused through the Frenchman's place. It follows that (to repeat myself) Faulkner casts the bovine as earth's orifice, not to sexualize the earth but to earth sexuality. He gives body to the earth, so that place shall be read as the materialization of what bodies do to the earth in that place. Where Ike and the men of the hamlet are "lovers," Mink, at least in relation to his stock, is a quasi-political agent. The proximity of Ike's cow both to Eula and to the disputed bull draws the three "beasts" into comparative alignment, with each providing an interpretative stencil through which the others may be read. Ike's passage into the cow casts the Bend's shared desire for Eula as an erotic autochthony in which the earth is animate and held in common. That structure of feeling, inflected through Ike's defense of his yearling, may be said to originate in the practices of subsistence production, and in the life-work of a class for whom the earth remains human—a "commonwealth" resistant to enclosure, to large means, and to speculation.

Even with three "cows" in place, my comparative study has yet to offer insight into Mink's putative slave revolt. Nor have I explained Ike and Mink's co-presence as the substance of book 3. These problems are, however, illuminated by Eula's place in the bovine series. Eula sits at its head (just as book 2, "Eula," comes before book 3, "The Long Summer"). Indeed, her departure from the Bend both jeopardizes the series that she initiates, and elicits the surfacing of autochthonic residues in the book that follows her marriage and removal to Texas. In order to understand why Eula's enforced departure from the Bend releases remainders of archaic social forms into the narrative of *The Hamlet*, one needs to recognize book 3 as Ratliff's complex elegy. "Eula" (book 2) closes with the sewing machine agent lamenting Eula's loss, first in Jefferson at the court house and station (867–69), and then, three months later, en route for the Bend (869). Ratliff's long lamentation introduces book 3 (875–78), where in conversation with Will Varner, he observes: "'You must have been desperate,'. . . . He meant no insult. He was not even thinking of Varner's daughter's shame or of his daughter at all. He meant the land, the Old Frenchman place" (875). On the first page of "The Long Summer," Ratliff subordinates Eula to her landed part, his staggered loss being Flem's cumulative gain. Flem's gain has been gradual but emphatic: book 1 ("Flem") ended on a singular image, conveyed to Ratliff from the gallery of Varner's store by a tenant: "'I passed them two horses [Flem's and Will's] and the buggy tied to the Old Frenchman fence this morning,' the fourth man said, he too leaned and spat carefully over the gallery-edge. Then he added, as if in trivial afterthought: 'It was Flem Snopes that was setting in the flour barrel'" (816). A shift between books serves to mark the silence of Ratliff's nonresponse. Ousted from the focal "flour barrel" of the coercive credit mechanisms through which Varner controls his lands,[24] Ratliff's attention (and the attention of the novel) shifts to Eula—as the iconic representation of those lands. But she too, in the space of book 2, falls to Flem. Doubly deprived, Ratliff's two-fold grief (for land and its female embodiment) seeks in book 3 to recover what has been lost, by way of substitutions which explore the ramifications of that loss—the cow and the bull. The second of the bovine substitutes (the yearling) extends the desire for a human earth, inherent in autochthony, toward political action. At which point the structural "cheering up" of the Ratliffian purview, from within which *The Hamlet* generally operates, fails.[25]

Ratliff's class position is complex, combining a tenant childhood with a merchant adulthood. The contradiction could hardly be more announced: apprenticed to subordination within the credit mechanism, he becomes that mechanism's agent. Like Varner in the commissary, Ratliff depends for the retail of his stock on a system which keeps Southern labor poor. Yet despite his structural role as an extension of what Faulkner calls "usury" (733), Ratliff, as a child, was Ab Snopes's semi-constant companion: "We lived about a mile from them. My pap and Ab were both renting from Old Man Anse Holland then, and I used to hang around Ab's barn with him. Because I was a fool about a horse too, same as he was" (757). Since Ab was also, and famously, "a fool about a barn," it is unlikely that the young Ratliff would have been deaf to Ab's "integrity" through "fire." As an adult, and outreach worker for the credit system which binds Varner's tenants to Varner's fields, barns, and store, Ratliff must suppress the populist aspect of his own past. But given his virtual adoption by a labor radical, he is likely to respond to populist resurgence in Mink. Hence the double trajectory of Mink's story, told from within the ambience of Ratliff's grief at land loss. The scrub-bull dispute results in populist violence, but equally, as I have argued, that violence may be reinflected as an expression of those problems of dependency associated with bondage. In effect, Ratliff's divided class position generates an extended split referent, or a sequence of events which can be read in two ways, having very different temporal and economic implications. Mink, the populist, seeks to revise and collectivize land use. Mink, the bound man, affirms that the land remains an extension of the body of its lord. The contradiction is emphatic, and mirrors Ratliff's class impasse: the child of the tenant longs for a shared and human earth; the merchant knows this desire to run counter to the proper conduct of dependency through coercive credit relations, he therefore (and subliminally) binds the laborer to the land and to its land lord.

At the close of Ike's story (book 3, chapter 1), Ratliff will re-enact his own social division, this time not by narrative proxy on the body of Mink, but directly on the body of Ike's beloved cow. Ratliff prompts the "beefing" of the cow as the "respectable" response to Lump Snopes's turning of serial bestiality in Miss Littlejohn's barn into a peep show. In effect, Ratliff does Flem's work for him by protecting the Snopes name (919). He does so only after witnessing the sodomizing of the cow:

> He [Ratliff] did look, leaning his face in between two other heads; and it was as though it were himself inside the stall with the cow, himself looking out of the blasted tongueless face at the row of faces watching him who had been given the wordless passions but not the specious words. (913)

Ratliff finds himself in Ike's position because, at residual levels, his class antecedents cast him as an autochthon desirous of unmediated relations with the earth. His self-displacement proves momentary: the merchant regaining ascendancy via an emphasis on verbal failure, which works to censor any remnant of affinity for the idiot's "passion." Not, however, before a degree of grammatical imprecision, operative in the phrase, "who had been given," allows that the passion and its censorship may be attributed both to the watchers (among them Ratliff) and to the watched (among them Ratliff). Of course, we know what the narrator means: that the voiceless desire in question belongs to the idiot, but for the space of a hesitation at least, syntactical leeway renders autochthonic desire generic— which is exactly the function of "The Long Summer" in relation to the larger narrative of *The Hamlet*.

Flem is absent from book 3, and in his absence (and through Ratliff's grieving), premodern social and political desires surface. It is as though Flem's departure weakens the hold of those modernizations, largely associated with a generalization of the viewpoint of exchange, undertaken in his name. Ratliff returns to the Bend at the start of book 3, effectively to recover the remainders and to police what he has recovered. To read book 3, as though from his perspective, is to be aware of the desirability and unsupportability of nonmarket impulses most typically associated with bovine stock. The disruptive co-presence of archaic and modern imperatives in Ratliff's behavior (and, via him, in the general structure and local semantics of the novel) is conclusively evidenced in his central act in book 4. Ratliff's attention to the earth of the Frenchman place has generally been read as indicative of his succumbing to the ploys and values of Flem. The argument runs that having been tricked by Flem's surrogate salting of the ground with coin, Ratliff and his companions, Armstid and Bookwright, dig because Flem dug before them, and because they believe that he would not work at anything that did not have considerable profit in it. By which accounts, Ratliff's digging ratifies Flem's discovery that land (like everything else) is "real" only insofar as it contains, somewhere about it, a price.[26]

All of which may be true, or (as I argued in chapter 1) only partially true, for Flem without being wholly true for Ratliff, whose digging is double digging in so far as it owes as much to Armstid as it does to Flem. What Ratliff excavates and buys is precious to him in a contradictory sense: he buys for speculative profit and to defeat a speculator, but he also buys Eula's dowry or marriage portion, purchasing, at one level, the landed body of Eula. Standing close to the foolish autochthon, Armstid, in a hole desirable to Ike, on property dedicated to Eula's earthy orifices— Ratliff cannot but partake of the residual bovine stories which disrupt the narrative of *The Hamlet*. For a moment he too digs back into the earth, perceivable as much more than price: part of Ratliff digs for the Frenchman's coin, but another part digs for the sweat of the tenantry, for that which his class of origin had literally buried in the earth. The moment passes. But not to recognize that moment for its antithetical class trajectories, positing opposed ways of life, is to fail to read the residual seriousness of the cows.

Revenants, Remnants, and

Counterrevolution

in "The Fire and the Hearth"

Revenant: a person who returns to a place; a person

who returns as a spirit after death; ghost.

I

THE Agricultural Adjustment Act (AAA) of 1933 initiated the transformation of southern labor and its place, prompting a labor revolution, driven by federal funds, and effectively exorcising black from white. To read sociological commentators in the early 1930s, addressing southern agriculture, is to hear black tenants described as "virtual slaves," held "in thrall," subjected to "almost complete dependence" and "incapable of ever achieving but a modicum of self direction."[1] Although the Civil War had freed the slave, it had done so only for southern landowners to bind him again in an alternative form of "dependency": for chattel slavery read debt peonage. Consequently, the postbellum agricultural worker, most typically living under forms of constraint, was, in the words of the economic historian Jay R. Mandle, "not slave, not free."[2] Mandle's fine distinction remained true until the second half of the 1930s, when New Deal agricultural programs finally unbound black laborer and white owner. Between 1933 and 1938, an influx of federal funds into the South sought to counter the overproduction of cotton: those funds reached only the landowners, who, instead of paying tenants in proportion to their acres left unseeded, fired the tenants. Between 1933 and 1940 the southern tenantry declined by more than 25 percent, while the number of hired laborers increased, though not proportionately, since landowners might simply evict any unnecessary "dependents," enclosing their farms to produce larger units, more viable for mechanized agriculture.[3] Drastically increased tenant mobility signalled structural change, as sharecroppers (bound by debt) were made over into cash workers, "free" to be under- or unemployed in a region where dependency was slowly ousted by autonomy as a cultural dominant.[4] The AAA produced systematic removals alongside unsystematic modernization and immiseration of workers. Less conspicuously, it gave rise to what I would call "revenants"—in that a radical restructuring of labor necessarily forces to prominence archaic and perhaps resistant features of the system which it displaces.

Central to a pre- or semimodern regime of constrained labor,[5] be it chattel slavery or debt peonage,[6] is a notion of dependency, growing out of what Mark Tushnett calls "total relations," that is, relations between binder and bound that extend to the whole life of the slave or tenant, and to the whole life of the master or land lord. Under wage labor, employer/employee connections are "partial" in that the wagepayer pays for, and assumes power over, only the working part of the worker's day.[7]

In 1935, Johnson, Embree, and Alexander surveyed cotton tenancy and concluded:

> The status of the tenancy . . . required no education and demands no initiative, since the landlord assumes the prerogative of direction in the choice of crop, the method by which it shall be cultivated, and how and when and where it shall be sold. He keeps the record and determines the earnings. . . . He controls the courts; the agencies of law enforcement . . . and can effectively thwart any efforts to organise to protect their [the tenants'] meagre rights.[8]

Or, as an Arkansas sharecropper put it in 1939, "De landlord is landlord, de policeman is landlord, de shurf is landlord, ever'body landlord, en we ain't got nothin."[9] To preserve "total relations," even at the level of class fantasy, is, however, to be liable to a contradiction inherent within them. Here Hegel's account of "Lordship and Bondage" is helpful.

Hegel has it that the lord seeks absolute, because independent, authority. However, at the moment of his supremacy, he is troubled because he recognizes, in the propertied objects through which he represents that supremacy to himself, labor that is not his own. He knows that his lordship depends on the labor of the bound man: "Just when the master had effectively achieved lordship, he really finds that something has come about quite different from an independent consciousness. It is not an independent consciousness, but rather a dependent consciousness that he has achieved."[10] Recognition puts him in an impossible position: the white lord must extract from his lordship those black materials which define it "in order to become certain of [himself] . . . as a true being."[11] To do as much is difficult, since the master's mastery depends on the body, labor, and consciousness of the bound man. As Jessica Benjamin has it, "[I]f we fatally negate each other, that is if we assume complete control over his identity and will, then we have negated ourselves as well."[12] It follows that, should the master negate his bondsman, allowing him no independent consciousness, then he will find himself enmeshed with a dead thing (a nonconscious being). And he, having deprived himself of the very goods and recognitions that represent his lordship, will discover himself close to death, since dead the slave cancels the master's means to mastery. However, perhaps held by some means between life and death, the slave might ratify that mastery (underpinning the substance of the lord), without troubling the master's independent consciousness. The solution to the master's impossible contradiction (that he and his are blacks in whiteface) is that the slave become all but a revenant, by which means the bound man, semidead, remains the latent proprietor of the owner's place, property, and person. Without the bound man's repressed and revenantial presence, southern property and place is simply modern—no more than the price it will fetch.

From the perspective of the early 1940s,[13] Lucas Beauchamp, a black tenant who for some forty-five years has worked the same section of the land on the plantation of the McCaslin/Edmonds line, remembers events surrounding the birth of his current land lord, Roth Edmonds, in 1898. The events that he recalls amount to an attempt to make of him a revenant: one who is dead and alive and tied to a place. I would stress that he remembers in 1941, toward the close of what for the economist Paul Schuster Taylor, in 1937, was the "greatest revolution since the Civil War" in "the cotton sections of the South"[14]—a "Second Reconstruction" (for the historian Donald Grubbs) launched by the Farm Security Administration's attack on "tenancy" as "a version of slavery."[15] Lucas, economically speaking, is unreconstructed; still bound, he remembers his revenanting from the perspective of a remnant, archaically at odds with emergent ways of working the land. Arguably, what he recalls expresses the structural core of what forty years of cropping have made of him.

In the winter of 1898, Roth's father, Zack, faced with a wife in difficult labor and a flood, calls on Lucas and his wife, Molly. Lucas crosses the river, "emerging from death" with a doctor,[16] only to find "the white man's wife dead and his own wife already established in the white man's house" (36). After six months, Lucas demands Molly's return, gets it, and subsequently decides, "*I got to kill him* [Zack] *or I got to leave here*" (38). The dispute is not primarily sexual; rather it turns on the white presumption that the physical properties of free black women are available for appropriation. Molly is nursing her own child by Lucas: Zack's child needs milk,

Zack takes that milk and presumes on the accompanying maternal labor. When Lucas makes his demand, he says "I wants my wife. I needs her at home" (36). "Want" and "need" have a sexual edge, but "home" is the key term—Lucas refers to Molly's labor, "keeping alive the fire which was to burn on the hearth until neither he nor Molly were left to feed it" (36). Born within a decade of emancipation, and to ex-slaves, Lucas and Molly demand the right not just to "home," but to marriage and to a hearthfire such as they know burns in the house that Cass Edmonds built for his son Zack (36). The political context of Zack's theft is that, under slavery, marriage between slaves was illegal, precisely because, in order to exercise property rights, masters had to ensure that their slaves were kinless. The slave who was socially dead, that is to say, without kin, was altogether more available for sale or transfer. As James Oakes puts it, "[B]y law . . . [the slave] had no brother or sister, no husband or wife, no son or daughter, no ancestors or posterity."[17] Zack, possibly without thinking, acts the antebellum lord in the postbellum south. He deprives Lucas not only of wife and son and posterity, but of ancestor and brother. It should be remembered that Lucas, though black, is descended from Lucius Quintus Carothers McCaslin, the white founder of the Edmonds dynasty. Moreover, he and Zack were born in the same year and "could have been brothers, almost twins too" (36).

Zack delivers Lucas a comprehensive "social death";[18] in Hegel's terms he "negates" him. Lucas reacts by deciding to kill or leave, where killing is the easier option. To leave would be to desert the artifact, the land which grants evidence of his own independence. Hegel catches the problematic liberation latent in objects of labor for the bound man. The slave, having experienced himself as a negation, or as nothing other than an extension of his lord's will (one "whose essence of life is for another")[19] may be troubled if he recognizes, in the independent existence of those things made by his own hand, evidence of his own capacity to "author" himself, and therefore to negate his own prior negation by the lord: "Shaping and forming the object has . . . the positive significance that the bondsman becomes thereby the author of himself and factually and objectively self-existent."[20] Such a moment is uncomfortable since it requires that the bound man experience both the death of his dependent self and the emergence of an independent self: "Precisely in labor, where there seems to be some outsider's mind and ideas involved, the bondsman becomes aware, through his rediscovery of himself, of having and being a 'mind of his own.'"[21] Where the master risks his masterful "self" in the appreciation that the objects of his desire are the product of the slave's hand, the slave risks his "abject" self in the consciousness that his labor not only postpones the master's satisfaction but also produces an object "that is permanent" and remains "after the master's desire is gratified."[22] Although the bound man's labor makes things that are aspects of himself, in a coercive system those properties are dedicated to the will of another. He who works for a year for a share of a crop that will not cover his living costs, or the cost of his previous year's debt, and so is bound for a second year . . . may find that the things in his hand represent at best a fuller identity which he cannot take, and at worst a slow death. Judith Butler notes that Hegel's discussion of labor "begins to show how the world of substance becomes recast as the world of the subject,"[23] but under debt peonage, circa 1898, the southern tenantry are subjects subjected, who, since they receive limited recognition from others, are likely to live in dread of that freedom which the objects of labor might teach them.

What emerges is revenantial rather that liberatory; Faulkner brackets the memory of the Lucas/Zack dispute with references to Lucas's work: he sharecrops on Edmonds's land (we are assured that he plows with Edmonds's mule and draws on Edmonds's commissary for cash and supplies), and does so despite having "more money . . . in the bank . . . than he would ever spend"(26). The bank contains, at the very least, the lump sum paid by Ike McCaslin to each of Lucius Quintus Carothers McCaslin's black descendants, but money and tenant status are irrelevant when placed beside the fact of his labor: "He had been born on this land. . . . He had worked on it ever since he got big enough to hold a plow straight; he had hunted over every foot of it" (28). As a tenant, whether in 1898 or in the 1930s, his own control over the land is constrained; we are told that "Edmonds" visits the field three times a week, and that during the growing season he gives advice which "he [Lucas] completely ignored, ignoring not only the advice but the very voice which gave it, as though the other had not spoken even" (28). Nominating which "Edmonds" visits is difficult since Lucas's perspective (considering 1898 and earlier from 1941) elides Cass Edmonds (born 1850), Zack Edmonds (born 1874), and Roth Edmonds (born 1898) into a single and intrusive managerial presence— a generic Edmonds." "Edmonds[5] "share" in the tenant product allows him to direct the laborer's hand and so to curtail his independence. Indeed, historically sharecropping developed as a compromise between landowners without cash to pay wages and freedmen without capital to buy land.[24] The compromise, which saw owners grant a season's access to land and credit, in return for a designated "share" of the crop at the season's end, was read by freedmen as a move toward autonomy, and by plantation owners as evidence of a continuing right to constrain a worker's mobility and require his deference. Jay R. Mandle describes the South's agricultural labor market, throughout the second half of the nineteenth century and for a third of the twentieth, as characterized by "confinement more than opportunity," adding that the will of the ex-master threatened to transform "authoritarian supervision" into servitude.[25]

Lucas's field, by his own account, therefore becomes the site of a Hegelian clash of wills. In 1898, Zack's will is dominant; he renders Lucas "socially dead" for six months. Reconsidered, from the time of the story's frame the wound is not mortal. Lucas has his wife, fire, and land back, and has had a further forty-three growing seasons during which, through labor, to establish his disputed title to a disputed independence. Hence his essential and always problematic relation to "his" land: "But it was his own field, though he neither owned it nor wanted to nor even needed to" (27–28).

In 1898 Lucas had to kill the master or leave that land. Finally, he does neither, since to do the latter would be to leave his laboring self and to do the former would be to kill himself, in that the act could result only in "the limb . . . [and] the coal oil" (41). However, he does risk the lynching, and Faulkner's account of Lucas's attempt on Zack's life turns on moments of positively Hegelian "recognition." A degree of proceduralism may help with dense textual materials. Place: Zack's bedroom. Time: dawn. Weapon: several—Lucas's razor (discarded), "nekkid hands" (demoted to arm wrestling [44]), Zack's pistol (misfired). Manner: protracted and verbal. Motive: Zack's, self-defense; Lucas's, ditto but with complications (both before and after the event Lucas claims to have been directed by "*old Carothers's blood*" as he "*spoke for me*" [45], though during the perpetration of the crime he insists, three times, that he has to "beat" that "blood"). Some illumination may result from consulting Faulkner's transcript at the point where Lucas, having got Zack's gun,

broke the pistol's breech and glanced quickly at the cylinder and turned it until the empty chamber under the hammer was at the bottom, so that a live cartridge would come beneath the hammer regardless of which direction the cylinder rotated. "Because I'll need two of them," he said. He snapped the breech shut and faced the white man. Again the white man saw his eyes rush until there was neither cornea nor iris. *This is it*, the white man thought, with that rapid and even unamazed clarity, gathering himself as much as he dared. Lucas didn't seem to notice. *He cant even see me right now*, the white man thought. But that was too late too. Lucas was looking at him now. "You thought I wouldn't, didn't you?" Lucas said. "You knowed I could beat you, so you thought to beat me with old Carothers, like Cass Edmonds done Isaac: used old Carothers to make Isaac give up the land that was his because Cass Edmonds was the woman-made McCaslin, the woman-branch, the sister, and old Carothers would have told Isaac to give in to the woman-kin that couldn't fend for herself. And you thought I'd do that too, didn't you? You thought I'd do it quick, quicker than Isaac since it aint any land I would give up. I aint got any fine big McCaslin farm to give up. All I got to give up is McCaslin blood that rightfully aint even mine or at least aint worth much since old Carothers never seemed to miss much what he give to Tomey that night that made my father. And if this is what that McCaslin blood has brought me, I dont want it neither. And if the running of it into my black blood never hurt him any more than the running of it out is going to hurt me, it wont even be old Carothers that had the most pleasure.—Or no," he cried. *He cant see me again*, the white man thought. *Now*. "No!" Lucas cried; "say I dont even use this first bullet at all, say I just uses the last one and beat you and old Carothers both, leave you something to think about now and then when you aint too busy to try to think up what to tell old Carothers when you get where he's done already gone, tomorrow and the one after that and the one after that as long as tomorrow—" The white man sprang, hurling himself across the bed, grasping at the pistol and the hand which held it. Lucas sprang too; they met over the center of the bed where Lucas clasped the other with his left arm almost like an embrace and jammed the pistol against the white man's side and pulled the trigger and flung the white man from him all in one motion, hearing as he did so the light, dry, incredibly loud click of the miss-fire. (43–44)

A number of questions remain unanswered, not the least of them, why did the gun misfire? However, to take problems in order of occurrence: Lucas's physical demeanor—loss of sight is the last in the list of symptoms evidencing acute physical failure ("rapid inhalations," "trembl[ing]," "strangl[ed] voice," "spent and frantic face" [43]). Hegelian diagnosis would indicate that Lucas was not in good health when he undertook the crime: Zack's two semimortal blows, delivered six months earlier at river and hearth, should have convinced him of the degree to which his reality is subordinate to the essential reality of the master. Given such dependency, the decision to kill the master amounts to self-murder, hence the symptoms of Lucas's protracted dissolution. One detail is particularly revealing: Lucas's eye turns inwards. The victim's claim, *"He cant even see me right now,"* is in keeping with complete cessation of gaze which, coupled with the perpetrator's concern for an inner voice associated with his own "white" blood, raises the question, "who or what does Lucas see as he stares inwards?" Clues are everywhere but don't easily add up: take, for example, the ventriloquized entry of old Carothers. Lucas imagines old Carothers, using his descendants as mouthpieces through which to negotiate the disposition of his lands. Presumably, Lucas, in his mind's eye, sees his namesake and founding father. The guise of the patriarch is complex, taking form through a three-fold elision: of "blood" which is seen and heard (Lucas's and his ur-master's); of "land" (that which manifests the continuity of the blood); and of lord (the body of the master implicitly eternal within the body of his land).[26] Lucas adds a fourth term at the instigation of Zack, the entire pistol-on-the-bed sequence having been prompted by the land lord's racial slur, "Or maybe you aint even woman-made McCaslin but just a nigger that's got out of hand" (42). The fourth term is "nigger": Zack's taunt deprives his attacker of most of his name, which but for "Beauchamp" is all but the name of the original white patriarch (Lucas Quintus Carothers McCaslin *Beauchamp*). Lucas counters with a complicated move to recapture both the name and its attendant terms, "blood," "land," and "lordship"; he insists that Zack, as "a woman-made McCaslin," descended not from old Carothers but from his sister, is pulling gender. His case runs that just as Zack's father, Cass Edmonds, demanded deference towards his female "blood" in the question of inheritance, so Zack expects Lucas to defer to him, since Zack too is "of the woman-branch." The move is adroit, Lucas regains the kinship that he, as mere "nigger," has been denied, along with the high-ground of the male McCaslin descent. Ascendancy is momentary since it implicitly begs the question, "Of what use is the name without the substance?" In his pursuit of a patriarch's authority, Lucas recognizes that without "farm" and "land," "the blood" is an illusion. He observes that "all I got to give up is McCaslin blood," and he is immediately carried back to the genealogical fount of that blood, to the point at which it "ran into [his] black blood."

Why does Lucas, gun in hand, bring to mind the miscegenated union of his grandparents? I call as evidence Quentin Compson's remarks concerning Dalton Ames in *The Sound and the Fury*: "Dalton Ames. If I could have been his mother with open body lifted laughing, holding his father with my hand refraining, seeing, watching him die before he lived."[27] Lucas intends a more violent constraint; gun in hand, he will substitute blood for semen, pain for pleasure. It is unclear, in the first instance, whether the blood is to be Zack's or his own. However, since talk of pleasure exacerbates Lucas's ocular symptoms ("*He cant see me again*"), we are required to repeat the question, "What does he see?" Given the break at the point of reference to grandpaternal pleasure, (the dash), and the immediacy of Lucas's subsequent and negative cry ("—Or no"), I would suggest that he witnesses the founding orgasm of the black McCaslin line and determines to prevent it. Method: suicide. Lucas speaks in parables, projecting his own death as an eternal conundrum for the planter class. Having denied his McCaslin genealogy, he speaks as pure Beauchamp and so as a bound man, and as one recently subjected to the extremity of his lord's will. His parable is as follows: the black bondsman who would kill his lord must first kill himself, since by doing so he deprives his lord of the pleasures that derive from the bound hand, those pleasures and properties that are his very substance. The bondsman who kills himself kills the lord who depends upon that self.

Beauchamp's parabolic death retroactively kills old Carothers. His logic is impacted but simple. To deprive Zack of labor strikes at what makes his mastery: his grip on the land will fail. Without land, which embodies McCaslin continuity, old Carothers's presence will fade. Withdrawal of labor exacts an apt revenge for the initial crime of miscegenation: although Lucas's death cannot remove Tomasina from the McCaslin bed, it can remove the founding McCaslin from the land, land which (through black labor) assured him of his quasi-seigneural mastery. Sexual crossing becomes a theft of pleasure, wherein the white master most exemplifies his readiness to exploit to the full the properties of a black body. So inflected, Faulkner's use of miscegenation (at least in "The Fire and the Hearth") addresses labor questions through the issue of sexual pathology Witness the capacity of the act to generate "pleasure" via which a black labor force is reproduced to ensure further "pleasures" for the master. So, Lucius Quintus Carothers McCaslin penetrates his slave Tomasina, who dies in childbirth: her son (Terrel) is old Carothers's property, and Terrel's son Lucas continues to work McCaslin land.

Whether Lucas intends to kill himself or is merely telling tales cannot be discerned, but it must be stressed that the tale he tells involves a politically creative kind of death , in that it marks a revolution in the bound consciousness. Why does Zack "spring" exactly as Lucas proposes suicide? Either to save himself or, if he has been attentive, to save Lucas, "the man whom he had known from infancy, with whom he had lived until they were both grown almost as brothers lived" (43). If he has been listening and has understood, the distinction is irrelevant: to save Lucas *is* to save himself pace Hegel:

> For just when the master has effectively achieved Lordship, he really finds that something has come about quite different from an independent consciousness . . . he feels that his truth is rather the unessential consciousness [of the bondsman], and the fortuitous and unessential action of that consciousness.[28]

Were Lucas to kill Zack he would become for those who find the body "just a nigger that's got out of hand" (42). Were he to escape lynching with his revolutionary consciousness intact, he could not sustain that consciousness within a labor system characterized by constraint (at least in 1898) and among laborers tied to separate units of production.[29] Moreover, within the Hegelian double bind, to kill Zack is suicide, and the manner of their "embrace" and separation indicates that Lucas senses as much. In such circumstances, the pistol's misfire represents an honorable draw, allowing Lucas to return to his field, wife, and hearth, the sources of a disputed independence. In the paragraph that immediately follows the "incredibly loud click," Faulkner has Lucas take stock of his labors during the good growing season of 1898, from the perspective of 1941, and then describe in some detail the process of plowing a field; his point being that in labor itself Lucas retains, at the very least, the material base for a revolutionary consciousness: "He plowed on until the plantation bell rang for noon. He watered and fed the mule and himself ate—the milk, the still-warm biscuit—and rested in the shade until the bell rang again. Then, not rising yet, he took the cartridge from his pocket and looked at it again, musing . . ." (45).

The postbellum land lord continues to direct his "free" labor in authoritarian fashion by means of an antebellum plantation bell. Lucas may ignore it, but his musings indicate that the landowning class has reclaimed its pre-eminence in his mind. His speculative recollection of the events leading up to the return of Molly erase all trace of the radical parable of self-murder. In its place Lucas puts a more conventional scenario—Zack dead, Lucas waiting "*even* [for] *the coal oil*" (45): "*I would have paid. So I reckon I aint got old Carothers' blood for nothing. . . . Old Carothers, . . . I needed him and he come and spoke for me.* He plowed again" (45).

This conclusion turns the story into a piece of counterrevolutionary revisionism. Lucas restores the very "voice" and "blood" that earlier he "beats."

While, allowing Lucas his conclusion, we should perhaps reconsider the process through which Faulkner traces its emergence. Detective work on two instances of temporary blindness and an exclamatory pause suggests that though the scene over the bed (in 1898) is recorded primarily from Zack's perspective, it retains within it a requirement that simultaneously we adopt Lucas's viewpoint. The episode as a whole is cast as that which Lucas "would never forget" (35)—a memory occurring in 1941 between the repetition of a name, and triggered by an authorial reference to Roth Edmonds's age: "'George?' Edmonds said. 'George Wilkins?' He came out onto the gallery—a young man still, a bachelor, forty-three years old last March. Lucas did not need to remember that. He would never forget it—that night of early spring following ten days of such rain" (35). Over ten pages later, having crossed "to the edge of the gallery," Roth repeats his enquiry ("'George Wilkins?'" [46]); in effect, his pause for breath contains Lucas's memory of 1898, triggered not by a date of birth ("Lucas did not need to remember that"), but by the gallery itself. Lucas has come to the front of the Edmonds's plantation house, a type of building referred to as "nigger sweat" by a white cropper in Faulkner's story "Barn Burning" (1938).[30] That "[h]e didn't go around to the back" (35) indicates a refusal of due deference which renders architectural space a disputed site. The meaning of the gallery divides, imposing double articulation on the framing name: for Roth, George Wilkins is an unproductive tenant, and as such an economic liability; for Lucas, about to protect his own still by betraying George's, Wilkins is a competitor. But in the context of a semantically unstable gallery, he can be recast as a cropper who uses liquor production to withhold labor from his land lord, while countering surveillance by and indebtedness to that land lord. Given that the events of Lucas's insurrection fall between the iteration of the name, its post-1898 recurrence as memory requires that we read "George Wilkins" (inflected as a question) through Lucas and against Edmonds, not as a "jimber-jawed clown" (57), but at least potentially as a black who tacitly refuses his place. Indeed, by the close of "The Fire and the Hearth," George has married into Lucas's family and is operating as his business subordinate.

Nouns are split and their objects divided by Faulkner's choice of free indirect discourse as a prevalent narrative option throughout *Go Down, Moses*. By exploring examples taken from the framing of the Zack/Lucas dispute, I have distracted from my earlier claim that the entire 1898 interlude should be articulated from both black and white positions. Zack believes that Lucas "*cant . . . see*" twice; but on each occasion Lucas sees sufficiently to forestall Zack's incipient motion toward the gun ("*He cant even see me right now*, the white man thought. But that was too late too. Lucas was looking at him now" / "*He cant see me again. . . . Now*. 'No!' Lucas cried"). Blind from a white perspective is anything but from a black. Doubleness is required because a free indirect narration moves strategically between options (here racialized), resisting specific determination of perspective. As the linguist V. N. Vološinov notes of what he calls "quasi-direct discourse," when an author simultaneously identifies with and yet retains distance from a creation (sidling up to and away from the consciousness or voice of a character), more is involved than a "mixture" or "average" of subject positions and modes of enunciation.[31] Instead, "an author and character speak at the same time."[32] And though, in particular passages and phrases, a single enunciation may take precedence, the reader is always likely to be aware that any word, as the potential locus of "two differently orientated voices," may carry a "double intonation" in which two speech acts interfere with one another.[33] "The Fire and the Hearth" compounds interference, turning dual voices quadraphonic, as an author forms temporary and double alignments with different characters, often within single phrases or words: witness "gallery," "George Wilkins?" or "*see.*"

Lucas and Zack, indirectly narrated and confronting one another within a particular and racialized regime of labor, do not belong to themselves: rather, they find themselves by oscillating between points of view on themselves—a movement enhanced by Faulkner's adoption of a mode of narration whose habit of covert cotelling breaks sentences across standpoints, and positions the meaning of words between speakers. Zack and Lucas, in Vološinov's phrase, are "double faced,"[34] being with, yet detached from, those to whom they respond. Consequently, within Faulkner's deployment of free indirect discourse, any utterance may contain "the accents of two differently orientated voices" (first and third; white and black; owner and owned). Whether characterised as "crossed utterance," tonal "collision," and "interference" (Vološinov), or as "assemblage" and "oscillation" (Deleuze),[35] free indirect discourse amounts to splitting: we hear two or more voices where we expect one.

It might be objected that I multiply wilfully and in ways that ignore Lucas's account. Plowing, after the confrontation in 1898, and with Molly restored, Lucas thinks, "*Old Carothers, . . . I needed him and he come and spoke for me*" (45). In effect, and in the first person, he trades the very ambivalence which he caused to be released into the semantic and social orders for a univalent term—the voice of the master.[36] His volte-face is depressing, but should not be ignored since it exactly reflects the counterrevolution claimed by the postbellum planter class, Lucas's employers. Union victory in the Civil War "produced a social revolution in the South,"[37] yet planters retained their lands and a coercive system of labor.[38] Consequently, with the restoration of the plantation mode of production, albeit in modified form, they could recast defeat as victory. As Redemption (1877) followed Reconstruction (1867–77), and a net of Jim Crow laws (1880–90) stabilized white political and economic supremacy, so Reconstruction's attempt to give the revolution an adequate social form was written as a "mistake," enacted by "Carpet Baggers" and "Scalawags" on "ignorant" freedmen.[39] Lucas partakes of a larger tradition of southern revisionism; he, in his concluding reliance on old Carothers, restores the masters even as and when they restore themselves. Yet Faulkner adds, "He plowed again," pointing out that, counterrevolution or not, the bound man has his liberation to hand in the work of that hand.

II

Plowing in 1941 is not what it was in 1898, as Faulkner carefully notes, via two appraisals—modernizing land lord of archaic tenant; archaic tenant of modernizing land lord. Reviewing Lucas's work over twenty years as one protracted labor dispute—an "unbroken course of outrageous trouble and conflict, not with the land . . . but with the old negro" (90)—Roth (Zack's son) notes the "clumsy old fashion" in which Lucas farms, his refusal to "let a tractor so much as cross the land," or a crop duster enter the air space above it (90). By 1941, mechanization and chemicals were the visible future of southern agriculture. Thanks to tenant displacement, care of the New Deal, land would cease to be that to which its owner bound labor in the extraction of profit. Rather, it would become that from which the owner cast labor out, in order to enclose his tenants' tracts in enlarged units of production, into which farms he must sink capital for the greater extraction of profit. Pete Daniel offers a useful summary: "for better or worse, World War II reconfigured Southern society. . . . Machines and chemicals assumed iconic importance as agribusiness relied on capital more than labor."[40] Perhaps predictably, Lucas's review of Roth reverses the emphasis. On the unstable "gallery" and about to betray George Wilkins, he notes that:

> In age he [Roth] could have been Lucas' son, but actually was the lesser man for more reason than that, since it was not Lucas who paid taxes insurance and interest or owned anything which had to be kept ditched drained fenced and fertilized or gambled anything save his sweat, and that only as he saw fit, against God for his yearly sustenance. (46)

Lucas bids for the superiority of "sweat" over capital: he insists that servicing land as a form of capital, or what the owner *does* in the early forties, is the lesser part of value taking. "Sweat," invested as labor "sees fit" produces "sustenance," where "sustenance" resists the notion of "profit." "Land" is the curiously missing term here; its synonym "anything" suggests the degree to which, perhaps even for Lucas, that which he plows is in effect a means of production cast into ambivalence by a transition in regimes of accumulation, from postbellum plantation to agribusiness. Lucas presents Roth as diminished in proportion to the degree to which he invests capital—draining and fertilizing his property, insuring his fixed assets (among them, perhaps, tractors). Yet by such standards Lucas is similarly diminished, or at least transformed. He reviews his land lord as a prelude to protecting his considerable investment (29) in corn-liquor production by ridding himself of market competition. We are told repeatedly that Lucas has three thousand dollars banked in Jefferson, two thousand of it from Lucius Quintus Carothers McCaslin's will. Croppers caught in debt structures do not accrue: the additional thousand is therefore moonshine profit,[41] rendering Lucas an economically split subject: a capitalist in credit, masked as a tenant in debt. Roth specifies the degree of indebtedness; for thirty years Lucas had drawn supplies from the commissary on an account that the ledgers record as unpaid (90). The land lord who neglected to collect on tenant debt at cropping time would fail. But Roth, in 1941 investing in tractors and chemicals, may begin to see the indebted cropper as an imminent anachronism, due for eviction though as yet retained. In which case, Roth also splits economically: a land lord whose profit resides in his control over low-cost production undertaken by a bound workforce; and an agricultural businessman whose profit derives from enforced labor migration, enclosure, and capitalization. Roth and Lucas are arguably alike, each caught between a version of land as "sweat" or land as capital. Which, structurally speaking, is where they should be in the early 1940s, if "sweat" is understood as labor retained, and "capital" as labor expelled.

Whatever the liberal reformers of the AAA thought they were doing, the planter bloc used New Deal measures to create a foundation for the neo-plantation complex, initially by dismantling the furnishing system, in order to end their responsibility for the survival and reproduction of black labor. Between 1930 and 1940, the tenantry declined by 62 percent in Mississippi.[42]

Black migrancy rates depended on the readiness of northern capital to draw low-cost labor out of the South. For as long as European immigration served northeastern labor needs, the planters retained their entrapped workforce.[43] World War I cut the labor supply to the North, with a consequent and drastic increase in out-migration from the South. Between 1916 and 1919, half a million blacks left the region, and Mississippi recorded its first ever decline in black population. During the 1920s, Mississippi alone lost over 14 percent of its black males aged 15–34—that is, ready to move and employable: the figure gains in dimension with the recognition that in 1910 over 10 percent of American blacks were Mississippians.[44] Neil McMillen, historian of African American Mississippi, notes of the wartime phase of the Great Migration: "To the reader who followed early local press accounts of this mass movement, it surely seemed that an entire people were abandoning the state for the packing houses and steel mills of Chicago, Detroit, and St. Louis as fast as the railroad could carry them."[45]

Rates of abandonment slowed during the 1920s and 1930s, though migration figures remained consistent with those recorded during the 1910s, that is, at levels higher than in any previous decade. Mandle describes the period from World War I until 1940 as

one in which an incremental chipping away at the structure of the plantation economy occurred. The structure remained intact with the planters continuing to control large numbers of dependent workers in the production of the cotton staple. Below the surface, however, large numbers of southern blacks had learned or were learning the route by which they could escape the plantation economy.[46]

Creative rejection of that economy in daily practice might involve a considered refusal of deference, or taking the time to go to the railhead to find a copy of the *Chicago Defender*: but most typically it turned on the idea of motion—"a persistent and overriding theme in [Southern black] conversations (as in their songs) was movement away from where they were living and working, if not always towards a clearly defined destination."[47] Motion remained for the majority conceptual, in that the Depression, with its attendant news of the immiseration of urban blacks, ensured that northern capital no longer needed to draw on the southern labor reserve. In effect the breakdown of the plantation economy stalled, although the influx of federal funds, associated with the New Deal, set in place a capitalization of the Southern owning class, which allowed a new regime of accumulation to emerge, even as World War II tripped bound black labor finally free of its rural entailment.

Black removals during early 1940s were effectively financed by capital inflows during the late 1930s. The 1940s saw over one million African Americans leave the six plantation states, while between 1940 and 1946 the national proportion of black males working on farms fell from 41 to 28 percent. Mississippi alone, in the first four years of the decade, experienced a decline in its farm population of over 23 percent.[48] We should set against this, as its enabling condition, federal payments made to a landowning class, and subsequently deployed to evict an increasingly workless labor force, and then, via welfare, to pay for the policing of its consequent impoverishment.

Government subsidies, administered by local elites, sponsored the dispossession of rural blacks in that initial payments for acreage reduction (1933), and subsequent acreage allotments for cotton growth after 1934, went not to black tenants but to white owners. The AAA and its acronymic successors cut cotton acreage to raise prices and reduce surplus, rendering many black producers redundant and forcing them from the land. The land was laid fallow for capital. Even as black Mississippians were displaced, federal funds restored the state:

As a result of the AAA and other related programs, bank deposits, farm values, and farm incomes all doubled. Between 1933 and 1939, the federal government's direct expenditure in Mississippi totalled $450 million, while an additional $260 million entered state banks through ensured loans.[49]

The landowning class shifted its pattern of dependency, from black labor to northern capital, while the tenantry, increasingly landless and welfare-dependent, waited on the pull of northern employment needs to renew its migration. "America's entry into World War II marks the principal point of discontinuity in the black experience in the United States,"[50] as a consequence of which December 1941 marks the imminent reconfiguration of southern land by capital-intensive agriculture.[51] With blacks less and less in their laboring place, and capital more and more in that place, the substance of southern land is transformed. To return to the distinction which prompted this historical interlude—land as "sweat" gives way to land as "capital," though agribusiness, and its attendant destruction of "the labor-intensive rural order born of Reconstuction," was not fully established until the 1950s.[52]

The growing season of 1941 frames "The Fire and the Hearth." Disputes over the management of Lucas's labor time (literally his "sweat") pepper the text, but center on Roth's discontent over his tenant's decision to concentrate not on his indebted crop but on the recovery of a cache of some $20,000, supposedly buried on the McCaslin land. The gold may be read in two ways: first, "as a token of the plantation riches that derive from the buried value of first slave, then tenant labor"[53]—such a reading is retrospective. Alternatively, a projective account might consider the cache as the hidden and emergent meaning of the earth itself, as capital. Certainly, it draws to it a northern machine, albeit only from Memphis. Lucas expends much stolen labor time using announcedly modern technology ("complex with nobs and dials" [63]). The machine fails to locate the buried treasure, implying that even as late as 1941 neither land nor labor is best characterized as price. I have argued that the archaic practices of dependency, as a system for organizing labor, produce revenants. I would add that Lucas, as a troubled expression of the logic of dependency (as both a laboring remnant and a self-revising revenant), remains a goldless standard.

Yet he does not have to stay. He has $3,000 in the bank, and it is a moot point whether $20,000, and then some, might see him join the migration northward. Certainly Molly, his wife, fears that finding it will be his destruction (79); in fact, it would be his modernization. But the point of the story is that Lucas remains a tenant, putting substance *into* McCaslin land. He is, by choice, caught in a contradiction—a revolutionary who resists his own "social death" (1898), only to accept it later in a counterrevolutionary revision. He is, therefore just enough of a revenant to ensure the viability of McCaslin property. Faulkner's continuing commitment to Lucas's story in 1942, after the adjustment of the Second Civil War and its attendant and radical Second Reconstruction, indicates the degree to which his work turns on and returns to the forms of "dependency" as they emerge from an archaic regime of accumulation and resist modernity.

"Resist," however, is overemphatic. Resistance would imply an authorially stable perspective on modernization—that Faulkner takes the "sweat" and not the "gold," or decides on the viewpoint of labor over that of exchange. Doubtless he will incline that way, but the free indirect discourse through which he approaches Lucas's position allows no such finality. Articulating *Go Down, Moses*, or in this instance "The Fire and the Hearth," produces split subjects and divided objects, in so far as we are required to see from within the perspectives both of the constrained and of those who constrain; to recognize the passage of one into the other, and to experience an attendant wrenching of syntax and subject. All of which yields disconcerting levels of textual undecidability. In 1942, on the cusp of a major economic transition, "things" are not comfortable, subjects are not decided, and voices (or at least Faulkner's authorial voice[s]) tend to talk from both sides of their mouths at once. Put another way: Faulkner's historical acuity produces a narrative problem founded on a dense or double temporality. His backward glance toward 1898 yields the black (Lucas) committed to the white (Edmonds) in the toil of dependency. His forward glance toward the war yields, on the evidence of previous migration of black from white, intimations of a racialized modernity . . . the black separated, the black in motion, the black urbanized, the black stranger, each of them spectral forms of a longed-for emancipation. "Freedom," it would seem, makes for difficult company by revising customary relations. In 1942 Faulkner's voice can only just take the strain of articulating the emancipation, not least because to free the black is to evacuate white substance as it has been realized in the South up to this point.

Joel Williamson, an historian of southern black/white relations, defines the legacy of those relations at midcentury—he proposes that for white to release black is to declare, "I am not going to be me anymore": "In order for an individual white person to let black people go . . . the white person, in a sense, had to die, had to cease to be in an important way what he or she had been. . . . How does one excise an integral and functioning part of the body and yet preserve the life of the patient?"[54] I have argued elsewhere that Quentin Compson could not do it, twice,[55] but that was in 1929 and 1936, before an agricultural revolution had completed one form of excision via funded eviction. The test case for Quentin in *Absalom, Absalom!* (1936), undertaken without much New Deal anesthetic, involves the death of Bon. As Quentin tells it, Henry Sutpen, confronted by his possibly black and probably fraternal companion's proposal to marry his sister, shoots the problem—but in so doing triggers the logic of dependency. He (white) who kills his brother (black) kills his own substance and therefore murders himself. Henry Sutpen is Lucas Beauchamp in whiteface; but whereas Lucas, care of his misfire, survives, awkwardly inside and outside the white body, Henry joins the living dead, full time. He fires in 1865 and vanishes, to the consternation of his narrators, returning to Sutpen's Hundred in 1909, little more than a corpse. In that year he becomes one, completing a forty-four-year career as a revenant. Bon's story causes Quentin to take to his Harvard bed. For those who witnessed his jump into the Charles River (in *The Sound and the Fury* [1929]), his sweating paralysis in Cambridge bodes early death. It would seem that in 1936, as in 1929, and in Williamson's terms, taking black from white proves fatal.

In 1942, abetted by the New Deal's cash inflows and labor outflows, through Lucas, Faulkner figures a modified solution. More properly, I should say that first through Zack and Lucas, and then through Roth and Lucas, he figures a formal solution, residing not in those characters and their actions, but in a mode of narration which, made meaningful by its historical moment, allows him to be "with" but not "in" those characters. He, at least, is formally free to move between racialized subject positions, conclusively bound at neither extremity, experiencing many small migrations in the modulation of his voice. So, for example, Faulkner passes behind the stereotypically rolled eye of the black to establish the logic of Lucas's proposed violence against his own person: he moves, therefore, quasi-directly out of "himself" and toward the consciousness of a bound man. Yet divided he moves again, almost at the same time, to exist close to the argued musculature of the labor lord's leap. Zack's instinctive decision, to defend himself by trying to stop Lucas from killing him (Zack) in and through his own (Lucas's) body, stands as a moment of Hegelian density. One consciousness moves into another to repossess itself. The days of Zack's authority may be numbered, in that he has seen himself as dependent on the boundman, and reclaimed himself by literally binding his own body to that of his subordinate. Faulkner does the leap from both perspectives, by being freely and indirectly committed to each. The mobile and variant inflections of his authorial voice structure his sympathy, but do not amount to an emancipatory bid. "Quasi" and "indirect" positions cannot be definitive, though they may incline incrementally toward definition. So inflected, "being with each" amounts to a "two-faced" device for liberation and retention.

Arguably, the dense modulations compacted within Faulkner's voice in "The Fire and the Hearth" confirm the rhetorical force of Williamson's question. The excision of black from white cannot be a final or absolute option other than in a ghettoized culture. Though the Jim Crow South might be defined as a place held in place by the very many lines with which whites put blacks in their place, its placedness is less a matter of separations than of binding tensions across labor-based lines, where each ethnic option defines its excluded other. Certainly, this remained the case in 1942, the Great Migration notwithstanding.

In labor terms, during the late 1930s and early 1940s, blacks very often had autonomy, under the worst possible conditions, forced upon them. Expelled from increasingly untenable forms of dependency, but lacking the emancipatory tug of war-prompted northern employment needs, they made what amounted to small migratory motions, from tenant contract to scarcer tenant contract, from cropping to welfare, from field to town—predominantly within the plantation states. Black labor was freed to be partially free and often destitute. Arguably, these historical conditions situate the black body between dependency and autonomy, where the former is the residual, and the latter the emergent, term. I would suggest that the same conditions generate Faulkner's vocal impasse in *Go Down, Moses*—his authorial shuffle between black and white, bound and binder, labor and labor lord—an inflective motion which establishes an emancipatory self-multiplication, and grants him the incremental option of being free from his white middle-class subject position, but does not and cannot amount to that emancipation associated with the release of the black from the white body, and of the white body from the black.

Lucas exactly embodies the intermediary solution. He exists within and beyond labor control. His name is all but contained within that of his founding labor lord, from which it differs—as Lucas (or money) differs from Lucius (whose varied forms, "lousious," "looshiouse," "lushious," and "luscious" together imply "pleasures or sweetness taken at leisure, but not necessarily earned").[56] His land is both "his" ("allotted [to him] . . . as long as he lived or remained on the place" [85]) and Edmonds's to contract out on shares. His bank balance constitutes a means to motion which remains immobile. He contains his revolt in a counterrevolutionary revision. He proposes suicide and lives to haunt a generic Edmonds with his independent dependency. It maybe said that he prompts Zack, Roth, and the narrator to find themselves in him, recovering ethnic and class differences as kinship, and thereby extending aspects of the self toward a self that contradicts that self's coherence. It might equally be said that possessors who discover themselves in the dispossessed are likely to mask or refuse that recognition. Lucas partakes of two dynamics, emancipatory and reconstrictive. He is impasse.

III

Within what I have called the "logic of dependency," laborer and land lord are creatures of the same impasse. Throughout "The Fire and the Hearth," and with increasing exasperation, Roth is reminded of what he would like to deny— that Lucas's conduct is essential to his own. In Hegelian terms, the degree to which he takes a holiday from Lucas is the degree to which he dies. Faulkner records the exact distances travelled by Roth on his Sunday away from "stewing and fretting" over his tenant: five miles to church; three more to dinner with friends, after which an afternoon spent discussing agricultural adjustment, or, as Roth would have it, "governmental interference with the raising and marketing" of cotton (95). To leave

Lucas is to enter a segregated sociability and to debate the capitalization of land; by way of which Roth tacitly consents to an intimation of his own demise as labor lord and reinvention as laborless land lord.

But not yet. When Molly confronts him with her decision to divorce Lucas, Roth cannot let him go. Indeed, the whole of the first section of chapter 3 is little more than a reactive and extended profile of Lucas from Roth's perspective, drawn up as Roth struggles to come to terms with Molly's instigation of severance. Edmonds in his commissary "glanced up from the ledger" (77) to see Molly. Having listened to her account of Lucas's treasure hunting and heard her request (78–80), he looks through her departing form to that of her husband (80–81), whose imagined figure sets the parameters of the rest of his day. At the close of the chapter, the commissary and the ledger have been replaced by the plantation house and a "solitary supper" (91). Though Roth has obviously moved, Faulkner offers no account of his movement, so that effectively he remains seated, from first to last, locked in consideration of Lucas's face, cast as the containing condition of the Edmonds's ledgers, buildings, and sustenance.

> Impervious to time too. It seemed to Edmonds, sitting at his solitary supper which he couldn't eat, that he could actually see Lucas standing there in the room before him—the face which at sixty-seven looked actually younger than his own at forty-three, showed less of the ravages of passions and thought and satieties and frustrations than his own—the face which was not at all a replica even in caricature of his grandfather McCaslin's but which had heired and now reproduced with absolute and shocking fidelity the old ancestor's entire generation and thought—the face which, as old Isaac McCaslin had seen it that morning forty-five years ago, was a composite of a whole generation of fierce and undefeated young Confederate soldiers, embalmed and slightly mummified—and he thought with amazement and something very like horror: *He's more like old Carothers than all the rest of us put together, including old Carothers. He is both heir and prototype simultaneously of all the geography and climate and biology which sired old Carothers and all the rest of us and our kind, myriad, countless, faceless, even nameless now except himself who fathered himself, intact and complete, contemptuous, as old Carothers must have been, of all blood black white yellow or red, including his own.* (91)

Roth looks to find his own face in a four-fold reiteration of Lucas's face. But the impulse to identify himself through his tenant is contradictory, since it involves casting himself as black *and* white, owned *and* owner. Consequently, the purpose of the portrait doubles toward confusion, as Roth decomposes the "composite" that he has composed, in order to take white back from black, or, in familial terms, to recover Lucius from Lucas. Roth, having found himself retained within the body of his retainer (on the wrong side of the structure of oppression that he administers), seeks to misrecognize what he has seen. Hence his confused terminology: the portrait may be a "replica," a "caricature," a reproduction, a "face," a statue made from stone or blood, having "fidelity" or none.

Initially Roth draws a generational distinction: Lucas is sixty-seven, he (Roth) is forty-three—but even here difference folds toward sameness as Roth appreciates that Lucas has the younger "face." Roth starts again, with another distinction: despite being Lucius's grandson, Lucas's face is not the face of Lucius. The appeal to genealogy looks a safe bet, in that, to adapt Foucault on knowledge, genealogical knowledge "is for cutting, not for understanding."[57] If Roth wants categorical difference, distinctions concerning who is whose heir seem useful. Except that "heired" effects a "shocking" reversal. "To heir" is a transitive verb whose transitivity is the problem; either the subject (Lucas's "face") is acted upon (passive voice), or it acts (active voice). Both options are available in the neologistic formulation "heired." If the black face is acted upon it is the heir to, and therefore descended from, Lucius: the founder and the founded are each in their places. If, however, the black face acts, it claims generative and reproductive primacy: genealogy turns upside down as Lucas, his class and his ethnicity, bid for supremacy. The dash punctuates desperation. Roth starts for a third time and Faulkner supplies support: Roth's portrait will echo Ike's—both interestingly undertaken at moments of severance. In 1941, divorce might initiate Lucas's departure; in 1895, on his twenty-first birthday, Lucas came to Ike for the inheritance that could have enabled him to quit the tenancy. Roth's third "face" should be read in the context of the face it follows. Roth first: confused by the instability of the family portrait, Roth casts Lucas as the type of Confederate soldiery (perhaps an "undefeated" army, dedicated to the preservation of a slave economy, can contain Lucas's unruly body). The fix eludes him: embalming and partial mummification rigidify without constructing either funerary art or a Confederate monument. In the place of a living black tenant, Roth makes a stiffening dead white soldier—a guard who cannot guard. His "horror" stems not just from the image, but from its structural implication. In his effort to police the black, subordinating the heir to the progenitor, he has made a white corpse. Again, the logic is impeccable. He who would assert mastery by excluding the mastered from that mastery will die, or produce emblems of imminent demise (as Henry Sutpen or his own father might have told him). But rigor is not mortis, and the white is presumably off-white, enabling Roth, in "amazement" at what he has done, to cancel and try again.

Before reviewing Roth's fourth and summative portrait, we should perhaps consider the derivation of his third figure from Ike's earlier version:

> Then Lucas was in the room, standing just inside the door, his hat in one hand against his leg—the face the color of a used saddle, the features Syriac, not in a racial sense but as the heir to ten centuries of desert horsemen. It was not at all the face of their grandfather, Carothers McCaslin. It was the face of the generation which had just preceded them: the composite tintype face of ten thousand undefeated Confederate soldiers almost indistinguishably caricatured, composed, cold, colder than his, more ruthless than his, with more bottom than he had. (83)

Much here is held in common; Lucas is not Lucius, though his "features" favor Confederate soldiery. The problem with the shared analogy is of course color: for the resemblance to work, black must turn white. "Syriac" effects the trick: Lucas looks "Syriac, not in a racial sense" (though it is difficult to say "not" in literature without foregrounding that which is denied). The equestrian allusion may be supposed to distract from the saddle's tint, while at the same time extracting Lucius from Lucas by setting "horse-men" in his (Lucius's) place: that is to say, the planter is displaced by the very type of mounted Confederate who defended the continuance of his property. The logic of the analogy that declares Lucas a Confederate is strained, ensuring that the resultant "composite" wears the marks of its construction on its "face." To read for those marks is to unmask the figurative mask, cast around Lucas, even as it is constructed, thereby revealing the secret that it would conceal—the black within the white. "Syriac," "composite," "tintype," and "composed" together form a lexicon of lettering. "Syriac" is "a printer's type or letter"; "composite" in the context of composed allows for "compositor" or "type setter" to emerge, extracting "type" from "tintype" and unsettling that term. "Tintype," or ferrotype, an early form of photography involving "an image taken as a positive on a thin tin plate," contains its own negation in the archaic colloquial phrase (American), "not on your tintype," or "certainly not," as in "not on your nelly." With "tintype" destabilized and tending to negation, its syllables redistribute: the proximity of "face" yields "typeface," though "tin," in the context of color values (albeit repressed) may tend to retains its "t." Consequently, the "tint" that the entire exercise sought to erase resurfaces to pervade the composition.[58] Like Roth, Ike would encrypt a secret that cannot be encrypted—white derivation from black. Like Roth, in doing so he contrives an image whose chill ("cold, colder") approaches the funerary, all but delivering a white corpse.

Ike faces Lucas in 1895 when the locked logic of dependency virtually ensured that an expelled black amounted to white death, at least for the owning class. Zack's leap and Ike's image share a single deep structure, grounded in a long economic moment. Roth faces Lucas in 1941, after out-migration and an influx of federal funds have partially unlocked that logic and its attendant structures of feeling. Born in 1898, Roth is a child of the coercive economy, but by 1941 he must outgrow his tutelage if he is to survive economically. How he imagines Lucas is vital to the forms of his future existence.

Roth begins his fourth attempt to face Lucas with a marked shift in emphasis. As with his earlier versions, his initial gambit is comparative, but where they strove, with varied success, to subordinate black features to white (Lucas's to Roth's face, Lucas's to Grandfather McCaslin's face; Lucas's to the face of the Confederate dead), Roth now compares in order to reverse and subsume his comparative terms. His projection of Lucas, as being "*more like old Carothers than all the rest of us put together, including old Carothers,*" masks white owners in blackface, where "*us*," at least initially, is a familial pronoun containing the McCaslin lines (male, distaff, and shadow). But genealogy, like the study of facial features, risks recovering identity as a number of "indelible marks" or "codes" written in the blood or on the skin of the carriers.[59] As discursive modes deployed in a racial comparison they are liable to discover incompatibilities and to yield "otherness" as latent destiny and necessary threat. Roth drops genealogy: he follows "*heir*" (free of its earlier and awkward transitivity) with "*prototype*," where "prototype," "the original of which another is a copy," appeals to a "model" or "standard" unencumbered by notions of "blood" or "name." (We should note that "*heir*" is not displaced by "*prototype*" since both are retained). Roth also drops close facial study; "types," in that they are "patterns" or "exemplars," do not necessarily have faces—a lack that enables Roth to find resemblances based on terms lacking overt racial triggers ("*geography*," "*climate*," "*biology*"). His third term, "*biology*," in the context of the retained "*heir*," may be said to require "*sired*"—an archaic form of the verb "to procreate," whose archaism arguably signals the passing of genealogy as an adequately explanatory device. Moreover, Roth makes the point that "*old Carothers and all the rest of us and our kind*" are children of an environment which is modelled on Lucas's prototypical form. (To revert for a moment, and improperly, to those terms that Roth has singularly set aside—from a black body came white bodies, without a caesural mark of panic, ["—"]). "*Biology*," read for "*sired*," yields "blood" and "name" as synonyms, but read in conjunction with "*geography*" and "*climate*," the term is as likely to generate "agriculture" or "horticulture," in which case the revised trinity results in a version of "the land" (their implied generic term) that has little or nothing to do with the body of the land's lord. "McCaslin" and "*Carothers*" are accordingly diminished ("name*less*," "face*less*"). If "*biology*" takes horticulture as its prevalent element, subordinating "blood" to the antonymic, "*us*" and "*kind*" are modified, shifting from family or race toward class. Roth distinguishes between an "*us*" or "*kind*" ("*sired*" by an environment of which Lucas is the "prototype"), and Lucas "*himself*," who, in a reversion to the genealogical, is said to have "*fathered himself, intact and complete*." One way of understanding how Lucas can be considered as a distinct and philoprogenitive body, from which the land and its owners derive, is to read Roth as acknowledging that the physical labors of the rural working class materialize the substance and wealth of those who own the land. Perhaps he can achieve such a recognition in 1941 because owners have less and less need of that class and of its works. Indeed, as a modernizing class, landowners must separate or die: in mundane terms, dependent croppers must be made over into occasional day laborers, care of the AAA. Roth is not Zack, nor if he is to succeed financially can he afford to be.

I have been reading Roth's fourth Lucas for its emergent implications; in Engels's terms, for "the laws of . . . future social development"[60]—that is, for implied revisions in patterns of work, ownership, and ethnicity (post-1940). Such a reading goes against some of the grain. Roth at the last appeals to "*blood*" and "*old Carothers*," though only to insist that as terms of differentiation "*blood*" and name are worthy of contempt. Nonetheless, I have had to lean on "*us*" and "*kind*" to produce class entities, and have pressured Lucas into being the type of a counterclass. I acknowledge that the collective pronoun might be read as referring to a generically southern "*kind*," above and over whom old Carothers and Lucas vie for foundational rights. But I would suggest that a familial, not to say patriarchal, reading of the passage represents a residual rather than the emergent option, and ignores Roth's sustained achievement. He recovers himself and his class within the class body of a deracialized tenantry, and does so in direct if internalized speech (italics indicate Faulkner's suspension of the preferred free indirect discourse). Recognition is achieved at the fourth attempt without panic, fear of contamination, or violent denial, though traces of these reactions have marked his first three Lucases. Instead, he balances "horror" against "amazement," where the latter need not, fourth time round, be read negatively.

Put at its most utopian, and probably mistakenly, Roth recognizes that his identity forms on both sides of the structure of oppression which he administers. The insight debilitates more than it liberates: to experience what Paul Gilroy usefully calls "identity's foundational slipperiness" is hardly comforting,[61] particularly when, as in this instance, the experience radically modifies the cultural codes of "soil" and "blood" within which Roth has been raised. Such recognition might split his identity, producing a multiplication of selves. In Du Boisian terms, Roth is on the brink of acknowledging his own "double life," with its "double thoughts" and "double duties," which, in the best of all possible worlds, require "double social classes," or, in practical terms, a redistribution of social goods.[62] He takes himself, through his consideration of Lucas, to the splitting point . . . and steps back. Chapter 3, section 1 closes as the italics close. Roth quits his reverie and leaves his house to deal with Molly's requested divorce: "It was full dark when he tied the mare to Lucas' fence and walked up the rock path neatly bordered with broken brick and upended bottles and such set into the earth, and mounted the steps and entered. Lucas was waiting, . . ." (91). The rest of "The Fire and the Hearth" details Roth's face-to-face efforts at marriage counselling, management of labor time, and revision of tenant contract—in effect, with the particularities of keeping Lucas tied to Edmonds's land.

No redistribution of goods occurs. In 1941, the structural conditions for social change are in place, but at least initially they will uproot and further impoverish rural workers rather than enrich them. Nonetheless, to persist with my utopian articulation of the text, Roth achieves a revolution in his own consciousness, rendered more painful and evanescent by its intimation of an as-yet-unachievable social transformation. But even this version of his achievement may be a step too far: perhaps it would be fairer to say that the implications of what Roth sees in his fourth portrait of Lucas remain hidden, or, more accurately, "come into hiding" (as an unknown, which, to the degree that it is at least in hiding, *can* be known)[63]—released as a frail exegetic option (in italics) by incipient emancipatory pressures arising from shifts in the southern regime of accumulation.

To know as much, albeit briefly, is to know what Du Bois claimed the African American knew:

[B]orn with a veil, and gifted with second-sight in the American world,—a world which yields him no true self-consciousness, but only lets him see himself through the revelation of the other world. It is a peculiar sensation, this double-consciousness, this sense of always looking at oneself through the eyes of others. . . . One ever feels this twoness—[64]

"Twoness" hurts by requiring an enlargement of the subject who suffers it. Malcolm Bull, considering Du Bois's debt to Hegel, offers a useful diagnosis of emancipatory pain:

The basic reason for double consciousness is that those who possess it have been possessed by others. They see themselves through the eyes of another because their minds have been taken over by others. However, the fundamental Hegelian move which Du Bois preserves is that emancipation does not take the form of throwing off this parasitic consciousness but of gaining one's own sense of self in addition to it, and as a result not only seeing the other in oneself, but seeing one's self not only in one's self but in the other as well.[65]

To see double in a social space not designed for it may result in self-damaging disorientation. Consequently, Roth's achievement remains largely hidden from himself and from the critics.[66] Its true measure lies in the degree to which facing Lucas causes him to "face" himself within Lucas's "face"—that is, to recover his deep memory of key moments from his tutelage within the Beauchamp household.

Roth was raised in doubleness, experiencing it for the first seven years of his life not as division, but as the fullness of a biracial childhood, lived unselfconsciously. His natal space is initially marked as maternal; a holding environment orientated to Molly's breast. Faulkner notes that she "suckled" Roth until he was "weaned," alongside her own child, Henry (77), adding that Molly "was the only mother that he [Roth] would remember" (85). Molly embodies nurture: yet it would be a mistake to identify the Beauchamp household too absolutely with the mammary and the kitchen, despite Molly's emphatic lactation and frequent cooking. In "accept[ing]" Molly, Roth also accepts her "adjunct[s]" (85), Lucas and Henry. "Adjunct" appears twice: "Still in infancy, he had already accepted the black man as an adjunct to the woman who was the only mother he would remember, as simply as he accepted his black foster-brother, as simply as he accepted his father as an adjunct to his existence" (85). There is little "simple" about an adjunctive acceptance of foster family relations: the term, meaning "joined" or "added," retains a hint of making "connection" through "subordination" or "annexation." Faulkner's use of it exactly catches how a white infant, whose "first of remembering [is] projected upon" the breast "of a single woman whose skin was . . . dark" (85), may well take in tacit assumptions of peremptory rights even as he latches on to a wet nurse's milk. It might be objected that Molly is exempt from the adjunctive term; Lucas being subordinate to her, and Zack being subordinate to Roth's "existence" with her. So read, Roth's two fathers are "adjunct[s]" to the maternal dyad. Yet caught between so curious a usage, might not the mammy also be seen as "essentially dependent upon" (*OED*) the authority of the white baby, who so absolutely depends upon her? Roth is "weaned" presumably between 1898 and 1899. "Adjunct" excruciatingly historicizes the racialized practice of his nurture within an economy dedicated to dependency. Faulkner continues: "Even before he [Roth] was out of infancy, the two houses had become interchangeable . . . [Roth] actually preferring the negro house, the hearth on which even in summer a little fire always burned, centering the life in it, to his own" (85) As Roth centers his early life on the Beauchamp "fire" and "hearth," so the black tenants sense the drift of their own symbolic center toward an oblivious white presence. The shift occurs as the merest intimation of a syntactical hesitation. "[P]referring" implies a comparison whose second term ("his own") is deferred. Syntactical delay grows uneasy with the intervention of another possible comparator ("centering"), which threatens to absorb the awaited object of preference ("his own") into its minor grammatical field (as in "centering the life in it [the negro house] to his own [life]"). A split syntactical decision divides the titular "fire and hearth," producing disputed entitlement.

I have been harassing "adjunct" and an instance of grammatical hesitancy in order to find fault with an early childhood that Roth finds perfect. Faulkner's free indirect mobility supplies the subsemantic fractures that derive from seeing what the white boy sees from the perspective of the black who sees and nurtures that boy and his seeing. For seven years Roth sees only support; or, more accurately, inhales and ingests a home identified as smell, food, and warmth (85). The Beauchamp place sustains him and is his substance. He sees Lucas "as much as and even more than his own father" (85), learns to hunt with his "foster-brother" Henry (86), and is fed by Molly. No mention is made of an equivalent education in the white house. Yet in 1905, aged seven, he separates, "and never slept in the same room again and never again ate at the same table" (87). Roth's break, involving the excision of "an integral and functioning part of his body" (Williamson),[67] is close to fatal. Faulkner offers no reason, since the reason is imminent in "adjunct," though he does allude to the seemingly arbitrary descent "one day" of "ancestral pride based not on any value but an accident of geography" (86). The term "geography," where one might have expected "birth" or "race," indicates that the childhood episode should be read as part of Roth's ongoing debate with Lucas. So read, "geography" intuits its own second usage in relation to Roth's culminating recognition that he exists within Lucas, where Lucas is conceived as the "*pro-*

totype" of a shared "*geography and climate and biology*," that is, as a place released from the discursive limitations of "blood," "name," and "soil." In 1941 and at the end of Roth's struggle to face himself within his tenant—without finding either of them close to death by dint of an archaic extractive impulse—"geography" all but speaks of a utopian "twoness." However, early in Roth's quasi-internal debate, and referring to an incident in 1905, "geography" can carry only the frailest intimation of "double consciousness." Rather, Roth aged forty-three, re-experiences separation from Beauchamp as partial death, and not as preparatory ground for the recognition of self as self-addition.

The break is instigated by Roth's refusal first to sleep at Henry's place, and subsequently to share his own pallet with Henry. After a month without contact, Roth returns to the Beauchamp house where, "trembling a little, lordly [and] peremptory" he instructs Molly, "I'm going to eat supper with you all tonight" (87). The meal is not what he expected. After a period "busy in the yard in the dusk" with Henry, Molly's voice, "as it had always been," calls him to supper:

> But it was too late. The table was set in the kitchen where it always was and Molly stood at the stove drawing the biscuit out as she always stood, but Lucas was not there and there was just one chair, one plate, his glass of milk beside it, the platter heaped with untouched chicken, and even as he sprang back, gasping, for an instant blind as the room rushed and swam, Henry was turning toward the door to go out of it.
>
> "Are you ashamed to eat when I eat?" he cried.
>
> Henry paused, turning his head a little to speak in the voice slow and without heat: "I ain't shamed of nobody," he said peacefully. "Not even me." (88)

The glass of milk is the equivalent of Zack's pistol. Where Roth's father "sprang" (44) to stop Lucas killing him by killing himself, Roth "sprang back" from Lucas's withdrawal ("But Lucas was not there"), experiencing it as a murderous extraction that leaves him "gasping," "blind," and at a loss for reality ("the room rushed and swam"). Milk, chicken, and biscuits are each in their place, but their fullness is diminished in that they are recognized now as objects of service due to a landlord nascent in a "lordly" child. Faulkner has Roth notice without noticing (at least in 1905) that a meal is labor before it is nurture—that Henry "killed and dressed the chicken"; that "Henry milked" (87). While the children are "busy" in the yard ("busy" is a "two-faced" word requiring double and racialized articulation), Roth smells the "cooking chicken" that Molly cooks. What is on the table, focused through the glass of milk, is the mammy and her place (the supportive body of black social practices), recast in abstract form as products of labor, available to the presumption of a white child. Henry glosses the single place-setting as the correlative of Roth's "shame." Glossed, his gloss might run: insofar as Roth is ashamed of Henry, and since he has lived in and through Henry (as Henry has lived in and through Roth), he, Roth, is ashamed of a part of himself. Having refused that part, he must subsequently live at a loss for the better part of his life. During his month-long trial separation, Roth acknowledged "shame" and "grief" (87). From the perspective of 1941, recalling 1905, he may realize that his has been a life in mourning for the lost fullness of his early years, with their intimation of alternative social practices.

Roth retains a residue of what he has set aside in the form of his monthly visit to "the only mother he ever knew" (77, 101), with its offerings of "soft cheap candy" (77) and iteration of an increasingly formulaic maternal connection. The candy is a dreg of the early sweetness, retained in memory. Roth's reverie over Lucas recovers that memory, drenched with milk, and retrieves from it an intimation of a utopian formula—the model for his fourth Lucas—redeemed from infancy and regression by way of separation, experienced as the onset of division; note that splitting might be thought to result in acknowledged addition, rather than a muted and partial expulsion of that part deemed darkly parasitic. Without separation from what might glibly be called "the other," Roth could not be aware that he had lived his life elsewhere (other than in his own name, race, and class), let alone have sensed that his life was fuller lived within the double articulation of felt hybridity.

I grow gnomic, yet my purpose has merely been to bring to exegetic light the impacted implication of seven lines of italicized and unspoken speech. Those lines constitute Roth's "Self Portrait as Another in Black." They take exception to the story as a whole, in that they accept, albeit mutely and momentarily, the emancipatory "twoness" that can exist only as an inference latent within the changing labor structure of the Jim Crow South. Roth cannot live with what he sees, anymore than Lucas, though for different reasons, could abide by the revolution in his own consciousness in 1898. Nonetheless, for seven lines, Roth's silent speech traces the social face inherent in Faulkner's tonal modulation. Free indirect discourse, Faulkner's formal response to the emancipatory energies inherent in black migrations and capital movements during the late 1930s and early 1940s, allowed him to move between ethnicities and toward doubleness. For a moment Roth carries him toward the utopian structural space of that duplicity.

The narrative resolution of "The Fire and the Hearth" recontains the liberatory traces released by the story. Roth, post-reverie, plays a minor managerial part in a divorce proceeding that results not in the separation of Lucas from Molly, and by proxy of Lucas from Edmonds (understood as land and person), but in his retention under the same marital and tenant agreements that ruled at the story's start. When Lucas interrupts the Chancellor and his clerk, as they are about to pronounce on his severance, with "We dont want no voce," Roth can only and "quickly" reiterate, "We dont want it now" (99). None of them has ever wanted "it" enough since "it," or "voce," Lucas's lack of Italian notwithstanding, is an independent African American voice. Within the residual and archaic structures that generate the multiform impasse that is "The Fire and the Hearth," a free black voice might be the death of the ventriloquial white subject as landowner or author.

"Pantaloon in Black" and

"The Old People": Migration, Mourning,

and the Exquisite Corpse of

African American Labor

I

IN the plantation South, by 1942 historical conditions existed for the extraction of black from white. For two decades, whiteness had whitened by way of steady out-migration. With the decline of tenantry and the relaxation of the structure enforcing dependency, white, in the last instance, had less reason to be black. The first three stories of *Go Down, Moses*, usefully described by John Matthews as the "plantation trilogy,"[1] feature black movement, much of it away from whites. "Was" (set in 1859) concerns Turl's annual runaway. Buck and Buddy McCaslin catch their slave, but not before black motion has disrupted two white households. "The Fire and the Hearth" is an anthology of journeys by foot, mule, cart, and car. Its fixed points, the Beauchamp cabin, the Edmonds's plantation, the Jefferson court, Memphis and Vicksberg are criss-crossed as a metal detector, a mule, a marriage license, and two stills, variously assembled and disassembled, are carted hither and yon. Her rest disrupted by Lucas's nocturnal trips, Molly, "without awakening," voices a useful critical caption, "'Walking the roads all last night. Walking the roads all tonight'" (48). Although the grief-stricken mobilities of Rider in "Pantaloon in Black" are brief and circumscribed by his desire to rejoin his wife in the grave, Rider too cannot rest. A giant of a man, he steps "over . . . three-strand wire fences" (103) and strides "fast as a horse . . . across the slopes of pasture[s]" and through "old abandoned fields" (107); fields abandoned, presumably by evicted tenants also now in varied motion.

It might here be objected that the perambulations listed are contained within narratives of pursuit and capture. Each story features whites successfully tracking blacks but in every case apprehension serves a black purpose. Turl gains a wife. Lucas exasperates his employer, turns a competitor into a trainee, retains his marriage, and may continue to hunt buried treasure on his own time (100). That he does not wish to do so is hardly a sign that he is anybody's tool but his own. Rider, having killed a Birdsong, is imprisoned and subsequently lynched by "Birdsong's kinfolks" (119). Since he intended only to die, they may be said perversely to have served his purpose (of which more soon). It remains the case that none of this independent black motion, though suggestive of restlessness and separation, heads conclusively to the North. In this it exhibits no better sense of direction than the "dark journey" of diaspora itself, which as the historian Neil McMillen argues was generally not a single, one-way trip:

> More often the migration seems to have developed in several stages, carrying a worker from a plantation in Coahoma County, say, to a turpentine camp in Hancock County, first to a cottonseed oil mill in Clarksdale or a lumber yard in Gulfport and then perhaps to a job as a hotel porter in Memphis or New Orleans, before finally terminating in a St. Louis foundry or a Gary steel mill.[2]

Nonetheless, where I chart restlessness another might locate repossession: which leaves me at an impasse, or, more correctly, at the same impasse that I recovered from Lucas. I feel as though I have been running on a critical spot, getting nowhere and descending for some time. My only comfort is that Faulkner is here before me, reworking a contradiction between dependency and autonomy, variously redescribable as stasis and motion; entrapment and escape; black labor held within the white body, or black labor expelled from the white body. Up to this point, and with increasing anxiety, I have argued that Faulkner resolves the impasse by two means. Firstly, he adopts a narrative voice which allows him to move across racialized class lines in a manner largely unavailable to those whom he describes— his are the compensatory poetics of a limited freedom. Secondly, he constructs revenants, "persons who return as spirits after death," among whom I would include Ike McCaslin (the framer of "Was"), Lucas, and Rider.

Let me recoup, but diagrammatically and only in relation to the plantation trilogy. Lucas (circa 1898), a black Jacobin, who because (in 1898) he lacked the conditions to realize the freedom that he recognized, continued to live in dread of that freedom, becoming (in terms borrowed from Gramsci) "a morbid symptom," or revenant, produced "when the old is dying and the new cannot be born."[3] For over forty years, declining the freedom of reciprocal recognition, he dies, burying the better part of himself (his "sweat") in a land that by 1942 has scant need of it.

Ike McCaslin, "past seventy and nearer eighty" (5), at the time of the narration of "Was," seems a more likely candidate for spectral status. The story's one-page frame makes a fast case for Ike's social death: he lives surrounded by genealogies, entitlements, and property relations, but has scrupulously refused most of them. "[F]ather to no one," twenty years a widower, he is, however, "uncle to half a county" (5), though the avuncular title should be read as disparagement rather than tie: Ike shares with African American males, deemed irrelevant to the point of invisibility, a gentle and generic epithet. Faulkner concludes his list of what Ike (his implied narrative perspective) lacks with voice and perspective. The content of "Was," we are assured, is "not something he [Ike] had participated in or even remembered except for the hearing, the listening" (5). Instead, his cousin, Carothers McCaslin, sixteen years his senior, was there, and speaks if not for then through him. Moreover, Ike does not even markedly occupy the position of a subject who receives the oral transmission that links him to his cousin as an implied and indirect co-speaker: a reiterated definite article displaces the possessive from "*the* hearing, *the* listening." Arguably, Ike is simply too spectral to warrant a personal pronoun—pronouns are referred to by linguists as "shifters" because of their referential instability.[4]

As one too shifty for a shifter, Ike might take gratification from the notion that the story he barely indirectly narrates was in one typescript titled "Almost."[5] Since "Was," among other things, tells the story of how Ike's parents almost married before they did, a term for the provisional stands as its apt provisional title. Buck McCaslin unsuspectingly lies down in Sophonsiba Beauchamp's bed. Thanks to the poker skills of his twin, Buddy, he avoids matrimony, but the brothers, as part of the deal, have to return to their plantation not only with the runaway, Turl, but with she for whom he ran, Tennie Beauchamp. From the nonmarriage of a white couple emerges the slave "marriage" of a black couple. Or, to pursue the deep logic of the outcome, from the nonbirth of Ike McCaslin emerges the multiple-birth of a line of black labor, most significant among them Lucas Beauchamp. Stated generically, the point of a story detailing the preconceptual abortion of its virtually absent quasi narrator would seem to be that from the white body, no matter how far withdrawn from social life, emerges black substance—and more particularly that black substance whose labor substantiates the white body. This is, arguably, the very scenario that Ike, in *Go Down, Moses* as a whole, withdrew from social life to resist. Ike chooses to live outside human relations, or to live a long death, in order not to inherit McCaslin property made from "nigger sweat." Yet, from its inception, or more properly from its preconception, his design is flawed. In the South, it would seem even in 1942, white can take substance only from black.

I have read "The Fire and the Hearth" as the story of the construction of Lucas as a revenant, through whom black work is problematically retained within white substance. "Was" shifts the dynamic, being in its deep structure about the inevitable failure of the withdrawal of white from black. Both stories turn on the historical specter of released black labor, though neither boasts a ghost. "Pantaloon in Black," the third of the plantation trilogy, *is* a ghost story. My case for a revenant would seem easily made, yet Mannie's ectoplasm proves difficult to pin down.

In a study of the sociology of haunting, Avery Gordon argues that "the ghostly gives notice that something is missing, that what appears to be invisible or in the shadows is announcing itself, however symptomatically."[6] I take him to mean that the spectral is a symptom of the social, making not quite plain that which we miss—"miss" not simply in the sense of mourning (though that too is involved), but "miss" as in "misapprehend." So read, the ghost ghosts the barely visible social sources of its own deprivation and incompleteness. Mannie, youthfully dead for no traceable reason, represents the arbitrary violence that haunts the social practices of successful black life. Rider, in labor terms, is mobile. Off the land, he receives a relatively high wage as the head of a sawmill timber gang. He and Mannie visibly improve their rented property (105), and each week Mannie banks a portion of their wage in Edmonds's commissary safe (104). Leon Litwack notes that the principal targets of coercive white violence were "blacks 'out of their place' and [that] these inevitably included . . . propertied blacks."[7] Mannie's ghost, "standing in the kitchen door" (106); "vanished but not gone" (103) from the footprints beneath the footprints on the dirt road to the commissary; present to Rider in "post and tree and field and house" (103) marks the items of everyday existence with black labor's fear that each gain might, for no reason, be exchanged for loss and grief. Mannie returns from the dead to make manifest the unlivable nature of aspirant black life in Mississippi in 1942, where arbitrary and violent death is a constitutive feature of black sociability.[8] To rejoin her, as a spectral partner, Rider must not simply die, he must do so in a manner that brings from hiding the meaning of her spectrality. Grief-stricken, he acts to ensure his own lynching. "Hanging from the bell-rope in the negro schoolhouse" (116), his corpse makes Mannie's educative point, evidencing that "extra-legal violence" operates as "an instrument for social discipline" in ways "guaranteed to serve the needs, and particularly the labor needs, of the white caste."[9]

For the two days between Mannie's funeral and his death, Rider is characterized as rogue labor. We first see him filling Mannie's grave:

Soon he had one of the shovels himself. . . . Another member of his sawmill gang touched his arm and said, "Lemme have hit, Rider." He didn't even falter. He released one hand in midstroke and flung it backward, striking the other across the chest, jolting him back a step, and restored the hand to the moving shovel, flinging the dirt with that effortless fury so that the mound seemed to be rising of its own volition, not built up from above but thrusting visibly upward out of the earth itself. (102)

I cannot improve on Michael Toolan's reading of the passage:[10] he notes that Rider is not, syntactically, the stable subject of the verbs "striking," "jolting," and "flinging," the first two of which find their subject in "one hand" and not "he," while "flinging" displaces the pronoun for "the moving shovel" as subject. Agency, as a result, is ascribed to a body part and a shovel. The grammatical strategy contributes to the conclusion that the mound has an independent will, "thrusting . . . upward out of the earth itself." I would merely add that, drawn to Mannie in the earth, Rider's body and the objects of his hand are animate with purposes beyond the purpose of those who customarily hire his manual labor. The "earth," albeit briefly, has more than one proprietor. Confronted on every side with artifacts no longer singly owned (or available for rent), Rider experiences a form of body loss. His physique, that of a giant, the very type of heroic labor, is temporarily beyond his own and his employer's control, in the sense that it is doubly occupied or at crossed purpose. Something else, encrypted as Mannie, exerts a pressure.

Faulkner details Rider's grief as a sequence of labor infractions; he shovels when he should mourn; he goes to work when he should absent himself; having started his shift, "he walks off the job in the middle of the afternoon" (118); he buys too much liquor at an inappropriate time (110). Rider's final violation of labor practice is to cut the throat of Birdsong, the night watchman and gambler who, working out of industrial premises, in the boiler shed/tool room (114, 115), takes back, on a nightly basis, a portion of black earnings. Like the deputy who partially frames the story, Birdsong is what Rider calls him, "boss-man" (115), evidence of the extent of the informal networks of control that constrain black work.

Yet it would be a mistake to cast Rider as the master of his own infringements. His is a body out of control, mastered neither by himself nor by his employers. Faulkner scrupulously records how the loss of Mannie takes Rider apart, and to what end. Mannie's ghost is promiscuous and specific. She makes one appearance and her instructions are clear. Unable to prevent her fading from the kitchen's threshold, Rider, "talking as sweet as he had ever heard his voice speak to a woman," asks, "'Den lemme go wid you, honey'": "But she was going. She was going fast now; he could actually feel between them the insuperable barrier of that very strength which could handle alone a log which would have taken any two other men to handle" (106). If Rider is to attend her as a lover, he must lose not just his body, whose very strength blocks its passage into the earth, but his body defined as an instrument of labor, twice as productive as that of any of his co-workers.

In that Mannie's presence remains tangibly within those objects that she so recently used, external reality, during the days following her death, solicits Rider with her breath, eye, and touch, "his body breasting the air her body had vacated, his eyes touching the objects—post and tree and field and house and hill—her eyes had lost" (103). In effect, Rider experiences his body as a faulty apperture into that which it is not (literally, into Mannie), rather than as an entity or tool. She, who is now quite "other" to him in her death, exerts a dispossessive power, drawing his perceptions toward self loss. At the risk of gilding the grave, Mannie occupies the earth as an exquisite corpse, offering herself through the body of the land, as a site of unworkable desire into which Rider must pass. He "breast[s]" her "air" (103), elsewhere "breasting aside the silver solid air which began to flow past him" (112); Rider is subject to that object (the air) which, in that it has passed through her as breath, takes erotic form as a skin whose touch calls his skin into felt existence (breast to breast). At times Rider feels that his spaces are so packed with memories of his six-month marriage that "there was no space left for air to breathe" (105). To inhale such scant air, "solid" and promise-crammed, is to be overcome with desire.[11]

On the day after the funeral, Rider seeks to rejoin Mannie by translating labor into an industrial accident—he lifts a log no one man should lift:

> [H]e nudged the log to the edge of the truck-frame and squatted and set his palms against the underside of it. For a time there was no movement at all. It was as if the unrational and inanimate wood had invested, mesmerised the man with some of its own primal inertia. Then a voice said quietly: "He got hit. Hit's off de truck," and they saw the crack and gap of air, watching the infinitesimal straightening of the braced legs until the knees locked, the movement mounting infinitesimally through the belly's insuck, the arch of the chest, the neck cords, lifting the lip from the white clench of teeth in passing, drawing the whole head backward and only the bloodshot fixity of the eyes impervious to it, moving on up the arms and the straightening elbows until the balanced log was higher than his head. "Only he aint gonter turn wid dat un," the same voice said. "And when he try to put hit back on de truck, hit gonter kill him." But none of them moved. Then—there was no gathering of supreme effort—the log seemed to leap suddenly backward over his head of its own volition, spinning, crashing and thundering down the incline. (110)

Faulkner so focuses our attention on the slow lift of the log that "its," in "its own volition," is oddly apt (logs are not volitional), reducing the more likely "his" to an antonymic inference. Since Mannie is mesmerically latent in most of the objects Rider encounters, her presence complicates the issue of "volition," allowing "its" to retain "her" ("her volition") within its redistribution of industrial agency. If Mannie is in the log, lifting that log is an erection. Two discourses vie for possession of the same object. Read through the optic of labor, the lift is either an accident about to happen ("hit gonter kill him"), or a particularly productive use of labor time; unless, of course, the sheer dimension of the log, compounded by the height and velocity of its drop, break the machine. "Crashing," "spinning," "thundering" pose an open question, in that Rider walks off site and takes us with him. However, Rider's labor makes him a column of muscle whose slow-motion straightening is surely intended, in its anatomical transposibility, to make plain why he is called Rider—a name understood by Faulkner as a synonym for a sexual athlete.[12] Neither discursive option ousts the other; instead Rider stands available for a profit or loss *and* for desire, and, consequently, as a real contradiction beyond our or Faulkner's semantic control.

Having tried to break the saw mill, or to make it break him, he takes to liquor for the same purpose. Whiskey is a "big boy" and a "better man" (111), used by Rider in the long shot that it will obliterate him. But, like the log, the liquor exhibits divided purposes, confirming Rider's inability to master his own body. The deputy identifies the liquor in question as "white-mule," that is to say, whiskey fit to keep a "nigger" so "bust-skull" that he will operate on weekdays as the white man's mule (118). Its purveyor knows its purpose, hence his unwillingness to sell more than a modicum on a working day. Rider, following Mannie's desire, puts the liquor to another purpose. Since, it seems, he cannot drink enough to drown his sorrow, he involuntarily casts from "the mold of his gullet" two "columns" which are silvered by the "moonlight," so that each "intact column sprang silvering, glinting, shivering" (112). On Saturdays, during their marriage, Rider used ritualistically to "ring . . . [a] bright cascade of silver dollars" onto Mannie's "scrubbed table" (104). Vomiting "bust-skull," he discovers coming from his mouth the contents of his recast pay packet, silvered by the moon for mourning and cascading into funerary forms—forms dedicated to Mannie gone into the ground, though still active therein.

The nature of her activity lies encrypted in her name. Mannie summons Rider into the earth. Through her he enters a conceit which casts the soil as a black vagina containing a black phallus. Entry may be read as signatory: given that Mannie is named for the conjunction of a male term and a first-person pronoun, Rider's death, in admitting him to the ground, admits him to a full identity (Man—I).[13] Since Rider's reclaimed body will doubtless be laid in Mannie's grave, their reunion is tacitly proprietorial. The grave, containing the embodiment of independent black work and desire, will be marked by "shards of pottery and broken bottles and old brick," unreadable by whites and "fatal to touch" (102). The space is narrow and the dedication an assemblage of refuse, but black encryption declares the place privately owned.

It may be objected that I have made the two syllables work both too hard and not hard enough. Afterall, the syllable "ie" is a diminutive. If I insist on punning, should I not acknowledge the rather obvious fact that death diminishes Rider's manhood? Yet the story makes no mention of castration, despite detailing the location of the body's recovery (116).[14] Nonetheless, whether or not Rider takes his phallus with him into the ground does not gainsay the punning presence of dimunition within the first-person pronoun. Perhaps, as with my utopian inflection of Roth's four-fold study of Lucas's face (91), the duplicity discovered within the pun catches at the impasse of black/white relations in 1941, and of Faulkner's response to those relations. What the pun gives—Rider's independence achieved through a rededication of his labor (Man—I [first-person pronoun])—the pun takes away with its inference of masculinity torn by "extralegal violence" servicing "the labor needs of the white caste" (Man-ie [diminutive]). That the pun gives and takes away in less than a breath marks the focal force of the real contradiction that was the burden of the previous chapter: Rider, as the embodiment of black labor, circa 1941, *is* independent and *must* be retained in dependency.

The nominal pun makes bids whose semantic weighting depends on the context of use, though Mannie's grave itself remains the orientating context. We should remember that "Pantaloon in Black" begins at her graveside with intimations of an autochthonic resurrection; Mannie, care of Rider's shovelling, all but springs from the soil she inhabits as her "mound" appears "to be rising of its own volition, not built up from above but thrusting visibly upward out of the earth itself" (102). Her "mound" "ris[es]" and "thrust[s]," perhaps because she quits it to draw her lover back into it. The "orifice" (29) whose "hurling," "striking," and "admonitory pat" initiates the action of the previous story, "The Fire and the Hearth," is part of a yet more active "mound" (29, 30). In both instances black work (Lucas digs to "fit" a "worm and kettle" into an "orifice" in an Indian burial "mound") causes the earth to "rise" or "loom" (30). The parallel is inescapable: each story begins with a tacit instruction that its protagonist enter the earth, by excavation or death, to take possession of it in a nonwhite form. Lucas's "mound" delivers "a fragment of an earthenware vessel" and "a single coin" (30). Location suggests that the coin derives from "the old earth, perhaps the old ancestors," and that as Native American currency it pre-exists white exchange. Read through the stencil of Rider's digging, Lucas's excavation recovers less an original and "uncorrupted source of value,"[15] or quasi gold standard, than a prompt to work outside the temporal and technological constraints of the coercive system within which Lucas most typically labors. Neither Molly nor Roth gets the coin's point. Molly seeks to divorce Lucas because she believes him cursed by contact with the coin, "God say 'What's rendered to My earth, it belong to Me unto I resurrect it. And let him or her touch it, and beware'" (79). Roth insists that Lucas merely wants easy money, "on which there was no sweat, at least none of it [Lucas's] own" (95). But the coin, "deposited in his palm as though it had been handed to him" by the mound (30), will elicit much sweat, the whole point being that the sweat in question is entirely "own[ed]" by Lucas, and in no part owned by his land lord. Such a prompt to independent labor, in the context of "Mannie," might be said to intimate, through the "sigh," "roar," and "whisper" of its worked medium—the earth (29)—that Lucas will become the monetary implication of his name (filthy lucre) only when he takes from the earth the "deposited" fruits of the labor that he has put into it. Such "whispering" is liable to sound like curse or sickness (79) to those who own the earth in question (Roth), or sustain the received forms of that ownership (Molly).

Lucas eventually ignores the coin's point. "The Fire and the Hearth" closes with his delivery of the metal detector into Roth's keeping, to "[g]et rid of it":

'I dont want never to see it again. Man has got three score and ten years on this earth, the Book says. He can want a heap in that time and a heap of what he can want is due to come to him, if he just starts in soon enough. I done waited too late to start. That money's there. Them two white men that slipped in here that night three years ago and dug up twenty-two thousand dollars and got clean away with it before anybody saw them. I know. I saw the hole where they filled it up again, and the churn it was buried in. But I am near to the end of my three score and ten, and I reckon to find the money aint for me." (101)

To turn the page is to be confronted, in the first paragraph of "Pantaloon in Black," with another "hole," with another "mound" or "heap," with more instruments of excavation, with further infill . . . with Mannie's "thrusting" grave (102). Lucas does not recover the money lodged in the earth and in his name, perhaps because "white men" stole it or a portion of it. He at least had nearly seventy years to get the point of his labor. Mannie, rendered briefly independent by Rider's "bright cascade of silver dollars" (104), summons her lover into an autochthonous space which, thanks to his work, rises.

I have excavated an up-rising from subsemantic whispering latent in key names and structural contiguities. Perhaps, care of my digging, the "fragment of earthenware vessel" that strikes Lucas "squarely in the face" before crumbling to yield the coin (29, 30) might be added to "the shards of pottery" surrounding Mannie's "mound." It too intimates that the earth has been and should again be owned in different ways. Just as the end of "The Fire and the Hearth" offers a context for the start of "Pantaloon in Black," in order to draw unbound black labor (or Rider's "I") from "Mannie," so the end of "Pantaloon in Black" is recast by its echo of the close of "Was."

In "Was" the pursuit of Tomey's Turl, attended throughout by a sustained vocabulary of hunting, parallels a framing pursuit through the McCaslin cabin of a semidomesticated fox by a pack of dogs. At Buck's return with Tomey, the fox is "tree[d]" (25). Both hunts suggest a certain strain in the capacity of the peculiar institution to retain its charges: indeed, the lead dog ("old Moses" [25]), in his keenness to catch the fox, enters its cage head-first to emerge, "wearing most of the crate around its neck" (25). The taking apart of a cage recurs at the close of "Pantaloon in Black," where old Moses's collar is revised during Rider's dismantling of a Jefferson jail cell: Rider grabs the "steel barred door," rips it from the wall, and walks from the cell "toting the door over his head like it was a gauze window-screen" (120). Rider, like Tomey's Turl, is systematically associated with or likened to animals, but unlike Tomey's Turl he remains the hunter not the hunted. In a telling analysis of *Light in August*, Jay Watson argues that Joe Christmas becomes a "nigger," at least in the collective imagination of Jefferson, because he bleeds and because he runs.[16] Rider conspicuously does neither: he cuts Birdsong's throat with a "sweeping blow," which ensures that "not even the first jet of blood touched his hand or arm" (116); expecting him to have "passed Jackson, Tennessee," the sheriff and his deputy apprehend him asleep in his own backyard (118)—my point being that Rider pursues his own death in the manner of his own choosing. As the leader not the led, he warrants, care of "Was," the structural analogy with the lead dog. Rider is a second Moses; his actions, therefore, merit reading through the template of Faulkner's titular instruction.

Go Down, Moses contains only one reference to Moses, the dog in "Was," arguably so named to trigger a tacit and subsequent allusion to a labor radical. The antebellum "old Moses" spoils the cage he seeks to police, just as his masters, Buck and Buddy, spoil their father's great house by converting it to a slave quarters without a backdoor (194). Dog and masters exist in a complicity with fox and slave, a complicity that allows the quarry (whether slave or fox) some latitude circa 1859. Rider, circa 1941, by analogy a *new* Moses, keeps to the letter of the chorus of Faulkner's titular song ("Let My People Go. A Song of the Contrabands"):

> —O go down, Moses
> Away down to Egypt's land,
> And tell King Pharaoh
> To let my people go!

For Egypt read the South (also a place of bondage); for Pharaoh, read the owning class; for Jews read blacks, and for Exodus read the Great Migration. This much is critical commonplace. to read Rider for Moses is less so, in that he, as the song instructs, "go[es] down" to obtain release and partial recovery of "Egypt's spoil."[17]

II

My reading of "Pantaloon in Black" as a lynching narrative that exactly offends its own generic imperative to keep the black in his place, dead and buried, depends upon what I shall call the "paratactic" arrangement of two cages and two graves, key elements in the beginnings and endings of three more and less discrete stories. Parataxis involves "the placing of propositions or clauses one after another without indicating by connecting words the relation of coordination or subordination between them."[18] The structure of *Go Down, Moses*, and of the plantation trilogy within it, may usefully be spoken of as paratactic in so far as any coordination of its parts depends upon inferences cast across pauses and changes in narrative direction, instigated by the gaps between the stories themselves. So, for example, a cage broken in 1859 ("Was") is fixed as a meaning by being broken again, but differently, in 1941 ("Pantaloon"); or, the value of a coin taken from a hole in "Fire" is to be inferred by its relation to quite another emergence from a second and contingent hole in "Pantaloon." Any and all such inferences are unstable, not least because the gaps between stories ensure that all connections are faulty since they subsume breaks. John Matthews borrows the term "stereoptic" from the text (221) to suggest the broken unity extant between the seven stories, which for him "remain tangential to each other . . . touch[ing] without coalescing."[19] The stereoscope traditionally effects coalsescence, being "a double magic lantern arranged to combine two images of the same object or scene on a screen, so as to produce the appearance of solidity. . . . [It was] also used to cause the image of one object or scene to pass gradually into that of another with dissolving effect." My own revision of the best available interpretive technology might be branded a paratactic stereoscope, or a stereoptic parataxis—a mechanism for generating incomplete connections.[20] The extent of my whimsy is a measure of my struggle to convey a process of reading for meanings that are hidden in plain sight, where the effect of hiding is produced not primarily by repression, but by the space between elements whose resemblance calls for their combination. Each of those elements . . . images, objects, scenes—a cage, a hole, a bed . . . remains partial until brought into conjunction with its semblance: the partiality of the combination ensures that solidity never results, in that the elements set side by side do not quite fit together. Instead, each realizes, in and through the other options, meanings that remain only inferential. The structure of *Go Down, Moses* is in effect designed to yield incomplete knowledge drawn from partial sight. Such a structure begs the question, what is it that Faulkner prefers partially to see and incompletely to know? Any answer will have to wait for more evidence to be put in place.

I have argued that Rider dies, descends into Mannie, and rises as Moses. My evidence rests on a combination of images resulting in congruence (an inferred image larger than its parts), but more may be drawn from hiding once the congruent elements (hole, cage) are seen together—indeed, a pattern can be constructed backward from the structural effect of their connection. Rider's death at the hands of unspecified Birdsongs enables his presumed burial in a grave gendered female but marked with a disguised male term (*Man*nie). To read Mannie's aperture as a space through which a black phallus enters into ambiguous union with an ambivalent body is to draw from the text a series of homologous resting places (or beds), in which males meet over the nominal body of a female, only for that body to dissolve or mutate. Working backward from "Pantaloon": in "Fire," Lucas, having recovered Molly from Zack, seeks vengeance for her removal by entering the McCaslin plantation house with a razor. Over Zack's bed—surely metonymic of Molly—male bodies "clasp" in an "embrace" (44). The "click" is "incredible" not least because ballistics barely contain coitus, albeit "dry" and interrupted. Read serially, Molly goes missing, perhaps absorbed euphonically into the acoustic provided by "Mannie." "Was" too yields its awkward bed: Buck McCaslin and his nephew McCaslin Edmonds, late from hunting Turl, make the mistake of lying down together on Sophonsiba's bed—the upshot, as I have argued, is a delay in conception for Ike and the resultant inception of Turl and Tennie's black line. Read through the optic of the subsequent resting places, Sophonsiba's bed also proves unstable; Hubert famously likens his sister's bedroom to a "den" in "bear-country" (19), by dint of which extended metaphor man and boy bed a bear, and Sophonsiba all but vanishes.

The three beds, set side by side, draw one another toward a "steroptic" clarity within which shared structural elements may be discerned. The elements are as follows: a woman, on a bed or herself a bed, in a state of transformative displacement.[21] (Aware that I am engaged in the semantic equivalent of joining-the-dots, I shall risk reiteration—Sophonsiba in bed as a bear ["Was"]; Molly as a bed, barely visible ["Fire"]; Mannie embedded in a grave ["Pantaloon"]). Two males on a bed—Buck McCaslin and McCaslin Edmonds ("Was"); Lucas and Zack ("Fire"); Rider buried with a woman whose name contains a male term ("Pantaloon"). Somewhat to the side of each bed, and perhaps as a consequence of the pairing on the bed, lies a male who is corpselike but undead. My third element, sightable but hardly in plain sight, requires fuller explication. The triangulation on Sophonsiba's bed stems from a misconception that yields an aborted conception. The story itself is framed by the all but absent abortee, introduced via a listing of social dislocations that renders him not only ancient but socially dead. Ergo: Ike, a living corpse at the margins on two counts. In "Fire" either Zack or Lucas might have died as a result of their meeting over a bed, but neither does. The corpse in question is discernible only subsequently and at a distance through Roth's conceptual rehearsal of his father's physical struggle: I allude to the already described Confederate, "slightly mummified," who features in the "composite" face drawn by Roth from his own and Lucas's face (91). Bodies proliferate in "Pantaloon," and all of them literally dead; but Mannie "be wawkin yit" (103) and Rider, on an inference, rises from the dead. Birdsong alone, it seems, stays dead and buried, though the incongruity of his name, sustained by the discovery that the arresting officer is one "Maydew," grants him nascent levity. Since the prior undead of the sequence (Ike and the Confederate) are white, Birdsong best fits: seen serially, he recovers the vibrancy of his name.

I have been engaged in a formal exercise, fabricating a scene from the recurrent parts of other scenes. The scene features a male pairing on a bed, a missing female, and a mortally wounded white body. The ethnicity of the male pair shifts: two white ("Was"); white and black ("Fire"); and black and black ("Pantaloon"), though it might be argued that, as with my partial revival of Birdsong, I should allow any element in the sequence to interfere with and literalize a distant option in any other element, where that option is available. Reinflected, the pairing of Buck and a bear in "Was" yields not just a near-dead white baby but black children. In which case, and logically, since the progenitive bear must be "black," the ethnicity of the sequential male couples stands corrected, the first two pairs now featuring a white and a black.[22] By implication the pairing of Mannie and Rider in "Pantaloon," though inferentially male on male, remains black on black, interrupting the coherence of the emergent sequence. I can only presume that the exception awaits correction. Such anticipatory dexterity among the parataxes smacks of optic trickery, yet I would argue that it results directly from the form of Go Down, Moses, where, since meanings must be made from broken parts, those meanings can retain only a mutating and miasmic solidity.

The objects that I have gathered into a scene take shape as composites created by a recursive reading and rereading as it moves backward and forward across separate narratives, understood as a single paratactic field of bits and pieces, waiting for extractive connections to be made. As such, the ur-scene, whose logic has yet to be read, subordinates narrative—both the narratives of the single stories, and the larger narrative implied by their sequence. Arguably, each instance of every object in the ur-scene (bed, cross-racial male pair, absented female, white body close to death) is modified by any version that follows it, even as that version clarifies aspects of prior versions by (re)covering them in itself. Such clarification depends on narrative; that is to say, on an order of occurrence and encounter between the elements in question. Consequently, having extracted the scenic elements, I must restore them to their narrative places if I am to trace the key conjunctions that generated their "appearance of solidity."

In the first section of this chapter, I read "Pantaloon" largely on its own terms. The separateness of the story has long been recognized: Rider is the only named African American in Go Down, Moses to have no family connection to the McCaslin/Beauchamp lines; he is without a cross, they are cross-bred; he is an urban worker among blacks who prevalently work the land; he is waged, they are tenants; he is autonomous, they are dependent. Rider therefore seems close to anomaly, particularly for those who see Go Down, Moses as "a novel of the McCaslin family" with miscegenation "holding all the episodes together."[23] How, then, to read "Pantaloon" as part of the larger narrative of the collection, given the yawning parataxis of its apparent nonrelation to "Fire" before it to and "The Old People" after it? The latter gap opens on several counts: Faulkner shifts focus from 1941 to 1879; from Jefferson to the Delta; from the plantation trilogy to the Big Woods trilogy. Of course, thematic ties can quite properly be made to bind: "hunting," "mourning," and "ritual" work as "connecting words," under which the lynching of a grief-stricken black may be bracketed with the initiation of a twelve-year-old into the lost ways of the woods, via the killing of a buck—indeed, ectoplasm links one buck to Mannie. Little ingenuity is required to operate the thematic dragnet, yet neither thematics nor the aesthetic panacea of "counterpoint," with its "pathos"

("Pantaloon") after "domestic comedy" ("Fire"),[24] catches the anxiety of Roth's "Self Portrait as Another in Black"—an anxiety driven by a comprehensive category collapse (chap. 3, section 1, 91) that "Fire['s]" two brief concluding sections (91–101) can barely contain in their account of marriage and tenant agreements renewed, and of candy given as a scant sweetener.

To recognize why "Pantaloon" necessarily follows "Fire," as part of its narrative *and* as an element in an emergent and unread ur-scene, I shall return briefly to Roth's discovery of his own face in the face of Lucas. In 1941, Roth's class no longer needs to operate as a collective labor lord: indeed, to make their land make money, they must recast themselves as land lords-without-labor. The war will act as a trigger to renewed out-migration among blacks, effectively completing the structural shift in the regime of accumulation initiated by the New Deal. But in 1941, when Roth imagines himself without labor—by taking Lucas out of Lucius—he renders himself "nameless." Far from white whitening with the incipient expulsion of black, white threatens to turn black; and where "blood" may no longer be relied upon to do the discursive work of ethnic difference, "name," "face," and "land" will rapidly diminish as secure distributive categories. *Nameless* and *faceless* corrosively call for a third term, latent in Roth's imagining of Lucas as the *prototype* of regional *geography*. That Roth cannot say *landless*, thereby articulating the social apocalypse available in his own name, is a measure of his realism. In the teeth of a class crisis, typified by his struggle with Lucas, Roth will retain "land" not "labor": he and his "kind" will reinvent themselves, but not without epistemic pain. Consider closely Roth's fantastical crimes. By putting himself in the place of his own undeclared but "adjunctive" "foster" father (85) he discovers Lucas as the "prototype" of Lucius Quintus Carothers McCaslin: in effect, he engages in speculative incest while tacitly perpetrating parricide, though at several removes.[25] To enter one father (black) in order to "[de]face" another (white) by declaring his own grandfather (and therefore his father) "nameless" amounts to a dissolution of difference worthy of the wrath of biblical last days.

Of course, Roth does no such things. He remains a criminal of perception who commits tacit crimes against terms—the very terms that have defined him and his "kind," but which no longer usefully do so. To go further would be to translate his own quasi-apocalyptic insecurity into a quasi-revolutionary call for that redistribution of goods latent in his imaginary founding of the southern social order ("*geography and climate and biology*" [91]) on a reinclusion of the previously excluded. Apocalypse can be read as a social forecast and teammate of revolution, insofar as its difference-dissolving crimes (among them parricide and incest) release a time of mixture, as a prelude to the return of the refused. In the book of Revelations it is "the lamb slain from the foundation of the world" (Rev. 13:8) who opens the seven seals and receives the Kindgom of God. Malcolm Bull notes of biblical and apocryphal apocalypses "[that] what is revealed at the end of the word frequently turns out to be what was hidden at its foundation. It is not the obvious figures of the patriarchal age who return as eschatological judges, but those whose memory has all but vanished—the missing and the sacrificed."[26] Roth, circa 1941, has need neither of old Carothers (as patriarch "come back to judge") nor of Lucas (as "hidden" and foundational labor). Indeed, both must vanish if he is to retain his land under revolutionary economic conditions.

Read narrowly from the viewpoint of an emergent owning class, Roth doubles his consciousness in order to rid himself of two archaic modes of thought. Stated diagrammatically, he detaches himself from his own values to project himself into the values of another: behind the mask of Lucas he finds Carothers, as a possible subordinate whose company he currently keeps ("us"). Faced with himself in the doubled face of a redundant unit of labor and an equally redundant patriarch, Roth, reaching in effect for the tractors and the cropdusters (90), discards himself as "he" whom he has encountered in no-longer-tenable versions of himself among discardable others. My reading is partial, not least because it edits anxiety out of the experience of hybridity. I witness an epistemic revolution in Roth, by way of a claim that he deploys Lucas to dispose of Carothers, and of the patriach's accompanying lexicons of "blood," "paternity," and "soil," terms necessary to mastery in the pre–New Deal economy, within which Roth was raised, but terms increasingly counterproductive among tractors and cropdusters. My misreading turns on an abrupt severance of italic from roman script. The italic signals Roth's interior monologue: the roman indicates Faulkner's deployment of free indirect discourse as the narrative means by which he has doubled and tripled his character's consciousness. So, to recap: "[I]t seemed to Edmonds," faced with Lucas's face in his mind's eye, "[that] the face . . . was not at all a replica even in caricature of his grandfather McCaslin's but [that it] . . . had heired and now reproduced with absolute and shocking fidelity the old ancestor's entire generation and thought" (91). "Heired," as I have argued, is a neologistic verb capable of articulation in active or passive form: the passive voice marks Lucas as the "old ancestor's" subordinate, and as a vehicle for the owner's continuities. The active voice renders Lucas the founder, potentially releasing sexual panic from the terms "reproduced" and "generation," a panic that subordinates both the master's mastery and his potency to that of the bound man. The very form of the verb contains a class conflict whose inflection depends upon a choice between differently orientated voices: the apparent undecidability of that choice dramatizes Roth's impossible position, caught in the throat of an antithesis.

To point out that "heired" contains a primogeniture dispute involving two parties, one black and one white, both of them represented by Roth, does scant justice to the disruption latent in the term. "Heired" is rich in semen and signifiers; indeed, at the distant end of its ocular effect two male bodies, one white and one black, struggle for primacy over a bed. That bed, on past evidence and evidence to come (and "biology" notwithstanding), contains the merest whisper of a female form. Once spotted the ur-scene in "heired" spreads panic through the attendant terms: "re-produced" splits as "coitus" seeps from "copy"; "shock[ed]," "fidelity" contradicts itself, being no longer able to "conform to truth" in matters of reproductive "verac-ity," where a moment of disputed reproduction casts the original, whether as model for "replica[tion]" or body, into doubt. It might be objected that Roth considers Lucas's "face," not his body and certainly not his member, but the latent lexicon of procreation (triggered by "heired") draws a founding phallus toward sight. Witness "generation": the noun arrives effectively policed by "entire" and "thought"—an ini-tial modifier that emphasizes a generic usage, as "a whole body of persons born about the same period," and a detumescent end-stop. Yet "generation" as "the act of procreation" withstands the chill of its bracketing abstractions to hint at carnal-ity. That is to say, "generation" puns. I am reminded of Malcolm Bull's account of hiddeness: "If something is hidden, it is not because the truth has eluded you and is unattainable, but because the truth is flirting with you, simultaneously offering and withholding."[27] Aided by "heired," "generation" flirts: now you see the found-er's phallus, now you do not. Of course, the shade of the member is open to dis-pute: where "heired" is passive and Lucas merely he who inherits grandfather Mc-Caslin's continuities, "generation" as generic entity subordinates the carnal. However, "heired" in the active voice declares Lucas a progenitor and eroticizes "generation," allowing the semblance of a black phallus to mark the inferential se-mantic space in which a white member might have been expected to rise.

Much here depends on whispers running through linked puns. A pun involves a small instance of parataxis in which speakers hear their own voices buckle, inter-rupting the pattern of their speech, to release a second word from a first. Because the second appears to be saying more than the first intended, a semantic excess results, stalling the narrative trajectory of the utterance. Puns are caesural sounds; by breaking a word across an acoustic they produce two words which sound the same but whose occurrence "one after another . . . lacks connecting words." Henry Krips follows Freud in linking puns to "an anxiety with no apparently appro-priate object."[28] He suggests that speakers who pun, overcome by what has sprung from their mouths (materials appearing to derive from somewhere else, quite other than their intentions), tend to reassess their words: "Speakers are thus transformed into listeners to their 'own' alienated utterances, and correspondingly a wedge is driven between the 'I' producing speech and the 'I' reflexively listening to what is being said."[29] Roth, "sitting at his solitary supper" (91), neither speaks nor thinks "generation"; rather, Faulkner's voice, in free indirect mode, divides so that author and character may "speak at the same time" in a form of split enunci-ation that ensures the co-presence of "two differently orientated voices" within any element of the utterance.[30] Within such an acoustic, puns may be expected to proliferate since the oscillation of the narrative utterance between social inflections requires that words and phrases be heard from contested positions. In the instance of "generation" and its linked terms, two voices incline to four, as the author, identifying with and yet retaining distance from a character (Roth), follows that character's attempt to identify with and yet retain distance from a racial other (Lucas), who may yet prove to be integral to him. To speak of "Faulkner," "Roth," or "Lucas" in this textured space of enunciative skid is to simplify since they are no longer discrete entities. In effect, Faulkner listens to his "own" utterances, "alienated" not into "a somewhere else which is nowhere," the nowhere of the presymbolic or unconscious (source of the puns according to Krips, out of Lacan by way of Zizek);[31] rather, he hears his voice tear on a real contradiction—itself the "appropriate object" of the anxieties that I have traced.

By 1941, although the lines of Jim Crow remained firmly in place, the regime of accumulation that gave foundational meaning to those lines was in recession; blacks in motion instilled a rebarbative fear of category collapse, even as their required migrancy demonstrated the economic archaism of those categories. In Roth's terms, and the terms of his class, ownership must change. The proprietors of 1941 must loose the bound body of black labor. The trick in the "creative destruction" of themselves,[32] required by a mutation in the form of their capital, is to expel their black substance without self-loss. But where the properties of that selfhood—from face to skin to sex to land—are determined by the laboring other, to lose that other is to lose the self's best parts, the parts that the self, in losing them, may learn through loss to love.

Again I have grown gnomic: better to turn back to Roth as he contemplates just such a severance. Finding his own face inextricable from the face of Lucas, Roth experiences epistemic panic as white turns black (skin failure); additionally unable to extricate Lucius from Lucas (name failure) in order to declare one the progenitor from whom he descends (phallus failure), he subjects himself to a failure of meaning that comes close to "horror." Matter and language shudder with an excess and "weight of meaninglessness about which there is nothing insignificant" ("heired" and its contagion).[33] In 1941 he who has given Roth meaning sues for "divorce," and Roth's meanings accordingly fail in a revelation of undifferentiation, ghosted by intimations of difference-dissolving crimes (parricide as Lucas vies with Lucius in "heired"; miscegenous homosexuality as black and white members rise together in "generation"). The semantic shocks produced by the contradiction (that I term "1941"), and registered through the supple splittings of Faulkner's narrative voice, may finally be resolved by Roth's achievement of a summative and univocal utterance (in italics).

Of course, to claim that the italics belong to Roth ignores how obviously they remain Faulknerian in idiom: "*myriad*" alone renders the vocal transference incomplete. Why then the italic subterfuge? I would suggest that Faulkner wants rid of the cognitive disruption in his own felt experience of contradiction. Since "heired" triggers the problem, Faulkner returns to it, masked in a modernizer's voice, to recover from it the less problematic *"heir"*: *"He* [Lucas] *is both heir and prototype simultaneously of all the geography and climate and biology which sired old Carothers and all the rest of us and our kind, myriad, countless . . ."* (91). By declaring Lucas *"heir and prototype,"* Roth engages in a flat contradiction: an "heir" derives property or person from a source or progenitor, whereas a "prototype" is that from which copies are derived. But the contradiction no longer hurts, since, read from the viewpoint of futurity, it contains only a redundant conflict. Whether Lucas inherits or founds the particular South that *"sired"* *"old Carothers"* matters not, where *"sired"* signals the archaism of that realm and of apprenticeship to it. Which is not to say that Roth's futurity is without ambiguities. As I have already argued, his eventual claim for the primacy of Lucas may dispatch Lucius, leaving *"all the geography and climate and biology"* of the McCaslin plantation available for redistribution to its tenancy. But Lucas and his class are remnants; as such, notwithstanding the owner's upbringing among them, they are the very stuff of dispossession. Lucas may stay on as resident revenant, "a mule farmer in a tractor world,"[34] while all around him a black tenancy will experience enforced migration at the hands of a modernizing class.

It will not have escaped attention that I have read, reread, and read again one paragraph, in order to do the words in the different voices generated by a particular contradiction. Such vocalization necessarily collapses categories, not least that of the individual subject, be he Faulkner, Roth, or Lucas. For each to find himself in the mouth of others is to be changed severally. That Roth emerges into italics from a passage of thought involving defacement, dismemberment, and the hint of a corpse says much for his readiness to move on historically. From the viewpoint of futurity, he has indulged in necessary cognitive crime. Yet Faulkner has Roth step not into the light of progress, but into the dark: "It was full dark when he tied the mare to Lucas' fence and walked up the rock path" (91). The italic may nominally belong to Roth, but the section break that immediately follows, prefacing Roth's progress in the dark, belongs to Faulkner. The author's decision to have his character pass into the "full dark" returns this reader to "the impossible place between knowing and not knowing" within whose "excess" he has so recently and lengthily been held.[35] I borrow the language used by the ethnographer Michael Taussig in his work on defacement. Taussig notes that he who "takes himself bodily into alterity" teeters "on the edge of stable knowledge":[36] at which point, as normative modes of understanding fail, absence and indeterminacy combine to generate the presence of an "irrecuperable force" which "spill[s] out . . . contagious, proliferating, voided." Taussig adds that "no matter how long the death is faced off, contradiction cannot be mastered and only laughter, bottom spanking, eroticism, violence and dismemberment exist simultaneously in violent silence."[37] The passage from "Fire" may be low on laughter and spanking, but the other elements of Taussig's "irrecuperable" pressure run discernibly through the semisilence of Faulkner's subsemantics.

III

I would contend that a "nickle's worth" of candy (100) and a renewal of marriage and tenancy vows do not recover (reface or rename) the "excess" released from Roth's self-portrait in black. Put as a pun: Roth cannot contain "Wrath," which may explain the structural need for "Pantaloon"—lynching, after all, is socially designed to put blacks back in place, a place that grounds white property and masculinity. But, as I have already argued, Rider will not stay put: he rises, tacitly, on two counts; as property (the grave marked Man-I-Moses), and as the phallus in the timberyard.

In his studies of scapegoating and sacrifice René Girard suggests that violence is inherent in a radical failure of distinctions. In effect, he argues that Taussig's "irrecuperable force" can be recuperated through the selection of a sacrificial victim who mirrors the first violator of the rules of difference. A similar surrogate must be found to act as a substitute. Selection involves nicety: "The sacrificial process requires not only the complete separation of the sacrificial victim from the beings for whom the victim is a substitute but also a similarity between both parties. The dual requirement can be fulfilled only through a delicately balanced mechanism of associations."[38] If the victim is too different he will not draw to himself and from the group the unanimously violent impulse of those who have experienced the difference-dissolving crimes. If too similar, he may be taken as a "scandalous accomplice" or co-propagator of those crimes, thereby initiating a "contagious sameness" and further "dissolution of regulations pertaining to the individual's proper place in society."[39] Girard lists the scapegoat's typical qualities: he should be a marginal figure, "incapable of establishing or sharing the social bonds that link the rest of the inhabitants."[40] He should be understood to attack symbolic authority, and/or stand accused of sexual offenses.[41] He should be marked by deformity: since "[t]he human body is a system of anatomic differences . . . disability [is] disturbing . . . because it gives the impression of a disturbing dynamism. It seems to threaten the very system . . . disturb[ing] the differences that surround it."[42]

Before measuring Rider against Girard's specifications, I had best identify he for whom Rider might substitute. Choosing a perpetrator is not easy since the crisis figured in Roth's self-portrait dissolves distinctions between those involved. Arguably, by becoming Lucius, Lucas causes Roth conceptually to violate the rules of difference. But in one possible inflection of Roth's italic, he, Roth, steps into a future free of monstrous twinning. And, in any case, is not Faulkner the perpetrator, since his vocal passage between Lucas and Roth causes differentiation to fail?

Though one should add that Lucas, adorned in "mohair trousers such as Grover Cleveland or President Taft might have worn . . . and the sixty-dollar handmade beaver hat which Edmonds' grandfather [Lucius] had given him fifty years ago" (75–76), prompts the entire crisis. Let us then, at least initially, blame the black. The accusation must remain mute on the established grounds that taking Lucas out of Lucius will yield a white corpse.

Rider is the apt surrogate for Lucas: he who is like enough but not quite like; one who, in Girard's memorable phrases, may act the "monstrous double" whose death produces a "protective misapprehension"—protective because it deflects category collapse onto a manageable object.[43] After all, Rider is a monster or giant, who knows of Lucas's fire and hearth but is not of his line (104). Grief and economic mobility displace him, and he is named for a sexuality that might easily become the stuff of the black beast. Added to which, he offends murderously against the ethnic order.

Except that Rider proves unmanageable because overtly erect and covertly resurrected. The manner of his erection may be a clue to his scapegoat failure. In the timberyard, Faulkner offers a segment by segment account of Rider's "straightening" body ("legs," "belly," "chest," "head" [110]) as he raises an outsized log, prior to tossing it from truck to skidway. Rider's "brace," "lock," "insuck," "arch," and "fix" leave him most erect when most laborful. Straightened until literally a column of muscle, he figures desire and yet remains excessive and unreadable, not least because his body is simultaneously engaged in suicide, gainful labor, an assault on the means of production and tumescence. I do not intend to repeat my case for the complexity of the image, merely to ask why Rider tumesces? I would point out that he is but one instance of a repeated inference: black *phalloi* have already been discerned contributing to a paratactically dislocated ur-scene involving problematic sexuality. But where earlier instances were semantically diminutive, Rider, in contradistinction, is heroically aroused and barely inferential. Why such laborious desire in plain sight?

My route to an answer, like *Go Down, Moses* itself, suffers from compulsive recursivity. I can only assure those who still read that I go backward to advance. Initially, care of Girard, I cast Rider as a surrogate for Lucas, one whose sacrifice might resolve "the crisis of unrecognised reciprocity" drawn from hiding by Roth's self-portrait in black (circa 1941).[44] But given that Faulkner's free indirect voice, trailing the anxieties attendant on movement between racialized subject positions, instigates the category collapse, could "Rider" better be understood, in an aurally tripped unmasking, as "writer"? The term "pantaloon" refers to " a kind of mask on the Italian stage, representing the Venitian" for whom Pantalone was a nickname.[45] Faulkner may mask himself in black as a prelude to casting the black from himself, through the invention of a twin or "monstrous double" who may be killed.[46] Except, even if Faulkner doubles as Rider in order to expel him, why should he desire that which he would expel?

As already argued, Rider's laborious tumescence involves a contradictory meeting of seemingly incompatible worlds: the world of labor in which black work yields white substance, and the world of desire in which a black male tumesces for a "Man," that is for "Mannie," drawn into focus through the stereoscope of a paratactic ur-scene. Incompatibility, so stated, seems startlingly compatible, since both elements are liable to a single summary, whereby white absorbs black by taking black into itself as property and phallus. But, in 1941, and thereafter throughout the 1940s, white ownership of black bodies grew increasingly redundant. Structurally speaking, whites, at least those raised with habits of mind deriving from an archaic regime of accumulation, had to find alternative modes for retention of the black body, even as they studied its departure. Rider's phallus figures a fantastical solution: "love," imaged in the eminently deniable form of homoerotic desire.

To read the image as a point of transfer between a residual form of dependency (as labor) and an emergent form of dependency (as desire) is to link the moment in the timberyard to other versions of a deep narrative of expulsion and retention; that is, to the structural device of the revenant and to the politics of the free indirect voice. Masked in Rider, Faulkner takes Lucas out of Lucius and the black from himself, and then discards it via sacrifice. But, masked in Rider, Faulkner cannot accept the death of his own better part: he needs must keep alive that hybridity whose departure causes unacknowledgeable pain. Concepts drawn from the work of the psychiatrists Nicolas Abraham and Maria Torok may help here. For Abraham and Torok, those who adjust to the loss of a loved one do so by "introjection": that is, they work through their grief, coming to terms with a void by filling their mouths with words. Able to turn away from the lost object of love, they get on with their lives. Those who cannot face the meaning of their loss deny that loss by "incorporation": they refuse grief by taking its cause (the object of love) into themselves. They get on with the illness of melancholia:

> There can be no thought of speaking to someone else about our grief. . . . The words that cannot be uttered, the scenes that cannot be recalled, the tears that cannot be shed— everything will be swallowed, along with the trauma that led to the loss. Swallowed and preserved. Inexpressible mourning erects a secret tomb inside the subject. Reconstituted from the memories of words, scenes and affects, the objectal correlative of the loss is buried alive in the crypt as a full fledged person, complete with its own topography.[47]

Abraham and Torok follow Freud in his observation that although "[m]ourning is regularly the reaction to the loss of a loved person," it may involve "the loss of some abstraction" which takes the place of the loved one, "such as one's country, liberty, an ideal."[48] They note of those who come to analysis sick with unresolved mourning, whatever its object, that "[e]verything unfolds as though a mysterious compass led them to the tomb wherein the repressed problem lies."⁴⁹

"Pantaloon in Black" departs from Mannie's tomb, and by implication ends there. Although sick with grief, Rider cannot mourn since to do so would be to acknowledge the finality of his wife's death. Instead, he incorporates her, turning his body into a preservative crypt. Unable to introject, or fill his mouth with words, he fills it with congealed pease (107) and liquor (112), only to have both "bounce . . . [from] his lips" (107) or spring from his gullet (112). In Abraham and Torok's terms, he tricks himself "with a magical procedure in which 'eating' (the feast) is paraded as the equivalent of an immediate but purely hallucinatory . . . 'introjection.'"⁵⁰ Moreover, his translation of himself into an extended muscle beneath a log animate with Mannie may be understood as an equally triumphal hallucination, inhibitive of mourning. By raising the log, Rider lifts Mannie locked in that log, a log whose curious "volition" unites them even as "its" (in "its volition" [110]) subsumes "his" and "hers." A refinement of Abraham and Torok's notion of "incorporation" offers a useful analytic tool: they note that incorporation can, in particular circumstances, involve the encryption of an "exquisite corpse." Sometimes the illness of mourning denied may stem not from *the affliction caused by the objectal loss itself, but rather from the feeling of an irreparable crime: the crime of having been overcome with desire . . . at the least appropriate moment, when it would behoove us to be grieved in despair.*⁵¹ Such an effusion of libido seeming "eminently illegal," particularly if the departed is a nonsexual associate, constitutes a "secret crime" or "blockage" to be hidden by incorporation: the libidinous mourner "preserves" his or her illegitimate desire in the form of an "'exquisite corpse' . . . lying somewhere inside."⁵²

Although Rider suffers libidinous grief "breasting" and tumescing as if amorously fulfilled by air and timber, his erection in the timberyard is hardly "illegal" since Mannie is his wife. But what happens to what might be termed Rider's "legal" instance of incorporation, if that instance is reviewed from the perspective of Faulkner as he who lifts the log while masked in black? I would suggest that the log vanishes, taking Mannie with it, though leaving her name. The departure, or more properly the transformative displacement of the female (her name remains), is in keeping with the imperatives of the ur-scene to which Rider and Mannie paratactically contribute. Reread, as a figure for the writers' desire rather than for Rider's, the focus of the scene shifts from the log to he who raises it. The black body as phallus recedes as he who desires Mannie, and emerges as he who is manifestly desirable: the "illegality" of the image grows in exact proportion to the degree that it can be seen to embody Faulkner's grieving desire. The extent to which a black member draws a white member from hiding (and I would stress that both are merely inferential) is the extent to which Mannie ceases to be a wife and becomes a gender caption, whose second syllable now nominates one who must not speak his name.

I have switched bodies in the crypt, or at least in the encryption, by extracting "Man-I" from "Mannie," in this inflection not as Moses but as an aroused white male. My purpose has not been to identify instances of homoeroticism veiled in workplace and name play. Rather, I seek to characterize structural arousal: if, after Freud, mourning (and so, blocked mourning) may result from the loss of an idea (be it that of nation or region), then incorporation can be understood as possibly occurring in response to radical economic change, particularly where that change implies an abrupt break in the social relations of production—involving a severance of white from black. Confronted with the necessary loss of the black body, and thrown into disarray by the recession of that object, Faulkner mourns through the mask of Rider's mourning.

Masked mourning might seem a tad detached, but masking has its risks: the anthropologist Michael Taussig links masks to the "mimetic faculty," as part of that urge not just to "copy" and "imitate" but to "yield into and become [the] Other."[53] Girard goes further, observing that "masks juxtapose beings . . . separated by differences," and do so "not merely [to] identify differences or efface them, but [to] . . . rearrange them in original fashion."[54] So defined, masks prompt participants to mix alterities. Under which circumstances, to "slip into Otherness, trying it on for size" could be to find that it all but fits,[55] and that, as a result, the very alterity that you sought merely to perform emerges from you as your twin-with-a-difference or "monstrous double." The anxieties attendant on Roth's impulse to self-portraiture imply as much.

Faulkner, masked as Rider, "yields" to what Rider does. Since Faulkner experiences Mannie, incorporated by Rider, only through the experience of the incorporator—one who consigns himself to death from the first—the author's mimicry of mourning attaches him to the male as living corpse, at least as much as to she whom he contains. Consequently, Rider plays "exquisite corpse" to Faulkner's systemic grief, but does so covertly since Rider's desire for Mannie masks Faulkner's desire for Rider. I would emphasize that the keeper of the tomb looks for his "exquisite corpse" "continually in the hope of one day reviving it."[56] Nonetheless, the corpse, as a constituent of "the recuperative magic of incorporation," remains secret (even as Rider's resurrection remains encrypted), the ultimate aim of incorporation being "to recover in secret" a lost object, "refusing both the object and reality's verdict" as to its loss.[57] Rider secretly recovers Mannie, through which process Faulkner secretly recovers Rider.

The worker's eroticized labor—for Rider evidence that Mannie is sufficiently alive within him to elicit libidinal effusion from him—represents for Faulkner a different but equally hallucinatory fulfillment of desire. Rider-as-erection, so anatomically detailed; so slow in rigidification; so close to rigor mortis; so nearly annotation as orgasm, embodies a secret repository of hope for the realization one day of a forbidden desire for the near-departed body of black labor. Like "heired" and "generation," Rider's tumescence, readable from both sides of a failing structure of servitude, is capable of two inflections, two temporalities, and two politics. To extract each from each is reductive in that the resultant and explanatory formula dispels the felt contradiction that generates the image or vocal impasse. Circa 1941, caught between retention and release of that which makes him what he is, Faulkner mourns, and through the structure of mourning retains what he frees. Read as an ethnic emergence (and with an eye to the war and beyond), Rider's labor-full phallus goes to Mannie in log and ground, from which it rises as Man-I-Moses, calling for Exodus and for the land that is owed to its labor. Expressed as a formula, the reading would run:

Rider → Mannie → Man-I → Moses → Canaan → Autonomy

Read residually (and with a backward glance), Rider's tumescence raises the Writer masked in his name, displacing Mannie so that Man-I serves only to encrypt a conjugal meeting of black and white males within a tomb. "Rider" takes "Writer" into the grave, where "Mannie" as "Man-I" declares the land an extension of their closeted bodies. Or, formulaically put:

Rider/Writer → M̶a̶n̶n̶i̶e̶ → Man-I (Rider/Writer) → Egypt → Dependency

My formulae are comic, not least because they imply that the vertiginous experience of a felt contradiction has two sides, which sides may be reduced to formulae. Instead, Faulkner's chosen names propose an endless semantic mobility, yielding interpretive excess as they automutate between the poles of what remains, in the last instance, a class contradiction. As proper names "Mannie" and "Rider" behave improperly because caught between the viewpoints of two classes, released from habitual alignment by a radical shift in the regime of accumulation: an owning class rendered self-conscious by a change in its substance and in persons previously owned; a laboring class displaced toward shared consciousness by migration. The author and his term are inextricable from the semantic discharge because an abrupt dissolution of controls within a shifting plantation system—controls associated with dependency—sets black and white within an altered and awkward proximity, where Du Boisian moments of "double consciousness" and its denial are culturally likely.

Malcolm Bull, addressing modernity as a liberatory impulse drawing into conjunction worlds previously kept apart, sees self-multiplication as the corollary of emancipation, but argues that such dualism inclines to elusiveness and duplicity: "We would acknowledge the master in the slave and the slave in the master, the colonizer in the colonized and the colonized in the colonizer, the white in the black and the black in the white, the man in the woman and the woman in the man." He adds that the result would be "extraordinarily complex and confusing."[58] Where proper names name severally, entitlement to property may be called into question

and the earth "boil" (29), "jeer" (30), "ris[e]," and "thrust" (102). I extrapolate regionally from two names and a burial plot in order to suggest what happens when,
for historically good reason, Faulkner finds the black in his own face and fears and
loves the resultant profile.

Yet the effect of category collapse in "Pantaloon," though undeniably complex,
is not finally confusing. For Girard, Taussig, and Bull, though in differing degree,
"monstrous mixing"[59] yields "mimetic crisis"[60] or "slippage" and "vertigo."[61] Where
"social order is secured by difference,"[62] indulgence in "lack of difference,"[63]
through "self-identity in otherness,"[64] grants "a revelation of undifferentiation"[65]—
a cultural symptom open to varied diagnosis: as "contagious sameness" productive of "monstrosities" requiring sacrificial excision;[66] as a general decline in "the
epistemic health and robust good cheer of realness";[67] or as an onset of "eschatological implications" attendant upon exposure to "the contradiction and indeterminacy at the limits of the existing order."[68] It should be understood that each diagnosis has its proposed cure; my point here is merely to evidence the extremity
of the cultural condition that may result from overindulgence in alterity. Faulkner,
finding that differences have become similar, sets the resultant semantic skid within
a narrative of grief. Admittedly, "Pantaloon" has elements of ritual sacrifice, Mosaic
eschaton, and perceptual collapse (in the matter of spectral manifestation), but at
its center Rider grieves, and in grieving provides a clue to Faulkner's management
of his own "mimetic crisis"—the crisis that migration made: or, more properly, that
Faulkner's movement "bodily into [the] alterity" of Rider, with its "attendant risk of
self-annihilation," made.[69]

IV

I am back with Rider's tumescence, erotic writing that may be
understood as involving Faulkner's co-tumescence, the product of an excitement
at discovering himself hidden in another, partial, incomplete, a creature of fluidity,
anonymity, and social mobility—that is to say, a creature of the modernizing South.
Such a degree of self-loss, compounded by the imminent loss of the vehicle that
contains that loss—the masking body of black labor, so much as part of the self's
prior substance—requires negotiation even as it elicits desire. I have offered two
explanations for tumescence: first, that Rider is an "exquisite corpse" produced by
Faulkner's blocked mourning (incorporation, care of Abraham and Torok); second,
out of Taussig, that high degrees of normative failure "spill" an "irrecuperable force"
akin to the erotic. Both explanations feature emptied mouths in which inarticulate-
ness swallows everything in "violent silence."[70] Yet Abraham and Torok's illegal libidinal effusion, like Taussig's "laughter . . . eroticism [and] violence,"[71] operates
as a clue made manageable by the release of *mute* signs. For example: "pan-

taloon," or mask, a device for hiding; but also, and more generally in American English, trousers. Faulkner masked in Rider's trousers. We are close to "Sophonsib[e]a[r]"; to coital "miss-fire"; to white and black members competing in the subsemantics of "generation," to shocked and silent laughter as *phalloi* rise from inference toward literalism via the reiterations of an ur-narrative. I would stress that the emergent *phalloi* strictly speaking attach to no one: as imaginary features of an ur-story, available piece-meal in several stories, and inherent in no single consciousness, these floating bits, strengthening with each emergence toward the emergency of full recognition, may best be understood as textual fetishes, figuring an insupportable structural deprivation.

A fetish is a semisecretive device for dealing with loss. Rider labors in the woodyard, trying literally to absent himself from life through an act of labor. Because he figures a regionally generic withdrawal of black labor from the plantation economy, he operates in a contradictory fashion as a token for the presence of that labor which conceals its increasing absence. In effect, Rider substitutes for what owners lack, replacing what they displace, and may therefore be thought of as a fetish, or an object which stands in for a lost thing, in the manner of a cotton reel for the maternal breast or fur for pubic hair. For Freud, desire stems from loss. What greater loss to an owning class than the loss of that body whose labor substantiates the class body of those who own? If the plantation trilogy, culminating in "Pantaloon in Black," may be read as Faulkner's struggle to manage anxieties associated with the out-migration of a culturally constitutive labor force, then we might expect to recover fetishistic items from the text. After all, the fetish is a technology for translating loss into desire, absence into erotic presence: most famously, a child, at a loss for its mother, throws a cotton reel, only to draw the reel back to itself on a piece of string. What Freud calls the "fort-da game" enables the child to master loss by infusing an object with anxiety over maternal departure and pleasure at maternal return. Of course, the child knows that the reel is not a breast, but its charged activities elide the wooden and the mammary, producing a curious object that is and is not mother. Such an object is subject to what Freud calls "disavowal"; that is to say, those who experience desire through the fetish "know that" the fetish is not in itself that which is desired, "but even so" know that it is.[72]

I can best gloss "disavowal" by way of an adaptation of Henry Krips's discussion of Lacan's recasting of Freud's fetish as the "*petit objet a*": the *objet a* stands in the way of what is desired; like a chaperone, it blocks the route to the loved one and so incites desire without itself being desired.[73] The foot excites but is not itself the forbidden *mons veneris*. As with the reel and foot, so with Rider's worked tumescence: each is an object of fascination, prompting pleasures inseparable from a disavowal of anxieties over loss and compromised control. In the case of Rider, a part object substituting for displaced plantation labor, the pleasure taken does not primarily involve "some deep truth too horrible to bear,"[74] the truth, for example, of interracial homosexual desire; rather, the homoerotic (captionable as the Writer inside Rider) is and is not the point. The black phallus, like the chaperoning *petit objet a*, is not desired for itself: instead, as a fetish, it invites you "to see through it[s pleasures] even as you see by means of [those pleasures]."[75] To desire Rider's phallus is to desire the labor through which it stands and to glimpse a consolatory fiction of amity between male bodies (the black in place within the white), even as black bodies circa 1941 are seen to depart from their place. Rider as fetish object allows a symbolic mastery of unmasterable economic reality, in the form of retention through deniable desire. John T. Matthews, applying Homi Bhabha's work on racial stereotyping as fetishized knowledge to Faulkner, comments:

> There is a kind of knowledge that can be held while being ignored, a kind of vision that looks but does not see. Such knowledge does not disappear into the depths of its repression—the prevailing model for the work of Faulknerian evasion or deferral. Instead such knowledge goes into open hiding on the surface of the Faulknerian text, where, like Poe's purloined letter, it is perhaps too obvious to see.[76]

Standing unseen in plain sight, Rider's phallus debilitates "Pantaloon" as a sacrificial text. The force of the epistemic panic which carried Roth into Lucas cannot be relieved by a further instance of that force recast as desire. Faulkner's passage into Rider compounds Roth's initial category collapse and its subsequent structural call for sacrificial correction. For Girard, a sacrificial surrogate emerges from a initially transgressive figure, for whom he substitutes.[77] But since Rider reiterates Roth's transgressions in altered from, he too must be substituted, generating an acceptable substitute. In Taussigian terms: with Roth and Rider both proving "paragons of transgression," Faulkner needs "a decent fix of straightforward othering."[78]

V

Superficially, the buck in "The Old People" fits. "Buck" refers to a male deer, but also and idiomatically to "any male, Indian or Negro." Since "buck" can also be used of a range of male animals—from goats to rabbits—male strength and sexuality may underpin its slang application to aboriginals. Rider's sexual repute readies him for sacrifice as a "nigger" thinly veiled in a "buck."[79]

The year of the sacrifice matters: Ike kills his first buck in 1879, on his third visit to the wilderness. However, the story focuses equally on the boy's initial entry at age ten into the big woods, perceived as a second birth (131). Ike is ten in 1877, the year in which Reconstruction ended. With the withdrawal of northern political and military influence, the South redeemed itself as an economy founded on coerced labor. In that year Ike is reborn. Two years later he becomes "a hunter and a man" (133) by killing a buck marked black and apt for punishment. Structurally speaking, to kill the buck is to kill what the buck contains—Roth, Rider, and the buck considered as a series, each element of which refines its predecessor in a move toward sacrificial preparedness. Put schematically: Roth achieves cognitive entry into Lucas; Rider sexualizes their liaison; the buck bestializes that release of desire. Of course, in terms of writing, the buck dies in 1941, and therefore its death needs to be understood also as a function of that year. Where Rider is Moses, his death in the buck silences a tacit appeal to African American exodus; where the dead buck contains Rider as Writer, its carcass censors a barely conceivable conjunction of male bodies. On either count, and for both years, the sacrifice appears to work insofar as it curtails deeply disruptive narrative trajectories.

However, recursively freighted with parataxes Ike's buck bifurcates, the second deer being primarily spectral. Leaving the big woods, the hunting party start a "fourteen[-]point" buck (133): after a day of stalking, the deer killed by Walter Ewell turns out to be a "yearling" (133), though it leaves tracks "pretty near big as a cow's" (137). The discrepant tracks are not made by the "little spike buck" (137) but by a "public secret" shared by those who hunt.[80] The spectral buck, seen by Ike and Sam Fathers "walking out of the very sound of the horn which related its death" (136), is absence made present by the collective will of the hunters. Like the small boy, according to the brothers Grimm, who on seeing the emperor in his new clothes cries, "He's naked!," those who protest of the buck that "there's nothing there" miss the force of the "perceptual cramp" that may result from a story told and retold to the point of materialization.[81] The death of the yearling releases the deep narrative of each and every kill from particularity, allowing it to walk free "slanting and tilting its head" (136)—a fragile public secret or fantasy hardening into a working fact, in exact proportion to the extent of its exposure. Like money, flags, or state statuary, the tracks are made visible by their unmasking: money counts as it burns; flags signify best when defaced; the politician's statue means again when graced with a green mohican. Abstract value, the state, politics, the code of the hunt—each, a quasi-spiritual public secret, materializes through exposure or defacement. So glossed, the ectoplasmic track is simply "an extension of whatever it is that makes matter matter" for these hunters.[82] The emperor stays an emperor even without a stitch, his imperiousness perhaps enhanced by the "contrived illusionism" of a crowd sharing a public secret, through which much of the real is really made up.[83] The yearling remains a fourteen-point buck thanks to an "ontological vehemence" induced by a public secret thrown forward into the world by some muddy prints.[84]

Ike kills his first buck and is marked with its blood as the last stage in an apprenticeship to the big woods, conducted in large part aurally. Sam Fathers would "talk to the boy . . . about the old days and People" (126–27). Talked to since he could remember, Ike remembers regressively: Sam's words take him into a pre-Columbian space which is necessarily prenatal: "[U]ntil at last it would seem to the boy that he himself had not come into existence yet, that none of his race nor the other subject's race which his people had brought with them into the land had come here yet" (127). The "here" in question is identifiably "land[ed]" matter made from speech: the "old people" drawn into Ike's "present" by Sam "actually walk" and cast an "actual shadow . . . in breath and air." "Breath" is the key medium: "[I]t would seem . . . that it was he, the boy, who was the guest here and Sam Fathers' voice the mouthpiece of the host" (127).

I am less concerned with the extent and rapidity of Ike's ahistorical regression than with the manner in which it is achieved—a manner that I shall argue is historically specific to the economy of the early 1940s. Sam's "voice" plays "host" to a "host" that is several: as one who has "guest[s]," Sam's mouth is occupied by "very many," but in the context of "consecrat[ion]" (122, 135), or "setting apart as sacred," that same "mouthpiece" may be thought to contain the eucharistic "host," or "bread . . . regarded as the body of Christ." Since Sam's talking will culminate in the buck's blood, and since his voice is metaphorically recast as a "mouthpiece" or part of a vessel, we may assume that Sam's speech transfers the "host" as blood rather than as wafer. Where Ike is the communicant and Sam the "mouthpiece," the lips of "guest" and "host" meet "forever" in a kiss by way of which "blood" transfuses from "breath and air."

Sam and Ike's exchanges, as reported by Faulkner, secrete variables. Yet nothing here can be said to be buried or repressed: The polyvocality of "host" hides in plain hearing at first reading to trigger the kinds of semantic transfer that I have sought to trace. Mapping is eased by the imperatives of an ur-narrative whose elements grow plainer with each iteration. The claim for an interethnic male kiss may offend as too literal an account of a latent option, though I wonder how often the conjunction of male bodies must occur before latency amounts to the all-but-overt which must be denied? Witness the gathering of the ur-narrative in the body of the buck itself, as a stencil through which that animal is made to carry apparently unmanageable meanings:

> At first there was nothing. . . . Then the buck was there. He did not come into sight; he was just there, looking not like a ghost but as if all of light were condensed in him and he were the source of it, not only moving in it but disseminating it, already running, seen first as you always see the deer, in that split second after he has already seen you, already slanting away in that first soaring bound, the antlers even in that dim light looking like a small rocking-chair balanced on his head.
>
> "Now," Sam Fathers said, "shoot quick, and slow." (121)

Figured through Genesis and sans antecedents, the buck is a luminous and seminal "source." But, "Let there be light" sits ill with a rocking chair. The antlers so described recall Buddy's favored furniture: Uncle Buddy, we are told, whether riding a horse or wagon, sits as he would "in his rocking chair" (19), perhaps because the "housekeeper" to the McCaslin home practices "sitting all day long in the rocking chair from which he cooked the food, before the kitchen fire on which he cooked it" (197). With Buddy balanced precariously in the horns of a buck, that buck, containing a black, must surely also nominate Buddy's twin? At which point, male bodies triangulate in a female shape marked male:[85] who will couple and who will play dead, in accordance with serial urgencies, remains moot. Since the dead buck does not conclusively die, but rather contributes to the ontological vehemence of its generically spectral recurrence, whoever or whatever Ike shoots survives his shot in altered form. Fraught with semantic slippage, the persistent buck should yield a "revelation of undifferentiation" plus an attendant "mimetic crisis" in which the distinctions that secure a racialized social order founder. Yet, notwithstanding intimations of patricide and of homosexual incest and miscegenation, glimpsed through the stereograph of the ur-narrative, the contents of the beast fall into predictable patterns.

The buck is a sacrificial surrogate, repeating at a distance Roth's (or rather Roth and Lucas's) initial dissolution of distinctions. Despite the increased distance that separates offender from surrogate (Roth/Lucas from Rider; Rider from buck), displacement fails, and with it the sacrifice. Rather than correcting category collapse, the buck maximizes undifferentiation in so far as its "blood"—a veritable "mixture of mixture"[86]—allows the movement of white into black into red; of man into man, and of man into beast. The sacrifice needs must be made again, and again to be made to fail, since, circa 1941, the intrusive body of the black has to be expelled, while being retained in forms displaced from the actualities of labor withdrawal. Those forms involve desires available for disavowal, not least because those for whom the masked black body operates as a revenant or exquisite corpse must recognize, while denying, that which they retentively contain. Hence Rider and the buck operate as fetishes: by standing in the way of a lost body, they attract into themselves desires that might more properly attach to that which has been lost, the sustaining body of black labor. The fetish counters loss by translating it into desire, though in these instances into one that cannot speak its name. To make that desire speak by locating it as occurring between identifiable male couples (Rider and Writer; Sam and Ike), each of them operating after the manner of the *petit object a*—as substitutes for a prior and missing physical exchange—risks fixing a flow of desire that is as duplicitous as it is pervasive: duplicitous because it mistakes its true and original object.[87]

One solution would be to argue that the indeterminately fantasmal pleasures that I have traced are finally textual, intimacies resident in verbal intimation alone; witness the passage of "guest" into "host" via "mouthpiece"; or the interference of "Rider" with "Mannie" with "buck." While the textual turn has its truths, I remain unconvinced that the homoerotic options of *Go Down, Moses*, emerge palimpsesti-cally, as *unrealised* and immaterial tropic possibilities, generated at the linguistic level and lost for a referent, either in personal practice or historical event. Indeed, without the instigatory force of material events, my textual stratagems—parataxes, puns, divisions and displacements—would skirt the pointless. An unwillingless to surrender the referent does not, however, require that I literalize what passes be-tween those several bodies who meet over or across several beds in the text (after all the mere fact of gayness or bisexuality is as uninteresting as the mere fact of heterosexuality). Rather, I would argue that the rapid and radical revision of labor relations in the plantation South, reaching a hiatus with the conjunction of New Deal reform and imminent global warfare in 1941, constitute an historical loosening of ethnic restraints and an attendant threat to sexual categories, insofar as those cat-egories turn substantially on notions of white male authority, themselves called into question by an internal transformation of the owning class. In such a context, what I have been calling the "ur-narrative" of *Go Down, Moses*—that recurrent scene made up from bits and pieces and featuring male conjunctions, uncertain corpses, and vanishing women—may be read not simply as a source of the felt intensities of the text, but as itself generated by an emergent and unformed historical transi-tion. By definition transition is evasive. One might speak with accuracy of inflows of capital and outflows of labor, or of the end of the postbellum plantation and the onset of a post-plantation South, or even of the demise of dependency as it gives way to autonomy as a "cultural dominant" in the region, while missing the felt ex-perience of change as realized in the material practices of an owning class whose continued and profitable ownership of land requires that they recast themselves, their land, and the labor relations through which they know themselves.[88]

Such practices are necessarily on "the very edge of semantic availability" inso-far as they are part of what Raymond Williams might have called a "preformation," lacking in specific articulation.[89] So, for example, by 1941 the coercive labor mech-anisms that had kept workers tied to the land since Redemption were economi-cally redundant, yet they remained residually essential to the typical experience of laborer and owner. Hence African Americans evanesce into those who must be in and out of place; and owners, as labor lords, become those who keep workers in their place while, as land lords, keen to capitalize their landed asset, encouraging their departure. Caught on the cusp of a fundamental class contradiction, work-ers and employers are liable to find their social experience indefinable—a matter of precipitate emergencies and dissolving residues. I would argue that "1941," as the moment from within which the key elements of *Go Down, Moses* are written, should be understood as the "preformation" of a structural crisis whose form or historical shape is realized only after the war. In 1941 the renewal of systemic out-migration of workers is merely imminent; worked things have yet to be rendered incomplete or quasi-spectral by the withdrawal of those who gave substance to things. Incipient structural loss, "on the very edge of semantic availability," may yet be countered by the recovery, from that edge, of forms of desire that stand in for, and allow the return of, that which has begun to go missing—the body of black labor. So read, "1941" provides a referent for a love, hidden in plain sight among the parataxes of the text, that binds white and black male bodies together in stressed, displaced, but sufficiently retentive, forms of amity.

CHAPTER **FIVE** ██████████████

Reading the Ledgers:

Textual Variants and Labor Variables

Richard Godden and Noel Polk

"THE Old People" opens with Buck and Buddy tangled on the horns of a latently black beast;[1] the story closes with two males in bed, dark hand to white "flank."[2] At either end, "The Old People" exhibits associative transformations rendered only slightly less shocking by their not being singular. The first four stories in *Go Down, Moses*, read cumulatively, release a whispered ur-narrative, or more properly an ur-narrative kit, whose constituent parts (bed; woman under erasure; male cross-racial couple; corpse) with each emergence advance toward emergency. The nub of that emergency, or so this argument has run, is to be found in the contradictory need of the planter class to loose *and* retain the bound body of African American labor, circa 1940–41. It is, therefore, perhaps unsurprising that the clarifying series, or rather the generative contradiction which is its final referent, should yield another variant in "The Bear," particularly since the fifth story of *Go Down, Moses* turns on an act of repudiation involving the systematic release of a black work force. The logic of the ur-narrative has been understood to require that any planter who vehemently and overtly repudiates the black body that is his substance risks not simply death (or material transformation) but the covert restoration of that body to him in alternative forms. Since in section 4 of "The Bear"

Faulkner gathers the documentary evidence for Isaac McCaslin's case against his class, and offers a clause by clause transcription of his making of that case, one might expect to find, among the finer points of the repudiator's argument, the emergent intimations of a countercase—or, more literally, beds, women in erasure, male couplings across racial lines, and corpses. Indeed, given the sustained and detailed nature of the repudiation, the recovery of an equally particularized and shocking emergency among the subsemantics of that case is systemically likely.

I

In 1888, aged twenty-one and in the commissary, Isaac McCas- lin begins arguing with his older cousin Cass over his, Isaac's, decision to repudi- ate his inheritance from his grandfather, Lucius Quintus Carothers (L.Q.C.) McCas- lin: as primary evidence he resorts to the commissary ledgers in which his forebears have recorded the business and personal affairs of the McCaslin family over the course of the plantation's life during the first half of the nineteenth century. He has read these ledgers before, mining them for what he believes are their records of his grandfather's perfidy toward his slaves: acts which have created a part-black branch of the McCaslin family whose history runs parallel with his own. To present Isaac's reconstruction, or memory, of the ledgers, Faulkner formally replicates the crude ungrammatical text of the ledgers that Isaac reads. He uses little capitaliza- tion and random punctuation (a few commas and full stops are replaced by colons): that is, he offers a text virtually unmoored from conventional linearity and periodicity. We have no sense that anything like *all* the ledgers are cited, or that those entries we do have appear in chronological sequence. As we shall see, Isaac, who goes to the ledgers to make his case about his grandfather, orders the en- tries and their appearance according to his own needs. Moreover, he takes these illegible, ungrammatical documents as something set "perhaps upon some apoc- ryphal Bench or even Altar or perhaps before the Throne Itself for a last perusal and contemplation and refreshment of the Allknowledgeable" (193). For Isaac the ledgers are quasi-sacred documents; yet, it becomes clear that they are far from "Allknowledgeable," even perhaps far from readable, since they present limited ev- idence for what Isaac wants to believe, and are more complex than he wishes to understand.

Isaac intends, of course, to go straight to that portion of the ledgers which he thinks documents his grandfather's incestuous exploitation of his slaves: his im- pregnation first of Eunice and then of his and Eunice's daughter Tomasina—which pregnancy, Isaac wants the ledgers to say, leads Eunice to commit suicide on Christmas Day 1832. That is, Isaac posits his grandfather's incestuous misce- genation as the immediate proximate cause of his own renunciation not just of the land and not even just of slavery, but of the entire history of land ownership—of the very idea of possession, which he believes to be embodied in the practice of slavery, as concentrated and focused in his grandfather's incest.

He cannot go there directly, though. First he turns to the "anomaly calling itself Percival Brownlee" (195) and to his unsettling appearance in the family chronicle. Brownlee is an "anomaly" in several senses, but most immediately in his being the only slave either of the twins had ever bought. The climax of the Brownlee episode comes in the revelation that Brownlee is homosexual, and that his homosexuality stands as an available reason for why Isaac's father purchased him. It is fairly clear that Isaac does not understand the full implications of this fact, or at least that he cannot face them. The Brownlee materials appear set aside in a parenthesis, as though merely a subsidiary clause; indeed, Brownlee turns up almost as an after-thought buried within and disrupting Isaac's lengthy, seven-page, one-sentence response to the ledger's putative evidence of the tangled triangulation of L.Q.C., Eunice, and Tomasina. The Brownlee prelude is thus, to say the least, recessive if not completely repressed. Critics over the years have followed Isaac in leaving the subsumed Brownlee all but alone. Yet the Brownlee episode (195–96) effectively prefaces those ledger entries offered by Ike as vital evidence for his repudiation. We shall transcribe the bracketed entries and offer commentary. The relevant entries may be understood to explain why Isaac's father bought Brownlee, his motives discernible through the consequences of the transaction. Initially, Buck records the transaction itself.

> *Percavil Brownly 26yr Old. cleark @ Bookepper. Bought from N.B. Forest at Cold Water 3 Mar 1856 $265. dolars*

It takes Buck barely two days to discover, or admit, that Brownlee not only is no "*bookepper*" but that he cannot even read: a fact he is likely to have suspected from the beginning since slaves were typically forbidden literacy, let alone accoun-tancy. Given a common (though not universal) prohibition on the education of slaves; and given also that the price is strikingly low for a healthy male slave, Buck could be seen as obscuring his reasons for purchasing Brownlee:[3]

> *5 mar 1856 No bookepper any way Cant read. Can write his Name but I already put that down My self Says he can Plough but dont look like it to Me. sent to Feild to day Mar 5 1856*

His second entry in two days indicates a keen need both to retain Brownlee and to find something for him to do, at least for his brother's eyes:

> *6 Mar 1856 Cant plough either Says he aims to be a Precher so may be he can lead live stock to Crick to Drink*

The next entry, over two weeks later, is Buddy's. The brothers, we learn, seem to use the "diurnally advancing pages" of the ledgers "to conduct the unavoidable business" of the plantation (194). Read as part of an ongoing conversation between the two, the occasional nature of the entries suggests that the twins are "long since past any oral intercourse" (194). Though Buddy may have been somewhat puzzled at his brother's purchase, he gives no hint that he has any idea why Buck bought any slave, much less Brownlee. His entry is concise:

Mar 23th 1856 Cant do that either Except one at a Time Get shut of him

Buck responds the next day:

24 Mar 1856 Who in hell would buy him

Buddy waits nearly a month before replying to his brother's almost certainly rhetorical question, and his response is markedly less concise:

19th of Apr 1856 Nobody You put yourself out of Market at Cold Water two months ago I never said sell him Free him

The increasing lapse of time between these entries raises serious questions about the twins' relationship. Do they speak to each other except in these journals? Is there no oral communication of any sort? What, then, are their days like? Has Brownlee come between them, and if so, in what sense?

In the ledger, at least, Buck maintains that his concerns are economic, his purchase an investment in labor:

22 April 1856 Ill get it out of him

To what does "*it*" refer? The term has its ambiguities, as does the body of the slave itself. Slaves, in their capacity to labor, constituted the master's accumulated wealth: as priceable, and therefore transferrable, items, like cotton, sugar, or tobacco, they linked the peculiar institution to the emergent and global processes of capital. Yet in labor terms, the slave's body, an ideological extension of the labor lord's will, was (in its less transferrable, because more intimate, bondage to the master's body), a premodern entity. Given Brownlee's sexuality, the intimacy of the labor tie may be understood, in the shiftiness of a single pronoun ("*it*"), to drift from labor time toward desire. Or, in other words, "*it*" is a split referent. "[*I*]*t*" refers to a quantity of labor time, debited against a sum prepaid. Yet "*it*['s]" indeterminacy, triggered by the double "anomaly" of Buck's purchase and Brownlee's sexuality, permits the inference that if Buck, even in fantasy, bought Brownlee for sexual purposes, then "*it*" refers to the work of a whore; that is, to a sexual practice extracted at a fixed price (defrayed against the original $265). We should perhaps recall that the final textual reference to Brownlee records that, twenty years after last encountering his slave, Buck "heard of him again, an old man . . . and quite fat . . . the well-to-do proprietor of a select New Orleans brothel" (217).[4] Buck's vocal inflection of the impersonal pronoun is unavailable, but the phrasing at least allows for his encrypted admission of a covert determination to recoup sexual pleasure.

To follow the connotation of "*it*['s]" duplicity would eventually be to question the nature of the twins' sibling intimacy. But, the ur-plot notwithstanding, such pursuit as yet lacks prompts.

Confronting Buck's economic confidence, Buddy's reply, nearly two months later, may well be sardonic:

June 13th 1856 How $1 per yr 265$ 265yrs Wholl sign his Free paper

Buddy's computation may simply mean that Brownlee is so worthless as laboring property that he could not live long enough to amortize his own market value: at Buddy's valuation of one dollar a year, nobody now living would be alive to free him after he had bought himself. Nonetheless, in the teeth of economic logic and his own manumitting tendencies, Buck keeps Brownlee. Four months later, Buck records perhaps the most curious of the entries:

1 Oct 1856 Mule josephine Broke Leg @ shot Wrong stall wrong niger wrong everything $100. dolars

Prompted by "*it*," "*Wrong*" yields plottable latencies. Mules do not generally break legs in stalls: had Josephine broken hers out in the field, she would have been shot where she lay. With little room in any stall for stock to fall, we may conclude that she damaged herself kicking at something or somebody. To recover a rationale for "*Wrong*," we suggest the following, aware even as we suggest it, that our case might readily be cast as carrying connotation too far, and as such as party to "the dominant signifying practice of homophobia,"[5] which tends, care of innuendo, to bring into being what it fearfully looks for, simply by looking for it. We will take the risk, hoping to counter the charge that we implausibly literalize what is at best a fragile subtextual inference, by way of a subsequent accumulation of inferences, even as we argue for the ultimate inseparability of the inferential from the denotative, within the materials in question.

Hostages to fortune in place, we therefore propose the following: wherever Buck sleeps, whether with Buddy or alone, in another room, it is doubtful that he brings Brownlee anywhere near his twin.[6] In accordance with the triggered inferences of "*it*," drawn into hiding on the page by the projective pressure of the ur-narrative, we might discern the barn as a trysting place . . . at night, and in the dark. On the evening of October 1, prior to his entry into the *right*, because prearranged, stall, Brownlee goes into Josephine's stall and begins to "diddle" her, or at least tries to do so; the mule kicks out at Brownlee, and missing, breaks her leg on the wall.[7] Assuming that Buck was waiting in another stall for Brownlee, he reacted rapidly to Josephine's distress. Seeing the mule crippled, he shoots her in the stall immediately. Hence sex in the "*Wrong stall*." By virtue of this complication, Brownlee finally proves himself even to Buck to be too problematic to keep—not only incompetent as either house or field slave, not only homosexual, but also, perhaps, given to bestial practices: he is thus the *"wrong niger,"* maybe even the wrong ho-mosexual Negro.[8]

Our explanation pivots *"wrong"* on the tacit triangle favored in earlier stories—that of "she" who vanishes (Josephine), making her bed (the stall) available for a miscegenous gay coupling. To extend the serial logic of the deep or counternar-rative would be to require a corpse, but previous corpses have tended to embody the death of the master's mastery as labor lord, in which case Josephine does not fit. Buddy, however, as the implied "wife" in the fraternal "marriage" between planters, might be seen as the requisite dead master, his love killed by Brownlee's presence. To backtrack on the bid for "marriage": Faulkner refers severally to the closeness of the twins, at one in handwriting (194) and appearance (87), though not, he reiterates, in gender—Buck named for a male goat, rabbit, or deer; Buddy carrying a feminine ending. As perhaps the more male of the pairing, Buck goes to war (he would not be the only male in Faulkner's work to look upon military ser-vice as an exit from marriage). Buddy stays at home as "cook and housekeeper" (18, 197), with a preference for "sitting all day long in the rocking chair from which he cooked the food, before the kitchen fire on which he cooked it" (197). Even on those occasions when Buck pursues Tomey's Turl to Sophonsiba's lair, Buddy, "who should have been a woman to begin with" (201), stays put, "though they all knew that [he] . . . could have risked it ten times as much as Uncle Buck could have dared" (7). Presumably, what "they all knew," in multiples of ten, is that given his gender preference, Buddy is less at "risk" of heterosexual entrapment than his twin. Certainly, Hubert Beauchamp notes that Buddy is not "woman-weak" (22). None of which amounts to a case for more than preferred celibacy: any inference of homosexual incest remains no more and no less than inferential. Nonetheless, having rendered *"wrong"* encyclopaedically suggestive, we can at least hypothe-size a reason for Buck's exasperation on October 1, while additionally recording an oddity in the dating.

At the onset of the Brownlee entries, Faulkner notes that they constitute "a sin-gle page" and cover "less than a year, not seven months in fact" (195). Running from "*5 mar 1856*" to "*Chrstms 1856*," they in fact cover ten months; a run of five entries in October, all dealing with the fallout from Josephine, extend Brownlee into an eighth month, with a final entry in December ensuring that he preoccupies the twins well into a tenth month. Since Faulkner narrates from within the purview of Ike as he gathers texts, specifies events, names and periodizes, in order to es-tablish due cause for repudiation, the slip goes to Ike; as does the iterative "in fact" which might be thought a sleight of emphasis, undertaken to obscure error. In which case, the resonance of an ill-disguised mistake raises questions not simply over what happened in a barn in 1856, but also as to what happened to the evi-dence for those events as Ike prepared his case in October 1883. We are told that his detailed preparations began at age sixteen when, having taken the commissary key from the bedroom of his sleeping cousin and stand-in father, McCaslin Edmonds, he ensconced himself in front of the ledgers, to read what he had read before, and, knowing "what he was going to find before he found it" (198), opened the ledgers, presumably (since they are the first entries appealed to in 1888) to the Brownlee page. The context for reading announces that his reading is furtive: adolescence, a stolen key, a locked door, the cover of darkness and "a forgotten lantern stinking anew." But, on the evidence of the seven months that is in fact ten, it may be that the furtive further announces the fixed. A dating error at least allows for an accompanying error concerning pagination, not least because period and page meet in the shared modifier "long":

> (It was a single page, not long and covering less than a year, not seven months in fact begun in the hand which the boy had learned to distinguish as that of his father:

"[L]ong"'s initial reference to spatial coverage shifts toward the temporal with the introduction of the mistaken month-count. If "long" contains a denied dating error, might not the "single page" be longer? A small matter, but one which if allowed credence at least implies that Ike's bracketed page has been put together from materials spread across one or more pages. The possibility that the "single page" is an editorial reconstruction, involving Ike's imaginative input, compounds a problem: the oddity of Ike's choice of a parenthetical "anomaly" as preface to the key evidence for his repudiation is enhanced by the possibility that Ike has had first to find and reconstruct his "anomaly," and further to misrepresent that reconstruction, before placing it as a "single page" (albeit bracketed) at the head of his textual case for setting aside his family, property, and class.

To return to the events of 1856, rather than to the nature of the evidence for those events—whatever happened in the barn would seem abruptly to persuade Buck of the need to dispense with Brownlee by freeing him:

> 2 Oct 1856 Freed Debit McCaslin@ McCaslin $256. dolars

Buddy hauls him up short, however, by insisting that the financial costs of the episode belong solely to Buck. But on the following day, noticing that Brownlee will not leave the plantation, he seems to soften, and, in an appeal to Father, perhaps bids for reconciliation with his twin:

> Oct 3th Debit Theophilus McCaslin Niger 265$ Mule 100$ 365$ He hasnt gone yet Father should be here

L.Q.C. McCaslin, dead nearly twenty years, dominates the final entries concerning Brownlee. Buck:

> 3 Oct 1856 Son of a bitch wont leave What would father done

Buddy, nearly a month later:

29th of Oct 1856 Renamed him

Buck:

31 Oct 1856 Renamed him what

Finally, Buddy, nearly two months later:

Chrstms 1856 Spintrius

The ongoing presence by invocation of their father in these entries, and the length of time over which the correspondents contemplate his presence, raises a question as to the nature of their appeal to him. At the close of his section in *The Sound and the Fury* (1929), Quentin Compson's invention of his father's voice offers one point of reference to Buddy's summons. Quentin invoked the father so that he might confess incest and thereby articulate his divided sense of that act as both sin and value. Any such parallel confession on Buddy's part would be entirely more problematic. If we understand Buddy's bid for paternal intervention, in the matter of Brownlee, as necessarily involving him in a phantasmal admission of tangled sexual preferences, we might usefully deploy Eve Kosofsky Sedgwick on gay confession. Sedgwick describes "coming out" to a parent as "a double-edged weapon" in that he who confesses expects both to wound and be wounded by the parent: "the fear of being wished dead by (say) one's parents . . . is apt to recoil [as] the more intensely imagined possibility of its killing them."[9] Where the parent in question is L.Q.C., any admission of incest, with its attendant imaging of bed, barn, and stall, verges on a "potent crossing and recrossing of . . . politically charged lines of representation," a representation whose lines meet in the body of Brownlee, as a figure not simply of desire but of labor.[10] The twins have, after all, acted on their doubts about slavery (doubts that their father did not apparently share), doing what they could, in their time and place, to ameliorate the practices of the institution. As soon as their father dies in 1837, the twins remove themselves into a "one-room log cabin which the two of them built themselves, refusing to allow any slave to touch any timber of it" (193). They quarter the slaves in their father's incomplete plantation house. Each night they conduct the occupants officially and ceremoniously in through the front door and lock it, while leaving the back door unlocked and unsupervised, so that the McCaslin slaves are free to roam, on the understanding that they will be back in the house by dawn. Such amelioration amounts to a systematic inversion of their father's world, via a particularized assault on the technology of his mastery: bound labor, house, and will stand modified. The twins substitute their own free labor for their father's bound labor in the matter of the cabin, thereby modifying the very substance of McCaslin property. They translate their father's white house into black quarters, in the process parodying the practice of the master's mastery. By renouncing the totality of their control over the body of labor, they abrogate their own authority, potentially setting black and white bodies in an altered state of intimacy, at least by night. On which grounds, Buddy's, "*What would father done*" might be said, care of Sedgwick, to solicit multiple harming—harm to the authority of a father, whose mastery the twins have already called into institutional question. Institutional authority within slavery should be recognized as involving face-to-face and embodied coercive practices, at once more total and intimate than labor control undertaken within a free market. To invert those technologies which extend mastery through the body of the master class is to assault the master's body, a body that liked to cast itself as paternal. A son who in 1837 undertakes an extended inversion of forms of authority associated with his father, and espoused by his neighbors, and who in 1856 even contemplates "outing" his twin's extension of their shared revision of master/slave intimacy, may anticipate harm from the father to whom he "confesses."

Whatever Buddy's case for L.Q.C's phantasmic presence, given the twins' difficult circumstance with regard to Brownlee, a summative name, issuing as though from the father, on Christmas day, seems likely to carry problematic authority. The entry "*Spintrius*" derives from the Latin "spintria," a male prostitute. Although Buddy uses the name in the name of his father, Faulkner probably took it from Suetonius's *The Lives of the Twelve Caesars*, of which he had a copy in his library. Suetonius makes three references to "spintrae," and in relation to Tiberius's love life details their pleasures: "In his retreat at Capri there was a room devised by him dedicated to the most arcane lusts. Here he had assembled from all quarters girls and perverts, whom he called spintrae, who invented monstrous feats of lubricity, and defiled one another before him, interlaced in a series of threes in order to enflame his feeble appetite."[11] One could, care of accumulating connotation, identify Buddy's long-pondered choice of name as the decision of a jilted lover, who, assuming the role of punative paternity, inscribes in the ledger an abbreviated synonym for "the threat of castration" in the father's name. Such a reading ignores the date: "*Spintrius*" is a Christmas gift. Presented by a brother to a twin who is emerging as a lover. Since Buddy plays a game with a name, we may be justified in pursuing the deep logic of his name game. "*Spintrius*," in the absence of glossaries, is a name devoid of easy referentiality; as such, at least for a time it stands empty and open for speculative reference along lines suggested by the sonorities of its phonemic mutations.[12] "Spinster," "sphinx," and "sphincter" lie residually available in its failure properly to name: "spinster" because Buddy, fearing Brownlee as a rival, sees in his presence his own decline into the loneliness of an old maid; "sphinx" because on the evidence of the ledger, Brownlee has at least tried to unite with a beast, though mule not lion; and "sphincter" because "Brownlee" is already anally colored—we can hear his name as the adverb "brownly," though to do so is to risk neglecting "lee," which may be understood either cloacally as "lees" ("dregs" or "refuse") or nautically (as in "lee shore," or place of safety or refuge).[13]

Since Buddy, at some level, attaches Buck to Brownlee when he writes "*Spintrius*," he may hear any or all of these emergences as they arise from the linked names, activated by his inscription. He may even recall that "buck" refers to the copulation of animals, most typically but not exclusively rabbits. Since Buck is probably as puzzled as we are by Buddy's choice of name, we may assume either that he too plays the phonemic permutations toward their promiscuities or that he turns away. He makes no subsequent entry on the page. In the latter case, Buddy effectively gives the gift to no one but himself, thereby rendering "*Spintrius*" autoerotic, and by inference indicating his own sense of himself as "interlaced in . . . [a] series of three." A pattern formed from the twins' names confirms such a tacit and substitutive triangulation.

Buddy's name, Amodeus ("I love God") is Latin; Buck's name, Theophilus ("Beloved of [or Dear to] God") is Greek. Indeed, the classical naming of the twins suggests that the loves of one are inextricable from the loves of the other: to translate, Amodeus loves what Theophilus is loved by, and, on the suggestion of the ledgers, God (whether "Deus" or "Theo") runs a distinct second to "*Spintrius*" as the object of Buck's affections. The triangulation formed by the trinity of classical names creates a riddle: "Amodeus" and "Theophilus" constitute a quasi-, or flawed, chiasmus:[14] as a clause "Amo deus" inverts and repeats "Theo philus," but where "theo" and "deus" exactly complement one another, "amo" (verb) and "philus" (adjective) do not. In an exact chiasmus Amodeus ("I love God") requires "God loves I (or me)" (Theophilus), but "Theophilus," literally translated means "Dear to God." That Buddy's love fails to find its inverse reflection in Buck's name displaces their whispered incest, even as "I," lost for its chiasmic partner, begs a question as to who is the "dear" whom Buck loves in the place of "I" (or me)? "*Spintrius*" fits.

"*Spintrius*" is the end of the ledger's account of Brownlee, but not of Isaac's story. Brownlee again interrupts the story that Isaac wants to tell, of his grandfather's sins, as Isaac moves his narration through the Civil War and Reconstruction, toward the issue of L.Q.C.'s descendants. It seems clear that before Isaac can discuss his grandfather's sexuality, anxieties concerning his father's sexuality intrude.

At some point Brownlee does leave the McCaslin plantation, though the ledgers do not suggest how or why. He must have departed some time before 1862, since in that year, "during the boy's father's absence," (216) Buddy discovers that Brownlee had been back on the plantation for at least a month. Brownlee has become the preacher he had told Buck he was called to be and is "conducting impromptu revival meetings among negroes, preaching and leading the singing also in his high sweet true soprano voice." He then just as suddenly disappears "on foot and at top speed" barely ahead of a "body of raiding Federal horse" (216) which he at least fears may be after him for reasons we can never know. He materializes one more time, after the war, in 1866, "in the entourage of a travelling Army paymaster, the two of them passing through Jefferson in a surrey at the exact moment when the boy's father . . . also happened to be crossing the Square." Brownlee and the paymaster give the impression of being on an "illicit holiday like a man on an excursion during his wife's absence with his wife's personal maid," a suggestion, surely, that the town—or Buck, at any rate—takes them to be lovers. Seeing Buck, Brownlee gives him "one defiant female glance" and then "[breaks] again, leap[s] from the surrey and disappear[s] this time for good" (216–17).

These concluding episodes, though resisting interpretation, at the very least raise questions that contribute to a connotative case for a secreted narrative, turning on a liaison between Buck and Brownlee. Why does Brownlee "break" *again*, leap from the surrey and run? Is he so afraid of Buck that he does not believe the paymaster can defend him? Or, to the contrary, is he also escaping the paymaster? "[A]gain" might suggest how he left the McCaslin plantation originally, "breaking" and fleeing under the threat of some kind of violence made by Buck or by Buddy? That he should resurface twice in relation to military bodies indicates that Brownlee has been pursuing an itinerant career as a camp follower: if so, Buck's attempts to make Brownlee yield a price appear to have paid off. As a whore to the Union troops, and eventually to a Northern "paymaster," Brownlee has achieved the autonomy by which one carries in one's person that labor which one may freely contract on the open marked. No longer bound as slave or tenant, he reappears in motion, and is free to "break" and run whenever he wishes. The next logical step is that he should manage the sexual work of others, hence his final destination and profession in New Orleans.

The Brownlee episode of the ledgers complete, Faulkner closes its intrusion into the larger narrative toward which Isaac moves by an anomalously placed close-parenthesis at the left margin of the prose roman passage (196). The resultant visual effect is curious:

the second:
   Chrstms 1856 Spintrius
) took substance and even a sort of shadowy life . . .

What follows the hung parenthesis resumes the sentence which the opening of the parenthesis had interrupted two pages earlier. But any attempt to convey that resumption by simply quoting across the parenthesis (omitting the parenthetical Brownlee materials) runs into difficulty, since the parenthesis about Brownlee occurs during yet another parenthetical intervention whose beginning is marked not by a parenthesis but by a dash (194): Isaac, remembering his reading of the ledgers, visualizes how "one by one the slaves which Carothers McCaslin had inherited and purchased—" (194). The dash signals the taking of an inventory,[15] but the list, undertaken in Ike's name, is interrupted by a need to elaborate on the purchase of Brownlee. Instead of naming names and moving on to his grandfather's abuse of human property, Ike must, it seems, deal with the emerging meaning of a figure who just may have been his father's lover. Faulkner specifies the details of the Brownlee ledger materials (number of pages, period covered, calligraphy), only to set them within an open-parenthesis, whose closure hangs at an awkward distance from the name "*Spintrius*." The strained punctuation leads back to the beginning of the sentence which, sans dash, would read: "as one by one slaves which Carothers McCaslin had inherited and purchased [194] . . . took substance and even a sort of shadowy life [196]. . . ." Isaac, reading the very particular "substance" and "shadow" of the ledgers, confidently announces that he has recovered "not only the general and condoned injustice and its slow amortization, but the specific tragedy which had not been condoned and could never be amortized" (196). The "specific tragedy," of course, is his grandfather's incestuous miscegenation. But the "specific" "substance" and detailed "shadows" from which Isaac recovers his grandfather's faults are inseparable from a sustained and problematical syntactical effort to occlude the Brownlee page. Faulkner's punctuation encrypts what he secretes, in both senses of both terms: a closing bracket placed at the start of a line, after a line space and between a shift from italic to roman type, looks anomalous and unlikely to retain "the anomaly" that it seeks to contain. ")" not only does not shut down the cryptic name "*Spintrius*," it begs to disclose it. Conspicuous in its syntactical displacement, the Brownlee episode hangs in an allusive state of partial censorship, its inferential resonances seeping through the more overt elements of Ike's repudiation narrative.

II

Having compiled inferences, let us overstate a case for their presence: that a "single page" of ledger entries constitutes an extended admission of an incestuous liaison between Isaac's father and uncle, a liaison drawn into the subsemantics of the page by Buck's homosexual miscegeny with a slave. The suggestion is shocking in its implausibility, yet the shock may be tempered by the recognition of a tacit parallel between L.Q.C.'s and Buck's miscegeny and incest, a parallel arguably recovered by Ike, which at least allows for a reading of the entire episode involving Brownlee and his father with significantly greater understanding. The Brownlee material thus runs counter to the narrative that Isaac wants to tell and to deploy in a condemnation of his grandfather: his own father has engaged in the same sexual acts (as a homosexual) for which Isaac condemns his grandfather (as a heterosexual). Since Isaac represses them, his father's notional acts would appear to be those he finds the more disturbing in his family chronicle.

We shall persist with our overstatement, in order to articulate the implications of the claim. If we suppose that Ike, at some level, distracts from one set of triangulated "lovers" (gay) with another (straight), two things follow. Firstly, the aptness of the fit indicates a degree of consciousness behind the impulse to hide: such an impulse is contradictory, since he who hides something does so because he presupposes that persons will look for it. Far better simply to forget or lose the item (be it a fleeting suspicion, a casual rumor, or a partial memory) than to conceal it—unless, of course, he who conceals wishes, at some level, to keep that which he hides. The snugness of the fit may, therefore, serve a double function: firstly, to match and conceal, where the very fact of matching may ensure an eventual revelation; and secondly, if the "single [ledger] page" can be made to carry the whispers which we claim, then the ledger entries that follow (as text after preface), may not actually say what Ike would have them say concerning his grandfather's culpability, since that culpability, within our revised dispensation of the ledgers, could be designed specifically to fit and conceal a more disruptive narrative.

Prior to testing the evidence against the grandfather, we should make good on one of our leading theoretical hostages to fortune—that concerning the truth value of connotation. To the charge that we overstate inference in the cause of the literal to produce the improbable (so that one word, "*wrong,*" in the phrase "*Wrong stall,*" may yield an entire scene, with Buck and Josephine lined up and awaiting Brownlee's ministrations), we would respond that there is about connotation, and more particularly sexual connotation, that which solicits sight. Witness "sphincter" as it plays among the antonyms released by innuendo from the troilistic "*Spintrius,*" or the glimpsed presence of mouth and anus as the puns in "oral intercourse" (194) and "Brownlee" expose, and in exposing censure, figures for what gay male sex may be imagined to involve. Indeed, puns, so readily dismissible as the most indecisive form of textual evidence, prove crucial to the visible yet immaterial nature of our case, insofar as they operate as textual closets. For Sedgwick, the closet famously involves "relations [between] . . . the known and the unknown, the explicit and the inexplicit" as they give rise to a "weighty . . . epistemological space," neither "vacuum" nor "blank," but a locus of "powerful . . . unknowing."[16] Puns, in this instance homosexual puns, exemplify the power of "unknowing" by making the sexual visible "only as a structure of occulation":[17] which is to say, for example in "Brownlee," that a second term slips by way of shared sound from a first, releasing the mistaken from the chosen, the unknown or unexpected from the known, while maintaining a motive, as tenuous as sound, for their implausible connection. We may cut the sonic excess, even as it inclines toward a semantic residue, but the cut (or "occultation") remains to mark our decision not to see and know, or show and tell.

D. A. Miller, addressing homosexual connotation in the visual medium of Alfred Hitchcock's *Rope* (1948) makes a useful general case for the manner in which connotative evidence works:

> Connotation . . . excites the desire for proof, a desire that, so long as it develops within the connotative register, tends to draft every signifier into what remains a hopeless task.

Hence the desire assumes another, complementary form in the dream (impossible to re-alize, but impossible not to entertain) that connotation would quit its dusky existence for fluorescent literality, would *become denotation*. Every discourse that speaks, every repre-sentation that shows homosexuality by connotative means alone will thus be implicitly haunted by the thing itself, not just in the form of the name but also, more basically, as what the name conjures up: the spectacle of "gay sex." Whenever homosexuality is re-duced to an epistemology, to a problem of *being able to tell*, this will-to-see never fails to make itself felt.[18]

We posit the existence of a "will-to-see" within the Brownlee materials. We do not and cannot claim that the consequent images, so much matter made from imag-inings, amount to a verification of literal bodies engaged in literal acts in literal barns. Perhaps we might most accurately speak not of liaisons between Buddy and Buck and Buck and Brownlee, but of clues that grant permission for the predication of a complex homosexual narrative, drawn from connotation toward denotation by a "will to see" figures and combinations imminent in the ur-narrative to which they contribute, and from which they take shape. By such figurative devices the Brown-lee page is made to mean all that it *can* mean,[19] without those predicative mean-ings being literally true or literally false. The nonverifiable/nonfalsifiable status of Brownlee, as we understand him, is essential to our case, insofar as the ultimate referents for his page and its implications are neither actual events in 1856 nor those events as glimpsed by Isaac in 1883: rather, the referent for Brownlee's prefa-tory existence is the out-migration of black workers from white land in 1940–41.

We had best recap in order to clarify. Reading within the McCaslin ledgers, we have identified a homosexual triangle involving incest and miscegenation. Reading within the same documents, Ike identifies a similar heterosexual triangle. For fifty years the latter has rendered the former invisible, perhaps because the structural imperative associated with an economic revolution in the South, and its attendant labor out-migration, has been insufficiently understood as a crucial determinant for Faulkner's writing in *Go Down, Moses*. Which is to say that the contradiction which requires Faulkner—apprenticed to a planter economy—figuratively to expel while retaining the black body yields the figure of a repudiator who sets aside properties derived from and invested in bound labor, while at the same time recovering the bound body as an object of deniable desire. Where the true referent of the tangled triangles is the generative contradiction "1941," neither triangle should be read as taking precedence; rather, each serves to suspend the other's full referential avail-ability in a semantic impertinence akin to that of an extended metaphor, whose two terms, and their accompanying fields of connotation, interfere with one another to create, in this instance, dislocated patterns of desire in which neither set of trian-gulated bodies comes to full and confident reference.

The issue, here, is neither the historicity of L.Q.C's double rape nor that of male bodies in bed and barn: the issue, rather, is the historicity of their required tension. So, for example, were the Buck-Buddy-Brownlee liaison read as literally true, two things might logically follow. First: L.Q.C's innocence, since his rapes would seem to exist primarily to match and obscure other bodies engaged in parallel acts. Yet for fifty years, L.Q.C's guilt has been accepted. Second: the emergence of Buck and Buddy from the closet, the secrecy of their jointed desire for Brownlee located solely within the consciousness and sexuality of Ike. If Ike reinforces the closet, then its existence is no more or less interesting than he is. Yet if the will to see and not to see Brownlee's anus may be said at some level to belong to Ike, the same cannot be said of the spectacle of Rider's tumescence. It follows, therefore, that the covert and erotic reach of the textual black body extends far beyond Ike's needs or fears. On both counts, to take the gay triangle as true is to ignore the fullness of the text and of critical responses to it.

On the other hand, to dismiss the gay triangle as nothing more than inference is similarly to reduce the text. So, for example, were L.Q.C. simply assumed to be guilty as charged, two things might logically follow. First: any gay revision of his acts could be deemed inconsequential or non-existent, casting Brownlee toward light relief. Second: Ike's repudiation would do what it bids to do, pay off a black labor force and repudiate the accumulated substance of its labor. With the centrality of the Brownlee materials to section 4 of "The Bear" denied, the emergent ur-narrative of cross-racial male desire might fail to become an emergency. Sans focal event, the novel's subterranean pattern of retentive love would remain lost rather than hidden, since without Brownlee no one might look for it, or, stumbling upon it, locate its rationale. True, *phalloi* would continue to float in the subsemantics of particular passages, but disconnected from a predicative scene, those members might drift to the margins of *Go Down, Moses*, reduced to oddities of authorial or character preference rather than recognized as elusive semantic erections containing the generative economy of the novel as a whole.

Our assertion that neither triangle should be taken as literal, because of the effect of each on the other, works most obviously in relation to the gay version, which as a product of cumulative connotation "enjoys or suffers from an abiding deniability."[20] In contradistiction, most readers of *Go Down, Moses* assume that the guilt of L.Q.C. stands proven by Isaac. Yet to make the case that the triangles are structurally linked, in their reference to "1941," we needs must establish not simply that our revision of Brownlee offers a more or less interesting reading of a generally ignored segment of text, but that the corrosion inherent in its inseparability from its heterosexual counterpart and hiding place calls into question the verifiability of L.Q.C's double rape—and in so doing undercuts the evidence validating Ike's expulsion of himself from black labor. Which is to say no more than Ricoeur says about the referent of poetic language more generally: that the first-order reference (here, the heterosexual triangle) is suspended in its ordinary reference as a condition of its relation to a second-order reference (here the homosexual triangle), through which extended moment of "negativity," or "abolition," their relation "reveals [or] unconceals . . . the deep [economic] structures of reality."[21]

III

That portion of the ledgers for which Isaac was presumably looking when he encountered Brownlee begins with his father's recording of his own father's death:

> *Father dide Lucuis Quintus Carothers McCaslin. Callina 1772 Missippy 1837. Dide and burid 27 June 1837* (196)

and continues with three other entries covering the slaves brought from Carolina:

> *Roskus. rased by Grandfather in Callina Dont know how old. Freed 27 June 1837 Dont want to leave. Dide and Burid 12 Jan 1841*

> Fibby Roskus Wife. bought by grandfather in Callina says Fifty Freed 27 June 1837 Dont want to leave. Dide and burd 1 Aug 1849

> Thucydus Roskus @ Fibby Son born in Callina 1779. Refused 10acre peace fathers Will 28 Jun 1837 Refused Cash offer $200. dolars from A. @ T. McCaslin 28 Jun 1837 Wants to stay and work it out (196–97)

We may assume that these entries, like the rest, have been made over a period of years, updated whenever something worthy of recording occurs. But, since Isaac is our source for the source, we cannot know the extent to which he elides or rearranges materials, the chronological relations of those entries he chooses to note, or the degree to which, like any historian, he weights and orders "facts" to make a convincing narrative. His knowledge of the documentation is not, however, to be doubted. He apparently began looking at the ledgers "even after nine and ten and eleven," but not reading them until much later—at some point between his eleventh and sixteenth year (198). Even so, his primer-simple preferred entries, seemingly little more than a record of deaths and burials, provide interesting and significant information. Through L.Q.C.'s father, they establish a family background in South Carolina, from which state slave-owning families often sent sons and extra slaves to farm in Mississippi on land bought cheaply. Though there is no suggestion of it here, from the settled perspective of Carolina, frontier Mississippi was often viewed as an apt destination for unruly sons.

Significantly, none of the members of the Carolina slave family wants to leave the McCaslin plantation after L.Q.C. dies, a fact which may merely reflect the poverty of choices confronting freed slaves. With few places of safety available, staying may represent their default option; it might also, however, indicate some esteem or even affection for L.Q.C. and/or his inheritors. What is really curious about the final entry is L.Q.C.s legacy to Thucydus of ten acres of land, which Thucydus, for some reason, refused, compounding his refusal by further refusing the twins' offer of $200 in its place, preferring instead to "*stay and work it out*." Perhaps he merely wants to stay with Roskus and Fibby, his parents. But why does L.Q.C. leave ten acres to him and not to his parents?

Since L.Q.C. is only seven years older than Thucydus, he cannot be his father, now indulging in his will a cheaper version of the payoff which Isaac believes he makes to his child by Tomasina. If what is commonly assumed about L.Q.C.'s relations with Eunice is true, the money might be a payoff to Roskus and Fibby for some earlier grievous violation of that family. Since Isaac will encounter a further ledger entry referring to "*Fathers will*" (199) and relating to L.Q.C.'s bequest to Turl (Tomasina's child), it is just possible that L.Q.C.'s legacy to Thucydus (declared the son of Roskus and Fibby) represents a payment made against the sins of *his* father.[22] Perhaps, too, it is simpler than that: perhaps he was doing what Joel Williamson says white men of property "in and after the 1830s" did with "amazing frequency": they "recognized their mulatto children as beneficiaries in their wills."[23] We have no record of why or when L.Q.C. left Carolina. We do know that he was born there (1772) seven years before Roskus (1779). We also know that he brought Roskus and Fibby with him, as a slave couple, to Mississippi, where, on his death, they were freed, whether by him or his sons the ledgers do not say. By implication, either the twins, as their father's executors, act on his will or, freed from his authority, they release three slaves, Either way, Buck and Buddy become managers of free rather than bound labor. Perhaps L.Q.C. left Carolina on discovering his father's "shadow family."[24] Taking them with him into exile, he seeks in his will to manumit the slave couple that his father had abused, and to provide for the slave child (his half brother) born to Fibby and fathered by his own (L.Q.C.'s) father. If this is the case, and there is much hypothesis here, the L.Q.C. who emerges looks, in his attitude toward slavery, more like his manumitting sons and his repudiating grandson, and less like Isaac's L.Q.C. But our excursus into Carolina still leaves us with troubling questions. Why didn't L.Q.C. give the land to Roskus and Fibby rather than to Thucydus? The answer might be that in 1837, at the time of the gift, while Thucydus is fifty-eight, his parents are likely to be in their mid-seventies, which does not explain what exactly Thucydus wants to "work out." According to the next entry, he accepts the $200 on November 3, 1841, not quite a year after Roskus dies, and sets himself up as a blacksmith in Jefferson, where he in turn dies thirteen years later.

Isaac apparently wonders about this too. He raises his eyes from the ledgers, and as he reads the relevant entries Thucydus comes to life for him as a slave who, offered $200 gratis, responds with $200 worth of labor, in order to translate an unacceptable gift into a wage—which sum he can then take, using it to purchase a blacksmith's shop. Isaac's brief meditation on Thucydus intervenes between directly recording ledger entries, though it is prompted by five pages of commissary accounting, presumably under Thucydus's name, featuring wages credited against goods debited:

> [A] slowly yet steadily mounting sum of balance (and it would seem to the boy that he could actually see the black man, the slave whom his white owner had forever manumitted by the very act from which the black man could never be free so long as memory lasted, entering the commissary, asking permission perhaps of the white man's son to see the ledger-page which he could not even read . . . (197)

The open parenthesis marks the point at which indirect summation of ledger material gives way to Isaac's imaginative recreation, the trigger for transition being the "very act" whose substance we can only surmise. What the ledgers have not yet been made to reveal is that Thucydus is Eunice's husband. If we are to believe what Isaac tells us, the "very act" is, at the very least, L.Q.C.'s miscegeny with Thucydus's wife. Therefore, in Isaac's reckoning, Thucydus will accept the terms of L.Q.C.'s will only if he can recast those terms through his own independent labor. Isaac "sees" him checking on the details of a labor contract because contracted labor, with its supposition that contracting parties do so "freely" on and "equal" footing, was ever a bourgeois fantasy for disguising the real facts of power.[25] That Thucydus's contract is for a cash wage (albeit deferred) enhances his bid for freedom. Money, abstract and metamorphic, reinforces contract in its displacing of the materiality of the actual human relations out of which it arises. Thucydus could have given lessons to Frederick Douglass: indeed, perhaps Faulkner names his unlettered but heroic self-inventor for the Greek historian Thucydides because by using his *own* $200 to buy a blacksmith's shop in Jefferson, out of which he works for thirteen years, Thucydus in his smithy *does* create an independent black history. We do not get that history, but we do get enough evidence to surmise it. We would add that each feature of our recreated Thucydus fits the surmiseable facts equally whether his acts are motivated by a desire to free himself from the will of a grandfather (L.Q.C.'s father), a half-brother (L.Q.C.), or a half-brother who slept with his wife (L.Q.C.). Isaac, of course will have none of it: believing that Thucydus would never be free, he proceeds to those entries which might be seen to point to the "very act" that binds him.

Isaac breaks from his reverie over the account-page entries against Thucydus's name to observe "the double pen-stroke closing the final entry" (197):

3 Nov 1841 By Cash to Thucydus McCaslin $200. dolars Set Up blaksmith in J. Dec 1841 Dide and buried in J. 17 feb 1854

Eunice Bought by Father in New Orleans 1807 $650. dolars. Marrid to Thucydus 1809 Drownd in Crick Cristmas Day 1832 (197)

Faulkner does not supply the stroke, however, and it remains open whether Isaac refers to the closing balance on Thucydus's $200 or to Thucydus's life. If, as a mere possibility, the "double pen-stroke" applies to the "final entry" on the life (i.e., to "*Dide and Burid in J. 17 feb 1854*"), the stroke's absence from the transcribed ledger foregrounds the issue of why the entry concerning Eunice's death should appear, out of all chronological sequence, so close to the record of her husband's death. We do not, of course, have any idea what the ledgers themselves look like, whether these two entries appear so juxtaposed there, or whether perhaps each person is allotted a whole page or merely space on a page. Perhaps wives shared pages with their husbands, although the lack of a legal status for slave marriage renders this option slightly less likely. In any case, Isaac's starkly achronological juxtaposition of these two entries no doubt reveals how closely Thucydus's death and Eunice's, more than two decades earlier, are related in his thinking about his grandfather's slaves.

The handwriting up to this point has been his father's. On Eunice's drowning, as a point of record, Isaac recognizes Buddy's hand; he notes the change in script as a gender change, recalling through Cass how Buddy has always taken the female role in the McCaslin household. We have no indication of when Buck recorded Eunice's drowning, but it seems likely that Buddy waits over six months to correct Buck's entry. Does the lengthy delay indicate some rift in the household perhaps over the nature of the death? If, as it appears, Buck, as supervisor of the commissary, customarily makes such entries, Buddy's intervention gains in significance. His entry is typically abbreviated. The absence of the question mark pitches the phrase between interrogation (of Buck) and assertion, where the latter might be accusatory and directed at Eunice ("*Drownd herself*" [our emphasis]). Such an emphasis would cast Buddy as his father's protector, one who cleanses the historical record, as it were.

June 21th 1833 Drownd herself

Buck, merely two days later, seems irate, perhaps defensive:

23 Jun 1833 Who in hell ever heard of a niger drownding him self (197)

Buddy responds, again abruptly but again after a lengthy wait of nearly two months, by simply reasserting what he either knows or believes:

Aug 13th 1833 Drownd herself (198)

We would stress that the twins' father does not die until 1837 and presumably has access to the commissary ledgers.

For Isaac, this and the following two entries comprise the heart of the ledger's chronicle, from which he extrapolates McCaslin family history, and his grandfather's guilt:

Tomasina called Tomy Daughter of Thucydus @ Eunice Born 1810 dide in Child bed June 1833 and Burd. Yr stars fell

Turl Son of Thucydus @ Eunice Tomy born Jun 1833 yr stars fell Fathers will (198–99)

The last two entries, recording Tomy's death in childbed and Turl's birth, are as problematic as the others. These events may carry astrological significance for their recorder, who appears to connect them to the meteor shower of November 12, 1833,[26] though we can only speculate as to what that significance might be. Nor do we know whether the entries were made in June, on or after November 12, or partially on both dates. Is the meteor shower merely an annalistic record, or is the writer magnifying earthly by heavenly incident? The position of the phrase "*Fathers will*" suggests that it was added on or after the rest of the entry—that is, on November 12 or later; either way, the juxtaposition at least implies that the writer makes a causal connection between "*will*" and the astral phenomenon. The star showers augur divine judgment, perhaps to Isaac (and almost certainly to the writer of the entry) as he looks to find evidence for his L.Q.C.'s sin. Perhaps Isaac believes that his grandfather, circa 1833, aware of the extent of his willful error and taking heaven's point, adds to his will a clause giving a thousand dollars to the newborn Turl. This, at any rate, is what Isaac believes later, when he describes the entry as a "pale sentence or paragraph scrawled in cringing fear of death by a weak and trembling hand as a last desperate sop flung backward at retribution" (223). The money, so read, operates as a sign of repentance, or at least a stay against judgment. But the text allows another reading, turning on the question of who wrote the two entries.

These linked entries, culminating in the cryptic "*Fathers will*," cast a complicating light over Isaac's whole purpose with regard to the ledgers. Following the entries, the text resumes, "and nothing more," an elocutionary punctuation whose form and purpose echo the phrase "and that was all" (200) which will terminate Isaac's vision of Eunice's drowning. But what follows "and nothing more" is a list of things that *are not* in the ledger, a piece of accounting such as *might* but *does not* fill the page: "no tedious recording filling this page of wages day by day and food and clothing charged . . ." (199). These non-entries may be inflected as a filibuster put in place after "*Fathers will*" to contradict the terminal punctuation of "nothing more" with a hypothetical something that serves to distract from the unstable referentiality of the entry's begged questions, whose "*father*" and which "*will*"? Isaac compounds the distraction by adding to the list of Turl's costs (which is not there) further ledger volumes by another hand (also not there) "which McCaslin kept," offered as evidence of what is omitted (Turl's obituary); McCaslin, it seems, "did not include obituaries" in his records. Our point is that Isaac at least appears to construct a false document from missing documents immediately after the phrase *"Fathers will"* and before returning to the phrase five lines later, where he construes the phrase to refer simply and singly to the legal document by which Carothers leaves $1000 to Turl—son of his incestuous union, Isaac thinks, with his half-black daughter. It is thus, according to Isaac's ethical accountancy, a payoff *"cheaper than saying My son to a nigger"* (199).

But if we leave out Isaac's record of what is not in the record, understanding his false document to be, like his parenthesis around Brownlee, an attempt at occlusion, we recover the following:

> *. . . Fathers will*
> and nothing more . . .: just *Fathers will* and he had seen that too: old Carothers' bold cramped hand far less legible than his sons' even and not much better in spelling, who while capitalizing almost every noun and verb, made no effort to punctuate or construct whatever, just as he made no effort either to explain or obfuscate the thousand-dollar legacy to the son of an unmarried slave-girl, to be paid only at the child's coming of age . . .
> (199)

The italicisation of the second *"Fathers will"* lodges the phrase in the ledgers in such a way as to ensure the splitting of its referent: *"Fathers will"* may refer either to a *second* handwritten ledger entry (required by "too") or to a legal document. To foreground the latter is to argue that Ike has seen L.Q.C.'s last will and testament, and that he indicates as much via the demonstrative pronoun "that." We should note that if Ike refers to a separate document, the italic and absent apostrophe are redundant signifiers—though their redundancy might be overcome were it assumed that Ike refers not to the will per se but to a reference to that document, entered elsewhere in the ledgers in L.Q.C.'s or Buck's or Buddy's hand (hands that would require italics and a missing apostrophe). In which case, "that" will refer to "hand" rather than will, and presumably to "old Carothers' bold cramped hand," as Ike has seen it here or elsewhere in the ledgers, since he goes on to detail its characteristics. Except that the situation of the split yet singular phrase *"Fathers will"* between "just" (meaning "only") and "too" (in "and he had seen that too")—a comparator which multiplies variables and sets the phrase within an absolute contradiction, requiring it to be one ("just") even as it is several ("too"). Let us first annotate the variables: "too," a comparator, plays on dualities, nominating at least three: two documents (ledgers and will); two out of three "hands" (Buck's, Buddy's, L.Q.C.'s); and two ledger entries. The combinatory options, though not legion, amount to obfuscation, which is surely the point. Having read two ledger entries concerning the birth of Eunice's child (Tomasina) and of Tomasina's child (Turl) in an unattributed hand or hands, and having conclusively punctuated his reading of those entries ("and nothing more"), Ike shuffles absent documents before repeat-ing the phrase "*Fathers will*" in a form which, to say the least, masks the hand that writes it. Since "too" introduces L.Q.C.'s calligraphy as a comparative item, its use may imply that the first instance of the focal phrase occurs in Buck or Buddy's script, but "just," in its emphasis on the abruptness of the phrasing, returns to "and nothing more," and so to the initial usage, characterized by a similarly abrupt ter-mination. Ike makes a tonal connection between the original ledger entry and his return to what may or may not be exactly that entry. The making of the connection at least allows that Ike repeats the first terse use in order to address exactly its terseness. If stars fell at the birth of Turl, and Turl's conception caused Eunice's death by water ("*Christmas Day 1832*" [197]), as recorded by Buck and Buddy on the previous page (198), "*Fathers will*" might be characterized as a minimal re-sponse, even in a ledger noted for its abbreviations. The problem remains one of attribution: to whom are we to attribute the terseness?

Much, here, may depend on a calligraphy that has been rendered exactly un-readable, although we cannot even be sure whether Ike's second use of "*Fathers will*" refers to a document, to handwriting, or to a recurrence in usage. What is cer-tain is that among the possible attributions, the inscriptions of the twins and their father are variously available, while the omission of Turl's paternity in the second entry may make L.Q.C. a primary suspect. In which case what Isaac recognizes as he reads, but would seem immediately to obfuscate, is that the two entries in question are made in his grandfather's "bold cramped hand," and that conse-quently "*Fathers will*" refers not to L.Q.C. but to, and only to, L.Q.C.'s father. Our claim is neither finally decidable nor conclusively deniable. Let us, for a moment, follow its logic: Isaac draws on his recollection of another and absent entry ("*fa-thers Will*" [197]), declaredly in his father's hand (196), in order (as in a palimpsest) to slide one entry under another. From the two available versions of the phrase (197, 199) he takes the wrong one, the one in Buck's hand, which best suits his case—a case that can be seen as resting on Isaac's heavily disguised abuse of the ledger's records. The implications of this reading are considerable.

To return to the original script, L.Q.C. seems, in his double and linked entries, to be meditating on what has been done to Tomy. We do not know exactly who did what to whom, though all reconstructions hinge upon the primary force of Tomasina's death in childbirth and Eunice's death by drowning. We should reiter-ate that if L.Q.C. is writing, "*Father*" in "*Fathers will*" the phrase without question refers to the Carolina patriarch; nonetheless "*will*" remains ambivalent, possibly re-ferring to a sum of money considered by L.Q.C. to be due by inheritance to the in-fant Turl, as a descendant of his father's sexual abuse of Fibby. L.Q.C. could, how-ever, mean that "*Fathers will*" *does not* provide for Turl and that he recognizes this as a shortcoming of both meanings of "will"; in this case, he may take it as his in-herited responsibility to remember Turl. By the same token, he may mean that "*Fa-*

thers will" does in fact remember and provide for Turl; in this case, *"Fathers will,"* as document and impulse, provides a model by which he, L.Q.C., can provide for his own miscegenated offspring, Turl. In any case, if *"will"* refers to the force of L.Q.C.'s father's willful acts in Carolina, it recasts the son as both repudiator of his father and as following his father's example. So read, *"will"* encrypts a variable in which L.Q.C. tacitly acknowledges that *he* fathered Turl on Tomasina. We point as evidence to L.Q.C.'s occlusive identification of Turl's parents: in effect, the entry comes preciously close to recording that Turl is the son of "Thucydus" and "Eunice's Tomy"—a double-headed monster created by an absent possessive and the contraction of *"Tomasina"* to *"Tomy."* Properly understood, of course, *"Thucydus@Eunice Tomy"* names Tomasina as the daughter of Thucydus and Eunice but *does not* name Turl's father. L.Q.C. here omits his own paternity, with reference to Turl, perhaps because he is troubled by his replication of his father's act, which act carried him, on a textual variant, out of Carolina in the first phase. We would add the proviso that this is a single option which renders *"will"* cavernous in its encryption, and that as an option it in no way makes a case for L.Q.C. as *also* the father of Tomasina by Eunice. Furthermore, these records do not *necessarily* convict L.Q.C. of miscegenation with Tomy. By invoking *"Fathers will"* at the birth of Thucydus's grandson Turl, L.Q.C. may simply be reminding himself that the McCaslin family owes Thucydus and his descendants whatever L.Q.C.'s father had left him in his will. On such grounds the whiteness of the black McCaslin could be understood to derive solely from L.Q.C.'s father, and not at all from L.Q.C. This reading lacks comprehensiveness in that it offers no traceable account of the absence of Turl's father's name. But the ledgers are chronicles, not registers.

Isaac will countenance none of the variables, since old Carothers is his villain of choice. The passage following the entry under discussion here continues:

> . . . to be paid only at the child's coming-of-age, bearing the consequence of the act of which there was still no definite incontrovertible proof that he acknowledged, not out of his own substance but penalising his sons with it, charging them a cash forfeit on the accident of their own paternity; not even a bribe for silence toward his own fame since his fame would suffer only after he was no longer present to defend it, flinging almost contemptuously, as he might a cast-off hat or pair of shoes, the thousand dollars which could have had no more reality to him under those conditions than it would have to the negro, the slave who would not even see it until he came of age, twenty-one years too late to begin to learn what money was . . . (199)

In this passage Isaac fools himself into thinking that these two ledger entries are in his father's, Buck's, handwriting so that he can believe that *"Fathers will"* refers to L.Q.C.'s will. Alternatively attributed to L.Q.C., the phrase, with its recollection of a culpable Carolina patriarch, entirely problematizes Isaac's account of Eunice's reasons for suicide. Only by occluding his grandfather's calligraphy can Isaac return to Christmas Day, 1832, and the frozen creek confident that he knows why Eunice died and why he (Isaac) must repudiate his grandfather. Within the variant reading, Isaac's moral authority rests on a crucial and critically missed act of deliberate misattribution (for one hand read and recognized he reads another). The misattribution, done in a flicker of false documents (199), allows him to assume an ethical high ground founded on a construction of L.Q.C. designed to mask, and in masking mime, and in miming retain, the features of his father's amities. To recognize that Isaac's case against his grandfather admits of a countercase, drawn from the same documentary evidence, is to appreciate that within the countercase Eunice's death, as the heart of Isaac's case against L.Q.C., must be open to for revision. Before revising we would stress again, concerning the linked triangulations from whose tensions our variants ultimately derive, that the ramifications of each undoes the literalness of the other, in an "abolition" that exposes deeper economic imperatives. Now we may read what we understand as that which has been forgotten in the ledgers; forgotten because Ike's constructive attention to those ledgers has occluded viable alternatives. Our act of unforgetting seeks to give to Eunice a different death.

From Eunice's drowning, of which *all* he knows is contained in his father's and uncle's four brief entries on the subject, and in those entries in his grandfather's arguably misrecognized hand (198), concerning related matters on "the next succeeding page" (198), Isaac begins to make his case against his grandfather. For reasons that should now be apparent, he accepts Buddy's flat statement that Eunice's death is a suicide rather than his father's hesitation over his twin's claim. Although Buddy does not explain his presumption of suicide, Isaac links the close chronological proximity of Eunice's death to the third month of Tomasina's pregnancy, and creates a narrative connection: Eunice commits suicide, Isaac believes, because she discovers that Tomasina is pregnant with L.Q.C.'s child. Isaac thus makes a further connection, positing that Tomasina is herself L.Q.C.'s child by Eunice, and that therefore his grandfather is guilty on two counts: first of miscegenation and then of miscegenated incest. L.Q.C.'s $1000 legacy to Turl, Tomasina's son, is, to Isaac, sufficient proof that his grandfather is Turl's father. From this sufficiency, Isaac supplies a romantic tragedy:

> the old man, old, within five years of his life's end, long a widower and, since his sons were not only bachelors but were approaching middleage, lonely in the house and doubtless even bored . . .; there was the girl, husbandless and young, only twenty-three when the child was born: perhaps he had sent for her at first out of loneliness . . . summoned her, bade her mother send her each morning to sweep the floors and make the beds and the mother acquiescing since that was probably already understood, already planned . . . (199–200)

In the next paragraph Isaac turns this May–December liaison into tragedy by identifying the young girl as the old man's daughter:

> The old frail pages seemed to turn of their own accord even while he thought *His own daughter. His own daughter. No No Not even him. . . .*(200)

Isaac works the story for all its worth: reiterating to prove by rhetorical extension that old Carothers violated not just his daughter, but innocence itself: he is *"Her first lover . . .* he thought. *Her first"* (200).

At this point Isaac seeks corroboration for his supposition by turning back to "that one [page or ledger entry] where the white man [L.Q.C. in 1807] (not even a widower then) . . . had gone all the way to New Orleans and bought one [a slave, Eunice]" (200). Joel Williamson suggests that Isaac may have some reason to be suspicious of L.Q.C.'s visit to New Orleans to buy a slave. New Orleans was well known for its trade in "fancy girls," which probably "reached its peak" in the 1850s. The price of "fancy girls" there "might be double that of a 'prime' male slave and might reach several thousand dollars."[27] Even if we assume that L.Q.C. visited New Orleans in 1807 in order to purchase a concubine, the bare factual phrasing of the ledgers does not actually say this, and Isaac's reconstruction of L.Q.C.'s motives and actions remains Isaac's reconstruction. To his imaginative recreation of L.Q.C.'s *"daughter,"* Isaac brings the historical record of her mother (Eunice). At the very moment when Isaac seeks corroborative evidence for his reconstruction, he does not turn back to the relevant ledger entry, the one which records Eunice's purchase and her death by drowning (197). Instead, Faulkner notes that "the pages seemed" to Isaac to "turn of their own accord" (200): that is, at the very moment Isaac constructs L.Q.C. as the villain of his piece, he attributes agency to the documentation. The ledger pages thus, for Isaac, constitute a coherent—and therefore true—history. We would simply point out, after Ricoeur, that "to make a plot is already to make the intelligible spring from the accidental, the universal from the singular, the necessary or probable from the episodic." Given that plots "do not see the universal [but] . . . make it spring forth," an adequate hermeneutics of suspicion should linger over the "episodic," "accidental," and "singular" (the elements of chronicular form), in order to trace "the play of discordance internal to concordance,"[28] as concordance mistakes "contingencies for absolutes and deviances for ends."[29] Isaac, exhibiting his limits as a reader of annals, and persuaded by the force of his idea about Eunice, visualizes the scene, a scene *nobody* witnessed: "[He] [s]eemed to see her actually walking into the icy creek on that Christmas day six months before her daughter's and her lover's . . . child was born, solitary, inflexible, griefless, ceremonial, in formal and succinct repudiation of grief and despair who had already had to repudiate belief and hope" (200). Let us say emphatically that the text—whether the ledgers Isaac reads or the prose account of his reading which we read—provides no reliable proof that L.Q.C. has had sex with *either* Eunice or Tomasina, Isaac's suppositions and accusations notwithstanding. The evidence of L.Q.C.'s links to Eunice is particularly patchy and insecure. The question we are left with, of course, is why Isaac reaches the conclusion he reaches. First, we note again that he has had several years of reading and pondering the ledger accounts; he comes to the ledgers when he is sixteen and knows "what he [is] going to find before he [finds] it" (198). He reconstructs the family— Roskus, Fibby, and Thucydus—that L.Q.C. brings with him from Carolina, then notes that his grandfather

> had travelled three hundred miles and better to New Orleans in a day when men travelled by horseback or steamboat, and bought the girl's mother [Eunice] as a wife for
>
> and that was all. The old frail pages seemed to turn of their own accord even while he thought . . . (200)

The paragraph breaks off sans full stop, to be completed by a separated and corrective termination, which will not allow Isaac to complete his unthinkable thought. Faulkner's free indirect discourse at this point mimes the process of Isaac's meditation concisely: he reaches an impasse, momentarily dwells within it, and finally emphatically contains it. As a spatialized iteration of closure, the phrase "and that was all" has about it something of the sprung rhythm of more than one option. Surely, he thinks he is about to say "wife for *Thucydus*," but stops at the moment of articulation with the realization that what he really means is more nearly "wife for *himself*," though clearly Eunice could not have lived with L.Q.C. as "wife" if only because he has just noted that L.Q.C. was "not even a widower" in 1807. We raise an alternate, though related possibility: if, as our variant of the ledger intimates, Thucydus is L.Q.C.'s father's child, over whom L.Q.C. went southwest into Mississippi, Isaac may have intended to say "wife for *his brother*." In any case Faulkner's visual representation of Isaac's omission marks Isaac's displacement of variables as a possible simplification: arguably, Faulkner deploys a textual space, readable as a paragraph break, though without supporting punctuation, to indicate a hiatus whose hesitation is subsequently repaired via the conceit of the self-turning pages—a conceit which allows Ike to overwrite any options that he might glimpse within his own hesitation.

Isaac accepts Eunice's death as suicide, following Buddy. But how does Buddy know? At the risk of literalism, but prompted by Ike's own imaginative reconstruction, let us consider "the play of discordance internal to [the] concordance" within Ike's version of the scene. Presumably, someone simply found Eunice's body in the creek. If that person, whether Buddy or anyone else, actually saw her, as Isaac envisions it, walking into the icy December waters, he or they would surely have prevented her, if for no other reason than that of her value as property. Since the time of year precludes swimming, accidental death or murder are at least, in the absence of witnesses, as likely as suicide. What follows results from our pushing Ike's denotative habits to different, but equally logical, ends—logical, that is, if we suspend the received order of reference as it devolves from Ike's preference for L.Q.C.'s guilt. To go with "murder" is to recover a parallel example in "The Fire and the Hearth." Zack deprives Lucas of a wife and a son by stealing Molly's maternal labor for his own newborn child; it is unlikely that Zack sleeps with Molly, though Lucas may at times believe that he does so. Lucas prepares to take his outrage out on Zack and on himself with razor and gun. Only a misfire prevents him from murdering over nominal and miscegenous adultery. Ike, Roskus, Eunice, and L.Q.C. exist in a related triangle. By structural analogy, then, it is possible to imagine that the helpless Roskus vents *his* rage on Eunice, another victim of the slave system—even as in "That Evening Sun" Nancy believes her husband Jesus waits to punish *her* for her pregnancy by another man, perhaps a white man. Buddy struggles to ameliorate the slave system with the contemporary means available to him. Whether or not he suspects his father's possible use of Eunice, he is unlikely to discover an accident or uncover a murder where suicide is an option. We should remember that close to two months separate his first ledger entry on the death from its reiteration in response to Buck's disbelief: the long delay, like the entries themselves ("identical" to the point of seeming produced by a "rubber stamp" [198]), is finally unreadable. Nonetheless, the cryptic manner of the twins' "handwriting" (194), from which they and their slaves "took substance and even a sort of shadowy life" (196), proves in its creation of "substance" and "shadow" from script the force of de Man's observation that flawed reference is "suspiciously text productive."[30]

But given that suicide is available as a logical assumption, does it follow that she committed suicide in despair over her lover's violation of their daughter's virginity? Is it not equally possible that she killed herself in despair: as a slave who may also have been her master's concubine, perhaps she could no longer tolerate the condition of her life.[31] The novel offers two exemplary and parallel white misunderstandings of black grief in response to violent death. In "Pantaloon in Black," the deputy whose account of Rider's apprehension and death closes that story manifestly struggles to understand what he equally and manifestly gets wrong—the substance of Rider's grief.[32] In "Go Down, Moses," Gavin Stevens, confronted with Molly Beauchamp's exacting and repeated observation that her nephew, Butch Beauchamp, was "sold . . . in Egypt" by Roth Edmonds (271, 278, 279), can only panic, before subsuming his initial reaction in the misguided and socially self-serving observation that Molly "*doesn't care how he died. She just wanted him home . . .*" (281). Molly not only cares, she *knows* how Butch died. She signifies on the book of Genesis (chapters 37 and 42), to accuse Roth of expelling Butch—a modern Benjamin—into captivity and execution, for the petty crime of commissary theft.

Isaac's recreation of Eunice's death by drowning should perhaps be set alongside Stevens's failure to take Molly's point about "Benjamin," despite his being an amateur translator of the Old Testament (271). Each black death is articulated in terms that best serve the interests of the white articulator. It suits the troubled conscience of the deputy in "Pantaloon," who has played a legal part in the extralegal killing of a man taken from civic custody, to try to cast that man as less than "human" (116) and as a beast (117). It suits Gavin Stevens, a Jefferson lawyer and county attorney, who therefore represents Jefferson's "official" voice, to remember Butch as a product of "bad" "seed" (272), rather than as one of many young migrant males for whom, in times of forced tenant migration, the city and crime in the city were among the few available economic options.[33] Similarly, it suits him to consider an old and illiterate black woman incapable of turning her biblical tradition into a tormented accusation of the landowning class, that class whose interest Gavin Stevens, as a public servant, in large part serves.

Similarly, it may well suit Isaac to bear witness to the unwitnessed drowning of Eunice as a "*suicide*" for which his grandfather is responsible:

> [H]e seemed to see her actually walking into the icy creek on that Christmas day six months before her daughter's and her lover's (*Her first lover's* he thought. *Her first*) child was born, solitary, inflexible, griefless, ceremonial, in formal and succinct repudiation of grief and despair who had already had to repudiate belief and hope
>
> that was all. He would never need to look at the ledgers again nor did he . . . (200)

Given how little we actually know, what Isaac "actually" and oxymoronically "seemed" to see should strain credibility.

To summarize: purchased in New Orleans in 1807, and married (perhaps already pregnant) to Thucydus in 1809 (she gives birth to Tomasina in 1810, though the entry specifies no month, for either marriage or birth), Eunice may or may not have been L.Q.C.'s concubine. Planters purchased female slaves of "breedable" age to renew their labor force. L.Q.C.'s sanctioning of the Thucydus/Eunice "marriage" may indeed have been a convenience within which to hide his own miscegenated daughter, but equally it may have been his attempt to give some semblance of social form to persons who within the peculiar institution were held to be "socially dead"—that is, as having no legal right to familial connection.[34] We should remember that the ledgers allow a reading in which Thucydus is L.Q.C.'s half-brother, one to whom L.Q.C. may feel that muted family acknowledgment is due. If L.Q.C.'s father had an unacknowledged "shadow family" (Thucydus from Fibby) over which L.Q.C. quit Carolina for Mississippi, the notion that L.Q.C. should travel all the way from Jefferson to New Orleans in order to purchase a wife for a valued half-brother is at least viable.

Isaac begs to differ, not least because in Eunice he finds himself. That Eunice happens to die on Christmas Day is grist to the creative mill of a repudiator who self-consciously adopts Christ's role as a celibate and propertyless carpenter (229). In effect, Isaac gives imaginative birth to Eunice-as-suicide so that she can stand in iconic and prefigurative relation to his own social suicide (more of this later). Not everything fits; Isaac is hardly "succinct" or "griefless." But, even so, the text raises doubts about critical assumptions that Isaac knows what he is talking about when he claims insight into Eunice's acts or motives.

With Eunice in place as she who suicidally repudiates L.Q.C.'s sustained abuse of the body of slaves, Isaac has grounds for his own parallel repudiation of McCaslin land, projected through the Eunice-Tomasina-L.Q.C. triangle as a serially raped and abused inheritance. For a second time on a single page of text, Faulkner uses "that was all" to punctuate Isaac's thought, abruptly and without punctuation. The phrase is a full stop. As in the first instance, the stoppage is followed by an immediate appeal to "the yellowed pages," previously perceived as "old frail pages"; where the earlier pages "turn of their own accord," here they "fad[e]" in "implacable succession" (200). Everything about our reading of the ledgers thus far argues that there is almost nothing automatic, inexorable, or sequential about the "succession" of their pages. Isaac disagrees: in 1883, "looking down at the yellowed pages spread beneath the yellow glow of the lantern," "chill" in the "midnight room (200), he finds his history and establishes, through his imaginary sighting of Eunice's death, that causality which will provide him with his own cause. The historian, traditionally, is he or she who can turn one thing (and its documents) after another thing (and its documents) into one thing *because* of another. The emergence of causation perhaps necessarily requires that some aspects of the documents recede from attention. Nonetheless, the suasion of that causality must surely depend on an available and traced relation to the documented evidence: yet Isaac's "actual" "sighting" of Eunice is based on his explicit refusal of "citation"; we are told that he would "never need to look at the ledgers again," and that he did not do so. Faulkner's attention to the historian's exact relation to his documents, at this crucial point, invites the reader to consider the extent to which Isaac fixes his evidence. We can have little confidence in the assurance that he has so internalized the ledgers that they are "as much a part of his consciousness . . . as the fact of his own nativity" (200). His own occlusion of his father's problematic sexuality—as "Was" affirms—would suggest that Isaac knows and wants to know as little as possible about his own "nativity."

But to return to the received reasons for Eunice's death. Much of the evidence for L.Q.C.'s miscegenation lies outside the ledgers in family lore, but the reading of that lore as implying a double and incestuous miscegenation is, again, exclusively Isaac's. In other words, and in terms of the evidence of the novel, family lore has it *only* that L.Q.C. fathers Turl from Tomasina. Isaac alone will have it that he also fathered Tomasina from Eunice. In "Was," Hubert Beauchamp insists that "he wouldn't have that damn white half-McCaslin [Turl] on his place even as a free gift"

(7): "half-McCaslin" implies a white father and no more. In "The Fire and the Hearth," Lucas Beauchamp mentions his "white half-brothers" (82) and here in part 4 of "The Bear," Isaac notes that Lucas has outlived Buck and Buddy, his "white half-brothers" (199). Family lore is not to be discounted, but if we are to take it seriously, we must also note that as Lucas prepares himself to die in his confrontation with Zack Edmonds over his wife Molly, he thinks, "All I got to give up is McCaslin blood that rightfully aint even mine or at least aint worth much since old Carothers never seemed to miss much what he give to Tomey that night that made my father" (44).

Lucas makes no mention of incest as he faces Zack and articulates his relation to the McCaslin/Edmonds line: the phrasing of his admission argues strongly for a sexual relationship between L.Q.C. and Tomasina, though not at all for one between L.Q.C. and Eunice. In any case, clear above all else is that L.Q.C.'s *utter* wickedness lies largely within Isaac's narrative gift—one that potentially allows him to displace onto his grandfather his father's acts of homosexual incest and miscegenation. Isaac's quarrel, then, is not exclusively with his grandfather (in fact he does not even mention his grandfather's depredations to Cass as they argue throughout part 4), but with his father, or, more properly, with a certain notion of masculinity, circa 1888, as that moment reflects and refracts a childhood and young adulthood (1867–88) spanning radical Reconstruction and Redemption. Ike's first two decades contain acute transformations in the mastery of plantation masters, as that mastery realized itself through changing patterns of authority over the more and less bound body of African American labor. If Ike is understood to refuse not simply his family property, nor planter property more generally, but the interethnic intimacies through which those properties were made, it becomes possible to see why, in a full semantics of his struggle to articulate a decision, he needs both a culpably heterosexual grandfather and a deniably homosexual father: each, in relation to the other, allows him to explore the polarities of a changing labor circumstance. His representation of L.Q.C. casts the antebellum labor lord as potent yet criminal in his potency; while his "will-to-see" his father's desire for a bound man recovers from abjection alternative modes of authority, verging on necessary love for the abjected (necessary in as much as the master's substance is, quite literally, the work of abjected hands).[35]

At the outset of this chapter we spoke loosely of the "repression" of the Brownlee materials; the manner of that repression now needs elucidation. "Repression" may not be the right term, since the Brownlee page is set to one side rather than rendered unreadable. What lies latent in its disclosure is not a "primal scene" or an early event misremembered through the screen of a later event because its materials are too shocking for conscious thought.[36] Isaac may not want to read about the "oral intercourse" of his father and uncle or to consider a love triangle terminated in a stall of the family barn, but he is not Wolf Man: nothing in the text indicates that he has seen the scenes of seduction which he would rather not face in reading the ledgers that may disclose them. Of course, the ledger entries are cryptic, after the manner of a chronicle or any drastically occasional jotting, and consequently their meaning has to be extracted hesitantly from abbreviation and aporia, and is therefore necessarily provisional. But the Brownlee entries are not encrypted by the force of a traumatic witnessing which works through them to deny witness. We do not take the language of the ledgers, though littered with errata, as the stuff of slip and error, best read through the psychoanalytic. Let us be very clear: bestiality in the barn does not here constitute a first event crucial to reference and yet unavailable to the act of reference. The phrase *"Wrong stall"* (196) does not enact a stand-off between the event and its representation. The erratic signs on the Brownlee page are not for Isaac under a contradictory pressure to reveal what they cannot finally reveal, an unavoidable first event, "which cannot be assimilated into the continuity of [Isaac's] psychic life."[37] This is not to say that they are unmarked by the work of concealment, but rather that their lack of transparency is lodged somewhere between the understandable evasions of the original scriptors and the equally understandable reluctance of their son and nephew to unlock the family closet.[38]

Yet at sixteen, by night, and by means of a secretly borrowed key, he takes down the ledgers that he has read before and, knowing what he will find (198), opens the book to the Brownlee page. The contents must, therefore, fascinate him, even though he simply rereads the page, virtually without comment, before passing to "the specific tragedy" (196) of Eunice, her daughter, and his grandfather. The two triangulated stories share affinities which allow the pattern of Isaac's reading to effect a structural occlusion: Buck, Buddy, and Brownlee enact in their permutations both incest and miscegenation; L.Q.C., Eunice, and Tomasina enact in Isaac's permutation of them a tighter miscegenous incest. In effect, the first page under Isaac's hand is dispossessed or overwritten by the later pages. Isaac cannot complete his act of concealment since he discloses that act by leaving the Brownlee page prominently in place as a prefatory note to his historical reconstruction of his grandfather's wickedness. Had the two stories been manifestly different, the second would not have matched and masked the first. Isaac's textual stratagem would be entirely pointless if the materials he sought to disguise did not possess for him an illicit and instigating force.

How, then, may the Brownlee page exert influence over our understanding of the ledgers, and why are its implications so troubling?[39] A recent strand of Faulkner scholarship based in the work, among others, of Judith Butler and Eve Kosofsky Sedgwick, would nominate "homosexual panic":[40] set among such readings, Isaac confronts Brownlee as a crisis in his own sexual definition. Once masculinity is thought of not as a given but as "a regulatory practice that produces the bodies it governs,"[41] or as a materialization of the effects of power, biology shifts toward performance. Recast, the gendered body becomes a social inscription, iterated and reiterated by way of the subject's acts of identification, and by that subject's disavowal of the other identifications. Butler's subject is therefore only as stable as the normative practices into which it is born, and through which it grows. Whatever the state of those practices, Butler makes the case that sexual identity retains the marks of that from which it "disidentifies."[42] To put her argument aphoristically: since bodies that matter do so by refusing to be other bodies, which are declared not to matter, those normative bodies remain haunted by the acts of refusal which tie them to what they exclude. She writes:

> This exclusionary matrix by which subjects are formed thus requires the simultaneous production of a domain of abject beings, those who are not yet "subjects," but who form the constitutive outside to the domain of the subject. The abject designates here precisely those "unlivable" and "uninhabitable" zones of social life which are nevertheless densely populated by those who do not enjoy the status of the subject, but whose living under the sign of the "unlivable" is required to circumscribe the domain of the subject.[43]

We prefer Butler's "exclusionary matrix" to Susan Donaldson's more user-friendly claim that "the whole of [Faulkner's] career is marked by his attraction to the blurring of sexual boundaries and by his horrified response to that possibility,"[44] because Butler's phrasing allows that "panic" involves a "horrified response" to "unlivable" forms and barely "uninhabitable zones." Isaac turns back to Brownlee, as though to a prefatory document incompletely refused, because from the Brownlee entries he might recover the very limits of the existing order within which he lives, and of the categories through which he thinks about that life. We would stress that, aged sixteen, alone, at night, furtively, in the commissary, he seeks evidence for a future repudiation, aged twenty-one, of his inheritance. He wants to effect a revolution, and will eventually do it (if only for himself) through the recovery of L.Q.C.'s founding and insufferable act of miscegenous incest. Yet on the Brownlee ledger pages, if released from the lock of sexual panic, he faces evidence of his father's and his uncle's local and revolutionary practices. Those practices, as they emerge from our variant reading, lack radicalism at the sexual level: Buck and Buddy appear harmlessly to replicate a heterosexual frontier marriage, into which Brownlee enters as adulterer. But the triangular intimacies carry an alternative politics in terms of the practices of slavery; an alternative available to Ike through the memory of his father's house. Indeed what frees him, momentarily and partially, from panic and its attendant attempt to exclude the Brownlee materials from relevance, is a recollection of the house his father and uncle create as an apt home for Percival Brownlee.

Just prior to commentary on the calligraphy and extent of the Brownlee page (195), Faulkner has Isaac recall the McCaslin plantation house, after L.Q.C.'s death (1837) and prior to his parents' marriage (probably in 1865 or 1866). The dates are important insofar as they establish this house as the house where Brownlee would have lived, but in which Isaac never truly lived, although he was born in a later man-ifestation of it. On L.Q.C.'s death the twins quit the incomplete "edifice" of their family home for a one-roomed cabin built primarily by their own labor. They rede-ploy the great house as a "domicile" for the McCaslin slaves. The arrangement pre-sumably runs from 1837 until Sophonsiba marries Buck; at which point Isaac's mother takes back the house, spending her Beauchamp dowry on its completion and furbishment. Isaac is born into a much changed house, but also into the his-tory of those changes. We will quote at length to establish his implied immersion in the lore of his birthplace—a place traceably haunted, for this child, by rumors of once-lived but not "unliveable" forms of life, and containing rooms where house-servants can only have whispered of abjected acts in "zones" beyond current "dominion":

> each sundown the brother who superintended the farming would parade the negroes as a first sergeant dismisses a company, and herd them willynilly, man woman and child, with-out question protest or recourse, into the tremendous abortive edifice scarcely yet out of embryo, as if even old Carothers McCaslin had paused aghast at the concrete indication of his own vanity's boundless conceiving: he would call his mental roll and herd them in and with a hand-wrought nail as long as a flenching-knife and suspended from a short deer-hide thong attached to the door-jamb for that purpose, he would nail to the door of that house which lacked half its windows and had no hinged back door at all, so that presently and for fifty years afterward, when the boy himself was big enough to hear and remember it, there was in the land a sort of folk-tale: of the countryside all night long full of skulking McCaslin slaves dodging the moonlit roads and the Patrol-riders to visit other plantations, and of the unspoken gentlemen's agreement between the two white men and the two dozen black ones that, after the white man had counted them and driven the home-made nail into the front door at sundown, neither of the white men would go around behind the house and look at the back door, provided that all the negroes were behind the front one when the brother who drove it drew out the nail again at daylight. (193–94)

Buck and Buddy know in 1837 what Ab Snopes knew during the 1890s, that a plantation house is "nigger sweat" with columns,[45] but they know it from the per-spective of the owners. Hence their decision not to live in their own house and, fur-ther, to display its ruin by inverting its purposes: they make their great house into the quarters. Faulkner's choice of the verb "to domicile" rather than "to quarter" (193) exactly catches the brothers' intent and its limits. The ledgers record that they freed Roskus, Fibby, and Thucydus, an act indicating their aim to manage free rather than bound labor, yet during the 1830s in the frontier South, manumission was difficult: the ledgers note that none of the freed were forced to leave. The twins' emancipations grow gestural, and the quarters remain a quarters, though recast as upmarket "domicile[s]." We should not, however, dismiss Buck's and Buddy's liberatory performances, since they are sustained, subversive, and founded on traced economic choices. They put the slave where the master should be, mastering their labor forces in a parody of bondage, whose expression "willy-nilly" mocks the inescapable fact that slavery in the 1830s and the 1840s was an embattled institution, held in place by compulsory pass systems, by complex patterns of surveillance, and by "the obligatory involvement of all white members of the community in the implementation of the laws."[46] One historian comments that the plantocracy administered "a strung-out society," strung-out because the blacks "were in the south in such number and manner as they were," and that manner "was recurrently rebellious."[47] It can hardly have helped the equipoise of planters that two of their members were by day mocking procedures for policing, and by night conniving at the release of twenty-four "skulking slaves" to play runaway with the Patrollers. The McCaslin slaves are, at the very least, emancipated on a nightly pass, and in some cases by name and fully. Our point is that the twins do the best they can, producing a labor force that though "not free," is, in the conventional sense, "not slave" either.[48] Their version of the peculiar institution is truly peculiar. Except, that is, for Brownlee, who is an exception because Buck buys him, considers selling him, and only eventually frees him.

How, then, can we speak of a house that Faulkner characterized as misruled as being apt to Brownlee? The key to Brownlee's affinity to the place, and to the place as prefatory to Brownlee, is the nail, read in the fullness of its innuendo. But before we draw that singular nail, let us briefly reprise what the ledgers establish about Brownlee. He is a homosexual. He is useless as labor, either in house or field. His sexuality compounds his uselessness in that he cannot serve in the reproduction of labor. The goods he yields involve neither work no product. His body, it would seem, is exclusively a locus of desire, increasingly accounted for in terms of price. He eventually achieves autonomy as a carrier of sexual labor power in his own body—that is, without dependency on property or person. On all these counts and because he is male, Brownlee is anomalous within the system of bound labor.

Unfit for slavery, he fits in a house where slave practices are subject to mirth and reversal. Indeed, the McCaslin plantation house would be the house that Brownlee built, were Brownlee capable of labor. It is designed for his body. The key "handwrought" to Buck's hand, lengthy and on display at the front, all but announces penile purpose, particularly since its function is to seal a front entrance while opening one at the back. L.Q.C. raised the house as an "embryo" "tremendously-conceived" (194) to express his "boundless conceiving": the rhetoric is vaginal, but if old Carothers's conception is to reach full term its inheritors must have sons and its slaves must breed, and neither looks likely in a house whose back door is so much used. Mere mention of the "unhinged" portal "fifty years afterward" is enough to give the young Isaac an editorially problematic hard-on. The text in the Library of America edition (1994) reads, "when the boy himself was big enough to hear and remember it," although the typescript setting copy and the 1990 Vintage edition both read, "when the boy himself was big to hear and remember": "enough" is just enough of a fig-leaf to cover Isaac's excitement at the "folk-tale[s]" that circulate about what went on around the back of the McCaslin "barn-like edifice" (193). Buck and Buddy run a gay house, in the old and perhaps the newer senses of that term, maybe a bawdy house, certainly a house that is the focus of sustained anal innuendo.

The innuendo is problematic, not in and of itself, but in that its focus and key is Brownlee, without whose page the plantation might pass as unruly, but not as anally so. Isaac will do his best to suppress the Brownlee entries. So how are we to take his responsiveness to the back-door anecdotes? Faulkner describes the house in free indirect discourse, that is, in a voice whose double orientation allows authorial speech and the consciousness of a character to coexist: they may "speak at the same time" from within single terms or phrases, producing split references whose meanings interfere with one another to yield oscillation within the word between the viewpoints of author and character. So, for example: Faulkner likens the elaborately phallic nail to a "flenching-knife," a comparison which renders the knife two-edged: a "flenching," or "flensing," knife was the instrument used to strip blubber from whales; Faulkner here draws on *Moby-Dick*,[49] whose very title is grist to innuendo (of author and character). The reference to an implement for flaying may, however, be taken as rebarbative, or as threatening to those who indulge in anal thoughts or desire. Here, Isaac's inflection could be considered dominant, though the "deer-hide thong" presages how the boy may sublate his illicit desire into the acceptable homosocial context of the hunting camp.

The text concerning the McCaslin house between 1837 and 1867 is unstable because two-faced in that it serves two consciousness. Identifying the operative consciousness at any point—author or character—is difficult and at times too close to call. As a result the source of the innuendo remains unresolved. We appreciate it but do not know to whom it should be attributed. The distinction matters because the degree to which Isaac responds to the tall-tales is the degree to which he receives his father's possible desires as something other than that which must be disavowed. The higher his degree of responsiveness, the more the nail unlocks; where the nail may be understood as the key to Isaac's capacity to realize the fullness of Brownlee's subversions—subversions which attach to the nexus of Isaac's sexuality and life, once the prohibition on that desire and its social implications is undone. We would note that the back door tales refer to the rear entrance of the house in which Isaac was raised: as "folk-tale[s] . . . in the land" they may be thought of as African American stories passed between field worker and house servant. Arguably, the boy Isaac overhears them from talkers who appreciate that they are letting the future master of the house listen-in on home-truths, dense with lives once lived and now unlivable. In Butler's terms, the tale-tellers excite the boy with news from an "uninhabitable zone," briefly repopulated with "abject[ed]" beings who may yet be admitted to social life, and who once lived in the rooms where he now lives.

The implications of Brownlee and of Buck and Buddy's involvement with him are dense. His story at least implicitly persists within the black speech community. As we read it, Isaac hears the tales and reads the relevant ledger page, but cannot face what he encounters. He obfuscates the radical potential of what through inference he might hear and see, encrypting and secreting his father's story within an altogether more tellable fiction about his grandfather. Incestuous miscegenation between a white man and two black women allows him a clear villain and a family narrative. Incestuous miscegenation involving white brothers and a black male strains the extant genealogical limits of the family plot, and potentially draws from hiding intimations of alternative ways of living within an abusive system. Since at age sixteen Isaac wants to quit that system, and looks to find justification for doing so, he leaves hidden materials that might have required him to read, think, and live in different ways.

Yet both his name and the novel's title may be heard to whisper of that which remains hidden. We have no wish to repeat the argument of the last three chapters: instead, and as a final instance of the contradiction from which Faulkner's text takes its instabilities, we invite a reconsideration of Isaac's subriet, "Uncle"—awarded with the novel's first sentence, "uncle to half a country and father to no one" (5). "Uncle," as an ethnic term, refers dismissively to a barely noticed African American male of advancing years.[50] "Uncle" also carries a gay inflection: used throughout the nineteenth century as a "common term [for] non conforming and non reproductive sexualit[y]," the avunculate may nominate same-sex preference.[51] Both usages fit. Each compounds its bearer's displaced dedication to lost ethnic and sexual possibilities, amounting to a new order, nascent in the textual and social inclusion of what has been excluded—the body of African American labor, recovered not as work but as amity. Such loving recovery also lies latent in the novel's title. *Go Down, Moses* famously cites the sung injunction that Moses instruct Pharaoh to free the Hebrew people from "Egypt's land." Yet the phrase "to go down" had currency in America, by 1910, as an idiomatic expression for oral genital contact.[52]

Before proceeding, a reminder: in 1939, Faulkner called his Hollywood novel, *If I Forget Thee, Jerusalem*. The titular phrase from verse 5, Psalm 137, addresses the Babylonian captivity. Verse 5 reads in full, "If I forget thee, Oh Jerusalem, let my right hand forget her cunning." The writer, Harry Wilbourne, imprisoned for killing his wife in a botched abortion, ensures that he will not forget her: he masturbates using his memory of her body as a stimulant. Faulkner render's Harry's "right hand . . . cunning" by confusing its onanistic and "wri[gh]terly" motions with the clashing of "wild palms" outside his cell. Faulkner, it would seem, has used a biblical phrase in order barely to occlude sexual innuendo in an earlier, albeit discarded, title.[53]

Go Down, Moses, as title and novel, read for its secondary gestures, yields floating *phalloi* emerging into hiding as both black and desirable. Yet the phalloi are themselves fetishes: open to disavowal, they stand in the place of a lost thing. To desire to "go down on" Rider's tumescence or to see Brownlee in his master's arms is to long for the lost labor for which such whispers stand, and to glimpse a consolatory fiction of amity between male bodies, black and white, even as black bodies are seen to depart from their place.[54]

Find the Jew: Modernity,

Seriality, and Armaments in *A Fable*

I

FAULKNER published *A Fable* in 1954. He wrote it over the ten years between 1943 and 1954, a period during which issues of "hot," "cold," and "total" war came to preoccupy American life. A brief list may serve to make the point that *A Fable*, though set during a single week of the Great War, addresses militarization in a more extensive sense. The eleven years of the novel's writing include: the last years of World War II (1943–45); the explosion of the first atomic bomb (August 1945); the Red Scare, reaching into the State Department and toward the Pentagon (1947–mid-1950s); the testing of the first hydrogen bomb (1952) by the United States, whose fallout (as feared) gave the Soviets clues on how to design an equivalent; the Korean War (1950–53), with its shifting of the theater of risk from Europe to Asia, and the onset of the Cold War (hard to date, but pervasive in the period), which split the globe into progressively militarized "alternative ways of life" (the phrase is Truman's).[1] The list could be extended, but with luck its point is made: that Faulkner's World War I allegory engages with the military even as militarization, in a plethora of guises—as "military keynesianism," the "military-industrial complex," "internal preparedness"—moves to the center of America's political and cultural economy. The historian Michael Sherry defines "militarization" as "the process by which war and national security become consuming anxieties and provide the memories, models and metaphors that shape broad areas of national life."[2]

A Fable turns on a "mutiny." Late in May 1918, on a Tuesday, at the instigation of one man, who converted twelve, who influenced a squad, a division of French foot soldiers disobey an order to attack. Their refusal initiates a ripple effect, from squad to battalion to division to regiment, and so on, along *both* lines of trenches, so that the "whole front stopped" and "by sundown," for all intents and purposes, "there was no more gunfire in France."[3] The hiatus in war is overcome by a temporary alliance between the supreme commanders, Allied and German (of which more later). Faulkner does not show the mutiny, and its extension along "that thousand kilometers of regimental fronts between the Alps and the Channel" (296); rather he concentrates on events in Chaulnesmont, and on a military decision over whether or not to execute by firing squad three thousand mutineers; central to that decision are the corporal and his twelve associates. Since A Fable is set around Passion Week and the Corporal is a Jew, intimations of Christ's crucifixion attend events. Allegorical signs proliferate to a degree that renders inventory, for its own sake, redundant.[4] An abbreviated curriculum vitae for the Corporal should serve to indicate the systematic nature of Faulkner's allegorical intent: conceived in quasi-immaculate manner (931); born on "the eve before Christmas" in a "cow-byre" (931); mothered by a Marya; raised a peasant; preceded by a John the Baptist (the runner); granted twelve followers (the squad); set between thieves, crowned with barbed wire, and crucified by firing squad (1023)—he is buried, only, after the requisite three days, to rise on a shell blast (1037), prior to ascending into national immortality as the unknown soldier, resting beneath the *Arc de Triomphe* (1069).

Much does not fit and more is omitted, but Faulkner's decision to employ the Gospels as a template ensures that the corporal will always mean more than he first meant. Given that Faulkner planned that A Fable's jacket "would show nothing but a cross,"[5] and that crosses punctuate the text (fifty-two in all), one thing that the corporal must mean is that he is—he who will be "crucified, dead and buried." Allegorically, the figure to whom armies incline and civilians move en masse is a death's-head, albeit one of some ambivalence. Brought before a British colonel, an American captain and a French major (920), the corporal is variously identified as Boggan (English), dead at Mons; Brzonyi (American), buried in the mid-Atlantic; and anonymous (French), resurrected to extract "miracles" of generosity from his regiment at the time of the first battle of the Marne. The Corporal answers to no name, but the sequential logic of the official accounts links him variously to the spectral bowmen of Mons (922), to the "archangels on the Aisne" (925), and to a resurrected corpse, with Christ-like habits. I would suggest that the Corporal *is* a corporal rather than a private or a sergeant because he is "corporeal," which in the context of A Fable means both marked for death and the incarnate manifestation of the Trinity.[6] The crowd in Chaulnesmont recognize the first option; their uncertainty resides in how many will die (one, thirteen, or three thousand).

As the masses, seen from above, gather to witness death, they encounter a line of cavalry "drawn up across the mouth of the wide main boulevard"(670):

> For another instant, the cavalry held. And even then, it did not break. It just began to move in retrograde while still facing forward, as though it had been picked up bodily—the white-rolled eyes of the short-held horses, the high small faces of the riders gaped with puny shouting beneath the raised sabres, all moving backward like martial effigies out of a gutted palace or mansion or museum being swept along on the flood which had obliterated to instantaneous rubble the stone crypts of their glorious privacy. (671)

In moving the cavalry line back, the crowd moves a mounted unit *and* the institutions that sustain it. Faulkner's simile throws a wide hermeneutic curve, clamping a raised saber onto an equine statue before locating that "effigy" in the grounds of the properties—a palace and a mansion—that it decorates and protects. Nor is the recuperative fracturing complete, since the sword arm, optioned as a museum piece or crypt accoutrement, indicates that a militarized state will necessarily be concerned to manage its dead (whether in gallery or cemetery), to the greater glory of its palaces—palaces like the *Hôtel de Ville*, policed by the cavalry in question. Faulkner raises arms, petrifies and fragments those arms into dissonant and quasi-allegorical signifiers, each converging on a tacit, but transcendent, signified, the armed state.[7] For an "instant," the crowd carries official history, in the form of the cavalry, like so many artifacts, plundered from palace, mansion, tomb, and museum, in triumph before it. But "the mounted officer free[s] himself," "the human river" parts, and although the cavalry is "flung aside," no death is recorded and no property is damaged, which raises crucial questions about the purposes, practices, and nature of the crowd in Chaulnesmont. Since, as Peter Nicolaisen has argued, *A Fable* is about "collective experience,"[8] how and why the crowd moves matters.

II

Synonyms for "flood" abound: the crowd "pour[s]" and "flow[s]" in various forms as "trickle," "stream," "wave," and "lake," all within the first two pages. The verbs "to void" and "to disgorge," allied to an emphasis on "mass," "mouth," and "congestion," add bodily fluids to the aquatic. Confronted with the crowd's oceanic ostentation ("sea" [682]), Richard Gray usefully reaches for Klaus Theweleit's account of the pathologies of the Freikorps—soldiers who successfully fought against the German working class in the years immediately after World War I.[9] These men, viewing the revolutionary mass as a red engulfing tide, feminized the collective body of the working class, translating it into "that which dissolves" those who stand against it: dissolution might take the form of drowning or vaginal absorption. The Freikorp member offered as a counternarrative rigidification: he became impermeable, defending himself "with a kind of sustained erection of his whole body, of whole cities, of whole troop units."[10] An iconography of "rock," "tower," "dryness," and "immobility" secures his "erection." *A Fable*, to a degree, fits. From the cavalry's "petrification" to the old general's inflexibility, Faulkner casts the army as a largely impregnable male body. Where its agents stand, "the human river" parts. My problem is that the crowd, though feminized, is not in any simple way the antagonist or antithesis of the military (stream to its citadel; female to its male). The mass "picks up" and "casts aside" the cavalry, it does not "break" it; it parts before motorcycle couriers; it watches the three allied commanders arrive; it stops at military perimeters (the steps to the palace; the wire of the prison camp). Indeed, Faulkner works to collapse the opposition between citizen and combatant as it applies to the regiment that has mutinied. We are told in the second paragraph that not only "the original regiment" but "its subsequent replacements" were drawn from the district of Chaulnesmont. The crowd is there-fore made up of "veterans," future conscripts, and the "parents" and "kin" of the regiment: "not only the actual old parents and kin of the doomed men, but fathers and mothers and sisters and wives and sweethearts whose sons and brothers and husbands and fathers and lovers might have been among the doomed men ex-cept for sheer blind chance and luck" (669). Since the regiment is the employer of choice to the district, and has long so been, all males and their extended female networks are economically and genealogically tied to "the doomed men." In mov-ing *against* the military who police, and *toward* the military who are policed, the crowd moves *against* and *toward* a part of itself.

Gauging the purpose and mood of the crowd's motion is difficult. We are later told, "[t]hey had no plan: only motion, like a wave" (786). No agent emerges to mo-tivate the collective act. No discrete voice articulates crowd decisions (if "deci-sions" is the right word); by and large "[t]he mass made no sound" (670). The ar-rival of the three generals elicits a "sound [that] was not voices yet so much as a sigh, an exhalation, traveling from breast to breast up the boulevard" (678). Only when they see the lorry containing the Corporal, and his twelve companions, the last vehicle in a convoy transporting the entire regiment to prison, does the crowd "yell" (682), and their "yelling" takes up the convoy's yell at the generals:

> the yelling passing from lorry to lorry as each entered the yelling and sped on, until the last one seemed to trail behind it a cloud of doomed and forlorn repudiation filled with gaped faces and threatening fists like the fading cloud of its own dust.
>
> It was like dust, still hanging in the air long after the object—the motion, the friction, the body, the momentum, speed—which had produced it was gone and vanished. Because the whole boulevard was filled with yelling now, not defiant now but just amazed and in-credulous, the two back-flung parallel banks of massed bodies and wan faces now gaped and frantic with adjuration. Because there was still one more lorry. (680)

"It," perhaps the most the difficult word in *A Fable*, recasts the yell as an imper-sonal pronoun in order to dislocate and depersonalize the source of the sound.

"It," in "it was like dust," refers shiftily to the sound (the yell), and to the object that raises the dust (the convoy). A second "it," in "it was gone," further divides or dissipates its referent, referring to lorries (and sound) as "motion," "friction," "body," "momentum," "speed"—"body" is the problematic term, having both a vehicular and a human referent. Two "it"s, capitalized and lower-case, liaise to defy the reader to extricate the sound made by the men from the sound made by the transport. To compound the tacit test, "Because," capitalized and causal, performs a seemingly absent causality. The crowd yells . . . apparently "Because" "it" has passed from collective subject (regiment), through military property (convoy), into collective subject (crowd), by way of some force (perhaps inhalation), best characterized by the syntactical path of a pronoun as it gathers into itself an excess of referents. "It" is the site of collection and collectivity, which helps much more than one might at first imagine, in that the impersonal pronoun catches Faulkner's sense that group action (here a "yell") passes between subjects along agentless routes ("it," not "he," "she" or "they") which are better defined syntactically (as sets of relations) than semantically (as points of definite reference).

"It," and all that "it" contains, culminates in the crowd's vocal "adjuration" (the act of adjuring), from "adjure" (to charge or entreat, solemnly). "Adjuration" is a complex term, not least because it releases both a euphonic synonym, "aduration," from "adure" (to burn completely, scorch, or parch; apt in so dusty a context), and a euphonic antonym, "adulation" (apt in that a civilian crowd greets the return of a regiment responsible for a cessation in hostilities). "Adjuration," plus sonic latencies, marks the crowd's solemn appeal (adjuration) as homage ("adulation") and self-immolation ("aduration"). I would add that "aduration" itself traditionally refers to entreaties made during exorcism. "Adjuration," like "it," though for a different reason, nominates excessively; yet, in all probability, the term takes readers to the dictionary and to a pattern made from sound, resulting in an urge to realize the referent that yields no attributable reference.

At the risk of trying my reader's patience, I would like to pursue a question raised by "it"—that of how content may be given to verbal structures which avoid (even as they seek) announced content (or, "where's the referent?"). A pronoun axiomatically stands in place of a noun. Not to do so, or to refer to too many nouns, triggers grammatical indecision which, if repeated, may in and of itself become the point of reference. Put another way: "it," slipping syntactically, may prompt a small but resilient structural anxiety. As the text grows and similar slippages accrue, a form of "ungrammaticality" produces as its referent the very anxiety over structure that "it" performs.[11] In order to give particularity to an abstracted claim, consider that which the crowd's yell ("it") seeks to adjure—to entreat, burn, praise, and exorcise ("Because there was still one more lorry"). However, before addressing the Corporal as the focus for collective action, Sartre's account of "seriality" may provide a useful and preparatory gloss. In a "series," as when I queue for a bus or listen to the radio, I am alone but I do what others do in the same situation—that is to say, I deliberately pattern my behavior on what I imagine another's to be. As Jameson points out: "The ontological irony of this mode of being is . . . that all the while I am modelling myself and my behaviour on the being of other people outside me, all the rest of them are doing exactly the same thing; in fact, there is no other, only an infinite regression, infinite flight in all directions."[12] Or, as Sartre summarizes, "each is the same as the others to the degree that he is other from himself."[13] What the crowd does in Chaulnesmont, or indeed the regiment does in refusing an order, may seem at some distance from queuing, though the crowd does wait in a by-and-large orderly fashion (for the generals, for the convoy, and for news of the judgment), and the regiment's refusal does look suspiciously like "the infinite flight in all directions" of another's act, re-enacted. However, if I add to the queue Sartre's version of panic and my own speculation on the effectiveness of loyalty oaths, the relevance of seriality to the events of *A Fable* may become clearer.

In a panic, an informer reports that three thousand men are to be executed. Neither he who speaks nor she who listens can verify the claim. If the listener believes the report to be true, she does so because of all the other reports extending, or about to extend, as a series, from this report. "The informer," as Sartre puts it, "*propagates* a material wave; he *does not truly inform*: his report is a *panic*; in a word, the truth, as Other, is transmitted as a state *by contagion* . . . and it is this *contagion* which grounds it [*the panic*] for everyone, in so far as it is ultimately the Other-Being of the series which realizes itself through it in him."[14] If an excited man runs toward me shouting, "They are all going to be shot!" and I, in a panic persuaded, and realizing my own helplessness before that fact, turn and run toward my neighbor, I behave like an other, and become that other for yet an other (ad infinitum). My action, insofar as it is not my own but other to me in its origin, is liable to return as something that may later seem alien. Jameson notes: "The structure of such phenomena as panics . . . can never be anything other than collective impotence . . . owing to the way in which each isolated individual feels being to be elsewhere, to be outside of him and serial action to be something to which he passively submits."[15] One has only to substitute for word of the three thousand news of "World Jewish Conspiracy," "Reds in the State Department," or "Soviet bombers" to recognize the centrality of serial panic to the period from which *A Fable* grew.

For example, President Truman's Executive Order 9835 (1947) created a Federal Employee Loyalty Program, having remit to screen two million government workers for evidence of political deviance. During the late 1940s and early 1950s, the net of loyalty checks extended to include many trades, professions, and businesses, and even (in Ohio) recipients of unemployment compensation. With every extension the red scare deepened, since each signature gave tacit credence to the claim of Truman's attorney general, J. Howard McGrath, that communists "are everywhere—in factories, offices, butcher stores, on street corners and private business. And each carries in himself the death of our society."[16] But why did so many sign? Michael Sherry properly argues that the red scare, and the loyalty oaths crucial to it, should be seen as a function of a postwar militarization. His argument runs thus: the supposition that reds are "everywhere," simultaneously explained both why America, despite ideological, nuclear, and economic superiority could not win the Cold War, *and* why the nation needed a clean up, on the path to future and "total victory."[17] Sherry's case is historically persuasive, not least because it overcomes the discrepancy between the number of signatures and the number of fellow travellers. "Reds," even as defined by the attorney general's list of subversive organizations, were few and far between; signatories were not. Sherry is less concerned with the felt structure of paranoia informing decisions to sign, structures that may be discernable through Sartre on seriality.

A signatory asserts his loyalty to the state. Not to sign—to leave the queue (or series)—is to become the Other who is feared: "disloyal," "alien," "red." Escalating opprobrium ensures rapid return and subsequent signature. Mine is a fantasy, since few will refuse to sign, where the social and employment stakes are high. To step out of the queue is to become "it" (the "red"), that impersonal "alien" whose very existence contagiously nominates hosts of putative employees, who are then also "it," in a game of infinite tag. My point is obvious: each member of the series invents the series by behaving as he expects others to behave, yet in so doing he introduces into the series (as an aspect of his sense, "What would happen if . . . ?") the very Other that he, like all the others, imagines himself becoming, if only in order to expel "it." In Sartre's terms, each signatory "is ultimately the Other-Being of the series which realizes itself through it in him." "Reds" then are "conceptual reds," serially produced as a fearful idea given substance by the act of signing. That substance, whether called "panic" or "paranoia," becomes a "real fantasy" placed at the heart of the state and its institutions by practices designed to affirm collective loyalty.[18]

Michael Rogin's study of U.S. political demonology firmly identifies the demon as the creature of those who cry his name, "the alien comes to birth as America's dark double, the imaginary twin who sustains his (or her) brother's identity."[19] Glossed, Rogin claims that cultural dedication to mobility, pluralism, and consensus, values arguably generalized by postwar consumption, generates anxiety over "boundary collapse." If the melting pot melts well and on a transnational scale, by what measure of difference may America recognize its own "exceptional" self? The "American," circa 1950, a suburban consumer and global policeman to future, exported suburbs, needs must invent the "Un-American," in order to guarantee his national edge:

> The alien preserves American identity against fears of boundary collapse and thereby allows the countersubversive [red-baiter], now split from the subversive [red] to mirror his

foe. Countersubversive politics—in its Manichean division of the world; its war on local and partial loyalties . . . its invasiveness and fear of boundary invasion . . . and its desire to subordinate political variety to a dominant authority—imitates the subversion it attacks.[20]

After my extended interlude on the serial demons of a nation, I would expect the objection that this chapter is about *A Fable*, an allegory written by a southerner during a period when the South hardly consented to plurality. In the 1940s and 1950s Jim Crow kept the South "solid" by drawing lines, in buses and cafeterias, between schools, across the entrances to polling stations and through idioms.[21] An inbuilt "black scare" ensured the policing of demarcations. Southern blacks, though neither "strangers" nor "aliens," experienced periodic translation into that "demon" against whom definitive white solidarity was achieved. I would suggest that even without Rogin's aids to demonology (pluralism and consensus), the region's readiness to cry "black devil" might usefully be read through the template of Sartrean seriality.

I take my example from the Mississippi summer of 1955, but the conditions and structures of feeling necessary for its manifestation pre-existed its expression. In May 1954, ruling on the matter of *Brown v. Board of Education*, the Supreme Court concluded "that in the field of public education the doctrine of 'separate but equal' has no place. Separate educational faculties are inherently unequal," thereby, as Numan Bartley notes, leaving "the legal structure of the southern caste system . . . without constitutional foundation."[22] Chief Justice Warren's words confirm what Dixiecrats and Neobourbons had confidently feared since, perhaps, Truman's recommendations on civil rights, delivered to Congress in February 1948—that their social system, founded in segregation, was under federal threat, in what amounted to a Second Reconstruction. That blacks should not cross the line into white space was central to the neopopulism of the Citizens' Councils and of Massive Resistance, during the mid- and late 1950s. When, on the advice of the NAACP, in the summer of 1955 some sixty petitions materialized in the South, requesting school boards to act on *Brown*, black petitioners frequently and rapidly found themselves without credit, jobs, or the questionable benefit of white "paternalism." Petitions were withdrawn. The storekeeper who refused credit or the employer who fired, effectively translating "our nigger" into "Nigger" and making a "demon" of a neighbor, did not *necessarily* act out of the belligerence, violent intent, or support for the Citizens' Council.[23] Rather, he saw himself as others would see him if he failed to *make* the "Nigger" from whose features "the stonelike unanimity of racial orthodoxy" might take its own justification.[24] I cite Bartley, the historian of the rise of Massive Resistance, to indicate that ideological "stones" take their stoniness, not from a fixed and unanimous idea, out there and available for co-option (like "racism"), but from particular social practices—resembling panics and queues—

in which isolated individuals feel their "being" to belong to an "o/Other-being," which occupies them (whether as "demon" or "companion") only long enough to ensure that their isolation turns into a solidarity which in no way frees them from collective loneliness. Now, finally equipped with social inferences concerning Faulkner's pronominal preferences, I return to the text and to that toward which "it" (the crowd) moves.

III

The focal object of what might be called a "queue to panic" is the Corporal. The final lorry carries thirteen men, split into two groups, four being chained separately. The thirteen are seen as "foreigners," "alien, bizarre and strange" (681), though nine of them are French, and from the Chaulnesmont district (669). Faulkner's point is that the crowd seeks to detach itself from the ringleaders of the mutiny, who are in fact part of its own body, by crying "foreigner" ("adjuration" as exorcism). "Then you saw that four of the thirteen were really foreigners, alien" (681). "You" turns readers into a better witnesses than the crowd: "we" mark the four as properly "alien," before adding "peasant" and "mountain man" to the list of epithets, as issued from the city on the plain. Of the four, "one was alien still somehow even to the other three" (681). "Somehow" is disingenuous: as essence of alien, in a Christian fable, the Corporal is jewish, or more properly "the Jew." Neither the crowd nor the text cries "Kike," because the Jew at the focal point (and origin) of the serially organized panic is the "other" who gives the crowd its form. We know from the first page that the regiment is, was, and will be drawn from Chaulnesmont. The regiment, to a man, has been convinced by the Corporal: effectively, each of the three thousand has placed himself at the point of view of that most other of others, the Jew, and has acted as that other acted. The crowd gathers and waits to see the regiment, a regiment that is, was, and will be a part of itself. The crowd may treat the Corporal as "the sole object of its vituperation and terror and fury" (681), but, as an extension of the regiment, it too has internalized the Jew ("adjuration" as aduration, or self-immolation).

Faulkner is exacting about the manner in which the crowd pursues "this one man" (681), and through him his regiment as an extension of themselves, from the square to the "man-proof pen" (787):

> like a wave; fanned out now across the plain, they—or it—seemed to have more breadth than depth, like a wave, seeming, as they approached the compound, to increase in speed as a wave does nearing the sand, on, until it suddenly crashed against the wire barrier and hung for an instant and then burst, split into two lesser waves which flowed in each direction along the fence until each spent itself. And that was all. Instinct, anguish, had

started them; motion had carried all of them for an hour, and some of them for twenty-four, and brought them here and flung them like a cast of refuse along the fence. (786)

The wire has recently been strung as part of a conversion involving "searchlight towers and machine-gun platforms and pits and an elevated catwalk for guards" (787). Caught on such wire in 1954, the members of the crowd, in a spatial and ethnic reversal, become the Jews on the inside rather than the French on the outside. As if it confirms the switch, Faulkner notes, they lay "along the barrier in an inextricable mass like victims being resurrected after a holocaust, staring through the taut, vicious, unclimbable strands" (787). By 1942 "holocaust" (a sacrifice wholly consumed by fire, or a whole burnt offering) was used by Jews with reference to Nazi atrocities; by the 1950s, historians, beyond the Jewish community, were applying the term to the Jewish genocide. Faulkner's usage triggers an associative network: the regiment is transported "packed like cattle," in lorries with "high slatted sides as though for the transportation of cattle" (679); they are destined for a soon to be electrified "pen" where they will "vanish . . . completely . . . as though they had never existed" (787). In such a context, the word "pits" resonates. One of the three killers of General Gragnon is called Buchwald, a Russian-American Jew, whose grandfather (a rabbi) died in a pogrom in Minsk (1011). Buchwald objects to the affinity of one of his coassassins (an Iowan) for pigs (1012). Buchenwald was liberated by American forces in 1945. If we are invited to see "them"/"it" as though from the outside through wire, they shift toward Europe's Jewry, figurable through U.S. newspictures of the liberation of the camps.

The context for this apparent misrecognition, or double vision, in which outside becomes inside so that French civilians may become Jewish survivors, stresses chiasmus, or the formal figure of inversion. The building and its guards variously change role and ethnicity, as if both were little more than functions of prefabricated building techniques or stagecraft. The compound has been variously a factory, a training-and-replacement-depot, and a prison. Its last conversion took a day, but is trumped by Faulkner's account of the perimeter and its environs as a "circum-ambience," featuring "a jocund morning," "lark-loud sky," and "glimmering pristine wire" en route to "gossamer" and "Christmas tinsel." "Working parties" in this figurative space might be "villagers decorating for a parish festival." Ricoeur, addressing tropes of resemblance, notes: "To see *the like* is to see the same in spite of, and through, the different. This tension between sameness and difference characterizes the logical structures of likeness. Imagination, accordingly, is the *ability* to produce new kinds of assimilation and to produce them not *above* the differences . . . but in spite of and through the difference."[25]

He adds that just as the "new compatibility" retains the "previous incompatibility," so "remoteness" is preserved within "proximity."[26] But what if the resemblance on offer bears no resemblance, as in "war is like peace" or "an internment camp is like a village festival"? In such instances, the distance between the terms, far from promoting a transfer of meaning from there to here, suggests a spatial and temporal dislocation amounting to a breakdown in perception of or collapse of those cognitive tensions that indicate imaginative activity. I am tempted to appeal to "loss of affect" (or at least to the performance of such loss)—where "affect" refers to a discharge of feeling, whether painful or pleasant, vague or well defined. So, for example, in early research on hysteria Breuer and Freud locate the hysterical symptom "in a traumatic event which has been met with no corresponding and proportionate discharge of affect [the affect, in other words, remains "strangulated"]."[27] Confronting a temporary prison that may also be a death camp; a French crowd that is Jewish, and an outside that is inside—Faulkner's affectless distention of our capacity to find "likeness" in his preferred resemblances is another example of this passage's requirement that we see double, pursuing misrecognition toward disruptive insight. That insight, coming into hiding through the text, dislocates his, and our, perceptions. The description of the Senegalese guards further enhances a distorted sense that we are not seeing it quite right; "lounging haughtily overhead along the catwalks" their "theatrical insouciance" resembles "that of an American blackface minstrel troupe dressed hurriedly out of pawnshops" (787). Black troops, according to the runner, have been brought from the edges of the French Empire to contain the threatened mutinies at its center: colonial regiments are disposed as a second front along and behind the French trenches (959–60). That Faulkner racializes the periphery/core distinction, having the blackened edge police the white center, is a measure of the revolutionary seriousness of a mutiny which threatens to turn the allied world outside in. Given such circumstances, Faulkner's simile looks inappropriate: why are we invited to see a desperate measure as minstrelsy in which black could be white?[28] I can answer my own question only by working back along the line of conversions and inversions which punctuate the passage: black into white; camp into theater (catwalks and lighting towers); engineers into village celebrants; outside into inside; gentile into Jew. The key reversal here, tripping the passage into its network of disruptive movement and spiraling contiguous displacements, involves the recognition that the crowd, like the regiment in whose place they are made to stand, are Jews in hiding—at least, if seen from the right perspective.

The notion of the hidden Jew recurs, receiving perhaps its most extended exploration in the case of Levine, the English flier, whose Jewishness remains undeclared to the point of denial. David Gerald Levine, alone among the characters, receives a full name, yet his very nomenclature entails ethnic contradiction: "David," Israel's military apogee versus "Gerald," of Germanic origin, meaning "to rule with a spear" or "mighty with a spear."[29] Neither the text nor the character use the word "Jew." Levine's thoughts on his own ethnicity constitute a trail of significant displacement. Refused admittance to an off-limits hangar, he thinks of Flight Sergeant

Conventicle and speculates on "the rapport, not between himself and Conventicle perhaps, but between their two races" (754), where the races in question are Jewish and Welsh. Conventicle is a "bog-complected man," one of a "musical people," often called "Evans or Morgan," who "knew dark things by simply breathing" or via a certain "rapport with man's sunless and subterrene origins" (755). Levine's ethnic analogy, minus its founding term, allows him "roots" ("bog," "dark thing," "subterrene"), but associates that rootedness with secrecy: the name "Conventicle" means "a secret or illegal assembly" or "hole-in-the-corner meeting," often among religious nonconformists or dissenters. Moreover, speculating on the fondness of the Welsh for Old Testament names ("Deuteronomy," "Tabernacle," or "Conventicle"), Levine notes that they "as no other people seemed at home" with "nouns out of the old fierce Hebraic annals" (755): the phrase "as no others" tacitly dislodges the Jewish "people" (present in all but name) from their Hebraic "home." Unprepared to speak his own ethic name, even to himself, Levine adds nominal cleansing to his expulsion of Jews from their textual source. Persisting in his felt affinity for the Welsh, he observes that they, having "names that no other men could pronounce . . . permitted themselves" to be renamed "out of the Old Testament," "as Napoleon in Austria had had his (the child's) people with their unpronounceable names fetched before him and said 'Your name is Wolf' or 'Hoff' or 'Fox' or 'Berg' or 'Schneider', according to what they looked like or where they lived or what they did" (755). Levine, aged eighteen, is earlier referred to as "(the child)" (749): the bracket, so close to bracketing out the subject of this complex syntax, locates Levine's family name as Austrian in origin. "Levine" is a pseudonym, Jewish only by French fiat; a name whose history obscures its bearer's original ethnicity. Aptly, given that the initial Judaeo-Welsh analogy allowed him to evade the genesis he sought, Levine turns directly from speculating on "Berg" and "Schneider" to an alternative and thoroughly English "source": "[b]ut he considered this [Napoleon's renaming] only a moment. There was only one sure source [for information on the ceasefire] . . . Bridesman and Cowrie's hut" (755). Again, the name matters: Bridesman is Levine's flight commander; as such, he will supervise his first aerial combat, referred to as "the valedictory of his maidenhood" (748) and as a "tumescence of valor" (752). Since Levine looks a tad "epicene" in an R.A.F. uniform whose hat-badge is held in place by gold pins resembling "lingerie clips" (746), Bridesman *is* as named, the "bride's" "man," who will "chaperone" (748) the "child" to the manhood of his first military erection. Faulkner's sustained innuendo at the very least implies that Levine, an assimilated Jew, will "marry" a gentile male who embodies English militarism. Here, the hidden switch which cast French citizens as Jews is revised, so that a Jew denied may marry into English citizenship.

Except that Levine's story ends in his suicide. His liaison with Bridesman *is* consummated, but in a manner whose perversity prompts the bride's death. The ceasefire, caused by the mutiny, necessitates that commanders on both sides meet to negotiate a continuation of hostilities. To ensure the German representative secret and safe aerial conduct across the front line, munitions must be disarmed. Levine flies in the fraudulent dog-fight that enables the conference between enemies which, in turn, ensures the war's resumption. He, therefore, witnesses his own impotence, experiencing what he sees from the air as a mismatch, or as evidence for the nonconsummation of his assimilation into "heroic" Englishness. What he actually *sees*, repeatedly and in detail, is that he fires blanks:

> and he pressed the button and nudged and ruddered the tracer right on to it [the German two-seater], walking the tracer the whole length of it . . .—the engine, the back of the pilot's head then the observor sitting as motionless as though in a saloon car on the way to the opera . . . then the observer turned without haste and looked right into the tracer, right at him, and with one hand deliberately raised the goggles—.(764–65)

Not trusting his own sight, once landed, he persuades Bridesman to fire a residue of the offending ammunition directly at him: the manner of the desired assault is erotically resonant. Levine, facing "the little black port out of which the gun shot" (769), tells Bridesman, "our hanger last night [was] locked tight as . . ."; Faulkner's ellipses make little effort to disguise the expletive ("arse"), particularly given the attendant sound track ("thock-thock-thock-thock"), as the pellets cover Levine's Sidcot with "stink" (770). As Bridesman "wrench[es] at the overall too, ripping it down," he asks "[a]re you satisfied now?"; and within a page, explaining his experiment, Levine tells a mechanic, "I had a stoppage . . . Captain Bridesman helped me clear it" (771). Anal interference is a textual option. Immediately after this conversation, Levine takes the stinking and still burning Sidcot "toward the incinerator behind the men's mess, then suddenly he turned sharply again and went to the latrines" (771). "Stink," "mess," and "latrine" are reiterated during the account of Levine's next thirty-six hours, after which time, he kills himself in the latrines, carrying the "slow thick smell" of the burning air jacket with him (292). More exactly, he shoots himself when, and only when, the Sidcot is consumed by the phosphorous:

> almost gone now—only a beggar's crumb but perhaps there had been an instant in the beginning when only a crumb of fire lay on the face of darkness and the falling waters and he moved again, one of the cubicles had a wooden latch inside the door if you were there first and he was and latched the invisible door and drew the invisible pistol from his tunic pocket and thumbed the safety off. (967–68)

In effect, the Sidcot serves as the uniform of Levine's adopted nationalism. When it is consumed, he will cease to be. As an assimilated Jew, once the mark of his assimilation has burned away, and lacking the insignia of state and subjecthood, he will no longer have reason to exist. Isolated during his last day, having refused all company, he speculates philosophically on the contradictory relation between the subject (himself) and its preferred objects (Sidcot, "night," "tree," "door," "pistol"). He calls his speculations a "dialectic" (289). Abbreviated, their logic runs: if I accept the perceptual authenticity of nothing other than my own directly accessible data, do I not, in the end, lose contact with external reality, and find myself imprisoned in the questionable realm of my own senses? Or, without me would night, tree, door, pistol, or Sidcot exist? Further, if I am led to lose confidence in the evidence of my senses (by bullets that do not kill), by what means may I take myself to be anything other than a dark vacuity?[30] Levine's world comes to bits on just such implied questions, after which, and invisibly in the dark, he follows it down the "invisible" latrine, by means of an "invisible" pistol (968). What interests me here is less Levine's youthful philosophy than the manner in which Faulkner figures his impasse—a smouldering Sidcot enclosed in a petrol can. At the very point where Levine voids himself, the signatory image for that cancellation is a miniature "holocaust," or an extended burning in the enclosed space of a temporary "incinerator." To strain the logic of the image: an Englishman burns, releasing a residual Jew encoded as fire, stink, and shit.

IV

If Richard Gray marks the crowd "female" for its liquidities, I would add that "slime" has been a traditional characteristic of the Jew. Zygmunt Bauman, in *Modernity and the Holocaust*, proposes "that the conceptual Jew has been historically construed as the universal viscosity of the Western World."[31] He argues that as "nationless foreigners" *inside* "[a] world tightly packed with nations and nation-states," Jews were "the non-national void."[32] Assimilation merely disguised and deferred their tendency to induce opacity, disorder, boundary-collapse, and slippage. Yet expulsion of the conceptual Jew proved impossible, since the order of the nation defined itself against what was alien to it, making the Jew, as an idea, the definitive guardian of what he transgresses. Faulkner's Corporal is a category mistake who rigidifies categories by transgressing their limits: able to "materialize" and "vanish," apparently at will, he crosses zonal lines and national boundaries, leaving "inspectors" and "inquisitors" at an impasse. They declare him an "incredible monstrosity" and a "monstrous incredibility" (784), and their argument by reiterated tautology might be read as the conceptual equivalent of the Freikorps' erection. Yet the Corporal—or viscous Jew—cannot be set outside the circle, since he is that Other who unites all the others. In Sartre's terms, he is a "unity object . . . the unity which is ever present but always elsewhere" and is the origin of the serial actions of regiment and crowd, as of the stylistics of "it."[33]

Yet like Levine (and the crowd and regiment) the Corporal is an unnamed Jew; in the first instance, a Jew by allegoresis rather than declaration. Many epithets attend his unit, each potentially a Semitic synonym: when first seen, the thirteen "looked not merely like foreigners but like creatures of another race, another species; alien, bizarre, and strange" (681). The race of four of the thirteen, chained separately in the last lorry, *can* be traced; they share a "middle-European nationality" (784), though Faulkner emphasizes that "[e]ven the army records did not seem to know what their nationality was" (783). I would speculate that the four, "none of [whom] . . . seemed to have any history at all" (784), are from the Russian Pale of Settlement, the Pale being that region of Russia where Russian Jews were compelled to live; it comprised central and eastern Poland, Ukraine, Belarus and Lithuania. Since the four contain a further distinction, between three and one (the Corporal), I risk the suggestion that he, "the fourth one . . . alien still somehow to the other three" (681), is a diasporic Jew—for example, if the three are Poles, he is a Polish Jew. I hasten to add that the Semitic term is a speculative recovery, unused in the text, though possibly encrypted in the Corporal's genealogy. We are told that he was born in Tibet, to a mother who died in childbirth. Her origins are obscure. Magda, his half sister, notes that her mother "had something in her . . . which did not belong in that village . . . that country" (931). She adds that "that something" (933) made her an "alien and a passing guest" in her Tibetan "home" (934). Magda's phrasing recalls the obfuscation that attends General Compson's version of Sutpen's account of his first wife—a French Haitian of supposedly Spanish extraction: "(and now Grandfather said there was the first mention—a shadow that almost emerged for a moment and then faded again but not completely away . . . so that Grandfather said it was like he had just seen her too for a second by the flash of one of the muskets—."[34] In Eulalia's case, the parenthetical maternal "shadow," seen obscurely in a "flash," is the mark of African "blood." Here, in Tibet, the "something in her" that is not a matter of facial features (934) may be gauged from the naming of the dead mother's daughters: Magda and Marya are German and Polish names, respectively; both point east, a direction affirmed by Magda's burial of her half-brother under the Polish name Stefan. By the close of the nineteenth century, Germany had a substantial Jewish population, at which time, what we now know as eastern Poland was Russian territory, and more particularly the location of enforced Jewish settlement. Arguably, the "something" in the mother is her Jewishness.

I say "arguably" because the clues are few, cryptic, and easily missed. The name Stefan is used twice in a dense and lengthy text. In France, Magda becomes Marthe, though just once, surprised at the gates of Chaulnesmont by the Corporal's common-law wife, she speaks, "not in French but in a staccato tongue full of harsh rapid consonants, which went with her face—a dark high calm ugly direct competent peasant's face out of the ancient mountainous central-European cradle, . . . though a moment later she spoke in French and with no accent" (863). The unidentified Central European language recurs once and in veiled circumstance. Incarcerated beneath the citadel, the squad are granted a last supper. One Pierre Bouc has apparently been imprisoned with them by mistake. When the sergeant summons Polchek (Judas), Pierre starts up and is identified by the Corporal as not being of the squad. He is removed from the cell. As always, the names matter. A Pole is "checked" and a Peter is allowed to deny his affiliation to the Corporal, except that this Peter, unlike the Peter of the Gospels, will re-encounter his Christ. Returning with the old general from their interview, the Corporal sees Pierre Bouc struggling with the guards to gain readmittance to the cell and the squad. According to the sergeant, he has "denied his name" (995) and the provenance of his "regimental order": "'You lie!' the man shouted again. 'My name is not Pierre Bouc. I am Piotr—' adding something in a harsh almost musical middle-eastern tongue so full of consonants as to be almost unintelligible. Then he turned to the Corporal . . . saying something else in the incomprehensible tongue, to which the Corporal answered in it" (995–96). Pierre, rechecked as Piotr, reveals a Polish Peter. Pierre/Piotr's French surname "Bouc" means "goat," which in New Testament parlance indicates that this particular goat is a sheep in goat-hide, seeking to rejoin the Corporal's apostolic flock. Biblical goats pass to the left, with unprofitable servants and foolish virgins, "into outer darkness" on the Day of the Judgment. Whereas sheep, profitable and wise, go right to "inherit the kingdom" (Matthew 25, 30–34). Bouc discards his pseudonym but appears initially not to regain his desired nomination. A dash stands in for the surname, subsequently supplied by the Corporal ("Zsettlani" [996]). Earlier and obscurely, at the start of their interview, the old general had spoken of "—one Zsettlani that had denied you," adding that he might be a "countryman," "blood brother," or "kinsman," since "you were all blood kin at some time there" (986). The reference renders Piotr one of the four, "alien even among the other nine" (681), held separately in the final lorry: although "there" remains dismissively directional, the linguistic clue goes east. Faulkner apparently mishears the language: Piotr, like Magda, speaks a harshly consonantal tongue; his name and the sound of his voice indicate Central Europe, or, more particularly, the Pale of eastern Poland. Yet "Central European" becomes "middle-eastern," converting a Pole into a Hebraic Jew, and Yiddish into Hebrew. With the crowd on the camp wire, we were required to see double; in this instance, we are required to listen for duplicity, hearing how Faulkner's apparent error effectively repatriates the diasporic Jew, while keeping the words "Jew," "Yiddish," "Hebrew," and "Israel" masked in the partial disclosures of a pseudonym.[35] I should add that the old general overhears the Corporal's words to Piotr and offers full translation, suggesting that he shares the Central European language (Yiddish) and its spectral Hebraic root—a linguistic facility that sets him among the sheep, with Piotr and the Corporal.

I started my pursuit of the Corporal's encrypted genealogy with his mother's ethnic status. Yet the Corporal's father is equally available as the cryptic Semitic fount for the son's more-than-conceptual Jewishness. Within *A Fable*'s scriptural sche-matic, the old general plays God, Father to the Corporal's son, but his divinity has political resonance. Orphaned, he is raised by an uncle and a godfather, one a cab-inet minister, the other chairman of an international federation producing munitions (893). His omniscience is, therefore, that of the militarized corporate state—Tru-man and C. Wright Mills would appreciate his political genealogy. In 1883, the old general (then a lieutenant-colonel) quit his military career (service at a colonial out-post) to vanish to a lamasery in Tibet, where the Corporal is conceived more im-maculately than Christ. Christ had a mother; the Corporal has aunts (Marya and Magda). Censorship of the mother's body extends to a remodelling of impregna-tion: Magda reports that the old general lived in a "eyrie," "a way-station to heaven," where "people—men—came as if through the air itself (you), leaving no more trace of coming or arriving (yes, you) or departing (oh yes, you), than eagles would (oh yes, you too" (933). At such a height, "eagles" incline to "angels," and females are barely acknowledged: men may "come," and, assisted by a parenthetical rhythm owing something to Molly Bloom,[36] need not notice that women do not. If the fa-ther is virtually the son's sole progenitor, then the Corporal's Jewishness (that "alien," "foreign," "bizarre" liquidity) derives also from the old general, whose om-niscience represents that of the military-industrial complex. The manner of the con-ception, though allegorically predictable, serves to reiterate the Corporal's insepa-rability, both from a Jewish story and from the institutional bodies that he appears to oppose. I repeat that the word "Jew" is unused in *A Fable*, though the concept of the Jew is everywhere, and everywhere in hiding.

To recount: I have tried to establish, first, that the Corporal is a death's-head and a Jew; second, that he is the seminal essence of that which he opposes—a mili-tarized state (in its combatant and noncombatant forms, as regiment and crowd). If further evidence were needed of his inseparability from the state-forms embod-ied in his father, I would simply point to the intermingling of their bones at the fable's end. From their joint tomb springs a "triumphal and enduring Arch" (1069), which leaves me with the problem of how to make sense of Faulkner's decision to situ-ate the focal point of resistance—the Corporal as mutineer, Jew, viscosity—at the center of the militarization that he resists. My present answer is that the mutiny is Faulkner's way of exposing the logic of twentieth-century military development as it stands circa 1953. What the Corporal causes is a kind of "technological fix," whereby the national administrations, engaged in conflict, are enabled to recog-nize that they are not one anothers' enemies: rather, they are all servants of a global system, whose chief concerns are control over citizenry and economic production for death. "Technological fix" is David Harvey's phrase:[37] he notes that an invest-ment in production innovation yields enhanced profit to the investor, until compet-itive catch-up results in profit equalization. The "fix" or "break" is the moment when an element of capital (a firm or nation) produces an innovation (technical or administrative) which results in competitive edge and super-profits. One firm's "technological break" is necessarily another firm's "devaluation," since those firms lacking the innovative element lose the value inherent in their own production process. They must rapidly scrap elements of what they do, devaluing their fixed capitals (perhaps before investment in the fixed bits—be they a production line or a distribution technique—has returned a profit), in order to introduce the new element, without which their rates of profit plummet. It follows that "devaluation," perceived as "creative destruction,"[38] is inherent in the "competitive" and "progressive" rhythms of capital accumulation. Innovation and devaluation are inseparable, the "technological fix" being that moment when a firm (or nation) gains the edge and enters a super-profitability which devalues the production processes of its rivals.

The mutiny in *A Fable* is an unexpected cessation of hostilities that threatens to stop military production. Faulkner is emphatic in drawing a correlation between the technology of war and the state-forms dedicated to its production. Two allusions will have to serve for sustained argument: the architecture of Chaulnesmont, center of the Allied High Command, rises less from rock than from the permanence of an arms economy. Standing at a window, high in the *Hôtel de Ville*, the old general envisages the city and its geology as a pile of institutional strata, descending from "the three flags and the three supreme generals who served them" (887) through an officer class and a military bureaucracy to a civilian body (dedicated to the provision of anything from "shells" to "shoes" [888]), and so on down to the "earth" of the working women (who are "all one woman," containing "still warm and living seed" [889]), and to the "dust" (889) of the casual laborers and the unemployable: "Out of that enduring and anguished dust it [Chaulnesmont] rose, out of the dark Gothic dream" (888). A similarly systemic impulse attends General Gragnon's sense of a single bullet. For Gragnon, whose regiment refused combat, the bullet that each of the three thousand deserves is the structural cornucopia of militarized production. One bullet contains, among other things, his military training, as well as the mining, smelting, and munitions industries:

> the Prime Ministers and Premiers and Secretaries, the cabinet members and senators and chancellors; and those who outnumbered even them: the board chairmen of the vast establishments which produced the munitions and shoes and tinned foods, and the modest unsung omnipotent ones who were the priests of simple money; and the others still who outnumbered even these: the politicians, the lobbyists, the owners and publishers of newspapers. (880)

The sentence detailing what makes a bullet runs for virtually two pages (880–81), and features seven semi-colons and four colons. I turn grammarian because a long sentence invites attention to punctuation; by straining syntactical leeway it pressures those signs through which pause and an inclination to stop are negotiated. In Fowler's *Modern English Usage* (1944), semi-colon and colon elicit the instruction, "See Stops," yet both are stops that do not; instead, they establish links across varying degrees of pause. The semi-colon separates parallel expressions— in this instance, negotiating a conjunction between administrative levels (political executives, corporate chairs, directors of public opinion). In effect, the punctuation performs like a social hinge, binding dissimilar managerial structures one to another within a state formation, perceived structurally as a syntax. The colon, marking a lesser discontinuity than that designated by a period, has the function, in this example, of delivering what has been proposed by previous words, and therefore substitutes for such verbal harbingers as "that is to say" or "ie": viz., "the board chairman" exemplify the "very many" who out number the political leaders, who in their turn are more numerous than . . . and so on, up the state hierarchy. The colon prefers not to stop: those grammatical units which it separates may be sentences, but its appearance between them denies their independence, by positing their relational dependency. Colons and semi-colons, particularly where multiple, might be read as expressive of a totalizing impulse since they proliferate connection, deferring completion in the cause of a greater completeness. Their capacity to carry meaning (as signs of "totalization") is inseparable from the rhythm they establish: here, that of interruption overruled.

Gragnon is a systemic totalizer. He watches from above and sees whole in order to make a case for the summary execution of his regiment. Having observed the mutiny from an "especially prepared . . . elevation" (687), he insists to his group commander that he be granted his legitimate right to submit his report and recommendation to the highest available authority (the commander in chief), even though that submittal will involve his own court-martial. Appropriately, where elevation empowers, Gragnon's regiment refused to fight for an "elevation of earth too small to show on a map" (881). One measure of Gragnon's assumption of power and its elevations is his expectation that his report will perform its deed in the moment of its utterance: that he will talk a bullet, which bullet will kill three thousand men. Despite his having had to repeat "for the fourth time" (879) his official request for the regiment's execution, "[i]n fact it seemed to him now that the two of them, speech and bullet, were analogous and coeval" (880). The phrasing of the supposition ("seemed") undoes its hypothetical status: "analogous" proposes a resemblance between terms at some distance from one another—a distance which "coeval," or "existing at the same time," reduces; "now" reiterates a temporal proximity between "speech" and "bullet," which "in fact" strains toward literal conjunction. Gragnon turns a simile into a metaphor and a metaphor into an illocutionary act. J. L. Austin defines the illocutionary as a form of speech in which saying is doing, to which Judith Butler adds the useful rider that the moment of such utterance takes its force from "a condensed historicity" coterminous with the "ritual" of law; she notes that "it exceeds itself in past and future directions, an effect of prior and future invocations that constitute and escape the instance of utterance."[39] Gragnon presumes that his utterance, "mimeographed" in "triplicate before the three generals" (879), will be injurious, because he views himself as no more than a citation from an institutional nexus whose totality ensures its own, and his, sovereignty. Colons and the impersonal pronoun combine, stylistically miming the reach of this assumption:

> inflexible and composed before the table on which lay the triumvirate markers of his career's sepulture, the triplicate monument of what the group commander had called his glory, he discharged for the fourth time the regiment from the rolls of his division as though it had vanished two mornings ago in the face of a machine-gun battery or a single mine explosion. He hadn't changed it. It had been right thirty-six hours ago when his honour and integrity as its (or any regiment's) division commander compelled him to anticipate having to make it; it was still right the second after that when he discovered that that which had given him the chance to become a commander of a division in exchange for the dedication of his honor and life, was compelling him to deliver it. So it was still right now for the very reason that it was the same honor and integrity. (879)

An iteration of conjunctive "it"s marks the passage, where "it," initially Gragnon's speech (written, typed, uttered), but rapidly also a monument, a grave, and a reported "mark of glory," is that which has not been changed. Since he "discharge[s] it," its metaphoric passage through the institutions of memorialization and military precedent credits the pronoun with the force of a "machine-gun" or "mine" (the choice of "mine" over mortar exhibits sweet, if possessive, reason). Five "it"s in the space of three lines (after the first sentence) requires Faulkner's parenthetical recovery of a referent for "its," in this instance that which pertains to the regiment ["(or any regiment's)"], except that his nomination is immediately problematized by the proximity of the previous and capitalized pronominal usage: "It" refers back to the speech (and all that "it" has accrued), so that the second and possessive "it" of the sentence (its/the regiment's) must be synonymous with the speech, and consequently with the bullet—which congruence yields the regiment dead (always Gragnon's illocutionary position). A third and fourth usage ("it; it") confirms the fusion of utterance, munitions, and summary execution, by deploying a semi-colon to create a balance between the speech, or better, "it" (as an act of such cumulative reference that nomination is deferred), and "it" as the "life" that qualified Gragnon for his commission. The ways in which "it" remains open to a broadening situation (and to a broadened base of referents) enacts the form of a pervasive power that grants Gragnon his un-self-conscious delusion of sovereignty. Central to such power is a capacity to operate without a subject, without a name beyond "it," in such a way that "it" constitutes a subject in the course of its operation— Gragnon as an extension or iterator of "it," where "it" is a power so diffuse as to

appear total. Were I to call the power in question that of a militarized state, my naming would fix, freeze, or delimit a range of state-forms (industrial, military, bureaucratic, religious, educational) whose convergence eludes nomination, but which is,
for example, caught in the architecture of Chaulnesmont as envisaged by the old
general, or in the architectonic procedures of "it," ";", and ":".[40] As Gragnon's
judge, the old general will deny Gragnon's word, shooting only one of the three
thousand, and ordering Gragnon's assassination. Yet the old general hears the
plaintiff; his secret agreement with the high commanders of Allied and enemy
forces ensures that, when a second regiment mutinies, Gragnon's illocutionary utterance will receive immediate expression in barrage form, though through other
mouths:

> "The regiment mutinied," the old marshal repeated again. "And suppose we do [shoot
> them]. What of the other regiments in your division, when they learn of it?"
> "Shoot them," the division commander said.
> "And the other division in your corps, and the other corps on either side of you."
> "Shoot them," the division commander said. (882)

As "the old Negro" stands with the runner in no-man's land, watching French and
German soldiers "crawling . . . empty-handed . . . through the wire":

> He never heard . . . the wailing rumble of the two barrages . . . nor saw nor heard little
> more of anything in that last second except the runner's voice crying out of the soundless
> rush of flame which enveloped half his body neatly from heel through navel through chin:
> "They cant kill us! They cant! Not dare not: they cant!" (963–64)

Gragnon's bullet, the old general's use of it, and Faulkner's understanding of "it"
independently and cumulatively comply with C. Wright Mills, who in 1956 was to
argue that "war lords," "corporate chieftains," and the nation's political executive
had formed a "power elite,"[41] whose "interlocking" directorates were responsible
for "the great structural shift of modern American capitalism toward a permanent
arms economy."[42] The figures at midcentury were compelling; since the run-up to
war in 1941, the element of the national budget marked for military purposes had
not dropped below 30 percent. Moreover, a considerable portion of that budget
was allocated to the South. Roosevelt's mobilization agencies used international
crisis to drive regional development, ensuring, via defense contracts, that war production moved increasingly south and west.[43] By 1954, 85 percent of government
expenditure on research (some five billion dollars [twenty times the prewar rate])
was for "national security," with the South as a major beneficiary.[44] The historian
James C. Cobb argues that World War II expanded the South's industrial capacity by 40 percent.[45] Nor should it be argued that the military-industrial complex is
a creature of the Cold War. The regulatory partnership between business and gov-

ernment, brokered by J. P. Morgan on behalf of Allied military provision between 1914 and 1916, meant that by 1918 it was

> emphatically clear that in twentieth century America, war much more than reform would shape the nation's values, institutions and ideology. During World War I the nation had taken a major and seemingly irrevocable step in the direction of becoming a warfare or national security state.[46]

But if that structure was to work, military production had to continue to be devalued by use: in effect, the mutiny instructs the old general in how to "fix" armaments so that they can continue to be made, perhaps forever. In order to ensure a conference with his German equivalent, he has to tamper with munitions along a lengthy sector of the Allied front. At his order, shells are disarmed in secret so that the enemy's commander can fly across Allied lines, be shot at from the air, and remain unharmed. The greater good of militarized production requires that enemies meet: at that meeting, they agree (presumably) to fire on their own men, if and where any subsequent mutiny breaks out. The runner initiates a second refusal, taken up by French and German troops. As the mutineers approach one another across no-man's land, they produce no serial ripple because they are immediately shelled from both sides. Continuing hostility and war production are thereby ensured.

The old general's "technological break," care of the mutiny, involves the recognition that, like military products, his military workers (the allied forces) should where necessary be devalued so that the permanent arms economy may be ensured permanency.[47] Prior to having the Corporal shot, he describes to him his vision of a technological dystopia in which machines fight machines, and man, reduced to a voice, "endures" only because of his capacity to quit a planet despoiled by war, and to militarize further planets:

> because already the next star in the blue immensity of space will be already clamorous with the uproar of his debarkation, his puny and inexhaustible and immortal voice still talking, still planning; and there too after the last ding dong of doom has rung and died there will still be one sound more: his voice, planning still to build something higher and faster and louder, more efficient and louder and faster than ever before. (994)

In a rewrite of his Nobel Prize Address (December 1950), entirely in keeping with the financial underpinnings of the Nobel Foundation, Faulkner has the old general insist that mankind's "endurance" is inseparable from the efficiency with which he produces munitions. In 1918, as seen from the perspective of in 1954, the old general has a very American point, a point that is also, by 1954, very southern.

A Fable offers no counterpoint, since the Jew—serially central to the father, the regiment, and the crowd—is the Other, not as opponent, antithesis, or even alternative. Rather, he is that serial other, an alien who defines the power elite, the military body, and the citizens of a militarized state, defines each of them (in serial relation to one another) as dedicated to expelling the alien, which alien makes them what they are. That the Jew is also a death's-head, eventually crowned with barbed wire (1023), marks his internalized otherness as a sign of the state's dedication to the delivery of destruction.

"The Bugger's a Jew":

A Fable as Melancholic Allegory

I

M Y ACCOUNT of *A Fable*, seeking the Jew and finding him in the potentially Semitic semen of the old general, risks simplifying the complex politics of the supreme commander's sexuality. In 1918, aged sixty-two, the "old" general apparently approaches what Faulkner elsewhere spoke of as ungendered peace, but the biography of his missing years (1877–circa 1914), fabricated over two meetings by his contemporaries (graduates of the St Cyr military academy) in Paris (1877) and Zermatt (1887–88), suggests a life founded on a systematic negation of sexuality. Since the life is collectively and substantially made up, its findings may be said to reveal as much about its composers, the cream of a military elite, as about its subject, the leader of that elite. Authors and authored were "classmates" at St Cyr:[1] he is "the last [and orphaned] male of his line" (893), destined for "the rigid hierarchy of an army" (895). Faulkner's choice of St Cyr implies that the making of military men requires an unannounced expulsion of the female. St Cyr was originally a very feminine place: the foundation of Madame de Maintenon, mistress and morganatic wife to Louis XIV, designed as a charitable institution for the education of impoverished young ladies of good family.[2] Judith Butler might say of what Faulkner does not say that we should "interrogate the exclusions,"[3] since among them are to be found the "constitutive antagonisms" from which the "sexed subject," or indeed the subject more generally, takes identifiable shape:[4] "The subject is constituted through the force of exclusion and abjection, one which produces a constitutive outside to the subject, an abjected outside, which is, afterall, 'inside' the subject as his own founding repudiation."[5]

I may be making too much of St Cyr's unmentioned history, except that Faulkner describes other military establishments whose architecture exemplifies gendered tensions, most notably the headquarters of the group commander, General Bidet. The chateau is entered via "a *porte cochere* at the back," "and so directly into the shabby cluttered cubicle not much larger than a clothes press, notched into the chateau's Italianate *bijou* like a rusted spur in a bride's cake, from which the group commander conducted the affairs of his armies" (694). A "*porte cochere*" is a carriage entrance. "*Bijou*", or "gem," colloquially means "little dear." Both terms will prove appropriate. At his second approach, through a park established by "a successful highwayman" having "distant connection" to a "French queen" (710), Gragnon, stopping his car like "an over-ridden horse," notices, in front of the "dark pile" of the building, "a pile of horse-droppings" (711). The synecdoche is ingenious, given that "Bidet," to whom the chateau has been requisitioned, means in French a "nag" or "small horse," but also and by English co-option, "a vessel in a long narrow stand, which can be 'bestridden' for bathing purposes."[6] The anuses of horses and men are plainly part of the architectural subtext, with rear entry, "notch," and the rigidification of the "clothes press" serving to sexualize the orifice of fecal emission. The bodies that matter here are male, and those that do not, pushed to the excluded margins in "*bijou*," "bride" and the "distant" French queen, are female. But, in excluding the vagina, Faulkner recessively foregrounds the anus, a pattern that recurs.

Gragnon's own headquarters, prior to military occupation, were the gift of a French millionaire to his Argentinean mistress. Gragnon's bedroom had previously been known as "the gunroom" and features suitably masculine accessories (though all them are flawed), a shotgun (unfired), a mounted stag's head ("not a very good one"), and "a *stuffed* trout" (706) [my emphasis]. Next to the bedroom, though still in Gragnon's "private quarters," is the room in which three of his aides slept: "the lovenest itself, which seemed to retain even yet something of the Argentine, though none could have said what it was, since nothing remained of her, unless it was some inconsolable ghost perhaps or what northerners conceived, believed, to be antipodal libidinous frenzy" (706). "[N]one could have said," "nothing remains"— the passage exerts a double censorship, declaring female sexuality first spectral and then the stuff of cliche, only to have what is refused return in mutated form. Gragnon goes to the "lovenest" (passing his own faulty phallic "closet") for a book belonging to a prior aide—a "couturier," who "made women's clothes," about whose "sexual proclivities the division commander had had his doubts (very likely wrong)" (706). The memory allows an "antipodal" switch, not just from South to North, but from female to male, so that the excluded female "libido" attaches to the male aides, whose occupancy of a "lovenest" implies that where the vagina had been, the anus shall be.[7]

The geography of the old general's career is likewise orifice-orientated. On graduation (1877), he goes directly to an African outpost of the French Empire, "as famous in its circles as the Black Hole of Calcutta" (900). Anality attends this "rim of oblivion" (903). After six years in a building made from "loop-holed clay" (900) and next to a "stinking well" (903) in a compound likened to a "midden" (905), functioning as a "hole" (904) for the "disposal" of that which is "self-proven to have no place in the Establishment of Man" (905), he departs, out of the army and beyond the empire, for a lamasery in Tibet. There, living on the roof of the world, he conceives a son. Despite the immaculacy of the place and act, conception retains vaginal traces: a parenthetically sexual rhythm underpins Marya's account of men "coming" there. Though they "leave no . . . trace" (933), the echo of Molly Bloom's climax restores a receptive female body, which the combined names of the child's surrogate mothers, Marya and Magda (or Mary Madgalene), translate from "virgin" to "whore."

The officers who author the oral biography describe the departure from Africa as a "defalcation" (the term is repeated three times [900, 901, 906]), their case being that the St Cyr graduate "diminishes" the "hope or dream" (900) of his adoptive family; for which "defalcation" ("short coming," or "failure")—the officers call it a "crime" (906)—he is punished by exile. They offer no account of the crime, nor do they propose grounds for their claim. "Defalcation" simply fills a gap. But the term itself, one which I suspect all but a few of the few readers of A Fable have to look up, is an odd choice. The OED offers, as variant kinds of "diminution," "the action of cutting or lopping off" and "a misappropriation of property in one's charge." The absence of a received referent, compounded by dictionary variables, legitimates enquiry along the lines of the word's sonorities, particularly where sound can be mapped in terms of the defalcator's career. In Africa "defalcate" is close to "defecate," though since "defalcation" leads eventually to Tibet, "deification" might be allowed a whisper, as a sonic antonym. I am prepared to chance my ear, hearing "dephallication" where others might prefer only "lopping off." By now, most of the readers of this chapter will be objecting, "On what grounds . . . ?"—evidence is imminent and African.

The account of the old general's service in the equivalent to a "Black Hole" features one event: a legionnaire from the garrison rapes and murders a female slave, belonging to the Riff. The tribe threatens a massacre, to prevent which the old general tricks the offender into volunteering to act as a messenger, seeking reinforcements from the next post. The Riff wait at a prearranged wadi, capture, torture, and kill the rapist, returning the body, "stripped of most of [its] flesh" (914), to the post. War is prevented and French Africa "saved" (912), in part by the suppression of a crime—a crime whose discovery remains unacknowledged both to its perpetrator (who dies not knowing that the old general knows) or to the military hierarchy (who seek to honor the perpetrator as a dead hero). Yet the crime undergoes a sudden and subsequently subtle mutation. The Norman, second in the old general's graduating year at St Cyr, and key carrier of the biography, defending the actions of his subject, resists the claim that since the rapist was "a man," a defender of the empire, and one who had "nothing in his [military] record but a little drunkenness, a little thievery—" (915), he deserved better. The manner of the Norman's objection resonates, "'Until now,' he cried '—only thievery, buggery, sodomy—until now'" (915). His stipulation that prior offenses involving anal penetration be taken into account in a rape case at the very least questions the nature of the particular crime "now" under consideration. The Norman's interjection revises who did what to whom. One who commits "buggery" is only and also a "sodomite" where anal penetration is effected between males. "Buggery" is not gender-specific.[8] The Norman's terminology confuses (in its implied relation to the legionnaire's crime) allowing vaginal rape to become anal rape, as a prelude to becoming the rape of a man by a man. Of course, the Norman is exasperated at having to defend his co-officer's actions. Of course, in a law court his citation of earlier and notional offenses might be ruled out, but Faulkner's text compounds the vaginal/anal switch. After all, the rapist was "spawned by," not "in" "a Marseilles cesspool" (903), posted to a "midden" and given to "rooting about" in "hog-wallows" (915); consequently, genealogy, location, and metaphor translate the focus of his violation.

It might be objected that the switch depends on the Norman's interjection and remains deeply cryptic, factors that could be explained by the objector's sustained "obsession" (901) for the old general, sustained since their first day at St Cyr, when the twenty-two-year-old Norman viewed the seventeen-year-old cadet, through "passionate eyes," as "a pubic unconscious girl" (901). The consistency of the gaze (1873) and the interjection (circa 1888), in their transformative focus on orifices, suggests that the fantasy belongs to the character rather than to the text. Yet the very officer whose casual defense of the rapist elicits the fantacist's protest offers an independent addendum which reiterates the partially hidden dynamic of the crime. Approving the army's decision to decorate the dead rapist, and noting to the Norman, "[y]ou were away at the time, so you have not heard this" (915), he recounts difficulties over signing the citation. Initially, a clerk "stumbled," overturning a liter bottle of ink and "blotting out not merely the recipient's name but the entire record of the achievement" (915). That an unwitting military cover-up of the old general's conscious concealment of a textually ambivalent crime should yield an encrypted erasure is perhaps unsurprising. The ink, by "blotting out," complements earlier excision, but in a form that announces stain. Moreover, the clerk who trips is an "Alpinist": since the first and punitive censor quits the "Black Hole" for the Himalayan peaks, it would seem that his moves to erase stain may equally be liable to slips and emissions. A second signatory attempt, on "new parchment," also failed, "even as the Grand Commander reached his hand for the pen" (915). This time a "draft of air" which "came from nowhere" blew the document twenty meters across the room into the fire, "where it vanished pouf!" (915). The account dwells on the draft, adding, "(if you know General Martel, you know that any room he stops in long enough to remove his hat, must be hermetically sealed)." Wind in a sealed room must have a human source. Since the parchment in question addresses doings in a "famous" hole (900), much mentioned as "cess" and "midden," and since the sound of its burning makes punning reference to a slang term for a male homosexual (in common usage since the early nineteenth century), I would argue that the text indicates the anus as the source of the offending wind. That the room belongs to a general named for a brandy long used to settle troubled stomachs further annotates afflatus. As with the ink, the medium through which the cover-up is cancelled contains elements of the obscured crime, though "draft" makes the clearer disclosure.

From St Cyr to Tibet, the map of the old general's career (1877–1914) possesses a subterranean anatomy, which, at the risk of sounding comically schematic, can be sketched as follows: he leaves St Cyr (the hymen) for Africa (the anus which is a vagina, which proves to be an anus). He leaves Africa for Tibet (the site of an immaculate conception involving "deification" as "dephallication" in an almost missing vagina). The unlikely Tibetan liaison between a Yiddish-speaking Pole and (at the very least) a French conceptual Jew yields a Semitic child—where the Jew has long been both eroticized and denigrated as refuse, waste, and excluded material.[9] In Tibet, anatomically speaking, a spectral phallus and a spectral vagina make spectral shit, which implies the return of the spectral anus. I am riding my cartographic luck, and indeed may have blown it several bids ago. But whether or not the more extreme ramifications of my point are accepted, that point remains simple and twofold. Firstly, that the legionnaire's crime in the African "hole[s]" speaks to the phantasmic needs of the old general and of his class. Secondly, that in *A Fable*, anus and vagina repeatedly exist in "undecidable" proximity.[10] One orifice does not cancel the other; rather, they turn into each other, so that each obscures and contains the other as its nonidentity.

Two more instances may serve to fix the pertinence of my claim to the old general's sexuality. Immediately after Gragnon's court martial, the narrator describes the supreme commander as a "boy": "a child, crouching amid the golden debris of the tomb not of a knight or bishop ravished in darkness but (perhaps the mummy itself) of a sultan or pharaoh violated by Christians in broad afternoon" (885). In the same section ("Wednesday Night"), the St Cyr contemporaries, speculating on what held him in Africa, presume "paradise within some camel-odored tent." The gender of the paradisal body is unspecified, though presumably female: "what limbs old and weary and cunning with ancient pleasures that Montmartre bagnios (and even St Germain boudoirs) knew nothing of, yet so ephemeral, so incipient with satiation and at last actual revulsion, that after only six years the sultan-master must vacate it" (903).

In both passages, a degree of syntactical leeway provokes a gender switch and subsequent orifice undecidability. In the earlier extract, the object of the verbs "to ravish" and "to violate" remains open—either the tomb or the entombed body. The distinction cannot be resolved. Since the corpses are male, the offense against them is either tomb-theft or homosexual necrophilia. The bracket, suggesting that a "mummy" is subjected to assault, opens a punning variable, whereby a vagina substitutes for an anus; or, more properly, whereby relevant orifices parenthetically and indefinitely pivot on one another. Much the same effect is achieved by the leeway in the hyphenate phrase "sultan-master," whose hyphen pivots, allowing the "master *and* sultan" to be also and equally the "master *of* the sultan," with obvious gender consequences. In the absence of a definitely sexed occupant for the tent, he who vacates quits neither a man *or* a woman, nor (after the manner of Jastrow's duck-rabbit),[11] one who is both at the same time—a manly woman *and* a womanly man. Rather, he leaves the site of erotic (and epistemic) movement, whose excitement devolves from the "sexing" of a tented subject, which, because it disavows its grammatically permissible opposite, grafts the disavowed onto its defining moment. So, if the old general is "a master *and* a sultan," "she" whom he quits is the vagina and *not* the anus. Whereas, if the old general is "he who masters a sultan," the "he" whom he quits is the anus *not* the vagina. In Judith Butler's phrasing, either way, the refused option "persists as a kind of defining negativity,"[12] or "internal dissonance,"[13] within the old general as he exits the desert fantasy. Except that the fantasy belongs to his St Cyr biographers, though its collective status and pervasion of diverse aspects of the old general's life allows that its structure characterizes the military elite as a whole—an elite who, in time of war (1918) and of preparedness for war (1954), threaten to become the ruling elite of the state.

I have spent considerable time turning over one orifice to find another, without finally addressing why *A Fable* demonstrates " a preoccupation with body vents and orifices" (713), or why it attaches that preoccupation to an officer class. Part of my problem is that much of the material is encrypted, and that decoding yields not an answer but "undecidability"—what I have been calling, care of Butler, the "return of the excluded," whereby gender identification depends on an exclusion which, far from excluding, takes that which it has put outside (or abjected) back inside, as its "*founding* exclusion" (my emphasis).[14] Put schematically, the rape of the Riff in Africa confronts the old general with a version of his own abjected other. Having, in effect, disembodied the culprit (who is returned sans flesh), he attempts his own disembodiment by quitting the empire for Tibet, thereby passing from "midden" (or vaginal anus as anal vagina) to its antithesis (from hot to cold, from low to high, from West to East, from genitalia to head). In Tibet, he discovers a secret Jewess and, all precautions unavailing, finds coming from himself, in the form of a Jewish child (denied), the very "shit" which he believed he had excluded from his domain. Since the old general's sexuality is imagined by a military elite who are also a ruling class, its structure may have resonance beyond the gender issue.[15] Were this not the case, I could happily follow Noel Polk's exemplary essay on the "feminine" in *A Fable*. Abbreviated, Polk's case is caught in his claim:

> The feminine in *A Fable* is a dark ferocious quality which resolutely insists, on page after page, that the battlegrounds of *A Fable* are far larger than the fields of northern France and that the casualty lists include those maimed and destroyed by something other than howitzers.[16]

Mothers maim, or their surrogates do. The oedipal struggle continues in the trenches, producing children who are the "victims of too-strong or too-weak or absent parents."[17] Polk's paradigm renders my vaginal/anal pivot eminently "decidable"—men, fleeing the vagina, find the anus; or, less contentiously, running from mother discover the pleasures of male groups, of which the novel features many (armies, officer corps, Masons, racing fraternities . . .). Polk's subtleties deserve more justice, particularly as those subtleties expose the final limitations of his revelatory gendering of the text. "Mama Bidet" may serve as exemplary: Polk takes the nickname as a "hermaphroditic epithet,"[18] representing the war between female and male. The equine aspect of the name, extending from Bidet's office like a "spur" in a "bridal cake" (694), through the dung pile at his door (711), marks him male. But "Mama," too, has a genealogy, involving a dominant wife, an affection for lavender shirts, a tendency to cook and clean, and being willing to conduct a military interview by candlelight from bed (712). So that when Gragnon enters Bidet's bedroom, "Mama" wins, becoming, for Polk, an "unmistakably . . . feminine punitive superego" supervising the activities of "an emasculate."[19] Gragnon *is* impotent in his wish to execute three thousand mutineers. Bidet *does*, in effect, send him to court martial and death, and *does* hold the word "Fatherland" responsible for war (716). But the bedroom scene is more undecidable than Polk permits. Take the name again. Mama Bidet brings to the health of armies "the dedicated asepsis of clinical or research laboratories" (713); where "asepsis" is "the state of not putrifying." "Bidet," as a device for cleansing anal and genital areas, is an apt name for a preventer of putrefaction. But how does "bidet" as a specialist water-closet sit with "bidet" as a small horse? Polk's answer is ingenious: it sits as a rider sits, since one straddles a bidet as one straddles a horse.[20] I would object that the response grants equine maleness temporary ascendancy at the expense of the nether regions. Yet Faulkner emphasizes Bidet's "cold, scathing, contemptuous preoccupation with body vents and orifices and mucous membrane as though he himself owned neither, who declared that no army was better than its anus, since even without its feet it could still crawl forward and fight" (713). Bidet's attention to "mucous" is reiterated: earlier he is described as exhibiting a "pitiless preoccupation with the mucous membrane buttoned inside his army breeches" (695). I would point out that breeches, military or otherwise, contain two mucoid orifices, and that "vent" is not necessarily a gender unspecific synonym for said holes. I quibble only to indicate, once again, that mention of the anus textually solicits other apertures, from vagina ("vent") to phallus (the second orifice in the "breeches"). Bidet's concern for holes in the military body outweighs his function as masculine or feminine. Indeed, interviewing Gragnon from his bed, he is both male and female, but not in the manner of the hermaphrodite who, in Polk's argument, embodies a gender war. The claim for androgyny naturalizes, albeit in an "unnatural" body, the oscillation between bodies that do and do not matter, as materialized in Bidet's name and gender. Neither "Mama" nor "Bidet" matter as much as "mucous" (a "viscous secretion" or "slime" common to each orifice), or as "mucous membrane" (a "lining" forming a continuity between the skin of the internal cavity and the external skin, and secreting said slime). Faulkner's mucoid emphasis is more remarkable than his revision of Napoleon's aphorism about armies and stomachs. "Mucous" and not "anus" is of the essence to Bidet, and to Faulkner, because it best represents the very slither between inside and out, a slither that exactly catches the movement by which the abjected is both excluded and contained.

I am reminded of the definition of "slime" as "the agony of water," by which Sartre sought to capture the contradictory experience of what is neither solid nor fluid, nor simply both; a sticky contagion dangerous to felt and thought catergories.[21] I am also reminded of Bauman's summation of the conceptual Jew as "the universal viscosity of the Western World."[22] The Chaulnesmont crowd, as it moves at dawn on the first Wednesday, "disgorg[ed]" (699) and "void[ed]" (700), will eventually flood; but the extended lexicon of liquidities through which it moves should not, perhaps, erase its initial and mucoid motion—particularly as the crowd will, via seriality and misrecognition, take on the collective body of the conceptual Jew. Indeed, Bidet's "mucous" is a vital and conjunctive figuration for what I can only call the novel's various strands of subsemantic whispering: for "it" and the cola as they constitute a stylistics of reference as slippage and incompletion; for sexuality as a pivoting product of what it negates and retains, and for the hidden Jew, essence of "it" in that (like the impersonal pronoun), Semitic viscosity slips among categories. Each whisper unfixes—syntax, gender, ethnicity, respectively—generating an experience of motion through categories and between viewpoints (and subsumptive of both), which amounts to the *practice* of an extending structure (and not its mere conceptualization), where structure, or better, structuration, like seriality or indeed modernity, carries "the truth, as Other . . . transmitted as a state by *contagion*."[23] "Mucous" joins "it" and "Jew" as a hidden key to *A Fable*.

To revert for a moment to the Bidet-Gragnon interview, and more particularly to Bidet's bedroom—the room would have divided its previous owners: the highway man and the marshal would have viewed the decor with "contemptuous unbelief"; the descendants of the Florentine "might or might not have slept" there, but the Levantine millionaire "without doubt did" (712) grace the "gaudy bed in the rococo room" (714). In slang parlance, "Levantine, equals jew, equals crooked."[24] Bidet, named for the cleansing of bodily orifices, lies in the bed of a masked Jew. Once again, encoded Semites and intimate emissions are drawn into a conjunction which tacitly implies that the military body, like the civic body, contains what it expels—the encrypted Jew—as its interalized otherness. To learn that Bidet has Levantine taste in bedding is structurally analogous to identifying a Jewess in Tibet, or to the deep logic of the old general's Semitic semen. But the discovery receives perhaps its closest analogue in the manner of the runner's demotion. Having been twice refused the right to give up his commission in order to "get back into the muck" (722), and on leave in London, he forces the hand of the authorities by engaging in unspecified sexual activity with a woman, three months pregnant, in a public place:

> the two of them taken in *delicto* so outrageously *flagrante* and public, so completely unequivocal and incapable of other than one interpretation, that anyone, even the field-rank moralists in charge of the conduct of Anglo-Saxon-derived junior officers, should have refused point blank to accept or even believe it. (723)

The prose insists on clarity yet provides none; the passage notwithstanding, an "unequivocal" act remains equivocally open to more "than one interpretation" when its substance so denies "acceptance" and "belief" as to escape nomination. The passage begs the question, what would be "outrageous" enough? Clues are available. On two occasions the runner quotes from Marlowe's *The Jew of Malta* (4.1. 41–43):

> Io, I have committed
> fornication. But that was in another country; and
> besides, the wench is dead . . . (730)

On the second occasion he omits the copulatory substance of the confession ("—but that was another country;—and besides / the wench is dead" [742]). His relation to the passage is complex and self-censoring: the initial usage allows him to displace combat, a "rearguard" action in which he uses his "heretofore unfired rifle" for the first time, by means of the memory of reading in Oxford ("he could even see the page" [730]). What he sees on the page, an admission of "fornication" by the Jew, Barabbus, might be said indirectly to refer to the runner's sexual activity, also "in another country," which activity might find displaced expression in those actions erased by Marlowe's page, so that displaced combat gives form to displaced sex. Put another way: since sex in London is linked via reading in Oxford to fighting on the Marne, the reference to Marlowe operates focally, ensuring that what defies "belief" and "acceptance" in London is an "[un]guard[ed]" "rear" action, or anal sex, culminating in orgasm (the "fired rifle"). That the runner (by allegoresis, John the Baptist) is marked as "*The Jew*" may also explain why "field-rank moralists," given the task of protecting the ethics of "Anglo-Saxon-derived junior officers," were quite so offended: intertextual revision compounds the offense, rendering the "bugger" (915) also a Jew. Faulkner's instance of intertextuality prompts a temporal distention whereby signifiers contain three times—a rifle on the Marne is script on the Oxford page and a phallus in London—in which context reference is necessarily destabilized and punning encouraged. We are told, for example, that the corporal paid the young woman twice what she asked, "which represented his whole balance at Cox's" (723). Where literary citation builds innuendo into "rifle" and "rearguard," "Cox" and "country" must surely follow? The corporal's second use of Marlowe's lines censors "fornication," but "another country" reinstates it, though in masked yet explicit form; by "trying" "another" "cunt" (or anus) the corporal has "[un]balance[d]" his circumcized "cock." I go this far, arguably too far, only because the text persists in bringing into hiding an encoded link between vagina, anus, and jew.[25]

The paragraph prior to the runner's distentive quotation from Marlowe has him anachronistically allude to Eliot's "The Waste Land" (1922). Coming across the corporal and his squad for the first time, he likens their uniforms, blue against "the khaki monotone . . . [of] the British zone" (728), to a "cluster of hyacinths" (728):

> He even knew what he was watching for: for the moment in the stagnancy when Authority would finally become aware of the clump of alien incongruous blue in its moat. Which would be at any time now; what he was watching was a race. Winter was almost over; they—the thirteen—had had time, but it was running out. It would be spring soon: the jocund bright time beginning to be mobile and dry underfoot; and even before that they in the Whitehalls and Quai d'Orsays and Unter den Somethings and Gargleplatzes would have thought of something anew . . . (729)

I quote at length to establish how a color is first gendered and then, as a result, ethnically shaded. The hyacinthine blue derives from Eliot's "hyacinth girl" ("'You gave me hyacinths first a year ago; / 'They call me the hyacinth girl'").[26] The squad, characterized by the "unresisting undemanding passivity" (728) of its requests that soldiers simply lay down their arms, are in effect intertextual "girl[s]," where the focal flower girl is also, and for Eliot, Lithuanian. Faulkner's "Unter den Somethings," by way of *Tender Is the Night*,[27] sketchily recalls a line from "The Burial of the Dead" in which spring prompts the child to claim Lithuanian nationality ("Bin gar keine Russin, stamm' aus Litauen, echt deutsch").[28] Lithuania, it will be recalled, is in the Pale, and therefore heavily Jewish. In which subterranean context, "alien" grows ethnically specific and "race" achieves a split reference. The syntax of the second sentence allows that what the runner watches is both a seasonal race between

winter and spring, and an ethnic group: note that the second and subordinate semantic option may draw its punning provenance out of the "blue" because reference to the competing seasons comes only *after* the sentence. Furthermore, with
female gender and Jewish race drawn into hiding at the semantic fringes of the
passage, anal association is necessarily close to hand. In the sentence immediately prior to the quoted passage, the runner speculates that as the winter lull in
combat draws to a close, each foot soldier, "lying almost quiescent in mud's foul
menopause," will recall the likely manner of his death, "panting, vermin-covered,
stinking with his own reek, without even privacy in which to drop the dung and
water he carried" (729). The burial mud, made largely from human emissions, provides the missing term; so that a traceable connection between the hyacinth girl
and the child who claims to be Lithuanian ensures that the hidden or residual Jew
shall surface through the postmenstrual mud and the fecal fall of waste to the earth,
to reunite anal, vaginal, and Semitic contiguities in the subsemantics of Faulkner's
page.

A similar mud, more effluent than soil, provides the substance for yet another
surfacing of the associative triangle. Incarcerated under the citadel and eating a
Last Supper, the squad turn their circumstance into a joke by arguing that they are
being fed merely to produce "manure." The thrift of the authorities will prohibit their
execution until they "digest" and "defecate" what they have consumed, thereby
making "fertilizer" for a "garden plot." The punch line is a pun, "'Christ assoil us,'
the fourth said" (978). To "assoil," or "absolve from sin," contains among its more
archaic usage allusions to "soilure" (to "discharge," "unloose," or "purge"), while
the sound of the phrase "assoil us," as "arse-hole us," specifies the orifice of release. Again, I risk crudity in the cause of a subtext, my excuse being the need to
demonstrate the systematic presence of a triangulated whisper. Witness the explicit trajectory of the corporal's corpse. Taken from Chaulnesmont, by Magda, to
a farm owned by her husband, near Vienne-la-Pucelle (1024), he is there buried
under "an ancient beech tree" (1034):

> Vienne-la-Pucelle [is] a name significant enough for Faulkner to have retyped a line of the
> final typescript in order to call it that. *Vienne* is the present subjunctive of the French verb
> *venir*, *to come*; *la Pucelle* means *the virgin*, so that, translated literally, the village's name
> means *if the virgin comes* or *should the virgin come*.[29]

Polk adds that La Pucelle was the chosen name of Joan of Arc, and I add that the
corporal's body, blown from its grave by shell-fire, becomes, by way of ingenious
contrivance, a substitute for the body of the unknown French soldier, exhumed
from Verdun and, in substituted form, eventually laid beneath the *Arc de Triomphe*.
Faulkner spends much of the final section of *A Fable* ("Tomorrow") detailing the
switched-body trick that puts the corporal's corpse under a national monument.
He places great emphasis on the exhumation of the original body from a fort on

the Meuse Heights (1043–48). The squad detailed to the task descend into what is essentially an *anus mundi*: references to "midden," "orifice," and "bowel" attended their every move, as does the "stink" of "old excrement": "they went on again between the sweating walls, the floor itself beneath the feet viscous and greasy so that there was a tendency to slip, passing the doorless orifices" (1046). Enabled by Polk's exemplary scholarship, and extemporizing among the funereal latencies, I would suggest that the course of the corporal's corpse copies the map made for the legionnaire by the old general. You will remember that the legionnaire entered an ambiguous or double "hole," was expelled, and returned skeletally to become the subject of official attempts to honor him—attempts that render him anonymous. The match is close rather than perfect. The corporal, first laid in land named for a virgin, is expelled and placed in a coffin recently occupied by a corpse taken from "the bowels of the earth" (1045), more bowel than earth. A state funeral declares the coffin's content anonymous.

Yet so much of all this remains a matter of whispers discerned at the lower semantic reaches of encrypted words ("rearguarded," "hyacinth," "assoil," "Vienne-la-Pucelle"), and of unlikely homologies founded on hidden links (anus, vagina, Jew), combined to speak, without speaking, to the imaginary of the old general and of his class. Moreover, and compounding my problem, the evidence gathered in this section, makes a case concerning a word which is available only as an omission. "Jew" is absent from *A Fable*. "Jewish" occurs once and in a significantly negated form. The old general, interviewing the corporal on the citadel, casually protests, "No, no, we are not two Greek or Armenian or Jewish—or for that matter, Norman—peasants swapping a horse" (988). A triple negative, followed by ethnic instances, each denied, amounts to protesting too much about what he thinks they are not, particularly where the secreted Jewishness of the speakers is arguably essential to their cojoined capacity to solve the overproduction problems of the permanent arms economy. Indeed, three of the denied terms encode the contradictory ground that renders denial so essential: Greek, Armenian, and Jew are each members of a populace famously subjected to genocidal purpose—the Greeks and Armenians by the Turks (1922 and 1915, respectively), the Jews by the Germans (1941–45). The old general (arguably Jewish) might deny what his son (a Jew) teaches him (by Jewish example) that citizens (like Jews) exist to be murdered by the state in the cause of maintained military production: nonetheless, his action embodies the insight, and serves to guarantee a regime dedicated to destruction.

II

Which returns me to my problem: I have argued that in *A Fable* "Jew" is a nomination which indicates that its bearer is marked for death by the state. Why then is "Jew" a banned term, discoverable everywhere in hiding? To recognize that each citizen and every enlisted man is either Semitic or conceptually so, and is therefore killable by a militarized regime, for the greater good of its economy, *is* unbearable—though central to the postwar emergence of U.S. preparedness and to the history of the last century. Confronting the global pervasiveness of mass killing during the modern period, the demographic historian Rummel coins the term "democide," from "demos," Greek for "people," and "cadere," Latin for "to kill." "Democide" denotes "public murder by governments acting authoritively" outside the immediate context of war.[30] Arguably, the shelling of the second mutiny is democidal insofar as it involves a joint agreement by the German and Allied states to kill enlisted citizens engaged not in war, but in a manifestly peaceful strike. The victims join a lengthy roster, among whom might be found the civilians of Hiroshima, though not the dead of Verdun. Rummel estimates that, in the first eighty-seven years of the twentieth century, 170 million men, women, and children have been put to death by government. He adds that "the dead could conceivably number nearly three hundred and sixty million people."[31] The figures are unbearable but do not pass beyond representation. Let the 170 million be gathered together as the citizens of a single nation. Call that nation Golgotha. In 1987, when Rummel counted, Golgotha was by population the sixth-largest nation state. My point is that the democidal fact of a murderous century, for which the Holocaust is the typical act, does not, in and of itself, resist representation. "Jew," in the late 1940s and early 1950s, may be a difficult term, but it is not unspeakable. Why then, in *A Fable*, is "Jew" unspoken yet pervasive, buried yet communicative? The manner of its frustrated communication offers grounds for a hesitant answer. Witness how the plausible structure, which I have called the vaginal, anal, Judaic triangle, comes into hiding from the unknown, and moves from encryption toward exegesis in forms whose content invites immediate re-encryption. To trace the triangle is to recover anal rape in Africa, consensual buggery in London, dephallication in Tibet, and mighty farts in the French military bureaucracy. Materials of such excess require rebuke for implausibility. Perhaps they are better left unspoken. Indeed, insofar as I have yet to establish a structure that will allow them to be understood as more than persistent aberrations, they *are* unspeakable.

Hidden, encrypted, rebuked, uttered yet without utterance . . . the terms of my discussion persuade me of an affinity between this material and melancholic speech. Before taking a psychoanalytic turn, however, I should stress that what I seek is less an explanatory model than an account of how an unthinkable, though historically specific, loss may result in a style of utterance, vociferous without being declarative, whereby, for *A Fable*, as perhaps for a melancholic, "unspeakability . . . organizes the field of the speakable."[32]

What the melancholic cannot speak is that loss which he cannot bear. In discussing who grieves for whom in "Pantaloon in Black," I have already deployed Abraham and Torok's distinction between "introjection" and "incorporation," the former addressing grief completed through spoken acknowledgment of loss, and the latter a refusal of grief achieved via an ingestion of the loved thing, which, secretly retained, cannot then be lost. Judith Butler offers a useful summation of melancholic ingestion or "incorporation": "If the object can no longer exist in the external world, it will then exist internally, and that internalisation will be a way to disavow the loss, to keep it at bay, to stay or postpone the recognition and suffering of loss."[33] For such postponement to work, Freud emphasizes that that which is preserved through repression, or placed in an internal crypt, must remain "withdrawn from consciousness,"[34] since to know it would be to lose it. Hence, Freud has it that the melancholic is a puzzle, since "we cannot see what it is that is absorbing [him] so entirely."[35] His absorption turns on himself as he becomes the receptacle that hides and encodes the lost object. Because the melancholic cannot acknowledge his loss, his anger at the unvoiced absence of the lost thing takes the form of "self-beratement," or "complaints [against the complainant] that are really plaints in the old sense of the word"[36]—laments for unarticulable loss. I nervously suggest that the pattern of emergence as rebuke, attendant on the coming into hiding of the vaginal, anal, Judaic triangle, has something of the logic of the melancholic's "disavowed rage," itself a disguised index of "attachment."[37]

Necessarily, the language of melancholy is duplicitous. Incorporation, or the continuing presence of the lost thing encrypted within the speaker, ensures that his language involves "double inscription," whereby "a founding silence [marks] . . . any act of signification," so that his utterances are liable to allude, while barely knowing it, to a concealed existence manifest only as a distortion on the surface of the utterance.[38] Once again, nervously, I would suggest that terms like "Conventicle," "Levantine," "Cox," "hyacinth," "assoil" . . . as their contiguities reach for triangulation, leave a refracted trail of the not-quite-said, leading to an "other" who is not quite named. But, if *A Fable* may even loosely be described as a melancholic text (centered, as it is, on a death's-head and preoccupied with mass killing), its melancholic speech encrypts, beneath the invisible yet legible word "Jew," a further and fully illegible term, whose absence, made barely present by the unspoken Semitic word, can neither be adequately uttered nor properly traced in the text. The unspeakable word arises from a truly contradictory loss, approachable only from beyond the text—that is, from the context of Faulkner's writing more generally.

Freud notes that though typically the founding loss derives from loss of a person, melancholy can be occasioned by "the loss of some abstraction . . . such as one's country, liberty, an ideal, and so on."[39] For "country" read "region," for "liberty" read "coercion," or more properly a regime of coerced labor constitutive of dependency between white and black. Faulkner's original and unspeakable term is "the black," for whom the unspoken "Jew" substitutes.

My Jewish question has elicited an African American answer, which carries its own difficulty. How to acknowledge the long withdrawal (1943–54) of an unacknowledged figure, whose nonacknowledgment was central to Faulkner's major fiction (1929–42), and to the regime of accumulation from which it sprang? The burden of *that* question forms the substance of work already done.[40] Here, my needs are twofold: to define the nature of the presence that has withdrawn, and to establish that absence as *A Fable*'s founding loss and ground for melancholy. Rather than rehearse the argument of *Fictions of Labor*, I shall approach the crucial presence of a shadowed figure, held economically in absence, via a summary of the workings of one word—but first, the context from within which that word works. *Absalom, Absalom!* (1936) describes how Thomas Sutpen builds a very white house. Its narrators know, but cannot acknowledge, that Sutpen and his house, the plantocracy and they as its descendants and inheritors (Shreve excepted), are created by black work. Put aphoristically, the white narrators and their subjects are blacks in white face, talking about much except what they know— their own dependency on a bound population who make them what they are. But I run ahead of myself, without offering the ghost of an argument.

Glossing even the plot of Faulkner's most canonical and modernist text is hard: *Absalom, Absalom!* tells the story of Sutpen, five times. Three versions are framed and revised by Quentin Compson in conversation with his Harvard roommate, Shreve, the fifth teller. Circa 1827, Sutpen, a poor white from west Virginia, quits his family as they migrate into the Delta. Arriving in the West Indies, he puts down an uprising among slaves on a French sugar plantation on Haiti. As due recompense, he marries the owner's daughter and achieves a son (1829). For reasons unspecified, but much speculated upon, he sets the marriage aside—eventually reaching northern Mississippi with a handful of Haitian slaves and sufficient capital to "buy" a hundred square miles of Indian land. A marriage and a plantation are made, only for the denied and (by Sutpen) never-acknowledged son of the first liaison (Charles Bon) to come to the door, court the daughter, and bring the house down. Incest and miscegenation did it, at least according to the five narrators as they work through, fill in, and guess at the story. Much is fabricated, compulsively and at length, but the impact of Bon is central and reiterated.

The name "Bon" (my focal term), given by Sutpen to his unacknowledged Haitian son, puns exactly to express the conundrum of a southern landowning class founded on constrained labor. To rehearse the puzzle retained within the pun (Bon-Good-Goods): if the white good of the owning class depends on the goods that the black makes, the owning class must deny it, while retaining that "good" (that Bon) in which their very substance resides, since without that unacknowledgeable good, they would cease to be what they are.

Pun and conundrum turn, as argued more substantively in *Fiction of Labor*, on the determining force of a coercive regime of accumulation, grounding a premodern culture of dependency. But during the second half of the 1930s, the regional form of labor, which in binding the black to the land bound him also to the land's lord, was transformed. A revolution in labor use, driven by federal funds, took black from white, one consequence of which was that white need never be as black again. But, additionally, removal took from Faulkner his problem, and with it a central tension from which his major work of the long 1930s was forced.

Faulkner wrote *A Fable* over the decade that followed the Second Civil War, and during a "Second Reconstruction" which "freed" the black from a premodern economy and culture to the raised expectation and overt racial antagonisms of the Civil Rights era.[41] The 1950s, in the South from the perspective of my argument, saw black break from white and prepare to rise, via the Movement, to that "freedom" associated with free wage labor rather than bound work. If the region's African Americans, during the 1950s, reconstructed themselves—through an economic revolution, self-assertion, and ultimately political organization—as their own masters, they left their masters (in Faulkner's terms) empty. That unbearable, unspoken, and necessary emptying (again, from Faulkner's perspective) is the subject that *A Fable* displaces into its own barely uttered Jewish question. That *A Fable*'s Jews are everywhere invisible; that their covert sexual manifestations are desired and disavowed, and that he who is central among them should be the son of the Allied supreme commander comes as no surprise once the text is read through the stencil of "Bon," itself a miniature focus for the generative problematic of *Absalom, Absalom!*. The corporal is to the old general what Bon is to Sutpen:[42] both are inheritors who cannot be acknowledged but who remain structurally central to their respective economies (modern and premodern). As an essence each is literally seminal, being the product of ambiguous pleasure, personal and systemic, which cannot be directly faced—a refused "*bonheur*" in Tibet and Haiti, respectively.

Yet their "returns" from Tibet and Haiti differ crucially. Where Bon, by report, brings down the planter's house, and with it by extension the plantocracy, the corporal's death shores up the *Hôtel de Ville* and the military-industrial complex for which it stands. Bon's death poses a fundamental threat to the persistence of the regime of accumulation in which he is involved, since his life represents the disavowed source of the planter's goods and pleasures. In contradistinction, although the corporal as Jew is, like Bon (and in Butler's terms) by "constitutive exclusion,"[43] internal to the system that has nominally displaced him, his structural centrality to the economy (though not to the sociability) of the militarized state depends upon his expungeability, both as an individual and as a race. If the Jew is executed, the state is dehumanized. Having killed the source of its serial sociability—that o/Other being which, in occupying the isolated individuals who make up its crowds and armies, translates those masses into social units capable of collective agency— the state as *socius* will fail, while prospering. The old general says as much: during his interview with the corporal, he sketches a militarized future in which war (as robotics), having "dispossessed" men of their bodies (993), will reduce them to "voices" whose "endurance" will consist of a capacity to plan "more efficient . . . louder and faster" means of destruction (994). The "voice" that emerges from the old general's voice is that of technological rationality,[44] a voice that seeks to become a machine for making death and money—a voice, that is, without an "o/ Other" to distract it from the legibility of its purpose.

At which point, although Bon may be said structurally to anticipate the corporal, his relevance as a precursive index of the corporal's meaning fails. When Henry Sutpen shoots Bon, Henry Sutpen effectively dies, and Sutpen's Hundred shrinks exponentially. When the old general executes the corporal and learns by extension to kill his own citizens, the war and related military production restart. Bon and the corporal are nominally the "sons" of fathers who exemplify regimes of accumulation. But Sutpen cannot say "son" to Bon, whereas the old general habitually greets filially officers and enlisted men, alike. For Sutpen to acknowledge a black son, and through him the inseparability of white goods from black work, is impossible and systemically ruinous. For the old general, such an acknowledgment has little to do with paternity or sociability, since the events of May 1918 indicate that his greeting might be glossed, "Those who are my sons are available for death at my command."

Yet despite their conclusive differences, I wish to persist with my claim that structural overlap casts Bon as the corporal's antecedent and secret sharer. Or, put another way, that in 1943, as Faulkner conceived *A Fable*, he may have realized the corporal *through* Bon, seeing him as a black Jew and therefore as subject to silent inscription.[45] In which straining case, the corporal's buried Jewishness encrypts the black. But, as economic grounds for secreting the black silently within the white fail—as, that is, an externally funded revolution in labor practices "releases" black from white—so the structural specter recedes, and the corporal minus his structuring revenant becomes he who must be put to death for the greater good of a transformed economy. The corporal remains a Jew without a name, but his missing Jewishness (circa 1954) is no longer haunted by a presence relevant to earlier forms of labor. Instead, he dies as an unacknowledged Jew, who is also and necessarily The Unnamed Soldier, or representative victim of a triumphalist state. His body joins that of the old general in the sepulcher under the *Arc de Triomphe*. Their reunion is not significantly that of father and child: rather, the Jew is placed with his killer under an official monument in the capital because, for Faulkner, their juncture conveys the democidal crime that makes the triumph of modernity possible and persistent. In 1954, the idea that the Jew might conceptually be every U.S. citizen cannot be brought to articulation, because the willingness of the government to kill him, or to persist in the production of the means to his destruction, is itself grounds for barely announceable grief.

In 1943, Faulkner has ample grounds for melancholy: his world is doubly dead. Melancholic writing inclines to allegory insofar as the duplicity of its script is complemented by the reinscriptions of allegoresis. He who suffers from melancholia experiences "a desolating loss of originary meaning,"[46] but swallows that loss in order to preserve the lost thing. Whatever he may say therefore distorts that which he silently retains, so that his speech might be though of as encoding the unspeakable, albeit often unspeakably. The allegorist departs from a comparable, though more conscious, sense of "doubleness."[47] Experiencing " a crisis of reference,"[48] he assumes that everything signifies something other than that which it represents: in the absence of referential confidence, each thing is made to intend another. My concern here is not with the cause of referential failure, but with the forms which failure yields.[49] Because meaning has lapsed for the allegorist as for the melancholic, both are haunted by the suspicion that any meaning found belongs not to the thing, seemingly lost to reference, but to their own constructive ingenuity. Where meaning is made, not found, anxiety as to its arbitrary and subjective nature undercuts its credibility. Double meaning triples, flawed reference being, as Paul de Man notes, "suspiciously text productive."[50] The allegorist, suspicious that he has become the source of the meaning which he cannot recover, effectively causes that meaning to recede as he buries it under renewed allegorical bids, each of them a gambit subject to denial. Or, as Max Pensky puts it:

> The more allegories the allegorist dedicates to this goal [of meaning recovery] the more the network of allegorical references multiplies and intertwines, the more distant this goal becomes, the more urgently the allegorist works, and the deeper the allegorist plunges into the well of subjectivity.[51]

Which "well" well suits the melancholic, for whom the incessant self-revision and rebuke of allegoresis may serve further to postpone recognition of the lost thing.[52]

By 1954, Faulkner's lost thing was lost and gone, separated from the white owning class by a decade of economic transition, and from Faulkner, in no small part, by the ten-year gestation of an allegorical text whose key subtext had involved him in scarcely conscious but persistent denigration of a barely present yet desired figure, eventually given up as dead. In Freud's terms, the buried presence of an unavailable love (the black Jew), encrypted in the vaginal, anal, Judaic triangle, is worked out of the textual system via a melancholic allegoresis whose rebukes amount to a sentence of death. Illegibly alive in 1942, but dead by 1954, the black Jew gives way to the barely legible Jew and to different grounds for grief, a grief sustaining the allegorical form in that it too may be spoken only indirectly and under erasure.

III

Inherent in my reading of *A Fable* are a number of quasi-cabalistic allegorical recuperations, extending through and far beyond Faulkner's overt Passion Week schematic. My Old Marshal plays Eisenhower as well as God. As a coda, and borrowing from Walter Benjamin's *The Origin of German Tragic Drama* (1925), I shall ghost a bare case for the claim that cultures dedicated to death are melancholic and liable to generate allegorical commentary.

Benjamin deals with literary responses to the Thirty Years War, and arguably, by analogy, to the Weimar.[53] Those on whom he comments confront a fallen world marked "impermanent" by historical catastrophe. For Benjamin, allegory renders the ruins runic:

> in allegory the observer is confronted with the *facies hippocratica* of history, as a petrified, primordial landscape. Everything about history that, from the very beginning, has been un-timely, sorrowful, unsuccessful, is expressed in a face—or rather in a death's head. . . . this is the form in which man's subjection to nature is most obvious. . . . This is the heart of the allegorical way of seeing, of the baroque, secular explanation of history as the Pas-sion of the world. The greater the significance, the greater the subjection to death, be-cause death digs most deeply the jagged line of demarcation between physical nature and significance.[54]

Where reality is hollowed out by death, and intrinsic meaning has been evacuated, the allegorist abridges loss by the arbitrary introduction of emblematic significance. For "ruin" read "rune."[55] From the "remnant" take "voluptuous . . . significance."[56] On the fragment write "eruptive expression[s] of allegorical interpretation."[57]

Benjamin's allegorists mourn the dead things that cause them grief, but do so with disrespect, since "[a]ny person, any object, any relationship can [to them] mean absolutely anything else."[58] Arguably, a three-legged racehorse might em-blematize the workings of abstract value within capital (but more of that, soon). I offer Benjamin's reconstruction of a poetics apt to a mortifying world, as a gloss on Faulkner's response to the "hot," "cold," and "total" wars of his first half-century.

But if the model is to seem appropriate, its hermeneutic reach should perhaps extend to the least likely facets of the text. *A Fable* is set primarily in France: allu-sions to Africa (Senegal), to Asia (Tibet), and to Eastern Europe (Poland) globalize the military nexus and render Alabama anomalous. Yet, close to the center of *A Fable*, Faulkner inserts the story of a racehorse, running "on three legs" through the back-country of the South (807), unbeaten, and attended by a black minister, a child jockey, and an English groom. The horse, stolen from "a United States oil baron" (806) and pursued by his agents, is capable of "complete invisibility" (808, 810, 812) and runs at "unbelievable speed" for "unbelievable odds" (812), amass-ing a presumed fortune, none of which is recovered. I would stress that the apoc-ryphal beast is repeatedly spoken of as "three-legged" and "running on three legs," which is rather more than lame: the fourth leg is likely to be a swinger not a limper, but since the animal, eventually shot by the groom, vanishes without trace, its anatomy is a matter of speculation.

The story seems out of place, though the trinity of attendants do make it to

France, where additional information is supplied. The groom is named Mr Harry, pronounced "Mistairy," or "Mystery" (853). The minister, originally Sutterfield, is re-named Tooleyman, a corruption of *Tout le Monde* (804). The jockey is anonymous. In France the minister pursues the groom (both in uniform), and waits for Mistairy to speak: we are offered no grounds for the pursuit, and no disclosure is forth-coming: "'He aint ready yet,' the old Negro said. 'We can wait. There's plenty of time yet.' 'We?' the runner said. 'You and God too?'" (853) Stretching it, or, care of Benjamin, engaging in an "eruptive expression of allegorical interpretation,"[59] all the world waits for Mystery to utter. The prophet may well talk of profit, because, while in France, Mr Harry (known simply as the private), has been running some-thing akin to a joint bank and insurance company. Each pay-day lengthy queues form around the ex-groom's billet (719, 797).

Let us suppose that I am part of one of those queues: the deal is that I borrow ten shillings. I repay six pence a day for thirty days (that is, fifteen shillings). I win if I die, since at my death elements of the loan are outstanding: my profit is my death. If I survive, his profit is my life, potentially worth five shillings. The typical "*client*" (801) reinvests each month, so that "the entire battalion role could have been called by anyone detailed to sit beside the man's bunk" (719). Nonetheless, the system works because I gamble on dying. My collateral may be my life, but I borrow be-cause I am likely to die: my expectation is perhaps tempered by a suspicion that via debt to a man ready to treat mortality as collateral, I somehow increase my chance of survival, if only so that I can pay off the debt and yield him a profit.

The private invests in the fact that in Picardy, in the late spring of 1916, just prior to the First Battle of the Somme (795), men expect to die. His bank prospers be-cause although very many die (proving to be negative or devalued assets), those who live (each, in effect, an exemplary "technological break" in the financial sec-tor) will advertise the private's "[a]ssociation" (798) among new conscripts.[60] The queues will reform and extend: at their edge are parked staff cars, containing var-iously a colonel delegated from Whitehall (719–20), a French cabinet secretary (798), a female American philanthropist investing in "air squadrons," with perhaps a Wall Street name (799), the Old Marshal, and the black minister (857). The pri-vate's financial arrangements attract agents of the state, in part because the ex-groom has a new "fix" on the extraction of profit from death. We are assured that his "worn money-belt" is "apparently inexhaustible, [and] anyway bottomless" (797), which may be why Tooleyman pursues him.

To float a bank, even an informal one, the private will have needed capital. His "bottomless" money-belt must rest on prior accumulation, whose unannounced source is likely to have been profits taken from betting on the horse. Those monies *are* a mystery; they vanish, perhaps with the groom, from America. Tooleyman tells the lawyer that there was "enough" (832), a "heap" (840); forty thousand dollars are mentioned (840). He tells the runner, "There wasn't no money" (849). I am less concerned with whether-or-not or how much than with establishing a connection between a three-legged horse embodying speed and a bank profiteering on expectancy of death. That the link is tenuous is virtually obligatory in a Benjaminian sense, since connections in allegory ("speculative," "enigmatic," "sententious," "abstract") are possible only because the material reality of the elements involved has been eviscerated by a destructive historical context.[61] The horse in question could not be more immaterial; indeed, the manner of its immateriality suggests a further allegorical layer, which I have space only to intimate.

For "horse" read "price," or, better, the concept of "abstract value." Tooleyman insists: "we couldn't have stole it [the horse], even if we had wanted to. Because it never belonged to no man to be stole from. It was the world's horse. The champion. No, that's wrong too. Things belonged to it, not it to things. Things and people both" (804). He might be describing the function not of money, but of that notional value, by way of which mean monetary sums (in the form of prices) are attached to all "[t]hings and people." Value is the abstracted essence of sociability under capital, in so far as its concept allows each and every thing to be drawn into relation with each and every other thing. Marx notes that "if one considers the concept of value, then the actual object is regarded only as a sign; it counts not as itself but as what it is worth."[62] Regarded as an actual object, the horse is an impossibility—three-legged, ubiquitous, tending to vanish, and having a body merely insofar as that body is a sign for speed ("only during those incredible moments against a white rail did the horse . . . become visible" [812]). Money, ever since Adam Smith, has been spoken of as velocity; except that not even money sticks to Mr Harry's horse—a beast that Faulkner resolutely *de*forms in order to remove it from all forms, save speed (a curiously formless horse). Again I am reminded of Marx, who noted that value might circulate outside those commodities through which it appears to realize itself: "[Value] suddenly presents itself as an independent substance, endowed with a motion of its own, passing through a lifeprocess of its own, in which money and commodities are mere forms which it assumes and casts off in turn."[63] The motion of the horse is presumably circular, since it runs on "white railed" circuits throughout the South. Without form save circulation "it" nonetheless draws toward itself a range of agencies who run in its tracks. Railroad and insurance companies, banks, the federal police and the United Press are among its pursuants (810). The list might serve to close my hermeneutic circle: if the three-legged racehorse emblematizes Value, it must contain not "an atom of matter,"[64] yet it must give form to all "things and people." Except that the allegorical curve ends in France with the private's bank, where the horse takes final and formless form as those monies made from and reinvested in the expectation of death. In France, Death is "the world's horse."

Like the Corporal's mutiny, the private's bank is a "fix," enabling high profits to be drawn from renewable and catastrophic levels of mortality. Having reached my conclusion, I feel that I have constructed a "schema" from "cyphers."[65] Nor am I reassured by Benjamin's observation: "And that is what the Allegorist does in this age drunk with acts of cruelty both lived and imagined. . . . He drags the essence of what is depicted out before the image in writing as a caption."[66] By now, Faulkner's captions, circa 1953, should be clear; consisting of variants on "Money makes mortification make Money." With luck, also clear is the degree to which *A Fable*'s allegory is economically determined, both in its substance and as an aesthetic choice.

IV

All of which leaves me, as a coda to my coda, with the horse's leg—or, more accurately, pulling it. Sayre Greenfield's *The Ends of Allegory* notes that allegoresis, by dint of extended contrivance, is always liable to an "air of the ridiculous."[67] Currently, my equine leg has comically little to stand on and much to carry. Though convinced that abstract value abstracts from the horse to the tune of one leg, in order to cast that deformation as an allegorical sign for its immaterial circuits, I am less convinced that I have convinced others. Interpreters of allegory, like allegorists themselves, fear the charge of mere ingenuity. More evidence is needed, if what fits is to avoid seeming "fitted up." A singular equine leg does singly appear elsewhere in the text, on a desk in the office or "cubicle" of the old general's aide: one of two bronzes, the first "a delicate and furious horse poised weightless and epicene on one leg," the second a head by Gaudier-Brzeska, "not cast, molded but cut by hand out of the amalgam" (928). Feminized, and marked weightless, secondary ("cast") and intellectual, in contradistinction to its male, weighty, primary ("cut") and manual counterpart, the leg is aestheticized to a degree that leaves it balanced on style alone. Since its presence in the room is also likened to that of a "beautifully-furled London umbrella," itself as unexpected there as a "domino" or "fan," the style of the leg grows sartorial, even as its "poise" turns deceptive: a "domino" is a cloak with a half mask, worn most typically at masquerades; a "fan" may be used to hide the face. In the case of the missing leg, this leg, at least initially, looks like a slightly artificial suspect.

A second single leg, also attached to a runner, makes a more conclusive appearance. In the final section, the runner, terribly scarred from the second attempted mutiny, visits both the corporal's graves, in Vienne-la-Pucelle (the emptied tomb) and in Paris (the "eternal" monument to the "permanent" arms economy). At the second tomb, whose contents he cannot know, he interrupts the state funeral for the old general. Faulkner describes him as "not a man but a mobile and upright scar": "on crutches, he had one arm and one leg, one entire side of his hatless head was one hairless eyeless and earless sear" (1070). The one-legged man, almost more leg than man, given the one-sided disposition of his scar, impedes the passage of the supreme commander's corpse into the tomb where the corporal's bones lie. Allegorically speaking, he blocks the final configuration of the economic "fix" that renders military production permanent. His objection to the symbolic union is itself symbolic and temporary. He is beaten and cast aside, but the form of his resistance remains interesting. Discovered in the gutter of a cul-de-sac by the Norman (second in the old general's year at St Cyr), he laughs at "the ring of faces enclosing him" and warns, "Tremble. I'm not going to die. Never" (1072). He delivers the promise from a pieta, "lying in the cradle of the old man's arm . . . head . . . turned a little." On the face of it, his claim is nonsensical: a limping wound who has just regained consciousness in the posture of the dead Christ would stretch credibility with a bid for longevity, let alone eternity. Yet Faulkner's logic is impeccable: the runner has interrupted the official Ascension of the Judaic couple, Father and Son, whose democidal union guarantees that production for destruction need have no foreseeable end. Given that a *permanent* arms economy may be said to take lasting profit from the manufacture of injury,[68] the runner offers the countereternity of the damage done. He, as the ruined corporeality of the ascendant Corporal, is that everlasting deformity that cannot die, at least not for as long money made from mutilation proves to be the motor that drives the dominant regime of accumulation.

The runner, so read, is the horse's leg, seen from below; seen, that is, from the viewpoint of the deformed rather than from that of the deformers. His outcry gives the lie to two equine lies, to the deceitful statuette and to the old general's denial that he and the Corporal should not be mistaken for "jewish . . . peasants swapping a horse" (998). Those who make a fast buck from death, in 1918 as in 1954, may need aestheticized versions of what they do in order to obscure what they have done or are about to do. The "poised" leg graces the desk of a military aide, from behind which the old general first receives Marya, Magda, and the Corporal's "wife." The three women watched him "while he went around the desk and sat down behind the two bronzes and looked at them—the harsh high mountain face which might have been a twin of the corporal's except for the difference in age, the serene and peaceful one which showed no age at all or perhaps all ages, and between them the strained and anguished one of the girl" (928–29). The old general "looks" at a version of the face he will execute, but sees it "masked" in the aesthetic, care of a pronounal shift punctuated by a pause which facilitates the splitting of the referent. "[T]hem—," paced by its caesural dash, refers doubly, to the art and to the supplicants, whose supplication is perhaps made bearable by the old general's contemplative moment of distraction. To pull the other one—the one about denial of horse trading—is to recognize the enormity of that from which the old general must distract himself. His equine aside goes to the nub of the allegory: read through the stencil of the story of the horse thieves, whose notional profits float a bank that banks on death, he, care of the Corporal, *is* a trader whose collateral (were it but seen as such) amounts to the democidally dead. The old general shares with the private a readiness to speculate on mortality—still, in 1954 as in 1918, "the world's horse." If leaders of the military-industrial complex were what they invested in, they *would* be Greeks, Armenians, and Jews, but since they cannot let themselves see the wound in the profit, they remain investors with decoration on their desks.

For a time between 1943 and 1954, Faulkner may have taken "puzzled" relief from his troubled and underarticulated exploration of "the Jew," since, and for a time, the Jew allowed him to retain the black, from whose work his own increasingly archaic South was made.[69] But, by the close of *A Fable*, the startling and partial recognition that he and his fellow citizens carry an illegible Jewish mark can only have been grounds for melancholia, whose impeded processes of mourning go some way to explain the subsumed political charges at *A Fable*'s core.[70] Articulated, those charges run as follows. The southern plantocracy, from slavery through debt peonage to Jim Crow, and with government sanction, proved itself capable of exterminating blacks (cognitively, experientially, and actually). Subsequently, and under linked pressures from out-migration and incipient African American demands for civil rights during the 1940s, whites, at a loss for their prior selves, sensed, in that loss, their own blackness. Such intimations, occurring coterminously with public absorption of facts concerning state-engineered Jewish genocide, exposed those who experienced their own darkening to melancholic wounds. To be black was to be vulnerable: vulnerablility, perceived through the jointed stencil of a militarized economy and the Holocaust, amounted to vulnerability to democide. The reverse proved equally true and offered an alternate route to the same mournful conclusion: for white southerners, between 1945 and 1954, to appreciate their vulnerability to democide was to recognize their blackness.

NOTES

Introduction

1. Karl Marx and Friedrich Engels, *The German Ideology* (London: Lawrence and Wishart, 1974), 51.

2. Mikhail Bakhtin, quoted in V. N. Vološinov, *Marxism and the Philosophy of Language*, trans. Ladislav Matejka and I. R. Titunik (New York: Seminar Press, 1973), 199.

3. Martha Woodmansee and Mark Osteen, *The New Economic Criticism: Studies at the Intersection of Literature and Economics* (New York: Routledge, 1999), 14.

4. Michel Aglietta insists that without expressing "the social content of economic relations" we cannot interpret "the forces and conflicts at work in the economic process." He adds, "[p]roduction is always the production of social relations as well as of material objects. To take these activities and relations as the starting point of scientific research in economics, instead of simply subjects, functions and goods, has a decisive bearing on this discipline." See Aglietta, *A Theory of Capitalist Regulation: The US Experience*, trans. David Fernbach (London: Verso, 1979), 4, 24.

5. Clyde Woods, *Development Arrested: Race, Power and Blues in the Mississippi Delta* (London: Verso, 1998), 127. See also Jack Temple Kirby, *Rural Worlds Lost: The American South, 1920–1960* (Baton Rouge: Louisana State University Press, 1987), 64. For an overview of the process see Pete Daniel, *Lost Revolutions: The South in the 1950s* (Chapel Hill: University of North Carolina Press, 2000), particularly chap. 2, "Creation and Destruction," 39–60.

6. Woods, *Development Arrested*, 143.

7. Jay R. Mandle, *The Roots of Black Poverty* (Durham, N.C.: Duke University Press, 1978), 84.

8. Woods, *Development Arrested*, 127.

9. Quoted in Stuart Kidd, "The Cultural Politics of Farm Mechanization: Farm Security Administration Photographs of the Southern Landscape, 1935–1943," in Tony Badger, Walter Edgar, and Jan Norby Gretland, eds., *Southern Landscapes* (Tübingen: Tauffenburg Verlag, 1996), 146.

10. Jonathan Wiener, "Class Structure and Economic Development in the American South, 1865–1955," *American Historical Review* 84, no.4 (1979): 970–1006.

11. Mark Tushnett, *The American Law of Slavery, 1810–1860* (Princeton: Princeton University Press, 1981), 6.

12. Charles Johnson, Edwin R. Embree, and W. W. Alexander, *The Collapse of the Cotton Tenancy: Summary of Field Studies and Statistical Surveys, 1933–1935* (Freeport, N.Y.: Books for Libraries Press, 1977), 22.

13. Karl Marx, *Grundrisse*, trans. Martin Nicolaus (Harmondsworth: Penguin, 1973), 749–50.

14. Joel Williamson, *The Crucible of Race: Black-White Relations in the American South Since Emancipation* (New York: Oxford University Press, 1984), 499.

15. Malcolm Bull, *Seeing Things Hidden: Apocalypse, Vision and Totality* (London: Verso, 2000), 207, 252.

16. Ibid., 180.

17. My phrasing derives from Bull: "for something inexperienced and or unknown hiding involves becoming more knowable. In other words, being hidden does not involve going into hiding, but coming into hiding," Ibid., 180.

18. Theodor Adorno, "Parataxis," in *Notes to Literature, Vol. 2*, ed. Rolph Tiedemann, trans. Shierry Weber Nicholsen (New York: Columbia University Press, 1992), 134.

19. Bull, *Seeing Things Hidden*, 294.

20. Immanuel Wallerstein "The Ideological Tensions of Capitalism: Universalism versus Racism and Sexism," in Etienne Balibar and Immanuel Wallerstein, *Race, Nation, Class: Ambiguous Identities* (London: Verso, 1991), 29.

21. Jay R. Mandle, *Not Slave, Not Free: The African American Experience Since the Civil War* (Durham, N.C.: Duke University Press, 1992).

22. Louis Althusser, "Ideology and Ideological State Apperatuses," in *Essays on Ideology* (New Left Books: London, 1976), 36.

23. Judith Butler, "Stubborn Attachment, Bodily Subjection: Rereading Hegel on the Unhappy Consciousness," in *The Psychic Life of Power* (Stanford: Stanford University Press, 1977), 35.

24. Fredric Jameson, *The Political Unconscious: Narrative as a Socially Symbolic Act* (London: Methuen, 1981), p. 79.

25. Theodor Adorno and Max Horkheimer, *Dialectic of Enlightenment*, trans. John Cumming (London: Verso, 1979), 24.

26. David Harvey, *The Condition of Postmodernity* (Cambridge: Blackwell, 1990), 105–6.

27. Marx, *Grundrisse*, 749–50.

28. Jacques Derrida, *Dissemination*, trans. Barbara Johnson (Chicago: University of Chicago Press, 1981), 70

29. Bull, *Seeing Things Hidden*, 38. See also Derrida, *Dissemination*, 70–75.

30. Mikhail Bakhtin, *Problems of Dostoevsky's Poetics*, trans. Caryl Emerson (Manchester: Manchester University Press, 1984), 32.

31. Bakhtin, quoted in Vološinov, *Marxism and the Philosophy of Language*, 199.

32. *The Cassell Dictionary of Slang*, ed. Jonathon Greene (London: Cassell, 1989), notes that "to go down" may refer both to fellatio and to cunnilingus. *The Random House Dictionary of Slang*, ed. J. E. Lighter (New York: Random House, 1994), grants the phrase currency from the first decade of the twentieth century.

33. See particularly: "—O go down, Moses / Away down to Egypt's land, / And tell King Pharaoh / To let my people go!"

Chapter One: Earthing *The Hamlet*

1. Edith Wharton, *The Age of Innocence* (Hamondsworth: Penguin, 1974), 216.

2. Ibid., 20.

3. Ibid., 216.

4. Ibid., 215.

5. Ibid., 183.

6. Ibid.

7. Ibid., 183.

8. Thorstein Veblen, *The Theory of the Leisure Class* (London: Unwin, 1970), 51.

9. Henry James, *The Bostonians* (London: John Lehmann, 1952), 33.

10. Veblen, *Theory of the Leisure Class*, 94–95.

11. Ibid., particulary chap. 3, "Conspicuous Lesure," 41–60.

12. William Faulkner, *The Hamlet*, in *William Faulkner Novels 1936–1940*, ed. Joseph Blotner and Noel Polk (New York: Library of America, 1990), 777. Hereafter, page references will appear in parenthetically in the text.

13. Mary Douglas, *Purity and Danger: An Analysis of Concepts of Pollution and Taboo* (Harmondsworth: Penguin, 1970), 48.

14. See Albert C. Smith, "'Southern Violence' Reconsidered: Arson as Protest in Black Belt Georgia, 1865–1910," *Journal of Southern History* 51, no. 4 (Nov. 1985): 527–64.

15. William Faulkner, "Barn Burning," in *Dr Martino and Other Stories* (London: Chatto and Windus, 1965), 13–14.

16. Ibid., 17.

17. Paul Ricoeur, "The Metaphoric Process as Cognition, Imagination and Feeling," *Critical Inquiry* 5, no. 1: 145.

18. The terms "focus" (a particular metaphoric term) and "frame" (or network of words "focused" by the initial term) are borrowed from Max Black. He adds that the frame's net may extend from the immediate context of the focal term to the outer limits of the work. See Max Black, "Metaphor," in *Models and Metaphors* (Ithaca, N.Y.: Cornell University Press, 1962), 25–47.

19. Smith, "'Southern Violence' Reconsidered," 528.

20. Considering de Spain's house, Ab instructs his son (Colonel Sartoris Snopes), "Pretty

and white, ain't it? . . . That's sweat. Nigger sweat. Maybe it ain't white enough yet to suit him. Maybe he wants to mix some white sweat with it" ("Barn Burning," 18).

21. Michel de Certeau, *The Practice of Everyday Life*, trans. Steven Rendall (Berkeley: University of California Press, 1988), 82.

22. Ibid., 86–87.

23. Ibid.

24. Paul Ricoeur, "Metaphoric Process," 144.

25. de Certeau, *Practice of Everyday Life*, 88, 86. The assemblage of brief quotations in the sentence prior to this passage is drawn from 84–89.

26. Richard Gray, *The Life of William Faulkner* (Oxford: Blackwell, 1994), 254.

27. James Snead, *Figures of Division* (London: Methnen, 1986), 159–60.

28. Louise K. Barnett, "The Speech Community of *The Hamlet*," *Centennial Review* 3, no. 3 (Summer 1986): 405.

29. Mauri Skinfill, "Reconstructing Class in Faulkner's Late Novels: *The Hamlet* and the Discovery of Capital," *Studies in American Fiction* 24, no. 2 (1996): 10.

30. Joseph Urgo, "Faulkner's Real Estate: Land and Literary Speculation in *The Hamlet*," *Mississippi Quarterly* 48, no. 3 (Summer, 1995): 450.

31. Richard Moreland, *Faulkner and Modernism: Rereading and Rewriting* (Madison: University of Wisconsin Press, 1990), 145.

32. See Hyatt H. Waggoner, *William Faulkner: From Jefferson to the World* (Lexington: University of Kentucky Press, 1959), 185; Olga Vickery, *The Novels of William Faulkner* (Barton Rouge: Louisiana State University Press, 1959), 169; Joseph Gold, "The Normality of Snopesism: Universal Themes in Faulkner's *The Hamlet*," *Wisconsin Studies in Contemporary Literature* 3 (Winter, 1962): 25–34.

33. Writing to Saxe Commins in October 1939, Faulkner notes, "Book Four happens in 1890, approximately. Have recollection of dating War somewhere in script as 40 years ago. Please watch for it. I will catch it in galley if you have not." *Selected Letters of William Faulkner*, ed. Joseph Blotner (New York: Random House, 1978), 115. The span of the novel is three years, hence 1887–90 ("approximately"). Richard Gray points out that while Faulkner could be "a little uncertain about dates . . . . he was much more certain and clear when it came to the processes of historical change." See Gray, *The Life of William Faulkner*, 256.

34. For useful discussion of sharecropping as a form of debt slavery, see Roger L. Ransom and Richard Sutch, *One Kind of Freedom: The Economic Consequences of Emancipation* (Cambridge; Cambridge University Press, 1977), particularly chap. 8, "The Trap of Debt Peonage," 149–70; Jay R. Mandle, *Not Slave, Not Free: The African American Experience Since the Civil War* (Durham: Duke University Press, 1992), particularly chap. 2, "The Limits to African American Freedom," 21–32; and Pete Daniel, *The Shadow of Slavery: Peonage in the South, 1901–1969* (London: University of Illinois Press, 1972).

35. Raymond Williams, "Base and Superstructure in Marxist Cultural Theory," in *Problems in Materialism and Culture* (London: Verso, 1980), 31–49.

36. See Steven Hahn, *The Roots of Southern Populism: Yeomen Farmers and the Transformation of the Georgia Upcountry, 1850–1890* (New York: Oxford University Press, 1983), particularly "Epilogue: The Contours of Populism," 269–89.

37. Ibid., 239–68.

38. Noel Polk suggests that the portion of Houston's land on which Will Varner foreclosed was purchased by Flem, who rents it to his cousin Mink. While acknowledging that Flem owns considerable acreage, I remain unconvinced that he is Mink's landlord. See Polk, "Around, behind, above, below Men: Ratliff's Buggies and the Homosocial in Yoknapatawpha," in *Haunted Bodies: Gender and Southern Texts*, ed. Anne Goodwyn Jones and Susan Donaldson (Charlottesville: University Press of Virginia, 1997), 352.

39. In fact, Faulkner began work on the Snopes novel in the mid-1920s (under the projected title, *Father Abraham*): arguably, Flem's ties of class loyalty to the tenants from whom he descends are enhanced by his inception in a period prior to the New Deal, with its federally induced mercantile incursions, and attendant, if limited, broadening of economic opportunity in agriculture. For the Agricultural Adjustment Program, see, Jonathan M. Wiener, "Class Structure and Economic Development in the American South, 1865–1955," *American History Review* 84, part 2 (October 1979): 970–1006; Harold D. Woodman, "Class, Race, Politics and the Modernization of the Postbellum South," *Journal of Southern History* 63, no. 1 (Feb. 1997): 3–22; and Gavin Wright, *Old South, New South: Revolutions in the Southern Economy Since the Civil War* (New York: Basic Books, 1986), particularly chap. 7, "The Interwar Years: Assault on the Low-Wage Economy," 198–238.

40. The casting of Flem as "naked aggression" and "undiluted acquisitiveness" [Cleanth Brooks, *William Faulkner: The Yoknapatawpha Country* (New Haven: Yale University Press, 1974], 190) stems in part from an understandable tendency to read *The Hamlet* through the rest of the trilogy. Nonetheless, to read backwards from *The Mansion* (1959) through *The Town* (1957) is to embourgeoisify Flem too soon and too emphatically. Crucially, such accounts both ignore the views of Flem's contemporaries at the close of the 1880s (the poor men on the rich man's porch), and avoid Faulkner's preoccupation with labor and its changing forms, a preoccupation he sustained over the late 1930s and into the early 1940s.

41. Michael Millgate, *The Achievement of William Faulkner* (London: Constable, 1966), 94–95.

42. Urgo, "Faulkner's Real Estate," 443–57.

43. Faulkner, "Barn Burning," 18.

44. Ransom and Sutch, *One Kind of Freedom*, 137.

45. Two price systems ran concurrently in country stores in the postbellum South: cash price and credit price, the latter including the price of credit charged to all those without money in hand. Figures detailing the increasing cost of southern credit between 1875 and 1896 (based on Georgia and Louisiana) read like larceny. See Ransom and Sutch, *One Kind of Freedom*, appendix D, "Calculation of Interest Charged for Credit Implicit in the Dual Price System," 237–43. See also, Thomas D. Clark, *Pills, Petticoats and Ploughs* (New York: Bobbs-Merrill, 1944), 316–18.

46. Calvin S. Brown, *A Glossary of Faulkner's South* (New Haven: Yale University Press, 1977), 179.

47. Ransom and Sutch, *One Kind of Freedom*, 170.

48. Faulkner, "Barn Burning," 13, 14.

49. For elaboration, see my *Fictions of Labor: William Faulkner and the South's Long Revolution* (Cambridge: Cambridge University Press, 1997), 123–29.

50. Ransom and Sutch, *One Kind of Freedom*, 187.

51. Umberto Eco, *A Theory of Semiotics* (London: Macmillan, 1977), 205.

52. Ricoeur, "Metaphoric Process," 153.

53. William Faulkner, *Go Down, Moses*, in *William Faulkner: Novels 1942–1954*, 245.

54. For "feice" and "fice," see Calvin S. Brown, *Glossary*, 80–81. Etymologically, "fice" contains Faulkner's pun, the alternate spelling "fise," meaning also "a breaking wind" (*The Century Dictionary*, vol. 3 [London: The Times, 1899]).

55. Faulkner had precedents for his liberties in that, as an allegorical figure of Liberty, Marianne has had several careers. Her role in representing the nation changed as the nation changed. She was variously a virgin and a mistress, a human and a divine. See Maurice Agulhon, *Marianne into Battle: Republican Imagery and Symbolism in France, 1789–1880*, trans. Janet Lloyd (Cambridge: Cambridge University Press, 1981), 40.

56. See Noel Polk, "Around, behind, above, below Men." While Polk's revelatory study deals in sociosexual areas outside the direct concern of this essay, my account of the vehicles and their word would not have been possible without his insights.

57. Stores were the first Southern outlets for "prepared" foods, considered a luxury. "Most popular of all . . . was the sardine packed in cottonseed oil, seasoned with pepper sauce and eaten with salty crackers. So popular was the combination that it was recognized as a popular characteristic of the entire country-store trade" (Thomas D. Clark, *Pills, Petticoats and Ploughs*, 45).

58. Fernand Braudel, *Civilization and Capitalism, 15th–18th Century. Volume 2: The Wheels of Commerce*, trans. Siân Reynolds (London: Collins, 1982), 229.

59. For the manner in which barter differs from other modes of exchange, see Caroline Humphrey and Stephen Hugh-Jones, "Introduction," in *Barter, Exchange and Value: An Anthropological Approach*, ed. Caroline Humphrey and Stephen Hugh-Jones (Cambridge: Cambridge University Press, 1992), 1–20. See also John Forrester, *Truth Games: Lies, Money and Psychoanalysis* (Cambridge, Mass.: Harvard University Press, 1997), particularly "Gift, Money and Debt," 101–71.

60. Ratliff's mirroring meditations occur at the close of "Eula, Book Two" (868–73), and at the start of "The Long Summer, Book Three," (877–82).

61. Noel Polk, "Around, behind, above, below Men," 357.

62. Planters argued for laws requiring the fencing of stock rather than of crops on the grounds that they wished to protect stock improvement and preserve timber. Small holders rightly saw this as a threat to their capacity to own livestock, because they "owned" no grazing land. See Hahn, *Roots of Southern Populism*, particularly chap. 7, "Common Right and Commonwealth," 239–68.

63. Ibid., 239.

64. A cropper might "crop" on a greater or smaller "share" agreement. The size of his "share" depended on the amount of capital he brought to the agreement. A cropper's capital might take the form of a plough, seed cotton, or stock.

65. See Frederick Douglass, *Narrative of the Life of Frederick Douglass* (London: Penguin, 1985), 114–15.

66. Karl Marx, *Grundrisse*, trans: Martin Nicolaus (Harmondsworth: Penguin, 1973), 749–50.

Chapter Two: Comparative Cows: Reading *The Hamlet* for Its Residues

1. Steven Hahn, *The Roots of Southern Populism: Yeomen Farmers and the Transformation of the Georgia Upcountry, 1850–1890* (New York: Oxford University Press, 1983), 243.

2. William Faulkner, *The Hamlet*, in *William Faulkner: Novels 1936–1940*, ed. Joseph Blotner and Noel Polk (New York: Library of America, 1990), 733. Subsequent references to this edition will be included in the body of the text.

3. Hahn, *Roots of Southern Populism*, 239.

4. J. Crawford King, Jr., "The Closing of the Southern Range: A Reinterpretation," *Journal of Southern History* 48, no. 1 (Feb. 1982): 63.

5. Quoted by Hahn, *Roots of Southern Populism*, 250.

6. Ibid., 288

7. Richard Godden, *Fictions of Labor: William Faulkner and the South's Long Revolution* (New York: Cambridge University Press, 1997), 53–66.

8. Mark Tushnett, *The American Law of Slavery 1810–1860: Considerations of Humanity and Interest* (Princeton: Princeton University Press, 1981), 6–7.

9. See G.W.F. Hegel, *The Phenomenology of Mind, Vol. 1* (New York: Macmillan, 1910), 175–88.

10. See C. Vann Woodward, *Origins of the New South, 1877–1913* (Baton Rouge: Louisiana State University Press, 1971), 211–15; Edward L. Ayers, *The Promise of the New South: Life After Reconstruction* (New York: Oxford University Press, 1993), 154–55, and "Chain Gang," *Encyclopedia of Southern Culture*, ed. Charles Reagan Wilson and William Ferns (Chapel Hill: University of North Carolina Press: 1989), 1501–02.

11. William Faulkner, *Absalom, Absalom!*, in *William Faulkner: Novels 1936–1940*, 306.

12. Ibid., 307.

13. William Faulkner, "Barn Burning," collected in *Dr Martino and Other Stories* (London: Chatto and Windus, 1965), 13–14.

14. The Agricultural Adjustment Act (1933) initiated a New Deal for southern agriculture, described by Jonathon Wiener as the South's "Second Civil War," and associated with shrinkage in regional cotton production and a consequent displacement of African American labor. I shall detail this transition, and its effects, in the next chapter. Here, suffice to say that falling cotton acreage and a drastically declining tenantry arguably initiated a Second Reconstruction. See Jonathan Wiener, "Class Structure and Economic Development in the American South, 1865–1955," *American Historical Review* 84, no. 2 (1979): 1006; Jay R. Mandle, *Not Slave, Not Free: The African American Experience Since the Civil War* (Durham, N.C.: Duke University Press, 1993), 89; Gavin Wright, *Old South, New South: Revolutions in the Southern Economy Since the Civil War* (New York: Basic Books, 1986), particularly chaps. 3 and 4, 51–123.

15. See "The Chambermaid's Second Song," "From pleasure of the bed, / Dull as a worm, / His rod and its butting head / Limp as a worm, / His spirit that has fled / Blind as a worm." *Collected Poems of W. B. Yeats* (London: Macmillan, 1967), 346. On Faulkner's early and "voracious" reading of Yeats, see Joseph Blotner, *Faulkner: A Biography, Vol. 1* (New York: Random House, 1974), 163, 203.

16. William Faulkner, *The Mansion*, in *William Faulkner: Novels, 1957–1962*, ed. Joseph Blotner and Noel Polk (New York: The Library of America, 1999), 691–720.

17. Donald M. Kartiganer, *The Fragile Thread: The Meaning of Form in Faulkner's Novels* (Amherst: University of Massachusetts Press, 1979), 119–24.

18. For a full account of Ike's first and autochthonic night with the cow, see my "Comparative Idiocy: A Phenomenological Reading of *The Hamlet* as a Rebuke to an American Century," in Joseph Urgo and A. J. Abadie, eds., *Faulkner in America* (Jackson: University Press of Mississippi, 2001), 1–23.

19. Charles Saunders Peirce, *The Collected Papers of Charles Saunders Peirce*, ed. C. Hartshorne, P. Weiss, A. Burks (Cambridge, Mass.: Harvard University Press, 1931–58), 3: 365.

20. Paul Ricoeur, "The Metaphoric Process as Cognition, Imagination, Feeling," *Critical Inquiry* 5, no. 1 (Autumn 1978): 143–59, particularly 146.

21. Umberto Eco, *A Theory of Semiotics* (London: Macmillan, 1977), 205.

22. "To the hegemony of the marketplace, Populism counterposed the vision of a producers' commonwealth achieved through cooperative enterprise and public regulation of exchange" (Hahn, *Roots of Southern Populism*, 282).

23. Like much of Mink's story, the "lightning" can be read from within the master/slave paradigm: issuing murderously from the ground, the "lightning/pain" might well embody that moment of recognition whereby the bound man appreciates that the objects of his labor (in this instance, the worked earth) stand as evidence of his independent will. Hegel notes, "Precisely in labor, where there seems to be some outsider's mind and ideas involved, the bondsman becomes aware, through his rediscovery of himself by himself, of having and being a 'mind of his own'" (*Phenomenology of Mind, Vol. 1*, 187).

24. Early in *The Hamlet*, the narrator comments of Varner that "he was a farmer, a usurer, a veterinarian" (733). The framing of "usury" within nominally more benevolent activities reveals more about the narrator than it does about the landowner.

25. Faulkner scholarship works to distinguish the various voices that make up *The Hamlet*: see Millie M. Kidd, "The Dialogic Perspective in William Faulkner's *The Hamlet*," *Mississippi Quarterly* 44, no. 3 (Summer 1991): 309–20; Charlotte Renner, "Talking and Writing in Faulkner's Snopes Trilogy," *Southern Literary Journal* 15, no. 11 (Fall 1982): 61–73; Louise K. Barnett, "The Speech Community of *The Hamlet*," *Centennial Review* 30, no. 3 (Summer 1986): 400–414. Nonetheless the prevalent view remains that the narrative voice follows the communal voice which follows the voice of Ratliff. Richard Gray notes, "We are told many tales by the people of Frenchman's Bend, by Ratliff in particular, and by an anonymous narrative voice that weaves in and out of the voices of the community, sharing its inclinations and idiom" (*Life of William Faulkner* [Oxford: Blackwell, 1996], 257).

26. For a fuller account, see Joseph Urgo, "Faulkner's Real Estate: Land and Literary Speculation in *The Hamlet*," *Mississippi Quarterly* 48, no. 3, (1995): 443–457.

Chapter Three: Revenants, Remnants, and Counterrevolution in "The Fire and the Hearth"

1. Norman Thomas, in a letter to Senator Robert F. Wagner, quoted in Vera Rony, "The Orgnization of Black and White Farm Workers in the South," collected in Thomas R. Frazier,

ed., *The Underside of American History: Other Readings, Vol. II—Since 1865* (New York: Harcourt and Brace, 1971), 165; Charles S. Johnson, Edwin R. Embree, and W. W. Alexander, *The Collapse of Cotton Tenancy: Summary of Field Studies and Statistical Surveys, 1933–35* (Freeport, N.Y.: Books for Libraries Press, 1972), 11; Charles S. Johnson, *Shadow of the Plantation* (Chicago: University of Chicago Press, 1960 [1934]), 4.

2. See Jay R. Mandle, *Not Slave, Not Free: The African American Experience Since the Civil War* (Durham: Duke University Press, 1982), particularly chap. 3, 33–43.

3. "The first stage in the consolidation of plantations was the wholesale eviction of tenants of all classes, especially sharecroppers. The process was protracted but it seems to have been underway all over the south by 1934, the first full crop year following the creation of the AAA" (Jack Temple Kirby, *Rural Worlds Lost: The American South, 1920–1960* [Baton Rouge: Louisiana State University Press, 1987], 64).

4. Gilbert Fite, *Cotton Fields No More: Southern Agriculture, 1865–1980* (Lexington: University Press of Kentucky, 1984), 210.

5. Constraint and dependency, not autonomy, defined the social relations through which freed black tenants were required to live their lives, at least until the AAA pushed labor from the South and increased the bargaining power of those who stayed. Between 1930 and 1940, the number of black sharecroppers declined by almost a quarter, in an out-migration which Jay R. Mandle equates with the final "undermining of share tenancy." He notes that "deference became increasingly anachronistic and irrelevant [as] . . . labor market relations began, for the first time, to resemble real relations" (Mandle, *Not Slave, Not Free*, 89–90).

6. See Pete Daniel, *The Shadow of Slavery: Peonage in the South, 1901–1969* (Urbana: University of Illinois Press, 1972), particularly chaps. 8 and 9.

7. "When a slaveowner purchases a slave, he or she acquires, not the use of the slave's labor-power—not, that is, only part of the slave's activities—but the slave's labor—all the activities in which the slave engages. The fundamental social relation of slavery is thus total, engaging the full personalities of the slave owner and the slave" (Mark Tushnett, *The American Law of Slavery, 1810–1860* [Princeton: Princeton University Press, 1981], 6).

8. Johnson, Embree, and Alexander, *Collapse of the Cotton Tenancy*, 22.

9. Quoted in Kirby, *Rural Worlds Lost*, 239.

10. G.W.F. Hegel, *The Phenomenology of Mind. Vol. I*. Trans. J. B. Ballie (New York: Macmillan, 1910), 184.

11. Ibid., 176.

12. Jessica Benjamin, *The Bonds of Love: Psychoanalysis, Feminism and the Problem of Domination* (New York: Pantheon, 1988), 39.

13. See Joseph Blotner, *Faulkner: A Biography, Vol. 2* (New York: Random House, 1974). Although "The Fire and the Hearth" appeared in *Go Down, Moses*, in 1942, it was probably written late in 1939. Roth Edmonds is aged forty-three at the time of his dispute with Lucas Beauchamp and George Wilkins; since he was born in 1898, Faulkner probably intended 1941 as the story's key growing season, though since the setting of the story is contemporary, initial readers might have taken 1942 as the likely year.

14. Quoted by Stuart Kidd, "The Cultural Politics of Farm Mechanization: Farm Security Administration Photographs of the Southern Landscape, 1935–1943," in Tony Badger, Walter Edgar, and Jan Norby Gretland, eds., *Southern Landscapes* (Tübingen: Tauffenburg Verlag, 1996), 146.

15. Donald H. Grubbs, *Cry From the Cotton: The Southern Tenant Farmer's Union and the New Deal* (Chapel Hill: University of North Carolina Press, 1971), 135.

16. William Faulkner, *Go Down, Moses*, in *William Faulkner: Novels 1942–1954* (New York: Library of America, 1994), 36. Subsequent references to this edition will appear in the body of the text.

17. James Oakes, *Slavery and Freedom: An Interpretation of the Old South* (New York: Knopf, 1990), 7.

18. Ibid., 4. To claim that Zack's "crime" is not sexual is to substitute "social death" for miscegenation. Yet, after the resolution of their confrontation, Lucas asks himself a question which points to a sexual offense: "'How to God . . . can a black man ask a white man to please not lay down with his black wife?'" (46). However, at no point in *Go Down, Moses* is there a sustained suggestion that Lucas considers Molly to have been Zack's mistress. I therefore would argue that miscegenation is being used by Lucas to focus much broader questions about white expectations of black deference and continuing quasi-chattel status. These are public questions, yet in 1898 they cannot be voiced by a black speaker; Lucas calls silently upon his god because he knows that whites expect his mute compliance in their control over his body, property, and sociability—a control which extends into the most intimate area of his life, and one which is tantamount to miscegenation.

19. Hegel, *Phenomenology of Mind*, 182.

20. Ibid., 182, 186.

21. Ibid., 187.

22. Ibid.

23. Judith Butler, *Subjects of Desire: Hegelian Reflections in Twentieth-Century France* (New York: Columbia, 1987), 58.

24. See Eric Foner, *Reconstruction: America's Unfinished Revolution, 1863–1877* (New York: Harper, 1988), particularly chap. 5, "Agricultural Reconstruction"; and Gavin Wright, *Old South, New South: Revolutions in the Southern Economy Since the Civil War* (New York: Basic Books, 1968), particularly chap. 4, "Plantation, Farm and Farm Labor in the South."

25. Mandle, *Not Slave, Not Free*, 58.

26. See Karl Marx, "Economic and Philosophical Manuscripts" (1844), collected in *Early Writings*, ed. Lucio Colleti, trans. Rodney Livingston and Gregor Benton (Harmondsworth: Penguin, 1974), 140. "The land is individualized with its lord, it acquires his status, it is baronial or ducal with him, has his privileges, his jurisdiction. . . . It appears as the inorganic body of its lord. Hence the proverb *nulle terre sans marte* (no land without its master), which expresses the blending of nobility and landed property."

27. William Faulkner, *The Sound and the Fury* (New York: Random House, 1984), 80.

28. Hegel, *Phenomenology of Mind*, 184.

29. Richard King, "Lucas Beauchamp and William Faulkner: Blood Bothers," in Arthur F. Kinney, ed., *Critical Essays on William Faulkner's the McCaslin Family*, (Boston: G. K. Hall, 1990), 237. King is perceptive on the systemic absence of "community" and "group support" within tenancy.

30. William Faulkner, "Barn Burning," in *Collected Stories of William Faulkner* (New York: Random House, 1977), 312.

31. V. N. Vološinov, *Marxism and the Philosophy of Language*, trans. Ladislav Matejka and I. R. Titunik (New York: Seminar Press, 1973), 142.

32. Ibid., 144.

33. Ibid., 144, 157. Bakhtin would define "double intonation" as a form of "hybrid construction": "an utterance that belongs, by its grammatical [syntactic] and compositional markers, to a single speaker, but that actually contains, mixed within it, two utterances, two speech manners, two styles. We repeat that there is no formal-compositional and syntactic-boundary between these utterances, styles, languages, belief systems. . . . It frequently happens that even one and the same word will belong simultaneously to two belief systems that intersect in a hybrid construction" (M. M. Bakhtin, *The Dialogic Imagination*, trans. Caryl Emerson and Michael Holquist [Austin: University of Texas Press, 1981], 304–5).

34. Vološinov, *Marxism and the Philosophy of Language*, 144.

35. Gilles Deleuze, *Cinema I: The Movement of Image*, trans. Hugh Tomlinson and Barbara Habberjam (London: Athlone Press, 1997), 73–74.

36. For a valuable alternative reading of the passage, see Karl F. Zender, *Faulkner and the Politics of Reading* (Baton Rouge: Louisiana State University Press, 2002), 92–94.

37. Foner, *Reconstruction*, 7.

38. Foner describes sharecropping as the South's "own distinctive system of repressive labor relations" (ibid., 596).

39. Faulkner writes "The Fire and the Hearth" even as historians of the South, prompted by Du Bois's *Black Reconstruction in America* (1935), are beginning to revise the prevalent William Dunning and John Burgess account of Radical Reconstruction as "mistake." The Dunning school version was produced at the beginning of the century. See Howard K. Beale, "On Rewriting Reconstruction History," *American Historical Review* 45 (1940): 807–27, and David H. Donald, "The Scalawag in Mississippi Reconstruction," *Journal of Southern History* 10 (1944): 447–60.

40. Pete Daniel, *Lost Revolutions: The South in the 1950s* (Chapel Hill: University of North Carolina Press, 2000), 20.

41. See John T. Matthews, "Touching Race in *Go Down, Moses*," in Linda Wagner-Martin, ed., *New Essays on* Go Down, Moses (Cambridge: Cambridge University Press, 1996), 31. Matthews's account contrasts with more typical readings which take Lucas's activities as comic "foolishness" (Myra Jehlen, *Class and Character in Faulkner's South* [New York: Columbia University Press, 1976], 122), or as "hapless shenanigans" (Arthur F. Kinney, *Go Down, Moses: The Miscegenation of Time* [New York: Twayne, 1996], 118).

42. Clyde Woods, *Development Arrested: Race, Power and Blues in the Mississippi Delta* (London: Verso, 1998), 127.

43. See Mandle, *Roots of Black Poverty*, 71–72.

44. Leon F. Litwack, *Trouble in Mind: Black Southerners in the Age of Jim Crow* (New York: Knopf, 1998), 487.

45. Neil R. McMillen, *Dark Journey: Black Mississippians in the Age of Jim Crow* (Champaign: University of Illinois Press, 1989), 262.

46. Mandle, *Roots of Black Poverty*, 83.

47. Litwack, *Trouble in Mind*, 482.

48. Mandle, *Roots of Black Poverty*, 84.

49. Woods, *Development Arrested*, 143.

50. Mandle, *Roots of Black Poverty*, 84.

51. See Daniel, *Lost Revolutions*, particularly chap. 2, 22–38.

52. Ibid., 141.

53. Matthews, "Touching Race," 32.

54. Joel Williamson, *The Crucible of Race: Black-White Relations in the American South Since Emancipation* (New York: Oxford University Press, 1984), 499.

55. See Richard Godden, *Fictions of Labor: William Faulkner and the South's Long Revolution* (Cambridge: Cambridge University Press, 1997), 44–48, 167–78.

56. See the *OED*, 2002.

57. Michel Foucault, "Nietzsche, Genealogy, History," in Paul Rainbow, ed., *The Foucault Reader* (London: Penguin, 1991), 76–100. Foucault's point is confirmed with the realization that Lucas may be Lucius Quintus Carothers's grandson or his great-grandson (or technically both), depending on whether the McCaslin patriarch rapes Eunice and/or Tomasina. Noel Polk and I argue in chap. 6 of the present volume that Isaac's ledger-based case for double rape, in the fourth section of "The Bear," is at least open to question. In "The Fire and the Hearth," Lucas assumes that his genealogical link to Lucius Quintus Carothers comes exclusively through "Tomey" (Tomasina; 43). Consequently, we must assume that the Beauchamp family history contains no account of Lucius Quintus Carothers McCaslin's (supposed) rape of Eunice.

58. "Syriac" may possibly reach toward "seriagraphy," whose adjectival form is "seriac." "Seriagraphy" refers to the art or process of printing designs by means of a silk screen. Inflected through "seriac," the typeface "syriac" infers that the irrepressible "tint" may be transferred to the surface of a soft membrane, whether silk or skin. I am thankful to Stephen Shapiro for pointing this out to me.

59. Paul Gilroy, *Against Race: Imagining Political Culture Beyond the Color Line* (Cambridge, Mass.: Harvard University Press, 2001) 104. The essay, "Identity, Belonging and the Critique of Pure Sameness," 97–133, may usefully be read in conjunction with any consideration of the racial problematics of *Go Down, Moses*.

60. See Engels's letter to Margaret Harkness (London, April 1888), in Marx and Engels, *On Literature and Art* (Moscow: Progress Publishers, 1976), 89–92. The letter lacks the phrase quoted: Raymond Williams, discussing Engels's use of the word "typical" (*tipichnost*) in the letter, notes, "Engels defined 'realism' as 'typical characters in typical situations' which would pass in quite ordinary sense, but which in this case has behind it the body of Marxist thinking. *Tipichnost* is a development of this definition, which radically affects the whole question of realism. For the 'typical,' Soviet theorists tell us, 'must not be confused with that which is frequently encountered'; the truly typical is based on 'comprehension of the laws and perspective of future social development'. . . . we can see that the concept of *tipichnost* alters 'realism' from its sense of the direct representation of observed reality: 'realism' becomes, instead, a principled and organized selection" (Williams, *The Long Revolution* [Harmondsworth: Penguin, 1961], 302–3).

61. Gilroy, *Against Race*, 106

62. See Malcolm Bull, *Seeing Things Hidden: Apocalypse, Vision and Totality* (London: Verso, 1999), 290.

63. For the concept of "the coming into hiding of the unknowable true contradiction," see Bull, ibid., 31–32.

64. W.E.B. Du Bois, *The Souls of Black Folk*, in *Three Negro Classics* (New York: Avon Books, 1965), 214–15.

65. Bull, *Seeing Things Hidden*, 246–47.

66. I know of no extended account of Roth in "The Fire and the Hearth": instead, critical attention focuses on his role in "Delta Autumn." Faulknerians tend to read Roth as a villain: he who sleeps with his second cousin, impregnates her (repeating the hypothetical miscegenated incest of his great-grandfather), and then refuses to acknowledge the child. I shall later argue that Roth is, at the very least, innocent of repetition.

67. Williamson, *Crucible of Race*, 499.

Chapter Four: "Pantaloon in Black" and "The Old People"

1. John T. Matthews, "Touching Race in *Go Down, Moses*," in Linda Wagner Martin ed., *New Essays on* Go Down, Moses (Cambridge: Cambridge University Press, 1996), 37.

2. Neil R. McMillen, *Dark Journey: Black Mississippians in the Age of Jim Crow* (Champaign: University of Illinois Press, 1982), 270.

3. Antonio Gramsci, *Selections from the Prison Notebooks*, ed. and trans. Quintin Hoare and Geoffrey Nowell Smith (London: Lawrence and Wishart, 1971), 276.

4. Roland Barthes, *Elements of Semiology*, trans. Annette Lavers and Colin Smith (London: Jonathan Cape, 1967), 22–23.

5. "During a visit with Faulkner which Meriwether and Millgate date July of 1940 . . . Dan Brennen pulled fifteen sheets of a typescript out of Faulkner's wastebasket; it was a revised form of 'Almost'. . . . This story, revised again, would become 'Was'" (Nancy Dew Taylor, *Annotations to Faulkner's* Go Down, Moses (New York: Garland, 1994), 9. See also Joseph Blotner, *Faulkner: A Biography, Vol. II* (New York: Random House, 1974), 1054.

6. Avery F. Gordon, *Ghostly Matters: Haunting and the Sociological Imagination* (Minneapolis: University of Minnesota Press, 1997), 15.

7. Leon Litwack, *Trouble in Mind: Black Southerners in the Age of Jim Crow* (New York: Knopf, 1998), 312–13.

8. I owe my argument here to Matthews's insight, which I merely gloss. See Wagner Martin, *New Essays on* Go Down, Moses, 29. Matthews's essay is the single most suggestive reading of the novel that I have encountered.

9. McMillen, *Dark Journey*, 242. See also, McMillen and Noel Polk, "Faulkner on Lynching," *Faulkner Journal* 8, no.1 (Fall 1992): 3–14.

10. Michael Toolan, *The Stylistics of Fiction: A Literary Linguistic Approach* (London: Routledge, 1990), 119.

11. Maria Torok uses the phrase "exquisite corpse" when referring to "[a]ll those who admit to having experienced . . . an 'increased libido' when they lost an object of love"; she argues that they respond in "shame, astonishment and hesitation" to the lost object as though to an "exquisite corpse" capable of eliciting erotic response. See Maria Torok, "The Illness of Mourning and the Fantasy of the Exquisite Corpse," in Nicolas Abraham and Maria Torok, *The Shell and the Kernel*, ed. and trans. Nicholas T. Rand (Chicago: University of Chicago Press, 1977), 109.

12. In *If I Forget Thee, Jerusalem* (1939), Charlotte Rittenmeyer, requesting that her lover and abortionist, Harry Wilbourne, apply his scalpel, links blade, phallus, and black masculinity with the observation, "What was it you told me nigger women say? Ride me down Harry." *If*

I Forget Thee, Jerusalem: William Faulkner Novels 1936–1940. ed. Joseph Blotner and Noel Polk (New York: Library of America, 1990), 645.

13. Anne Goodwyn Jones (on hearing a spoken version of this material), pointed out that the pun more properly yields "Man-he." I retain the "I," though acknowledging the force of her suggestion. Arguably, first and third persons vie within the acoustic, choice depending on Faulkner's authorial distance. That is to say, decisions concerning the extent to which Faulkner masks himself in Rider's grief (approaching Rider's consciousness, via free indirect discourse, while remaining variously detached from that perspective), will predicate whether a reader hears "I" or "he." To hear the former is to reduce the distance (maintained in "he") between author and African American consciousness.

14. Rider's body is "found . . . hanging from the bell-rope in a negro schoolhouse about two miles from the sawmill" (116)—positioned strategically as an educational and disciplinary instance for both black labor and black trainees.

15. Arthur A. Vanderveen, "Faulkner, the Interwar Gold Standard, and Discourse of Value in the 1930s," *Faulkner Journal* 12, no. 1 (Fall 1996): 44.

16. Jay Watson, "Writing Blood: The Art of the Literal in *Light in August*," in *Faulkner and the Natural World: Faulkner and Yoknapatawpha 1996*, ed. Donald M. Kartiganer and Ann J. Abadie (Jackson: University Press of Mississippi, 1999), 66–96.

17. The third verse of the song reads, "No more shall they in bondage toil / Let my people go! / Let them come out with Egypt's spoil / Let my people go." For full lyrics and the melody see, http://my.homewithgod.com/heavenlymidis/songbook/moses.html.

18. *Oxford English Dictionary* (*OED*) (Oxford: Oxford University Press, 2002). Subsequent dictionary definitions will be drawn from this edition.

19. Matthews, "Touching Race in *Go Down, Moses*," 22.

20. My procedure has advanced from a range of critical advice on what to do with these "loosely related stories" (Richard P. Adams, *Faulkner: Myth and Motion* [Princeton: Princeton University Press, 1968], 8), whose "over-all unity" (Cleanth Brooks, *William Faulkner: The Yoknapatawpha County* [New Haven: Yale University Press, 1963], 244) may be more "complexly" structured than their initial "self sufficiency" implies (Joseph Reed, *Faulkner's Narrative* [New Haven: Yale University Press, 1973]), 186–87). Terms for the connection of the parts to the whole, the stories to the novel, are various: written between 1935 and 1942 (with a concentration of stories written and revised in 1941–42), the collected elements of *Go Down, Moses* exist in relations of "anomaly," "parallax," and "disjunction," whose sum is "generically and formally unstable" (Matthews, *New Essays on* Go Down, Moses, 21). As "analogy and juxtaposition" (Eric J. Sundquist, *Faulkner: The House Divided* [Baltimore: The Johns Hopkins University Press, 1983], 150) lattice the text with instances of déjà vu, so recursivity attends the turning of the pages: I find myself going back to note a disjunction within what looked to be a conjunction, deviations among the parallels. David Minter comes close to this experience, describing *Go Down, Moses* as a novel that "defines [each of] its text[s] as an ur-text and pretext, and then requires us to begin to make connections that we must revise or even repudiate" (*William Faulkner: His Life and Work* [Baltimore: The Johns Hopkins University Press, 1980], 189–90). Revision ensures that the novel "holds itself on the brink of *dis*integration" (Sundquist, *Faulkner*, 158). Sundquist deploys italics carefully, to intimate an homology between aesthetic and social structure, one that Jack Matthews comes closest

to exploring. See also James Early, *The Making of* Go Down, Moses (Dallas: Southern Methodist University Press, 1972); Arthur F. Kinney, *Go Down, Moses: The Miscegenation of Time* (New York: Twayne, 1992), 31–33; John Limon, "The Integration of Faulkner's *Go Down, Moses*," *Critical Inquiry* 12 (Winter 1986): 422–38; John Carlos Rowe, "The African American Voice in Faulkner's *Go Down, Moses*," in J. Gerald Kennedy, ed., *Modern American Short Story Sequences* (Cambridge: Cambridge University Press, 1995), 76–97; James A Snead, *Figures of Division: William Faulkner's Major Novels* (Methuen: New York, 1986), 180–83.

21. For *Go Down, Moses* as an anthology of missing women, see Minrose Gwin, "Her Shape, His Hand: The Shape of African American Women," in Wagner Martin, *New Essays on* Go Down, Moses, 21–47.

22. The brown bear should be sexed male, despite Sophonsiba's status as its metaphoric vehicle, since in this sequence women tend to vanish and men to predominate. More particularly, as Hubert's metaphor extends ("bear-country," "den," "bear," "claw-mark" [99]), so its associative framework reaches toward Old Ben as the apt and displacing focus (or tenor).

23. Kinney, *Go Down, Moses: The Miscegenation of Time*, 42, 47–48.

24. Early, *Making of* Go Down, Moses, 11.

25. René Girard notes, "Incest is also a form of violence, an extreme form, and it plays in consequence an extreme role in the destruction of difference. It destroys that other crucial family distinction between the mother and her child. Between patricide and incest, the violent abolition of all family difference is achieved. The process that links violence to the loss of distinctions will naturally perceive incest and patricide as its ultimate goals. No possibility of difference remains; no aspect of life is immune from the aspect of violence" (*Violence and the Sacred*, trans. Patrick Gregory [Baltimore: The Johns Hopkins University Press, 1972], 74–75.

26. Malcolm Bull, *Seeing Things Hidden: Apocalypse, Vision and Totality* (London: Verso, 2000), 76.

27. Ibid., 19–20.

28. Henry Krips, *Fetish: An Erotics of Culture* (London: Cornell, 1999), 37.

29. Ibid., 38.

30. V. N. Vološinov, *Marxism and the Philosophy of Language*, trans. Ladislar Metejka and J. R. Titunik (New York: Seminar Press, 1973), 144–57. See also Malcolm McKenzie, "Free Indirect Speech in Fettered Insecure Society," *Language and Communication* 7 (1987): 153–59. McKenzie notes that "the intermingling of voices in speech representation . . . leads directly to FIS [Free Indirect Speech] . . . FIS allows a greater degree of vocal blending than any other speech representation form" (154).

31. Krips, *Fetish*, 39.

32. Karl Marx, *Grundrisse* (Harmondsworth: Penguin, 1973) 749–50.

33. Julia Kristeva, *The Power of Horror*, trans. L. S. Roudiez (New York: Columbia University Press, 1982), 2.

34. I borrow from Theodore Rosengarten's account of Nate Shaw on his release after ten years in prison (circa 1942). Rosengarten transposed the oral history of Shaw's life as a sharecropper in Alabama. See James C. Giesen, "Creating Nate Shaw: The Making and Remaking of *All God's Dangers*," in Richard Godden and Martin Crawford, eds., *Writing Southern Poverty Between the Wars (1918–1945)* (Athens: University of Georgia Press, 2006).

35. Michael Taussig, *Defacement: Public Secrecy and the Labor of the Negative* (Stanford: Stanford University Press, 1999), 196.

36. Michael Taussig, *Mimesis and Alterity: A Particular History of the Senses* (New York: Routledge, 1993), 40.

37. Taussig, *Defacement*, 41.

38. Girard, *Violence and the Sacred*, 39.

39. Ibid., 39, 56.

40. Ibid., 12.

41. René Girard, "Stereotypes of Persecution," in *The Girard Reader*, ed. James G. Williams (New York: Crossroads, 1996), 109–10.

42. Ibid., 115–16.

43. René Girard, *The Scapegoat*, trans. Yvonne Freccero (Baltimore: The Johns Hopkins Univeristy Press, 1986), 20.

44. Girard, *Violence and the Sacred*, 165.

45. Judith L. Sensibar first alerted me to the potential significance of the names Mannie and Rider. For Sensibar, "Mannie" crucially goes to "Mammy," and so "TO MAMMY, CAROLINE BARR," to whom the novel is dedicated. I can see little of the maternal in Mannie's tie to Rider. Nonetheless, Sensibar's essay is striking. See Judith L. Sensibar, "Who Wears the Mask? Memory, Desire and Race in *Go Down, Moses*," in Wagner Martin, *New Essays on* Go Down, Moses, 101–27.

46. The phrase is Girard's. "Under the heading *Monstrous Double* we shall group all the hallucinatory phenomena provoked at the height of the crisis by unrecognised reciprocity. The monstrous double is also to be found whenever we encounter an 'I' or an 'Other' caught up in a constant interchange of differences. . . . The subject watches the monstrosity take shape within and outside him. In his efforts to explain what is happening to him, he attributes the origin of the apparition to some exterior cause. Surely, he thinks, this vision is too bizarre to emanate from the familiar country within. . . . The whole interpretation of the experience is dominated by the sense that the monster is alien to himself" (Girard, *Violence and the Sacred*, 165).

47. For a further account of "incorporation" and "introjection," see Nicolas Abraham and Maria Torok, "Mourning *or* Melancholia: Introjection *versus* Incorporation," Abraham and Torok, in *The Shell and the Kernel*, 115–38. The extended quotation occurs on 130.

48. Sigmund Freud, "Mourning and Melancholia," in *The Complete Works of Sigmund Freud*, Vol. 14 (London: Hogarth Press, 1981), 243.

49. Abraham and Torok, *Shell and the Kernel*, 118.

50. Ibid., 115.

51. Ibid., 110. See also Torok, "The Illness of Mourning and the Fantasy of the Exquisite Corpse," in Abraham and Torok, *Shell and the Kernel*, 107–24.

52. Ibid., 118.

53. Taussig, *Mimesis and Alterity*, xiii.

54. Girard, *Violence and the Sacred*, 167.

55. Taussig, *Mimesis and Alterity*, 33.

56. Abraham and Torok, *Shell and the Kernel*, 118.

57. Ibid., 114.

58. Bull, *Seeing Things Hidden*, 283.

59. Williams, *Girard Reader*, 11.

60. A phrase used by Bull and Girard. See Bull, *Seeing Things Hidden*, 63, and Williams, *Girard Reader*, 11.

61. Taussig, *Mimesis and Alterity*, 126.

62. Bull, *Seeing Things Hidden*, 63.

63. Girard, *Violence and the Sacred*, 116.

64. Taussig, *Mimesis and Alterity*, 37.

65. Bull, *Seeing Things Hidden*, 84.

66. Girard, *Violence and the Sacred*, 168.

67. Taussig, *Mimesis and Alterity*, 77.

68. Bull, *Seeing Things Hidden*, 84.

69. Taussig, *Mimesis and Alterity*, 40, 111.

70. Taussig, *Defacement*, 41.

71. Ibid.

72. For useful accounts of "disavowal," see Krips, *Fetish*, 7–8, 45–46; Leo Bersani and Ulysse Dutoit, *The Forms of Violence: Narrative in Assyrian Art and Modern Culture* (New York: Schocken Books, 1985), 66–72.

73. Jacques Lacan, *The Four Fundamental Concepts of Psychoanalysis*, ed. Jacques Alain Miller, trans. Alan Sheridan (New York: Norton, 1981), 198.

74. Krips, *Fetish*, 61.

75. John T. Matthews, "Recalling the West Indies: From Yoknapatawpha to Haiti and Back," *American Literary History* 16, no.2 (Summer 2004): 241. Matthews's work on the structures of fetishized knowledge in relation to "Carcassone" and *Absalom, Absalom!* has been formative for my understanding of linked aspects in *Go Down, Moses*.

76. Ibid., 239.

77. Girard, *Violence and the Sacred*, 103.

78. Taussig, *Mimesis and Alterity*, 143.

79. Eric Sundquist argues that "the strategy of the hunt is to obliterate distinctions between hunter and beast, hold them posed in reflective postures as the ritual dance, the loving communication approaches its climax, and then to reassert those distinctions in an act of murderous violence. . . . the violent act that culminates the hunt necessarily destroys the loving intimacy that precedes it and upon which its sacrificial significance depends" (*Faulkner: The House Divided*, 145). Sundquist suggests that Rider's transposition as buck be read in relation to postbellum white hysteria over the "black beast."

80. My discussion of the "public secret" is heavily dependent on Michael Taussig's work in *Defacement*, particularly part 3, "In That Other Time: Isla Grande."

81. The phrase is Umberto Eco's: discussing icons, he notes, "[a]t a certain point the iconic representation, however stylised it may be, appears to be more true than the real experience, and people begin to look at things through the glasses of iconic convention . . . [in] a sort of perceptual cramp caused by overwhelming cultural habits" (*A Theory of Semiotics* [London: MacMillan, 1977], 205). Shared narratives, underarticulated because tacitly realized through repeated social practices, might be thought of as "cultural habits" or "public secrets": in either formulation they are the stuff of iconicity. The spectrality of Ike's buck may usefully be considered as a species of iconicity.

82. Taussig, *Defacement*, 193.

83. Ibid., 103.

84. Paul Ricoeur, *Time and Narrative*, Vol. 1, trans. Kathleen McLaughlin and David Pel-lauer (Chicago and London: University of Chicago Press, 1984), 48.

85. In describing a triangulation in the buck's horns as "a female shape marked male," I effect a sleight of time (1879 into 1941), by way of a visual affinity (between antlers [male] and ∇ [female]). The buck is manifestly male, but as one of a series of beasts referred to (in its re-manifestation at the story's close [1879]) as "Oleh" (137), the buck joins Old Ben and the snake as materializations of the Big Woods in essence, where that essence resides in the grave space of Old Ben and Sam Fathers, itself stereoptically recast as the "ultimate fun-nelling tip" of "∇" (253) (circa 1941). By such paratactic means does the ur-narrative redis-pose bodies in *Go Down, Moses*.

86. Bull, *Seeing Things Hidden*, 72.

87. Bersani and Dutoit note, "In fetishism . . . negation takes the form of intense sexual in-terest in certain objects or parts of the body—underclothing or feet for example—which 'take the place' of the missing phallic organ. Desire for these objects is, then, not really desire for the objects themselves, but rather for the presence of that object whose absence they both designate and deny" (*Forms of Violence*, 66–67).

88. The phrase is Fredric Jameson's; see Jameson, "Postmodernism, or the Cultural Logic of Late Capitalism," *New Left Review*, 146 (July–August 1984): 55.

89. See Raymond Williams, *Marxism and Literature* (Oxford: Oxford University Press, 1977), particularly "Structures of Feeling," chap. 9, 128–35. The quotations are drawn from 134.

Chapter Five: Reading the Ledgers: Textual Variants and Labor Variables

1. Sections 1, 3, and 4 of this chapter were co-written with Noel Polk and published as "Reading the Ledgers," *Mississippi Quarterly* 55, no.3 (Summer 2002): 301–59. Despite con-siderable revision, I would stress that the current version of those materials would not have been imaginable without Noel Polk's work. I thank him for that work and for his permission to redeploy it here.

2. William Faulkner, *Go Down, Moses*, in *William Faulkner: Novels 1942–1954*, ed. Joseph L. Blotner and Noel Polk (New York: Library of America, 1994), 139.

3. In New Orleans, the primary market along with Natchez for Mississippi slaves, average probate value of a prime bondsman aged 21–30 was $1,419 in 1856 and $1,639 in 1859. See Richard Follett, *The Sugar Masters: Planters and Slaves in Louisiana's Cane World* (Baton Rouge: Louisiana State University Press, 2005), 60.

4. With reference to "select": Allen Williams, associate curator of the Historic New Orleans collection at Loyola University, writes: "In all of the Historical New Orleans Collection's sources on New Orleans prostitution *circa* 1880, not one addresses male prostitution. Of course, the situation certainly existed, but [we] can't say there was an exclusive male brothel in the city. Al Rose's definitive study of Storyville doesn't discuss it, nor is there a reference in any of the Blue Books. This was verified by Pamela Arceneaux, head librarian and authority on the New Orleans flesh industry. . . . In fact, our only resource concerning the gay scene is a "Fess" Manetta interview, "Queers in the District," in the Bill Russell oral history cassettes. Manetta, she says, describes the scene then (*circa* 1915) in terms which make it sound very much like

the bar scene today. . . . Young men were sometimes kept in European female brothels to service interested clients, and I wouldn't be surprised if that were also the case here" (email communication, April 10, 2002).

5. D. A. Miller, "Anal Rope," *Representations*, 32 (Autumn 1990): 119.

6. At the death of their father, the twins build themselves "a one-room log cabin" to which they "added other rooms . . . while they lived in it" (193). In 1837 they, therefore, shared a room. By 1856, their sleeping arrangements have become a matter of choice rather than necessity, and are no longer mappable.

7. Perhaps Brownlee's entry into the "*Wrong stall*" is a mistake: intending to open another gate, he opens the gate to a stall housing Josephine who, surprised, kicks out at the intruder, misses, and injures herself. Such an explanation does little to catch the reiterated wrongness of "*Wrong*." Furthermore, the scenario seems unlikely since Josephine is almost certainly a working mule and so accustomed to human intrusion into her stall: though we do not forget Faulkner's paean to the mule in *Flags in the Dust*, in which he asserts that a mule, both "vindictive and patient," will "labor ten years willingly and patiently for you, for the privilege of kicking you once" (ed. Douglas Day [New York: Random House, 1973], 268).

8. Homosexual activity between masters and slaves (or between slaves) is almost impossible to detail accurately. Prevailing historiographic interpretations of slavery tend to gloss over homosexuality, along with domestic violence, divorce and intercommunity theft within the quarters, because such issues might be thought to distract from what is taken to be the slave's single domestic problem—that of his enslavement. It seems likely that documented examples of homosexual activity exist in the historical record, but as yet slave studies awaits its queer history because the prevalent paradigm requires that slaves be viewed as worker-agents, whose agency must be analytically celebrated even as the institution to which they are bound must be analytically condemned. In *Incidents in the Life of a Slave Girl*, Harriet Jacobs records an incident powerfully suggestive of miscegenous homosexuality: "As he [the master] lay there on his bed, a mere degraded wreck of manhood, he took into his head the strangest freaks of despotism; and if Luke [the slave] hesitated to submit to his orders, the constable was immediately sent for [to whip him]. Some of these freaks were of a nature too filthy to be repeated. When I fled from the house of bondage, I left poor Luke still chained to the bedside of this cruel and disgusting wretch." Before this we learn that "some days he was not allowed to wear any thing but his shirt, in order to be in readiness to be flogged" (Jacobs, *Incidents in the Life of a Slave Girl, Written by Herself*, ed. Jean Fagan Yellin [Cambridge and London: Harvard University Press, 1987], 192). We are grateful to Theresa Towner for calling this to our attention, and to Richard Follett for his observations concerning slave studies.

9. Eve Kosofsky Sedgwick, *Epistemology of the Closet* (London: Harvester Wheatsheaf, 1991), 80.

10. Ibid., 71.

11. *The Lives of the Twelve Caesars*, ed. Joseph Gavorse (New York: Modern Library, 1931), 145. Suetonius specifies that spintria should specialize in arcana and troilism. His *Lives*, of which Faulkner had a copy in his library, makes three references to "spintrae." As so often throughout this chapter, we are grateful to the scrupulous work of Nancy Dew Taylor. For fuller details on possible sources for "Spintrius," see her note to the name, *Annotations to William Faulkner's* Go Down, Moses (New York: Garland, 1994), 151.

12. Eve Kosofsky Sedgwick offers a useful gloss on our activity: she notes that "the potency of any signifier is proven and increased, over and over, by how visibly and spectacularly it fails to be adequate to the various signifieds over which it nonetheless seeks to hold sway. So the gaping fit between on the one hand the Name of the Family, and on the other the quite varied groupings gathered in that name, can only add to the numinous prestige of a term whose origins, histories, and uses may have little in common with our recognizable needs" (Sedgwick, *Tendencies* [Durham, N.C.: Duke University Press, 1993], 72).

13. "Lee" signals contradiction since it refers both to the sheltered side of any object (most typically a vessel), and, in conjunction with the shore, to that coast onto which high winds might carry a vessel, converting safety into wreckage.

14. We thank Mark Clark for pointing out the chiasmus in these names, and Sally Gray and Anne Goodwyn Jones for advice on translation.

15. Faulkner did not close the break begun by the dash. In editing the Library of America text, Noel Polk came close to supplying one, to follow the close parenthesis on 196, which would have read, ") —." Polk left the irregularity, against the possibility that Faulkner might be trying in his own prose to replicate the ragged jottings of the ledger entries.

16. Sedgwick, *Epistemology of the Closet*, 74. Elsewhere, Sedgwick argues that the semantic circumlocutions associated with the closet grant their recipients, "the privilege of unknowing" (Sedgwick, *Tendencies*, 23).

17. Miller, "Anal Rope, 74.

18. Ibid.

19. See Paul Ricoeur, "Metaphor and the Central Problem of Hermeneutics," in his *Hermeneutics and the Human Sciences*, ed. and trans. John B. Thompson (New York: Cambridge University Press, 1981), 163–81. Ricoeur argues for an analogy between the explanation of metaphorical statements and that of a literary work as a whole: "In both cases, the construction rests upon 'clues,' contained in the text itself. A clue serves as a guide for a specific construction, in that it contains at once a permission and a prohibition; it excludes unsuitable constructions and allows those which give more meaning to the same words. . . . In both cases, one construction can be said to be more probable than another, but not more truthful. The more probable is that which, on the one hand, takes account of the greatest number of facts furnished by the text, including its potential connotations, and on the other hand, offers a qualitatively better convergence between the features which it takes into account" (175–76). Ricoeur follows Monroe Beardsley in adding a "principle of plentitude" to that of "congruence" (defined above), which principle he describes as follows: "all of the connotations which are suitable must be attributed; the poem [or literary text] means all that it can mean" (176). Such an understanding of interpretive plenitude addresses the issue of reference as well as that of "making sense," insofar as it measures those aspects of experience "which demand to be said and to be equalled by the semantic density of the text" (ibid.). For Ricoeur, such density (or plenitude) derives from an absence of ostensive reference: where speech necessarily refers to a situation, texts are about that which is "freed from the limits of ostensive reference" (177). His claim, rather than dematerializing the textual referent, opens that referent to historical incompleteness—that is to say, to the recognition that materiality (the stuff of the referent) as subject to human action, is a work in progress (or a human fact, temporally and semantically distended with options, many of them denied). Where speech

refers ostensively, text is about "the totality of references" which it "opens up." Thus we write of "the 'world' of Greece [or of the plantation South], not to indicate what the situations were for those who experienced them, but to designate the non-situational references which outlast the effacement of the first and which then offer themselves as possible modes of being, as possible symbolic dimensions of our being in the world. . . . Interpretation thus becomes the apprehension of the proposed worlds which are opened up by the non-ostensive references of the text" (ibid.).

20. Miller, "Anal Rope," 119.

21. "To summarize, poetic language is no less *about* reality than any other use of language but refers to it by means of a complex strategy which implies, as an essential component, a suspension and seemingly an abolition of the ordinary reference attached to descriptive language. This suspension, however, is only the negative condition of a second-order reference, of an indirect reference built on the ruins of the direct reference. This reference is called second-order reference only with respect to the primacy of the reference of ordinary language. For in another respect it constitutes the primordial reference to the extent that it suggests, reveals, unconceals—or whatever you say—the deep structures of reality" (Ricoeur, "The Metaphorical Process as Cognition, Imagination, and Feeling," *Critical Inquiry* 5, no.1 [Autumn 1978]: 153).

22. Here we depend heavily on Taylor's annotation of "*Refused 10acre peace fathers Will*" in her *Annotations to Faulkner's* Go Down, Moses, 153, and on Evelyn Jaffe Schreiber's "'Old Carothers's Doomed and Fatal Blood': The Layers of the Ledgers in *Go Down, Moses*," *Faulkner Journal* 2, no. 12 (1997): 87–88. Schreiber uses her detection of L.Q.C.'s putative crime to ratify Isaac's version of L.Q.C.; her case being that incestuous miscegenation is a transgenerational sin. We extend Taylor's insight, and deploy Schreiber's hypothesis about what happened in Carolina to very different ends.

23. Joel Williamson, *William Faulkner and Southern History* (New York: Oxford University Press, 1993), 25.

24. The phrase seems to be Williamson's; he is, at any rate, the first scholar we know of to use the terms in Faulkner studies. See his *New People: Miscegenation and Mulattoes in the United States* (New York: Free Press, 1980), 44–45.

25. Our thinking here is informed by the work of Evgeny Pashukanis in his *Law and Marxism*, trans. Barbara Einhorn (London: Ink Links, 1978), particularly the chapter on "Commodity and the Subject," 109–33.

26. Taylor, *Annotations to Faulkner's* Go Down, Moses, 156.

27. Williamson, *William Faulkner and Southern History*, 383.

28. Paul Ricoeur, *Time and Narrative, Vol. 1*, trans. K. McLaughlon and D. Gellauer (Chicago: University of Chicago Press, 1984), 41, 38.

29. Frank Kermode, "Forgetting," in Kermode, *Pieces of My Mind: Writings 1958–2002* (London: Penguin, 2003), 310.

30. Paul de Man, *Allegories of Reading: Figural Landscape in Rousseau, Rilke, and Proust* (New Haven: Yale University Press, 1979), 200.

31. Faulkner studies—that is, nearly all commentators on *Go Down, Moses*—have agreed with Isaac in following Buddy's belief that Eunice committed suicide, and nearly all readings of *Go Down, Moses* of which we are aware are based upon Isaac's interpretation

of that suicide as having been caused by old Carothers's incestuous union with his and Eunice's daughter Tomy. See Michael Millgate, *The Achievement of William Faulkner* (New York: Random House, 1966), 201–14, and Thadious M. Davis, *Faulkner's Negro: Art and the Southern Context* (Baton Rouge: Louisiana State University Press, 1983), 239–47, for honorable exceptions to this general rule, but neither writes directly about the problem of genealogy in the novel.

It is worth noting that Faulkner himself provided somewhat contradictory extratextual evidence. Right after *Go Down, Moses* was published, he wrote a letter to an inquiring neighbor on June 23, 1942, who wanted to know about the ledgers. Faulkner wrote: "The ledger exerpts [*sic*] in Go Down Moses were a little to set a tone and an atmosphere, but they also told story, of how the negros became McCaslins too. Old McCaslin bought a handsome octoroon and got a daughter on her and then got a son on that daughter, that son was his mother's child and her brother at the same time, he was both McCaslin's son and his grandson" (Noel Polk "'How the negros became McCaslins too . . .': A New Faulkner letter," *Southern Cultures* [Fall 1999]: 103–8). Faulkner here returns to his practice in interviews of answering as simply as possible; even if he intended Carothers to be taken as an incestuous miscegenator, the novel provides no conclusive evidence of it, nor does it suggest that Eunice is a "handsome octoroon." Apparently, while he was writing *Go Down, Moses*, he drew at least three different genealogical charts; they at any rate appear on the versos of pages of preliminary typescripts of that novel (Thomas L. McHaney, ed., *William Faulkner Manuscripts*, 16: *Volume 1*—Go Down, Moses *Typescripts and Miscellaneous Typescript Pages* [New York: Garland, 1987], 240–41). The two apparently earlier (241) genealogies do not deal with the part-black McCaslins at all, but they introduce other McCaslins—for example, Lucius I (b. 1845) and Lucius II (b. 1895)—who were dropped from the family. The third genealogy (240) clearly claims L.Q.C.'s fathering of Turl: it draws a line directly from old Carothers to Tomey's Turl, who appears on the same generational line as Buck and Buddy and their white sister—that is, as one of their siblings; but no line connects him with Eunice or Tomey, just as no line to any of the siblings goes through a named mother. This genealogy has been in print since 1961, in James B. Meriwether, *The Literary Career of William Faulkner* (Princeton: Princeton University Press, 1961), 31.

32. See Noel Polk, "Man in the Middle: Faulkner and the Southern White Moderate," in Polk, *Children of the Dark House: Text and Context in Faulkner* (Jackson: University Press of Mississippi, 1996), 238–41.

33. For an illuminating reading of Butch as displaced labor, and of *Go Down, Moses* as a whole in relation to the economics of the late 1930s and early 1940s, see John T. Matthews, "Touching Race in *Go Down, Moses*," in *New Essays on* Go Down, Moses, ed. Linda Wagner Martin (Cambridge: Cambridge University Press, 1996), 21–47. See also Cheryl Lester, "*If I Forget Thee, Jerusalem* and the Great Migration: History in Black and White," in *Faulkner in Cultural Context*, ed. Donald M. Kartiganer and Ann J. Abadie (Jackson: University Press of Mississippi, 1977), 191–219, and idem, "Racial Awareness and Arrested Development: *The Sound and the Fury* and the Great Migration (1915–1928)," in *The Cambridge Companion to William Faulkner*, ed. Phillip M. Weinstein (Cambridge: Cambridge University Press, 1995), 123–45.

34. James Oakes, *Slavery and Freedom: An Interpretation of the Old South* (New York: Knopf, 1990), 4.

35. The literalness of what Isaac "sees" through his focal use of Brownlee continues to have its liabilities. We do not mean to suggest that Ike, having knowledge of bestiality in the barn, or of incestuous homosexual acts, ignores what he knows. Rather, he is a subject at odds with himself, because of a childhood packed with secrets and transitions. His sexuality, so much the matter of "The Bear," is at an impasse whose patterns may best be traced through evidence of occlusion, parataxis, and semantic slippage. Ike fantacizes variant forms of sexuality, where "fantasy" should be understood (after Jacqueline Rose, following Freud), not as a "lie," nullifying the event, but as an attempt to materialize those sites of conflict at which the subjectivity of the fantasist—coming to the end of itself—splits, diffuses, and returns with what it has discovered at its own edge, cast as a "hidden" scene. The events of molestation or love, heterosexual and homosexual, that will haunt Isaac's later sexual celibacy, may or may not have happened; their reality, a recurrent and typifying reality for *Go Down, Moses*, does not depend on external and traceable couplings. Instead, those realities, caught between inner and outer life, are generated by the interaction of semantic fields held in suspended alignment by changing patterns of social and economic authority, as manifest in 1888, and seen from the perspective of 1942. See Jacqueline Rose, *Sexuality in the Field of Vision* (London: Verso, 1986), 12–23.

36. See Ned Lukacher, *Primal Scenes: Literature, Philosophy and Psychoanalysis* (Ithaca: Cornell University Press, 1968), particularly 19–44, 68–96.

37. Nicholas Rand, "Introduction: Renewals of Psychoanalysis," in Nicolas Abraham and Maria Torok, *The Wolf Man's Magic Word: A Cryptonomy* (Minneapolis: University of Minnesota Press, 1986), 21.

38. For Eve Kosofsky Sedgwick, closets are designed from the silence they preserve: "'Closetedness' itself is a performance initiated as such by the speech act of silence—not a particular silence, but a silence that accrues particularity by fits and starts, in relation to the discourse that surrounds and differentially constitutes it" (*Epistemology of the Closet*, 3).

39. Isaac and generations of critics have refused to think about the Brownlee entries: the annotational work of Taylor is an exception. See her entries on "mule Josephine Broke Leg @ shot" and "Spintrius," which are crucial to our argument, in *Annotations to Faulkner's* Go Down, Moses, 150–51. Note also Catherine G. Kodat's unpublished paper, "Faulknerian Homotextuality: The Saming Change in *Go Down, Moses*," delivered at the American Literature Association's annual meeting, Cambridge Massachusetts, May 2001.

40. See John Duvall, "Faulkner's Crying Game: Male Homosexual Panic," in *Faulkner and Gender*, ed. Donald M. Kartiganer and Ann J. Abadie (Jackson: University Press of Mississippi, 1996), 48–72. See also Neil Watson, "The Incredible Loud . . . Miss-Fire": A Sexual Reading of *Go Down, Moses*," *Faulkner Journal* 9, nos. 1–2 (Fall 1993–Spring 1994): 113–23.

41. Judith Butler, *Bodies That Matter: On the Discursive Limits of Sex* (New York and London: Routledge, 1993), 1.

42. A Butlerian neologism: in *Bodies that Matter*, she speaks of the persistence of the disavowed, or of "disidentification" (4).

43. Ibid., 3.

44. Susan Donaldson, "Faulkner and Sexuality," *Faulkner Journal* 9, nos. 1–2 (Fall 1993–Spring 1994): 5.

45. William Faulkner, "Barn Burning," in *Collected Stories of William Faulkner* (New York: Random House, 1950), 12.

46. Sylvia Fry, *Water from Rock: Black Resistance in a Revolutionary Age* (Princeton: Princeton University Press, 1991), 235.

47. Joel Williamson, *The Crucible of Race: Black-White Relations in the American South Since Emancipation* (New York: Oxford University Press, 1984), 31.

48. In pursuit of Buck and Buddy's social radicalism, we should indicate that the twins make an earlier and sustained appearance in *The Unvanquished* (1938), and more particularly in the story "Retreat." Several are the differences: Buddy goes to war, not Buck; the twins are without contrasting nuances of gender; property, rather than sexuality, lies at the center of the three-page account; see Faulkner, *The Unvanquished*, in *William Faulkner: Novels 1936–1940*, ed. Joseph L. Blotner and Noel Polk (New York: Library of America, 1990), 350–53. "Retreat" specifies that Buck and Buddy operate a system for freeing their inherited slaves, whereby these slaves "buy" "liberty" "not in money . . . but in work from the plantation" (351). In addition, the earlier text notes that the twins persuade white "dirt farmers" to "pool their little patches of poor hill land along with the niggers and the McCaslin plantation" (352). Pooled land results in "white trash," whose families have shoes and some of whose children go to school. Faulkner adds that such "ideas about men and land . . . didn't have a name . . . yet" (352). We are reminded of the cross-racial activities of the Southern Tenant Farmers Union (1934–35). The point to make here, however, is that between *The Unvanquished* and *Go Down, Moses*, Faulkner's characterization of Buck and Buddy shifts in emphasis from labor to desire. Perhaps the years between 1938 and 1941 (in that they see large-scale southern enclosure and the dispossession of black tenantry) prompt his revision of the twins. Since the black body, by 1941, is increasingly neither held by debt to the land nor essentially a laboring body, that body (still the body whose work had created the white landowning class) needs to be retained by means other than labor—hence the emergence of the desirous Brownlee and the desiring twins. We thank Peter Nicolaisen for reminding us of the twins' earlier appearance, and different representation, in *The Unvanquished*.

49. See Calvin S. Brown, *A Glossary of Faulkner's South* (New Haven: Yale University Press, 1977), 83.

50. John N. Duvall argues that "[b]y the end of *Go Down, Moses*, Ike has become a 'funny uncle' indeed, one his white community consciously misrecognizes yet unconsciously recognizes as a 'black' white man" (Duvall, "Was Ike Black? An Avuncular Racechange in *Go Down, Moses*," in Michael Zeitlin, André Bleikasten, and Nicole Moulinoux, eds., *Études Faulkneriennes, No.4: Misrecognition, Race and the Real in Faulkner's Fiction* [Rennes: Presses Universitaires de Rennes, 2004], 39–51). See also Thadious M. Davis, "The Game of Courts: *Go Down, Moses*, Arbitrary Legalities and Compensatory Boundaries," in Linda Wagner-Martin, ed., New Essays on *Go Down, Moses*, (Cambridge: Cambridge University Press, 1996) 129–54. Davis raises the question as to whether Faulkner was "inscribing himself into the text of *Go Down, Moses* as "nigger" (151), but leaves it unanswered.

51. Eve Kosofsky Sedgwick, "Tales of the Avunculate: Queer Tutelage in *The Importance of Being Earnest*," in *Tendencies*, 59, 60.

52. *The Cassell Dictionary of Slang*, ed. Jonathon Greene (London: Cassell, 1989), notes that "to go down" may refer both to fellatio and to cunnilingus. *The Random House Dictionary of American Slang*, ed. J. E. Lighter (New York: Random House, 1994), grants the phrase currency from the first decade of the twentieth century. Hyman E. Goldin, ed., *Dic-*

tionary of American Underworld Lingo (New York: Twayne, 1950), notes additionally that "to go down" is "to commit oral sodomy," though this suggestion remains undated.

53. Faulkner's editor, Robert Hass, decided to change Faulkner's preferred title to *Wild Palms*. See Joseph Blotner, *Faulkner: A Biography*, Vol. 2 (New York: Random House, 1971), 1002.

54. "Uncle" and "Go Down," like the ledger triangle, operate as split signs. It would seem logical, given Ike's expenditure of equal educative effort on ledger and woods, that the woods (and their iconic bear) might likewise divide. Since the woods gain significance from their antithetical relations to the set-aside plantation, their arborial shades may be expected to shelter displaced variants of the repudiation and its documents. Moreover, insofar as the founding transgression, on which Ike based his withdrawal from inheritance, took double and masked form, perhaps the woods, too, are duplicitious after the manner of the ledger pages from which they derive. If so, Old Ben himself should split, releasing a problematic African American male body, set to one side in order to be retained in veiled and erotic form. Take, for example, the bear's death. Old Ben is repeatedly "the man" (145, 193, 230): at his final appearance he "stands erect," "rising and rising as though [he] would never stop" (177). Faulkner's reiterative insistence recalls Rider's segmented straightening (110) in the timberyard, an echo which operates stereoptically to hybridize two images, drawing a black through a beast, so that a deeply problematic desire can be figured. For readers who neither hear the echo of Rider's slow erection nor witness the consequent paratactic sleight of sight, there can still be no escaping the copulatory manner of the death. The bear "caught the dog in both arms almost loverlike," prior to "rising and rising": at which point Boon, who shared his bed with Lion (162–63), straddles the bear's back, "working and probing" his "blade" into its throat. The three figures fall backwards with Boon beneath the bear, only for the man to reassume the dominant position "astride" the beast's back, and affixed to that which "surged erect" (178). A thinly veiled ursine erection, held in triangulation and containing a more heavily veiled African American phallus, reaches back toward the commissary ledgers displaced by the life of the hunt. Just as those documents can be read as offering evidence of two heterosexual rapes (both miscegenous, one incestuous) *and* as containing counterevidence for matching, though arguably consensual, homosexual instances of miscegency and incest, so, too, does Old Ben operate "stereoptically." Named "Oleh" (Grandfather) (178), or the mimic bearer of a grandpaternal phallus, Old Ben warrants dismemberment. As black (or Rider/Brownlee), he solicits desire, albeit in barely discerned form.

Chapter Six: Find the Jew: Modernity, Seriality, and Armaments in *A Fable*

1. Quoted in Norman Sherry, *In the Shadow of War: the United States Since the 1930s* (New Haven: Yale University Press, 1995), 128.

2. Ibid., 265.

3. William Faulkner, *A Fable*, in *William Faulkner: Novels, 1942–1954*, ed. Joseph Blotner and Noel Polk (New York: Library of America, 1994), 676. Subsequent references will be from this edition and will appear in the body of the text.

4. For critical response to *A Fable* as a sustained religious allegory, see Rosemary M. Magee, "A Fable and the Gospels: A Study in Contrasts," *Research Studies* 47 (1979): 98–107; Carl Fricken, "The Christ Story in *A Fable*," *Mississippi Quarterly* 23 (1970): 251–64; Olga Vickery, *The Novels of William Faulkner: A Critical Interpretation* (Baton Rogue: Louisiana State University Press, 1959), 195–210; Cleanth Brooks, *William Faulkner: Towards Yoknapatawpha and Beyond* (New Haven: Yale University Press, 1978), 230–50.

5. See Malcolm Cowley, *The Faulkner-Cowley File: Letters and Memories, 1944–1962* (London: Chatto and Windus, 1966), 105. Cowley reports a conversation (Oct. 25, 1948) in which Faulkner concedes that if the cross could not stand alone, the jacket might perhaps have "below in the right-hand corner, and not in large type, the two words 'A Fable.'"

6. A military death's-head is central to Faulkner's first novel, *Soldiers Pay* (1926). Mahon, the terminally wounded aviator, returns home to die and to indicate that the wages of war are death. In 1926, for Faulkner and arguably for American culture, production for death was not yet perceived as structurally central to the national economy. I am thankful to the members of John T. Matthews's Faulkner graduate seminar at Boston University (2002) for their insights on corporeality, and particularly to comments by Randy Boyagoda, Wade Newhouse, and Jonathan Dyen.

7. My reading of the allegorical impulse in the passage owes much to Deborah Madsen's terminology in her *Allegory in America: From Puritanism to Postmodernism* (London: Macmillan, 1996), 104–5.

8. Peter Nicolaisen, "Collective Experience and Questions of Genre in *A Fable*," in Agostino Lombardo, ed., *The Artist and his Masks: William Faulkner and Metafiction* (Rome: Bulzoni Editore, 1992), 397–414.

9. Richard Gray, *The Life of William Faulkner: A Critical Biography* (Oxford: Blackwell, 1996), 327–32.

10. Klaus Theweleit, *Male Fantasies, Volume I: Women, Floods, Bodies and History* (Minneapolis: University of Minnesota Press, 1987), 224.

11. See Michael Riffaterre, *Semiotics of Poetry* (London: Methuen, 1980), 2. Riffaterre uses "ungrammaticality" as a generic term referring to various forms of semantic indirection, that is, "displacing," "distorting," and "creating." Although "displacing" is plainly relevant to Faulkner's use of the impersonal pronoun, "creating" is useful in relation to my later discussion of colons and semicolons as routes to a semanticized rhythm in *A Fable*. "Creating, when textual space serves as a principle of organization for making signs out of linguistic items that may not be meaningful otherwise (for instance, symmetry, rhyme or semantic equivalences between positional homologues in a stanza)" (2).

12. Fredric Jameson, *Marxism and Form: Twentieth Century Dialectical Theories of Literature* (Princeton: Princeton University Press, 1971), 248.

13. Quoted in Jameson, *Marxism and Form*, 248.

14. Jean-Paul Sartre, *Critique of Dialectical Reason, Volume 1: Theory of Practical Ensembles*, trans. Alan Sheridan-Smith (London: Verso, 1982), 299.

15. Jameson, *Marxism and Form*, 248.

16. Quoted in Sherry, *In the Shadow of War*, 174.

17. Ibid., 174.

18. See Louis Althusser, "Ideology and Ideological State Apparatuses," in *Essays on Ideology* (London: New Left Books, 1976), 1–60. See also, Joseph Urgo, *Faulkner's Apocrypha*:

A Fable, Snopes and the Spirit of Human Rebellion (Jackson: University Press of Mississippi, 1989), particularly chap. 3, 94–125. Urgo's study was helpful in directing me to the possibility of *A Fable* as a sustained reaction to U.S. state forms during the Cold War. I would also like to thank him for his illuminating response to an earlier version of this chapter.

19. Michael Rogin, *Ronald Reagan, the Movie: And Other Episodes in Political Demonology* (Berkeley: University of California Press, 1987), 284.

20. Ibid., 284.

21. The phrase "the solid South" is Clement Eaton's.

22. Numan V. Bartley, *The Rise of Massive Resistance: Race and Politics in the South During the 1950s* (Baton Rouge: Louisiana State University Press, 1969), 58.

23. Ibid., 85–86.

24. Ibid., 83

25. Paul Ricoeur, "The Metaphorical Process of Cognition, Imagination and Feeling," *Critical Inquiry* 5, no. 1 (1978): 148.

26. Ibid.

27. J. Laplanche and J. B. Pontalis, *The Language of Psychoanalysis*, trans. Donald Nicholson-Smith (London: Hogarth Press, 1980), 13.

28. Ann Douglas's remarks on minstrelsy are useful here: "It was the essence of minstrelsy that whites played blacks and blacks played whites-playing blacks. . . . Black minstrels not only imitated whites-playing blacks but also burlesqued them; minstrelsy involved stereotype upon stereotype, opponents as look-alikes, mocking and criticizing each other" (Douglas, *Terrible Honesty: Mongrel Manhattan in the 1920s* [New York: Farrar, Straus and Giroux, 1995], 75–76).

29. I borrow from the work of Keen Butterworth, *A Critical and Textual Study of Faulkner's A Fable.* (Ann Arbor: UMI Research Press, 1983). In addition, Butterworth usefully notes a conversation, concerning Levine's suicide, between Shelby Foote and Faulkner. Foote could see no reason for Levine to kill himself; Faulkner replied "by asking him what the pilot's name was, 'David,' '*No* . . . Last Name.' Shelby couldn't remember, but said he was Jewish. 'Yes' Faulkner said, 'That's it. He's a Jew.'" (89).

30. My account of Levine owes much to Ernest Gellner's discussion of the relation between Wittgenstein's linguistic philosophy, his cultural antecedents in Viennese jewery, and nationalism. See Gellner, *Language and Solitude: Wittgenstein, Malinowski and the Hapsburg Dilemma* (Cambridge: Cambridge University Press, 1998), 41–107.

31. Zygmunt Bauman, *Modernity and the Holocaust* (Cambridge, Mass.: Polity, 1989), 41.

32. Ibid., 55–56.

33. Sartre, *Critique of Dialectical Reason*, 207.

34. William Faulkner, *Absalom, Absalom!* (New York: Vintage, 1990), 199, 201.

35. In 1918 no Jew could be repatriated. In 1948, with the creation of Israel, those Jews resident in the Middle East, chiefly in the British Protectorate of Palestine, gained a Jewish state. Hebrew was instituted as the national language, to distinguish Israeli Jews from the Yiddish-speaking Jews of the diaspora.

36. "[A]nd then I asked him with my eyes to ask again yes and then he asked me would I say yes my mountain flower and first I put my arms around him yes and drew him down to me so he could feel my breasts all perfume yes and his heart was going like mad and yes I said yes I will yes" (James Joyce, *Ulysses* [Harmondsworth: Penguin, 1969], 704).

37. David Harvey, *The Limits of Capital* (Oxford: Blackwell, 1982), 443.

38. Karl Marx, *Grundrisse*, trans. Martin Nicolaus (Harmondsworth: Penguin, 1973), 749–50.

39. Judith Butler, *Excitable Speech: A Politics of the Performative* (London: Routledge, 1997), 3.

40. Like the procedures of the crowd, though by reason of a different convergence of structures, the power of "it" is perhaps best represented as mobility, where I would define mobility as the trace left by the impersonal pronoun as it inclines to refer diversely.

41. C. Wright Mills, *The Power Elite* (Oxford: Oxford University Press, 1956), 123.

42. Ibid., 218.

43. Numan V. Bartley, *The New South, 1945–1980* (Baton Rouge: Louisiana State University Press, 1988), 8–12.

44. For figures, see Mills, *The Power Elite*, 215–20. See also David Horowitz, ed., *Corporations and the Cold War* (New York: Monthly Review Press, 1970), particularly Lloyd C. Gardner, "The New Deal, New Frontiers and the Cold War: A Reexamination of American Expansion," 105–41, and David W. Eakins, "Business Planners and America's Postwar Expansion," 143–71.

45. James C. Cobb, *Industrialization and Southern Society, 1877–1984* (Lexington: University Press of Kentucky, 1984), 52.

46. Paul A. C. Koistinen, *Mobilization for Modern War: The Political Economy of American Warfare, 1865–1919* (Kansas: University Press of Kansas, 1997), 298.

47. The runner appreciates as much, but from below: he recognizes that in the context of a permanent arms economy, troops are simply workers laboring to consume by their labor (in part the labor of dying), the output of military production. Theirs is production for destruction. He tells Tooleyman: "It's because they cant afford to let it stop like this. I mean, let us stop it. They dont dare. If they ever let us find out that we can stop a war as simply as men tired of digging a ditch decide calmly and quietly to stop digging the ditch—" (954). His analogy between field workers and infantry is apt. The trench diggers of the Great War were the agricultural laborers of their respective peace-time economies; even as miners, once in uniform, found work undermining the earthworks of their class allies, now dubbed "enemies." For such workers to "stop" is to mutiny: a mutinous withdrawal of labor is a strike. See, Geoff Dyer, *The Missing of the Somme* (Harmondsworth: Penguin, 1994), 59–60.

Chapter Seven: "The Bugger's a Jew": *A Fable* as Melancholic Allegory

1. William Faulkner, *A Fable*, in *William Faulkner: Novels, 1942–1954*, eds., Joseph Blotner and Noel Polk (New York: Library of America, 1994), 894. Subsequent references will be from this edition and will appear in the body of the text.

2. See Jacques Derrida, *Given Time: I. Counterfeit Money* (Chicago: University of Chicago Press, 1994), 2–4.

3. Judith Butler, *Bodies That Matter: On the Discursive Limits of Sex* (New York and London: Routledge, 1993), 3.

4. Ibid., 206.

5. Ibid., 3.

6. See Noel Polk, *Children of the Dark House: Text and Context in Faulkner* (Jackson: University Press of Mississippi, 1998), 203.

7. In the context of such declarative architecture, the old general's "study" seems muted, having "probably been the chamber, cell of the old marquise's favourite lady-in-waiting or perhaps tiring woman" (945). However, as part of a gendered series, the double use of the room, involving male displacement of a female who waits on or attires a female body, should be noted as part of a wider feminization of the old general himself. For example, after two years in Africa he is "girlish-looking," retaining fragility "in the same way that adolescent girls appear incredibly delicate" (899). At the very least, his reiterated fragility and child-like quality problematize his masculinity.

8. See the *Oxford English Dictionary*, 2d ed.

9. See Joshua Trachtenberg, *The Devil and the Jews: The Medieval Conception of the Jews and its Relation to Anti-Semitism* (New Haven: Yale University Press, 1943).

10. For "undecideablility," see "Plato's Pharmacy," in Jacques Derrida, *Dissemination* (Chicago: University of Chicago Press, 1981), 63–172.

11. Jastrow's famous drawing usefully focuses the notion of how a subsemantic meaning may be both present and hidden. The duck-rabbit can be seen only as duck or rabbit, and not as both simultaneously. Yet even as we see one we are aware of the other; that is, we recognize something rabbity about the duck, or something ducky about the rabbit. We see one *or* the other, but truthfully say, "That is a duck *and* a rabbit." Experientially, we sense both at the same time in such a way that one is perceptible and one disguised; cognitively we recognize both at the same time, in such a way that one is perceptible and the other concealed. Puns operate similarly, depending on movement between two options. See Malcolm Bull, *Seeing Things Hidden: Apocalypse, Vision and Totality* (London: Verso, 2000), 19–26.

12. Butler, *Bodies That Matter*, 190.

13. Ibid., 188.

14. Ibid., 3.

15. Why Tibet? My reading is gender-orientated, but, given the military context, Faulkner's choice sustains his sense of the globablization of preparedness in the 1950s. Between 1949 and 1950, China's newly established communist government sent troops to invade Tibet. The United Nations ignored an appeal by the Tibetan government. A treaty in 1950 forced the Tibetans to acknowledge Chinese sovereignty in the region. The old general conceives his son (the ethnic other) in a place which, at the time of writing, had been occupied by the political other. In each instance, that other constitutes the subject, even as that subject (personal and national) repudiates it in an act of "constitutive antagonism" See Butler, *Bodies That Matter*, 12–17.

16. Polk, *Children of the Dark House*, 198. The essay, "Woman and the Feminine in *A Fable*," 196–218, transformed my reading of the novel. Although disagreeing with several of Polk's conclusions, I would not have been able to make my case without his insights. I would also like to thank him for letting me use his unpublished "A Chronology for *A Fable*," and more generally for his response to drafts of my two chapters on the novel.

17. Polk, *Children of the Dark House*, 198.

18. Ibid., 203.

19. Ibid., 204.

20. Ibid., 203, n 1.

21. Jean Paul Sartre, *Being and Nothingness: An Essay on Phenomenological Ontology*, trans. Hazel E. Barnes (London: Methuen, 1977), 607.

22. Zygmunt Bauman, *Modernity and the Holocaust* (Cambridge, Mass.: Polity, 1989), 41.

23. Sartre, *Critique of Dialectical Reason: Volume I: Theory of Practical Ensembles*, trans. Alan Sheridan-Smith (London: Verso, 1982), 299. My discussion of structure as a "practice" borrows from Roland Barthes: "There exist certain writers, painters, and musicians in whose eyes a certain *practice* of structure (and no longer merely its conceptualisation . . .) represents a distinctive experience, and that both analysts and creators should be placed under the common sign of what we might call *structural man*, defined not by his ideas or his languages, but by his imagination, or better still, by his *imaginary*—by the way, that is, in which he mentally experiences structure" (Barthes, *Critical Essays*, trans. Richard Howard [Evanston, Ill.: Northwestern University Press 1972], 214–15). My thinking is informed by Douglas Tallack's argument in "'A sense, through the eyes, of embracing possession': Views from a Distance," in Tallack, *New York Sights: Visualizing Old and New New York* (Oxford: Berg, 2005). Any convolution in my argument does not derive from Tallack.

24. *The Cassell's Dictionary of Slang*, ed. Jonathon Green (ed.), (London: Cassell, 1989).

25. I borrow my phrasing from Malcolm Bull's work on "the coming into hiding of the unknowably true contradiction" (Bull, *Seeing Things Hidden: Apocalypse, Vision and Totality* [London: Verso, 1999], 31–32). Bull reads "coming into hiding" as the realization of modernity (43). Given that the "emancipations" of the twentieth century necessarily involve the dissolution of boundaries and traditional mechanisms of order, social meanings, exposed to their own limits, become increasingly "undecideable." Such ambivalence is, for Bull, "just the necessary hiddeness of true contradiction" (290). Put simply, he proposes that expanded "relationality" must lodge contradiction at the center of ourselves and alienness at the center of our friends. Bull's case is particularly pertinent to Faulkner's encounter with the "relationality" of military globalization and with the South's changing status within it.

26. T. S. Eliot, "The Burial of the Dead," from "The Waste Land," in *Selected Poems* (London: Faber, 1997), 52.

27. Visiting the trenches at Beaumont-Hamel, Dick Diver assures his companions that to have fought here, "You had to remember Christmas, and postcards of the Crown Prince and his fiancée, and little cafes in Valence and beer gardens in Unter den Linden" (F. Scott Fitzgerald, *Tender is the Night* [London: Penguin, 1998], 67).

28. See Grover Smith, *T. S. Eliot's Poetry and Plays: A Study in Sources and Meaning* (Chicago: University of Chicago Press, 1967), 76.

29. Polk, *Chilren of the Dark House*, 213.

30. R. Rummel, *Death By Government*: *Genocide and Mass Murder Since 1900* (New Brunswick, N.J.: Transaction, 1992), 42.

31. Ibid., 9. I would like to thank Richard Crownshaw for conversations on the difficulty of articulating the Holocaust in the United States during the 1950s. See his unpublished PhD diss., "Tracing Holocaust Memory in American Culture," University of Sussex, U.K., 2000.

32. Judith Butler, *The Psychic Life of Power: Theories in Subjection* (Stanford: University of California Press, 1997), 186.

33. Ibid., 35.

34. Sigmund Freud, "Mourning and Melancholia," in *On the History of the Psycho-Analytic Movement*, vol. 14, *The Collected Works of Sigmund Freud* (London: Hogarth Press, 1981), 245. I should emphasize that Freud's work on melancholia developed as a response to World War I.

35. Butler, *The Psychic Life of Power*, 246.

36. Ibid., 248.

37. Ibid., 180.

38. For the language of melancholy, see particularly Butler, *The Psychic Life of Power*, chap. 6, "Psychic Incipations: Melancholy, Ambivalence, Rage," 167–98, and idem, *Bodies That Matter*, chap. 7 "Arguing With the Real," 187–222.

39. Freud, "Mourning and Melancholia," 243.

40. See my *Fictions of Labor: William Faulkner and the South's Long Revolution* (Cambridge: Cambridge University Press, 1997), particularly chaps. 2 and 3, 49–114.

41. The phrase is Donald H. Grubbs's. See his *Cry From the Cotton: The Southern Tenant Farmers' Union and the New Deal* (Chapel Hill: University of North Carolina Press, 1971), 125.

42. See, John T. Irwin, *Doubling and Incest/Repetition and Revenge: A Speculative Reading of Faulkner* (Baltimore: The Johns Hopkins University Press, 1980), 144–45, and Noel Polk, *Children in the Dark House*, 197–99, 204–5.

43. Butler, *Bodies That Matter*, 3.

44. For technological rationality, see Herbert Marcuse, *One-Dimensional Man: Studies in the Ideology of Advanced Industrial Society* (Boston: Beacon, 1966), 144–69. For a striking argument concerning the relation between the language of *A Fable* and that of bureaucratic reason, see Joseph R. Urgo, *Faulkner's Apocrypha: A Fable, Snopes and the Spirit of Human Rebellion* (Jackson: University Press of Mississippi, 1989), 94–125. See also Noel Polk, "Faulkner at Midcentury," in *Children of the Dark House*, 242–72.

45. The passage of black into Jew may seem slightly less incongruous once grounds for their quasi-metaphoric linkage are recognized. Between 1943 and 1945 much of Europe's Jewry "vanished" into over ten thousand camps, by far the majority of which were designed as sites of labor rather than (in the first instance) of extermination. Jews, unlike bound black labor, were purposely worked to death. Nonetheless, Jew and black maybe said to meet on the ruinous ground of brutally extractive regimes of labor. In a metaphoric relation, as Aristotle argues, one is led to see resemblance through and within difference.

46. Max Pensky, *Melancholy Dialectics: Walter Benjamin and the Play of Mourning* (Amherst: University of Massachusetts Press, 1993), 27.

47. Deborah Madsen, *Allegory in America: From Puritanism to Postmodernism* (London: Macmillan, 1996), 8.

48. Ibid., 1.

49. For Paul de Man, referential failure is an epistemic and linguistic given: "The ability of the mind to set up, by means of acts of judgement, formally coherent structures is never denied, but the ontological or epistemological authority of the resulting systems, like that of texts, escapes determination" (de Man, *Allegories of Reading: Figural Language in Rousseau, Nietzsche, Rilke and Proust* [New Haven: Yale University Press, 1979], 237). By this account allegory simply foregrounds a wider epistemological abdication. I would stress, in relation to Faulkner, that any referential opacity on his part should not be linked to that absence so per-

vasive among the varied poetics not simply of allegory but of the very many modernisms. The systematic assumption, informing much modernist innovation, that language operates in the absence of an available signified has tended to produce practices of reading for which a certain dematerializaion and abstraction are the inevitable concomitants of language's actual incapacity to refer. Yet, arguably, where the absence of the referent is too readily assumed, too little concern may be shown for the residual vehemence with which signs attend to the world. In effect Faulkner's allegory (like his "it") returns deviously to reference, delaying and dispersing, but not refusing, referential meaning. I am undebted here to conversations ith Peter Nicholls, and more generally to his work in *Modernisms: A Literary Guide* (London: Macmillan, 1995).

50. Paul de Man, *Allegories of Reading*, 200.

51. Pensky, *Melancholy Dialectics*, 127.

52. See Butler, *The Psychic Life of Power*, 179–86.

53. See Eugene Lunn, *Marxism and Modernism* (London: Verso, 1985), 184–87.

54. Walter Benjamin, *The Origin of German Tragic Drama*, trans. John Osborne (London: New Left, 1997), 166.

55. Ibid., 176.

56. Ibid., 184.

57. Ibid., 175.

58. Ibid.

59. Ibid.

60. I am aware that I make no mention of the Masons, though Masonic signs and references attend Mistairy (as groom and private). See Catherine Gunther Kodat, "Writing *A Fable* for America," in *Faulkner in America: Faulkner and Yoknapatawpha, 1998*, ed. Joseph R. Urgo and Ann J. Abadie (Jackson: Univerity Press of Mississippi, 2001), 82–97.

61. Benjamin, *The Origin of German Tragic Drama*, 161, 171, 197, 232.

62. Quoted by Susan Bucks-Morse, *The Dialectics of Seeing: Walter Benjamin and the Arcades Project* (Cambridge, Mass.: MIT Press, 1997), 179.

63. Karl Marx, *Capital*, vol. 1, trans. Ben Fowkes (Harmondsworth: Penguin, 1976), 1:256. I prefer, and have therefore quoted, the translation offered by K. Heinzelmann, *The Economics of Imagination* (Amherst: University of Massachusetts Press, 1980), 177.

64. Marx, *Capital*, 1:138.

65. Benjamin, *The Origin of German Tragic Drama*, 184.

66. Ibid., 185.

67. Sayre N. Greenfield, *The Ends of Allegory* (Newark: University of Delaware Press, 1998), 144.

68. Elaine Scarry argues that "war is relentless in taking for its own interior content the interior content of the wounded and open human body" (Scarry, *The Body in Pain: The Making and Unmaking of the World* [Oxford: Oxford University Press, 1985], 81). See particularly chap. 2, "The Structure of War," 60–157.

69. Freud, "Mourning and Melancholia," 246.

70. I am thankful to John T. Matthews for his detailed response to my materials on *A Fable*. He not only persuaded me to conclude by articulating the novel's "swallowed" charges, but seemed to understand my own purposes better than I did.

INDEX

Note: In addition to concepts and persons discussed in the text and notes, this index indicates, by italicized page numbers, first appearance of full citations for sources to the text.

grief. *See* mourning/grief
Grimm, brothers, 114
ground: in *The Hamlet,* 34, 36, 43, 59; in
"Pantaloon in Black," 93, 110. *See also*
dirt; earth; land; soil, the
Grubbs, Donald, 62, *212n15, 233n41*
gun, in "The Fire and the Hearth," 65, 66,
67, 68, 69
Gwin, Minrose, *217n21*

Hahn, Steven, 39, 42, *206n36*
Haiti, 193, 194
Harkness, Margaret, *214n60*
Harvey, David, 172, *204n26, 230n37*
Hass, Robert, *227n53*
hearth, 63, 68, 84, 106
Hegel, G.W.F., 44, 46, 47, 61–62, 63–64,
65, 66, 68, 76, 77, 83, *209n9,* 210n23
Heinzelmann, K., *234n63*
heir/heired: in "The Fire and the Hearth,"
78, 79, 81, 101, 102, 103–4; in "Pantaloon in Black," 109. *See also* inheritance; will/last testament
Hell, 35, 37, 39
hermaphrodite, 185, 186
heterosexuality, 124, 132, 133. *See also*
sexuality
hidden. *See* concealment
Hitchcock, Alfred, *Rope,* 131
Hoare, Quintin, *215n3*
hole: in *A Fable,* 181, 182, 183, 190; in
"The Fire and the Hearth," 97; in *The
Hamlet,* 26, 28, 29, 30, 31, 33, 34, 38,
56, 59; in "Pantaloon in Black," 95, 97
Holocaust, 191. *See also* democide; genocide
holocaust, 165, 169
home, in "The Fire and the Hearth," 63, 84
homosexuality: in "The Bear," 121, 123,
124, 127, 130, 132, 133, 134, 148, 149,
152, 153, 154, 225n35; in *A Fable,* 183,
184; in "The Fire and the Hearth," 103; in
Go Down, Moses, 117, 155; in "The Old
People," 116; in "Pantaloon in Black,"
107, 109, 113; Sedgwick on, 126; and
slavery, 221n8. *See also* anus; buggery;
sexuality; sodomy
Horkheimer, Max, *204n25*
Horowitz, David, *230n44*
horse(s): in *A Fable,* 180, 185, 197–98,
199, 200, 201, 202; in *The Hamlet,* 25,
39–41, 49. *See also* animals
horticulture: in "The Fire and the Hearth,"

81; in *The Hamlet,* 34, 53. *See also* agriculture
Hugh-Jones, Stephen, *208n59*
Humphrey, Caroline, *208n59*
hunting, 95, 99, 113–14, 153
hyacinth/hyacinth girl, 188, 189, 192
hybridity, 17, 25, 86, 101, 107, 213n33,
227n54
hymen, 25, 26, 183. *See also* vagina
hysteria, 166

icon/iconic, 15, 25, 37, 38, 41, 53, 54, 57
iconoclasm, 40, 41
identity, 75, 81, 82, 111
illocutionary, the, 174–75, 176
impregnation. *See* pregnancy/impregnation
incest: in *Absalom, Absalom!,* 193; in "The
Bear," 120, 121, 124, 126, 130, 132, 139,
142–43, 148, 149, 154, 223n31; in "The
Fire and the Hearth," 100, 148; Girard
on, 217n25; in "The Old People," 116;
in *The Sound and the Fury,* 126
incorporation, 107–8, 109, 191–92
independence: in "The Fire and the
Hearth," 63, 65, 77; in *The Hamlet,* 47.
See also autonomy; freedom
inference, in "The Bear," 122, 123, 124,
128, 130, 131, 132, 133, 154
inheritance: in *Absalom, Absalom!,* 194; in
"The Bear," 120, 147; in *A Fable,* 194; in
"The Fire and the Hearth," 66–67, 81,
101, 104. *See also* heir/heired; will/last
testament
introjection, 107–8, 191–92
Irwin, John T., *233n42*
italics: in "The Bear," 139; in "The Fire and
the Hearth," 82, 83, 86, 101, 103, 104,
105; in *The Hamlet,* 35, 37

Jacobs, Harriet, *221n8*
James, Henry, *205n9*
Jameson, Fredric, 161, *204n24, 220n88,
228n12*
Jastrow, Joseph, 184
Jehlen, Myra, *213n41*
Jews: assimilation of, 169; and blacks,
195, 233n45; conceptual, 169, 172,
183, 186, 191; in *A Fable,* 4, 157, 164,
165, 166, 167, 168, 169–70, 171, 177,
183, 185, 186, 187, 188, 189, 190–91,
192, 194, 195, 196, 201, 202; repatria-
tion of, 229n35. *See also* Semite/Semitic
Jim Crow South, 70, 76, 86, 103, 163, 202

tie. *See* garments
tintype, 80
Toolan, Michael, 91, *215n10*
Torok, Maria, 107–8, 111, 191, 215n11, *218n47, 225n37*
total relations, 61
Towner, Theresa, *221n8*
Trachtenberg, Joshua, *231n9*
triangle: in "The Bear," 124, 132, 133, 134, 145, 147, 148; in *A Fable,* 191, 192, 196; in "The Fire and the Hearth," 145; in *The Hamlet,* 51
triangulation, in "The Bear," 128, 130, 142, 149, 150
trousers, 112
Truman, Harry S., 156, 161, 163, 172
tumescence, 111; in *A Fable,* 167; in *Go Down, Moses,* 155; in *The Hamlet,* 45; in "Pantaloon in Black," 106, 107, 110, 111, 112, 133, 155. *See also* erection; phallus
Tushnett, Mark, 44, 61, *204n11, 209n8, 211n7*
twinning, 105
twoness, 83, 85, 86. *See also* double

uncle, 89, 130; in "The Bear," 130; in "Was," 89
undead, 98. *See also* revenant(s)
unknown/unnamed soldier, 157, 189, 195
ur-elegy, 32–33, 35, 38
Urgo, Joseph R., 18, 20–21, *206n30, 210nn18, 26,* 228n18, *233nn44, 60*
ur-narrative: in "The Bear," 123, 132, 133; in *Go Down, Moses,* 117, 119; in "The Old People," 115, 116; in "Pantaloon in Black," 112. *See also* narration
ur-scene: in "The Fire and the Hearth," 102; in *Go Down, Moses,* 99, 100; in "Pantaloon in Black," 106, 107, 108
use rights. *See* common-use rights
usury, 19, 22, 29
utopianism, 41, 86

vagina: in "The Bear," 152; in *A Fable,* 180, 182, 183, 184, 185, 186, 188, 189, 190, 191, 192, 196; in *The Hamlet,* 25, 26, 33, 34, 46, 52, 53; in "Pantaloon in Black," 93
value, 199, 200
vampire, 49
Vanderveen, Arthur A., *216n15*
Veblen, Thorstein, 12, 13, *205n8*

vent, 186
Vickery, Olga, *206n32, 228n4*
Vienne-la-Pucelle, 189, 200
violence: in "The Fire and the Hearth," 76; in *The Hamlet,* 23, 32, 43, 57–58; in "Pantaloon in Black," 90
virgin, 189, 190
visualization: in "The Bear," 143, 144. *See also* perception; sight
voice(s): in *A Fable,* 195; in "The Fire and the Hearth," 66, 69, 70, 75, 76, 86, 101, 102, 103, 104; in *Go Down, Moses,* 77; in *The Hamlet,* 17; in "Pantaloon in Black," 107; in "Was," 89
volition, 92, 94, 108
Vološinov, V. N., 7, 70, *203n2, 212n31, 217n30*
Vygotsky, Lev, 7

wage: in "The Bear," 136; in *The Hamlet,* 18, 49, 50. *See also* money
wage labor: and Agricultural Adjustment Program, 2; and *The Hamlet,* 19; partial connections in, 3; partial relations in, 61. *See also* labor
Waggoner, Hyatt H., *206n32*
Wagner, Robert F., *210n1*
Wagner-Martin, Linda, *213n41*
Wallerstein, Immanuel, 5, *204n20*
war, 157, 173, 194
Warren, Earl, 163
Watson, Jay, 95–96, *216n16*
Watson, Neil, *225n40*
wealth, 20
weapons, 49
Weinstein, Phillip M., *224n33*
welfare, 73
Wharton, Edith, *The Age of Innocence,* 11–13, *205n1*
whites: in *Absalom, Absalom!,* 75, 193, 194, 195; as absorbing black, 107; in "The Bear," 154; as blacks in whiteface, 3, 193; and black substance, 89; and Civil Rights era, 194; extraction/excision of blacks from, 3, 60, 62, 75, 76, 77, 87, 88; in *A Fable,* 192; failed withdrawal of from blacks, 90; in "The Fire and the Hearth," 75, 79, 80, 81, 84, 100, 101, 106; in *Go Down, Moses,* 77, 88, 155; in *The Hamlet,* 14, 23, 43; and migration, 87; and New Deal, 60–61; in "Pantaloon in Black," 90, 93, 94, 107, 109, 112, 113; release and retention of blacks by,